THE CAMB[RIDGE COM]PANION TO UTO[PIAN LITERA]TURE

Since the publication of Thom[as More's genre]-defining work *Utopia* in 1516, the field of utopian literature [has grown i]nto an ever-expanding domain. This *Companion* presents an e[xtended histo]rical survey of the development of utopianism, from the publica[tion of *Utop*]*ia* to today's dark and despairing tendency towards dystopian p[essimism epit]omized by works such as George Orwell's *Nineteen Eighty-Four* and Margaret Atwood's *The Handmaid's Tale*. Chapters address the difficult definition of the concept of utopia, and consider its relation to science fiction and other literary genres. The volume takes an innovative approach to the major themes predominating within the utopian and dystopian literary tradition, including feminism, romance and ecology, and explores in detail the vexed question of the purportedly 'western' nature of the concept of utopia. The reader is provided with a balanced overview of the evolution and current state of a long-standing, rich tradition of historical, political and literary scholarship.

GREGORY CLAEYS is Professor of the History of Political Thought at Royal Holloway, University of London. He has edited *Utopias of the British Enlightenment* (1994), *Modern British Utopias, 1700–1850* (8 vols., 1997), *Restoration and Augustan British Utopias* (2000), *Late Victorian Utopias* (6 vols., 2008) and other works. He has written several studies of aspects of the Owenite socialist movement, of the French Revolution debate in Britain and of Thomas Paine's thought. His most recent book is *Imperial Sceptics: British Critics of Empire, 1850–1920* (Cambridge, 2010).

A complete list of books in the series is at the back of this book

.RIDGE CO
PIAN LITERA

as More's genre
has evolved i
xtensive histo
tion of *Utop*
ssimism, epit

THE CAMBRIDGE
COMPANION TO
UTOPIAN
LITERATURE

EDITED BY
GREGORY CLAEYS

CAMBRIDGE
UNIVERSITY PRESS

CAMBRIDGE UNIVERSITY PRESS
Cambridge, New York, Melbourne, Madrid, Cape Town, Singapore,
São Paulo, Delhi, Tokyo, Mexico City

Cambridge University Press
The Edinburgh Building, Cambridge CB2 8RU, UK

Published in the United States of America by Cambridge University Press, New York

www.cambridge.org
Information on this title: www.cambridge.org/9780521714143

First published 2010
3rd printing 2011

Printed in the United Kingdom at the University Press, Cambridge

A catalogue record for this publication is available from the British Library

Library of Congress Cataloguing in Publication data
The Cambridge companion to utopian literature / [edited by] Gregory Claeys.
p.   cm. – (Cambridge companions to literature)
ISBN 978-0-521-88665-9 (hardback) – ISBN 978-0-521-71414-3 (pbk.)
1. Utopias in literature.   2. Dystopias in literature.   3. Utopias – History.
4. Science fiction, English – History and criticism.
I. Claeys, Gregory.   II. Title.   III. Series.
PN56.U8C36 2010
809'.93372–dc22   2010021486

ISBN 978-0-521-88665-9 Hardback
ISBN 978-0-521-71414-3 Paperback

CONTENTS

v

CONTENTS

NOTES ON CONTRIBUTORS

GREGORY CLAEYS is Professor of the History of Political Thought at Royal Holloway, University of London. He has edited *Utopias of the British Enlightenment* (1994), *Modern British Utopias, 1700–1850* (8 vols., 1997), *Restoration and Augustan British Utopias* (2000), *Late Victorian Utopias* (6 vols., 2008) and other works. He has written several studies of aspects of the Owenite socialist movement, of the French Revolution debate in Britain and of Thomas Paine's thought. His most recent book is *Imperial Sceptics: British Critics of Empire, 1850–1920* (Cambridge, 2010).

J. C. DAVIS is the author of a major study of early modern utopian writing, *Utopia and the Ideal Society 1516 to 1700* (Cambridge, 1981/1983). His publications also include essays exploring the relationship between utopia and history, science and social science. Most recently, he has published an essay on travel as a theme within utopian writing. In addition, he has written studies of individual utopian writers such as James Harrington, Gerrard Winstanley and Thomas More. He is also well known for his work on religious and political radicalism in the period of the English Revolution and is currently working on a book on English political discourse in that period. He is Emeritus Professor of History at the University of East Anglia.

JACQUELINE DUTTON lectures in French Studies at the University of Melbourne, Australia. She has published widely on utopianism in French literature and thought, including a monograph in French on the utopian writings of the 2008 Nobel Laureate in Literature, *Le Chercheur d'or et d'ailleurs: L'Utopie de J. M. G. Le Clézio* (2003). Her research interests range from travel writing and contemporary world literature in French to comparative utopias and Japanese imaginaries of the ideal. She is currently completing a book-length study of French visions of Australia as utopia, and editing volumes on representations of time in postcolonial and Francophone travel writing, and on comparative utopian studies.

PETER FITTING is an Emeritus Professor of French at the University of Toronto and the former Director of the Cinema Studies Program. He is the author of more than fifty articles on science fiction, fantasy and utopia – from critical analyses of the works of various SF and utopian writers (from P. K. Dick to Marge Piercy); to theoretical examinations of the reading effect in utopian fiction, the problem of the right-wing utopia, or gender and reading; to overviews of cyberpunk and of the turn from utopia in the 1990s, on the Golden Age and the foreclosure of utopian discourse in the 1950s; as well as articles on SF and utopian film and architecture, and the work of Fredric Jameson. He has recently completed a critical anthology of subterranean world fiction and is at work on a collection of his writing on science fiction.

ALESSA JOHNS is Associate Professor of English at the University of California, Davis. She has published *Women's Utopias of the Eighteenth Century* (2003) and edited *Dreadful Visitations: Confronting Natural Catastrophe in the Age of Enlightenment* (1999). She is currently completing a book on Anglo-German exchange in the late eighteenth and early nineteenth centuries and is serving as Reviews Editor for *Eighteenth-Century Studies*.

PATRICK PARRINDER grew up in London and north-west Kent and has had a lifelong interest in H. G. Wells and his literary contemporaries. He is a past chairman of the H. G. Wells Society, and his books on Wells include *Shadows of the Future* (1995). More recently he has been general editor of the Wells texts published in Penguin Classics. He has written on science fiction and many other topics in modern literature, and is the author of *Nation and Novel: The English Novel From Its Origins to the Present Day* (2006). He is also General Editor of the forthcoming *Oxford History of the Novel in English*. He is an Emeritus Professor of English at the University of Reading.

NICOLE POHL is Senior Lecturer in English at Oxford Brookes University. She has published and edited books on women's utopian writing in the seventeenth and eighteenth century, European salons and epistolarity, and is currently editing the complete letters of Sarah Scott. Her publications include *Women, Space and Utopia, 1600–1800* (2006); with Brenda Tooley (eds.), *Gender and Utopia in the Eighteenth Century: Essays in English and French Utopian Writing* (2007); with Betty Schellenberg (eds.), *Reconsidering the Bluestockings* (2002); with Rebecca D'Monté (eds.), *Female Communities 1600–1800: Literary Visions and Cultural Realities* (2000).

KENNETH M. ROEMER, an Academy of Distinguished Teachers and Academy of Distinguished Scholars Professor at the University of Texas at Arlington, has received four NEH grants to direct Summer Seminars, has co-chaired a utopias seminar at the European Alpbach Forum, and has been a Visiting Professor in Japan and a Japan Society for the Promotion of Science Fellow, a guest lecturer at Harvard and a lecturer in Vienna, Lisbon, Brazil and Turkey. He is the author of four books on utopian literature: *The Obsolete Necessity* (1976, nominated for a Pulitzer in American history); *America as Utopia* (ed., 1981); *Build Your Own Utopia* (1981) and *Utopian Audiences: How Readers Locate Nowhere* (2003). He is a past President of the Society for Utopian Studies and founding editor of *Utopus Discovered*.

LYMAN TOWER SARGENT is Professor Emeritus of Political Science at the University of Missouri-St. Louis and a Visiting Research Fellow, Centre for Political Ideologies, Department of Politics and International Relations, University of Oxford. He has also been a visiting professor and research fellow in Europe, New Zealand and the United States. He was the founding editor of *Utopian Studies* (1990–2004), and is author of *British and American Utopian Literature, 1516–1985: An Annotated, Chronological Bibliography* (1988); *Contemporary Political Ideologies: A Comparative Analysis* (14th edn, 2009); co-author with Lucy Sargisson of *Living in Utopia: Intentional Communities in New Zealand* (2004) and author or editor of other books and over 100 articles, mostly on aspects of utopianism.

BRIAN STABLEFORD has published more than sixty SF novels, twelve short-story collections, twenty non-fiction books and twenty-five volumes of translation from the French. He is currently translating a series of classics of French scientific romance, including works by Maurice Renard, Albert Robida, Theo Varlet, Jean de la Hire and J. H. Rosny, all of which are published by Black Coat Press, which also issued one of his recent novels, *Sherlock Holmes and the Vampires of Eternity*. Other recent fiction, including the novels *The Dragon Man* and *The Moment of Truth*, has been published by Borgo Press, which also issued his essay collection, *Heterocosms*, and his non-fiction book, *The Devil's Party: A History of Satanic Abuse*.

FÁTIMA VIEIRA is Associate Professor at the Faculty of Arts of the University of Oporto, where she has been teaching since 1986. She is currently the director of the Department of Anglo-American Studies of that Faculty and the Chairperson of the Utopian Studies Society/Europe. She is the co-ordinator of two research projects on utopianism funded by the Portuguese Ministry of Education: 'Literary Utopias and Utopianism: Portuguese Culture and the Western Intellectual Tradition' and 'Mapping Dreams: British and North-American Utopianism'. She is the director of the collection 'Biblioteca das Utopias', of the Portuguese publishing house 'Quasi' and the director of *E-topia*, an electronic journal on Portuguese utopianism, as well as of *Spaces of Utopia*, a transdisciplinary electronic journal on utopia written in English.

PREFACE

Although its notional point of departure is often Thomas More's genre-defining work, *Utopia*, published in 1516, the field of utopian literature today encompasses a far wider and ever-expanding domain. Platonism, classical mythology, golden ages both eastern and western, ideals of lost worlds, fantastic voyages, inhabited moons and planets, imaginary social and political experiments, nations, empires and ideal commonwealths, and satires upon all of these, jostle besides an enormous outpouring of later fictional and science-fiction works, a plethora of actually existing communitarian experiments across the ages, and a dark, despairing tendency, arising in the past century, towards dystopian or anti-utopian pessimism and the fear that all utopianism somehow eventuates in totalitarianism of one form or another. Utopia, often conceived after More's pun to be both a 'good place' and 'nowhere', seems paradoxically to be equally potentially a very dismal place found practically everywhere, and less a sanctuary of holiness than an emptying out of the evils of Pandora's box, in which hope alone remained restrained.

Whether taken as a branch of intellectual history concerned chiefly with the 'ideal commonwealth', as a literary genre, as a reflection of the history of religious consciousness or of an essential psychological aspiration of hope for a better state of existence in this life or elsewhere, notably in the form of the quest for 'community', the field of utopian studies has come to reflect discussions about the progressive or regressive aspects of historical development in microcosm. Modernity's endorsement of the ideal of progress has been counterbalanced by its disenchantment with the fruits of 'development' and 'growth'. Yet in a process of constant dialectical interaction, the angst of later modernity, generated by confronting genocide, nuclear war and ecological catastrophe, has been met with renewed visions of possible solutions. Though it has been intertwined with religion throughout their long collective histories, utopianism is not now usually assumed to involve salvation, perfectibility or the millennium, so much as the imagined, improved reordering of society in this world, and the more harmonious reconstitution of human relations and of attitudes towards nature. This, centrally, is the tradition of the ideal commonwealth most commonly identified with Thomas More, and with various revolutionary movements from the sixteenth through the twentieth centuries. But as wavering faith in science produced the scientific dystopia, so faltering faith in political engineering engendered the modern political dystopia of totalitarianism. With the collapse of the greatest of modern utopian political ideals, Marxism, came the triumphalist proclamation of an end of both history and utopia, a culmination of human desire, effort and progress in the liberal-democratic, capitalist worldview and the plenitude provided by a self-rectifying market mechanism. But this perspective, too, now rings hollow, as the spectres of global economic crisis and, far worse, environmental destruction, loom once again over us. New dystopian threats swarm upon us, to be met in due course, perhaps, by renewed efforts to imaginatively rework our concepts of other possible, alternate futures. To witness the juxtaposition of these bleakly negative and richly positive images is to see, yet again, how utopia and its negation have served so centrally as foci of human aspiration throughout the ages.

The volume

This collection of eleven essays aims to explore utopian literature, and to a lesser degree utopian thought and communitarian experimentation, in the western and, more briefly, non-western traditions. It is divided into two sections, the first more historical, the second more contemporary and thematic. Part I commences with an overview of some of the conceptual and theoretical issues associated with the utopian tradition. It then examines the definitive text which both gives its name to the tradition and radically exemplifies the rich ambiguity of many of its exemplars, Thomas More's *Utopia*. Subsequent essays in this section move forwards through the seventeenth, eighteenth, nineteenth and twentieth centuries, exploring the mutation and proliferation of the various sub-genres of utopia, satire, Robinsonade, Gulliveriana, and so on, and concluding with a re-examination of the 'turn' towards dystopianism in the latter epoch. In Part II the most important leading controversies in modern utopian studies are extensively explored, including the relationships between utopias, romance and science fiction; the contribution of feminist writers and thought; colonial, postcolonial and non-western utopian literature, and the bearing of ecological themes on utopian writing. The essays are thus intended to give a balanced sense of the evolution and current state of a long-standing, rich tradition of historical, political and literary scholarship, and how this tradition has been reconstructed, and what the chief intellectual disputes which have dominated it have been. Once confined to a relatively narrow range of texts, the interpretation of an ever-increasing number of works and proliferation of sub-genres has made the study of the subject more complex and contentious, as the actual movement of history has shifted our perspectives on how the past should be viewed. The contributors here, collectively, hope the volume's readers will agree at least that utopian writing remains nonetheless a challenging, exciting and provocative take on the human condition.

BRIEF CHRONOLOGY OF KEY WORKS
OF UTOPIAN LITERATURE AND THOUGHT

1759	Samuel Johnson, *Rasselas*
1762	Sarah Scott, *Millenium Hall*
1764	[James Burgh], *An Account of the First Settlement ... of the Cessares*
1771	Louis-Sébastien Mercier, *Memoirs of the Year Two Thousand Five Hundred*
1772	Denis Diderot, *Supplement to Bougainville's 'Voyage'*
1793	William Godwin, *Enquiry Concerning Political Justice*
1795	Thomas Spence, *Description of Spensonia*
1798	Thomas Robert Malthus, *Essay on Population*
1808	Charles Fourier, *Theory of the Four Movements*
1811	James Henry Lawrence, *The Empire of the Nairs*
1818	Mary Shelley, *Frankenstein*
1826	Mary Shelley, *The Last Man*
1827	Charles Fourier, *The New Industrial World*
1836–44	Robert Owen, *The Book of the New Moral World*
1840	Etienne Cabet, *Voyage en Icarie*
1848	Karl Marx and Friedrich Engels, *The Manifesto of the Communist Party*
1852	Nathaniel Hawthorne, *The Blithedale Romance*
1864	Jules Verne, *Journey to the Centre of the Earth*
1871	Edward Bulwer-Lytton, *The Coming Race*
1872	Samuel Butler, *Erewhon*
1880	Mary Bradley Lane, *Mizora*
1888	Edward Bellamy, *Looking Backward 2000–1887*
1890	Theodor Hetzka, *Freiland*
1890	William Morris, *News from Nowhere*
1890	Ignatius Donnelly, *Caesar's Column*
1895	H. G. Wells, *The Time Machine*
1896	H. G. Wells, *The Island of Doctor Moreau*
1898	H. G. Wells, *The War of the Worlds*
1901	H. G. Wells, *The First Men in the Moon*
1905	H. G. Wells, *A Modern Utopia*
1905	Gabriel Tarde, *Underground Man*
1908	Jack London, *The Iron Heel*
1915	Charlotte Perkins Gilman, *Herland*
1916	Charlotte Perkins Gilman, *With Her in Ourland*
1923	H. G. Wells, *Men Like Gods*
1924	Yevgeny Zamyatin, *We*
1930	Olaf Stapledon, *Last and First Men*
1932	Aldous Huxley, *Brave New World*

1933	H. G. Wells, *The Shape of Things to Come*
1937	Katharine Burdekin, *Swastika Night*
1948	B. F. Skinner, *Walden Two*
1949	George Orwell, *Nineteen Eighty-Four*
1953	Ray Bradbury, *Fahrenheit 451*
1954	William Golding, *The Lord of the Flies*
1958	Aldous Huxley, *Brave New World Revisited*
1962	Aldous Huxley, *Island*
1962	Anthony Burgess, *A Clockwork Orange*
1970	Ira Levin, *This Perfect Day*
1974	Ursula Le Guin, *The Dispossessed*
1975	Joanna Russ, *The Female Man*
1975	Ernest Callenbach, *Ecotopia*
1976	Marge Piercy, *Woman on the Edge of Time*
1986	Margaret Atwood, *The Handmaid's Tale*
1987	Iain M. Banks, *Consider Phlebas*
1992–6	Kim Stanley Robinson, *The Mars Trilogy*
1996	Jack Halperin, *The Truth Machine*
1997	Ronald Wright, *A Scientific Romance*
2000	Brian Aldiss, *White Mars*
2003	Margaret Atwood, *Oryx and Crake*
2005	Kazuo Ishiguro, *Never Let Me Go*
2007	Chuck Palahniuk, *Rant*
2009	Margaret Atwood, *The Year of the Flood*

PART I

History

I

FÁTIMA VIEIRA

The concept of utopia

Utopia: the word and the concept

The study of the concept of utopia can certainly not be reduced to the history of the word coined by Thomas More in 1516 to baptize the island described in his book. However, a careful consideration of the circumstances in which the word was generated can lead us to a better understanding of what More meant by the word as well as of the new meanings it has acquired since then.

It must be remembered that in 1516 the word utopia was a neologism. Neologisms correspond to the need to name what is new. By revealing the changes that the shared values of a given group undergo, the study of neologisms provides us not only with a dynamic portrait of a particular society over the ages but also with a representation of that society in a given period. There are basically three kinds of neologisms: they may be new words created to name new concepts or to synthesize pre-existing ones (lexical neologisms); they may be pre-existing words used in a new cultural context (semantic neologisms); or they may be variations of other words (derivation neologisms).[1]

Utopia, as a neologism, is an interesting case: it began its life as a lexical neologism, but over the centuries, after the process of deneologization, its meaning changed many times, and it has been adopted by authors and researchers from different fields of study, with divergent interests and conflicting aims. Its history can be seen as a collection of moments when a clear semantic renewal of the word occurred. The word utopia has itself often been used as the root for the formation of new words. These include words such as eutopia, dystopia, anti-utopia, alotopia, euchronia, heterotopia, ecotopia and hyperutopia, which are, in fact, derivation neologisms. And with the creation of every new associated word the concept of utopia took on a more precise meaning. It is important, thus, to distinguish the original meaning attributed to the word by Thomas More from the different meanings that various epochs and currents of thought have accredited to it.

The problem is that the first meaning of utopia is by no means obvious. More used the word both to name the unknown island described by the Portuguese sailor Raphael Hythloday, and as a title for his book. This situation resulted in the emergence of two different meanings of utopia, which became clearer as the process of deneologization occurred. In fact, though the word utopia came into being to allude to imaginary paradisiacal places, it has also been used to refer to a particular kind of narrative, which became known as utopian literature. This was a new literary form, and its novelty certainly justified the need for a neologism.

It is interesting to note that before coining the word utopia, More used another one to name his imaginary island: Nusquama. Nusquam is the Latin word for 'nowhere', 'in no place', 'on no occasion', and so if More had published his book with that title, and if he had called his imagined island Nusquama, he would simply be denying the possibility of the existence of such a place. But More wanted to convey a new idea, a new feeling that would give voice to the new currents of thought that were then arising in Europe. More's idea of utopia is, in fact, the product of the Renaissance, a period when the ancient world (namely Greece and Rome) was considered the peak of mankind's intellectual achievement, and taken as a model by Europeans; but it was also the result of a humanist logic, based on the discovery that the human being did not exist simply to accept his or her fate, but to use reason in order to build the future. Out of the ruins of the medieval social order, a confidence in the human being's capacity emerged – not yet a capacity to reach a state of human perfection (which would be impossible within a Christian worldview, as the idea of the Fall still persisted), but at least an ability to arrange society differently in order to ensure peace. This broadening of mental horizons was certainly influenced by the unprecedented expansion of geographical horizons. More wrote his *Utopia* inspired by the letters in which Amerigo Vespucci, Christopher Columbus and Angelo Poliziano described the discovery of new worlds and new peoples; geographical expansion inevitably implied the discovery of the *Other*. And More used the emerging awareness of otherness to legitimize the invention of other spaces, with other people and different forms of organization.[2] This, too, was new, and required a new word. In order to create his neologism, More resorted to two Greek words – *ouk* (that means not and was reduced to *u*) and *topos* (place), to which he added the suffix *ia*, indicating a place. Etymologically, utopia is thus a place which is a non-place, simultaneously constituted by a movement of affirmation and denial.

But, to complicate things further, More invented another neologism, which was published in the first edition of his seminal work. This second neologism derives from the first, in its composition, and is to be found in the poem published at the end of *Utopia* which is presented as having been written by the poet laureate Anemolius, nephew to Hythloday on his sister's side. In the six verses that constitute the poem, the island of Utopia speaks and states its three main characteristics: (1) it is isolated, set apart from the known world; (2) it rivals Plato's city, and believes itself to be superior to it, since that which in Plato's city is only sketched, in Utopia is presented as having been achieved; (3) its inhabitants and its laws are so wonderful that it should be called *Eutopia* (the good place) instead of Utopia.

By creating two neologisms which are so close in their composition and meaning – a lexical neologism (utopia) and a derivation neologism (eutopia) – More created a tension that has persisted over time and has been the basis for the perennial duality of meaning of utopia as the place that is simultaneously a non-place (utopia) and a good place (eutopia). This tension is further stressed by the self-description provided by Utopia in the poem: Utopia, the isolated place (where no one goes because it is a non-place) is also the place where we will not find sketches but plans that have been put into practice. As Utopia and Eutopia are pronounced in precisely the same way, this tension can never be eliminated. Again, this is an aspect which is completely new, and which justifies the need for a neologism. We are, in fact, very far away from *Nusquama*.

Utopia: the concept and the word

In the above mentioned poem, the island of Utopia points out its affiliation to Plato's city; the quality of this attachment is clearly defined: both Plato and More imagined alternative ways of organizing society. What is common to both authors, then, is the fact that they resorted to fiction to discuss other options. They differed, however, in the way they presented that fiction; and it could not have been otherwise, as More created the word utopia because he needed to designate something new, which included the narrative scheme he invented. In spite of that, the word is used nowadays to refer to texts that were written before More's time, as well as to allude to a tradition of thought that is founded on the consideration, by means of fantasy, of alternative solutions to reality. This is in fact an odd situation: normally, neologisms are used to designate new phenomena. Still, utopia seems to be of an anamnestic nature (i.e., the word refers to a kind of pre-history of the concept); this situation can easily be understood, as More did not work on a *tabula rasa*, but on a tradition of thought that goes back to ancient Greece and is nourished by the myth of the Golden Age, among other mythical and religious archetypes, and traverses the Middle Ages, having been influenced by the promise of a happy afterlife, as well as by the myth of Cockaygne (a land of plenty). It is thus certain that although he invented the word utopia, More did not invent utopianism, which has at its core the desire for a better life; but he certainly changed the way this desire was to be expressed. In fact, More made a connection between the classic and the Christian traditions, and added to it a new conception of the role individuals are to play during their lifetime.

Apart from this aspiration to better life, More's concept of utopia therefore differs from all the previous crystallizations of the utopian desire; these can in fact be seen as pre-figurations of utopia, as they lack the tension between the affirmation of a possibility and the negation of its fulfilment. Although they are part of the background of the concept of utopia, Plato's *Republic*, and St Augustine's *The City of God* differ from More's *Utopia*, as Plato does not go beyond mere speculation about the best organization of a city, and St Augustine projects his ideal into the afterlife (thus creating not a utopia but an *alotopia*).

The concept of utopia is no doubt an attribute of modern thought, and one of its most visible consequences. Having at its origin a paradox that does not really require to be solved (caused by the tension described above), from the very beginning of its history it showed a facility for acquiring new meanings, for serving new interests, and for crystallizing into new formats. Because of its dispersion into several directions, it has sometimes become so close to other literary genres or currents of thought that it has risked losing its own identity. Its diffuse nature has been at the basis of debate among researchers in the field of Utopian Studies, who have found it difficult to reach a consensual definition of the concept.

Historically, the concept of utopia has been defined with regard to one of four characteristics:[3] (1) the content of the imagined society (i.e., the identification of that society with the idea of 'good place', a notion that should be discarded since it is based on a subjective conception of what is or is not desirable, and envisages utopia as being essentially in opposition to the prevailing ideology); (2) the literary form into which the utopian imagination has been crystallized (which is a very limiting way of defining utopia, since it excludes a considerable number of texts that are clearly utopian in perspective but that do not rigorously comply with the narrative model established by More); (3) the function of utopia (i.e., the impact that it causes on its reader, urging him to take action (a definition that should be rejected as it takes into account political utopia only); (4) the desire for a better life, caused by a feeling of discontentment towards the society one lives in (utopia is then seen as a matter of attitude). This latter characteristic is no doubt the most important one, as it allows for the inclusion within the framework of utopia of a wide range of texts informed by what Ernst Bloch considered to be the principal energy of utopia: hope. Utopia is then to be seen as a matter of attitude, as a kind of reaction to an undesirable present and an aspiration to overcome all difficulties by the imagination of possible alternatives.[4]

Utopia as a literary genre

By opting for a more inclusive definition of utopia, we are not disregarding the merits and particulars of utopia as a literary genre, but recognizing the literary form as just one of the possible manifestations of utopian thought.[5] More established the basis for the steady development of a literary tradition which flourished particularly in England, Italy, France and the United States, and which relies on a more or less rigid narrative structure: it normally pictures the journey (by sea, land or air) of a man or woman to an unknown place (an island, a country or a continent); once there, the utopian traveller is usually offered a guided tour of the society, and given an explanation of its social, political, economic and religious organization; this journey typically implies the return of the utopian traveller to his or her own country, in order to be able to take back the message that there are alternative and better ways of organizing society.[6] Although the idea of utopia should not be confused with the idea of perfection, one of its most recognizable traits is its speculative discourse on a non-existent social organization which is better than the real society.[7] Another characteristic is that it is human-centred, not relying on chance or on the intervention of external, divine forces in order to impose order on society. Utopian societies are built by human beings and are meant for them. And it is because utopists very often distrust individuals' capacity to live together, that we very frequently find a rigid set of laws at the heart of utopian societies – rules that force the individuals to repress their unreliable and unstable nature and put on a more convenient social cloak.

In order to create the new literary genre, More used the conventions of travel literature and adapted them to his aims. Over the centuries, utopia as a literary genre has been influenced by similar genres, such as the novel, the journal and science fiction. In fact, it became so close to the latter genre that it has been often confused with it. At the advent of science fiction, it was not difficult to distinguish it from literary utopia, as the former made a clear investment in the imagination of a fantastic world brought about by scientific and technological progress, taking us on a journey to faraway planets, while the latter stayed focused on the description of the alternative ways of organizing the imagined societies. Still, in recent decades, science fiction has been permeated by social concerns, displaying a clear commitment to politics; this situation has given rise to endless debates on the links that bind the two literary genres: researchers in the field of Utopian Studies have claimed that science fiction is subordinate to utopia, as the latter was born first, whereas those who have devoted their study time to science fiction maintain that utopia is but a socio-political sub-genre.

One of the main features of utopia as a literary genre is its relationship with reality. Utopists depart from the observation of the society they live in, note down the aspects that need to be changed and imagine a place where those problems have been solved. Quite often, the imagined society is the opposite of the real one, a kind of inverted image of it. It should not be taken, though, as a feeble echo of the real world; utopias are by essence dynamic, and in spite of the fact that they are born out of a given set of circumstances, their scope of action is not limited to a criticism of the present; indeed, utopias put forward projective ideas that are to be adopted by future audiences, which may cause real changes.

The fact that the utopian traveller departs from a real place, visits an imagined place and goes back home, situates utopia at the boundary between reality and fiction. This fiction is in fact important, not as an end in itself, but as a privileged means to convey a potentially subversive message, but in such a way that the utopist cannot be criticized. In this sense, utopia, as a literary genre, is part of clandestine literature. Anchored in a real society, the utopist puts forward plausible alternatives, basing them on meticulous analysis and evaluation of different cultures. But although literary utopias are serious in their intent, they may well incorporate amusing and entertaining moments, provided they do not smother the didactic discourse. Utopia is, in fact, a game, and implies the celebration of a kind of pact between the utopist and the reader: the utopist addresses the reader to tell him about a society that does not exist, and the reader acts as if he believes the author, even if he is aware of the non-existence of such a society. Still, the reader's notion of reality cannot be pushed too far as otherwise he will refuse to act as if he believed the author. In fact, the fiction cannot defy logic, and the passage from the real to the fictional world has to be gradual. This passage can be softened by the introduction, into the imagined world, of objects and structures that already exist in the real world, but which now have a different or even opposite function. Out of this situation, satire is inevitably born, as conspicuous criticism of the real society's flaws is part of the nature of the genre. When satire is not confined to real society, and is aimed at the imagined society, when the satirical tone becomes dominant and supersedes pedagogy, satire ceases to be a means and becomes an end – and we are then pushed out of the realm of utopian literature.

From space to time: euchronia

By inviting us to take a journey to an imagined better place, literary utopia gives rise to a rupture with the real place. This topographical rupture engenders a break of another different kind, a fracture between the history of the real place and that of the imagined society. In fact, at the onset of literary utopianism, we can but find static, ahistorical utopias. Such utopias reject their past (faced as anti-utopian), offer a frozen image of the present, and eliminate the idea of a future from their horizon: there is no progress after the ideal society has been established. There is a reason for this situation: the imagined society is put forward as a model to be followed, and models are frozen images that don't allow for historical change after they have been instituted. The relationship between these utopias and the future is indeed problematic, since the model is offered as a term of comparison with real society, i.e., it is used by the utopist to criticize the present and not to open new paths to the future. In fact, we can say that the concept of time, as we know it, has been banished from these utopias.

In order to understand the nature of this temporal rupture, we have to distinguish the concept of time from its correlates. To St Augustine time is successive; eternity exists simultaneously, being deprived of an anteriority and a posteriority; and perpetuity has a beginning but no ending. So, it is true to say that it is perpetuity that we find in the utopias of the Renaissance, as the inhabitants of those imagined places have an existence, but do not envision their lives as a process of becoming. Those utopias must then be seen as a means for the expression of the utopist's wishes, not of his hope. Confined to remote islands or unknown places, utopian wishes fail to be materialized. Only in the last decades of the eighteenth century are utopias to be placed in the future; and only then does the utopian wish give place to hope.

The projection of the utopian wishes into the future implied a change in the very nature of utopia – and thus a derivation neologism was born. From eu/utopia, the good/non-place, we move to euchronia, the good place in the future. The birth of euchronia was due to a change of mentality, presided over by the optimistic worldview that prevailed in Europe in the Enlightenment. In the Renaissance, man discovered that there were alternative options to the society he lived in, became aware of the infinite powers of reason and understood that the construction of the future was in his hands. In the Enlightenment, man discovered that reason could enable him not only to have a happy life, but also to reach human perfection. More's *Utopia* is the result of the discovery that occurred in the Renaissance; euchronia is the product of the new logic of the Enlightenment.

These discoveries of the Enlightenment were stimulated by another revolution that took place in the field of science. In fact, it was the development of the sciences (in general, and more specifically in the fields of geology and biology) that prepared man to outline new perspectives of the world and of himself. During the Enlightenment, by transferring scientific conclusions to the purely intellectual field, man grounded his optimistic worldview on a global theory of evolution, thus reaching relevant conclusions not only regarding the splendour that would await him in the future, but also regarding the social organization and the economic order of the society he lived in.

The theories of progress that pervaded European thought in the eighteenth century were born in France, a politically unsubmissive country, which was preparing its revolution. Describing the logic of progress in his lectures at the Sorbonne in 1750, Anne-Robert Turgot associated the idea of the inevitability of progress with the idea of infinite human perfectibility. And later in the century, in 1795, in his *Sketch for a Historical Picture of the Progress of the Human Mind*, the Marquis de Condorcet added to this belief the idea that man has an important role to play in the process. According to Condorcet, progress was already being ensured by history; still, by resorting to science, man would be able to accelerate this improvement.

Inspired by the feeling of trust that characterized the Enlightenment, in 1771 the French writer Louis-Sébastien Mercier published the first euchronia, *L'An 2440: Un rêve s'il en fut jamais* (translated into English as *Memoirs of the Year Two Thousand Five Hundred*).[8] By favouring the notion of time and offering a vision of a future of happiness, euchronia acquired a historical dimension. History was now envisaged as a process of infinite improvement, and utopia, in the spirit of euchronia, was presented as a synchronic representation of one of the rings in the chain of progress. By this process, the imagined society came closer to the historical reality the utopist experienced. By projecting the ideal society in the future, the utopian discourse enunciated a logic of causalities that presupposed that certain actions (namely those of a political nature) might afford the changes that were necessary in order to make the imagined society come true. In this way, utopias became dynamic, and promoted the idea that man had a role to fulfil.

Inherent in this projection of utopia into the future, and aiding the process of convergence of the utopian discourse with the historical reality, was a change at the spatial level, at which Mercier's utopia operated: it no longer made sense, at a time when the utopist believed that his ideals could be rendered concrete with the help of time, to place the imaginary society on a remote island or in an unknown, inaccessible place. Man's trust in his intellectual capacities was thus stretched to the social possibilities of his country, and it was there that utopia was now to be located. Furthermore, as historical progress was believed to be inevitable, it affected not only the utopist's country, but all nations. The utopian project thus took on a universal dimension.

In France, the turning of utopian discourse towards the future took place in the second half of the eighteenth century, but in England this idea of infinite progress was only to be found among the intellectual elite, with strong connections to French theorization. In fact, this philosophy only took the shape of a popular ideology in England in the nineteenth century, associated with the benefits that were reserved to the nation by the process of industrialization. The optimistic logic that at the end of the eighteenth century led French utopists to the conception of an imaginary ideal society located in the future was thus not shared by the British utopists; and here lies the explanation for the fact that, for a whole century, euchronias were exclusively French.

Although intellectually linked to French optimism, the British idea of progress has a story of its own, and is deeply rooted in British intellectual thought. We can find these roots, with some variants, in the writings of men such as Shaftesbury, Locke and Hume. And it was certainly this optimism that Pope and Swift criticized at the beginning of the British eighteenth century, giving way to a whole set of satirical utopias that made the reader disregard the idea of a perfect future. Indeed, the aim of these texts was to satirize the present through the criticism of an imagined society, and the result of this situation was that the constructive, positive spirit that should preside in utopian texts was in fact lost. It is true that in the utopias of the British Enlightenment we can still find a few examples of the Renaissance aim of suggesting serious alternatives to real society.[9] However, with very few exceptions, these utopias were still based on the idea that only law would ensure social order, thus conveying a negative vision of man; in fact, it can be said that the prevailing tone of the eighteenth-century utopia was satirical, and so more destructive than constructive.

But although British literary utopias only revealed the influence of euchronic belief towards the end of the nineteenth century, this belief was incorporated into political and philosophic essays of the last decades of the eighteenth century and of the whole nineteenth century. The reception of the French and the American revolutions in England undoubtedly played a very important role in this process. The announcement, by Thomas Paine, that his generation would 'appear to the future as the Adam of a new world' (*Rights of Man*, Part II, 1792), actually corresponded to his belief in a renovation of the natural order of things and his conviction that a system combining moral with political happiness would ensure a magnificent future.[10] Through the words of William Godwin (*Enquiry Concerning Political Justice*, 1793), the idea of human perfectibility was promoted in Britain, providing the basis for the confidence that if man is properly raised and educated, he will wisely be able to put moral laws (that emanate from reason) into practice, making all the repressive artificial governmental laws irrelevant.[11] Godwin thus replaced the idea of the need for a political revolution with the idea of the need for a revolution of opinion. Although based on different premises and aims, both Paine and Godwin announced the birth of a new man and the coming of a new era. But it is important to note that this man was not to live on a remote or unknown island, but in the real, historical world of the future. With Paine and Godwin, British utopian thought thus became truly euchronic.

The wish to build euchronia, to make it real, can also be found in the thought of the so-called 'utopian socialists'. In fact, when Henri de Saint-Simon put forward the idea that the Golden Age was not to be found in the past but in the future, he was conveying the belief that it is up to man to conceive plans for the reconstruction of society and to put them into practice. Utopian socialism clearly cannot be seen as a homogeneous movement, not only because it was promoted by intellectuals with rather different backgrounds and dealing with divergent realities (Henri de Saint-Simon and Charles Fourier lived in a still rural France whereas Robert Owen defined his thought within the framework of industrial Britain), but also because their plans for the reconstruction of society were dissimilar. They all believed, though, that those who, like themselves, were able to conceive strategies in order to change society were morally obliged to do so. These plans were put forward by the utopian socialists based on a scientific analysis of the way society was organized. It cannot be forgotten that it was Marx and Engels who considered their plans utopian (in a negative sense), as they disregarded the forces of history and were rooted in the belief that strategies conceived by men of genius would be enough to change the world; for the modern socialists, who claimed for themselves a scientific view of history, the idea that history might obey reason did indeed seem absurd. But if possible the so-called utopian socialists would have refuted that label, as they conceived plans to be effectively put into practice. Indeed, Robert Owen, in particular, was not only a seer, but also a doer. In the community of New Lanark in Scotland, as well as in that of New Harmony in Indiana, Owen set the basis for the creation of what he called 'a new moral world', inhabited by those who would have adhered to a new religion, which would have given them the needed ethical support – the religion of humanity.

Owen's utopian thought is important for an understanding of how British political thought was impregnated with a utopian perspective at a time when Owenism and socialism were seen as synonymous and interchangeable words. And even though Marx and Engels criticized Owen and his contemporaries for having believed that a single man could change the world, they recognized that the utopian socialists were revolutionary for their time, as they put forward valid and innovative proposals and experimented with alternative communitarian ways of organizing society, paving the way for the acceptance of the idea that things might effectively be changed.

Although they claimed their theories to be scientific, the truth is that both Marx and Engels's thought was clearly utopian, in that it pointed to the future and offered promising images of freedom, stability and happiness. Based on the idea that as the capitalist modes of production caused the feudal world to disintegrate, so would industrial competition cause the destruction of the capitalist system, Marx and Engels believed that the improvement of machinery – an imperative dictated by the laws of competition – would lead to cyclical situations of a surplus of production, and eventually to the collapse of capitalist society. History itself would cause the destruction of capitalism (theory of historical materialism) but men would necessarily have to help in order to speed up this process (theory of dialectical materialism). After a period of revolution, the state would temporarily be the only owner of all the means of production (dictatorship of the proletariat). There would be no more class division, as the state itself would be revealed as dispensable. New, ethical men and women would be born and would fully assert their humanity.

If Marx and Engels's theories of historical and dialectical materialism are supposed to be scientific, the images of the future resulting from the political revolution are no doubt speculative. In fact, in *The German Ideology* (1845), the description of the psychological revolution that would inevitably follow the political one can only be described as a socialist-communist utopia: the alteration of the economic relations between individuals would lead to the birth of a new species, capable of harmoniously interacting with others; once the system of the division of labour – which forces individuals to assert themselves as a mere extension of the process of production – is extinguished, the differences between the countryside and the cities would be diluted, and people would be able to assert themselves as spontaneous, voluntary and eclectic workers; this transformation of the way man faces work would be reflected in a myriad of harmonious relationships with other men and women and with nature itself.[12]

The idea that both Marx and Engels incorporated a utopian perspective into their thought is particularly important for the understanding of the development of utopian thought and literature; indeed, the fact that Marxism (which in the second half of the nineteenth century was the predominant form of socialism) systematically insisted on an anti-utopian discourse could lead us to the erroneous conclusion that it would cause the progressive emaciation of utopia, until its irreversible disappearance. However, Marxism not only did not provoke the death of utopian thought, but instead forced its transformation, a situation that was crucial to its success. As Karl Mannheim pointed out in *Ideology and Utopia* (1929), this transformation was denoted in the way the future came to be perceived: as the time of fulfilment of ideas that were not to be faced as mere dreams or wishes, but as something that was to be achieved.[13] Marxism in fact merged the sentiment of determinism provided by its scientific theories with the idea of a utopia set in the future, thus redefining utopia in terms of reality: on the one hand, the idea was presented as something essentially accomplishable at the end of the historic process; on the other hand, the way this would be done had already been clearly delimited. The present should therefore be seen in terms of its fulfilment in the future.

This perception of time was the most important change that Marxist thought effected in utopian literature, as it saw the fulfilment of utopia as part of historical development. Having absorbed the way Marxism conceived the future, literary utopias of the last decades of the nineteenth century – of which William Morris's *News from Nowhere* (1890) is no doubt the best example[14] – faced history as a process of growth of humanity, until it would reach a mature state, from which the ideal society would finally emerge. These utopias were thus truly euchronic, as they normally described a post-historical socialist-communist society on a world-scale. In fact, for Marx, as for Engels, history would only make sense if it was universal.

The turning of British literary utopia towards the future, at the end of the nineteenth century, must be seen as the climax of a change that gradually took place at the end of the eighteenth century. In reality, many of the ideas that integrated the Marxist doctrine, and particularly those that we have described as the socialist-communist utopia (the birth of a new man, the non-essential nature of the state, the importance of work for the affirmation of man's humanity), were but reformulations of ideas that Paine, Godwin and Owen, as well as the other utopian socialists, had already put forward in a different way. All these men had, in fact, already looked at the future with a hope they all tried to justify and divulge. But only Marxist thought was able to find in the laws of historical evolution a basis for that hope, thus taking on the role of the most important promoter of the idea of the possibility of a future full of happiness. We are, no doubt, very far away from the French literary euchronia written by Mercier. In fact, the French writer looked at the future motivated by a feeling of hope arising from the theories of infinite improvement of the Enlightenment, and which was reflected in material (scientific) and moral progress. To Mercier, progress was in fact to be faced as an attribute of man himself, and was reflected in his ability to change social and political institutions. English literary utopias, influenced by Marxism, regarded the future as a promise of history, and were based on a logic which opposed that of Mercier: the birth of the new man would only take place after the economic situation of society had changed. It was then urgent for man to take action, and to hasten the transformation. In this sense, socialist-communist utopias were particularly revolutionary; but they were also dynamic: utopia was no longer seen as a rigid, finished model, but as a guiding principle that could even be transcended. In fact, it has often been forgotten that communism was presented by Marx as the active principle for a short-term future that could be transcended by a later evolution towards a positive humanism.

From hope to disbelief and despair: satirical utopia, anti-utopia and dystopia

So far, we have merely looked at the positive side of utopia – utopia as a better place or time, a portrait of a happy society. But utopia also has a 'dark side', which was only overtly disclosed in the literary utopias of the nineteenth century. As we will see, the dark side is related to the turning of utopia towards the future, on the one hand, and to the idea of scientific and technological progress, on the other. The story of the darker side goes back to the eighteenth century, though, and is related to two other literary subgenres: satirical utopia and anti-utopia.

As we have seen in the previous section, the eighteenth century was characterized by an unusual trust in man's capacities. This confidence led man to think highly of himself and to believe that he would be able to transcend his human limitations. For many intellectuals of the eighteenth century, man was aspiring too high, which would inevitably lead to his fall. Although, as we said above, there were a few examples of serious proposals for the reordering of society, the majority of the literary utopias of that period offered a mirror where man would not be able to see his reflection but only that of a much distorted image of humanity. In those literary utopias, the journey to utopia, as well as the setting and nature of the utopian space, had no particular social relevance. While the utopias of the Renaissance had tried to confer verisimilitude on the description of the imaginary society by setting it in a distant, unknown part of the world, the satirical utopia overtly set the imaginary society in places which could neither possibly exist nor be reached, due to technological and biological impossibilities. Those places were really not important *per se*; in fact, they were only worth looking at insofar as they existed as opposite worlds. That is why the description of the organization of the imaginary society was quite often discarded as irrelevant, the narrative being centred on the adventures of the utopian traveller. Such was the case, for example, of the protagonist of *Gulliver's Travels* (1726); in this book by Jonathan Swift, the reader's attention is in fact captivated by Gulliver's presumably brilliant – but in reality very narrow-minded – schemes to survive in the rather silly worlds he visits. The result is that, in the end, it is the real world which is valued, and thus the positive dynamic which is typical of utopia is lost.[15]

But the scepticism of the conservative eighteenth-century intellectuals also gave birth to anti-utopia. This literary form could never have come into existence without the literary utopia, as it shares its strategies and its narrative artifices; it points, however, in a completely opposite direction. If utopia is about hope, and satirical utopia is about distrust, anti-utopia is clearly about total disbelief. In fact, in the anti-utopias of the eighteenth century, it was the utopian spirit itself which was ridiculed; their only aim was to denounce the irrelevance and inconsistency of utopian dreaming and the ruin of society it might entail.

When the idea of euchronia came to be systematically promoted (i.e., when utopian thought turned towards the future), it was inevitably accompanied by the imagination of darker times. The idea of 'utopia gone wrong' was not naturally born then, though: from time immemorial people have thought about the possibility of the construction of a better world, but they have also been aware of the likelihood of a future which might be worse than the present. As in the case of utopia, the concept of dystopia preceded the invention of the word.

The first recorded use of dystopia (which is another derivation neologism) dates back to 1868, and is to be found in a parliamentary speech in which John Stuart Mill tried to find a name for a perspective which was opposite to that of utopia: if utopia was commonly seen as 'too good to be practicable', then dystopia was 'too bad to be practicable'.[16] In that speech, Mill used the word dystopia as synonymous with cacotopia, a neologism that had been invented by Jeremy Bentham; and the two words have in fact a similar etymology and intention: *dys* comes from the Greek *dus*, and means bad, abnormal, diseased; *caco* comes from the Greek *kako*, which is used to refer to something which is unpleasant or incorrect. Since Mill's speech, many other designations have been put forward by different authors to refer to the idea of utopia gone wrong (such as negative utopia, regressive utopia, inverse utopia or nasty utopia), but Mill's neologism has prevailed.

In the last decades of the nineteenth century, euchronias had gained their place both in France and in England (but also in the United States), although, as we have seen, the idea of a better future was nourished by different per-spectives and beliefs. Predictably, the contemplation of a worse future also affected utopia as a literary genre. Thus, the word dystopia came into usage not only to refer to imaginary places that were worse than real places, but also to works describing places such as these.

Literary dystopia utilizes the narrative devices of literary utopia, incorp-orating into its logic the principles of euchronia (i.e., imagining what the same place – the place where the utopist lives – will be like in another time – the future), but predicts that things will turn out badly; it is thus essentially pessimistic in its presentation of projective images.

But although the images of the future put forward in dystopias may lead the reader to despair, the main aim of this sub-genre is didactic and moral-istic: images of the future are put forward as real possibilities because the utopist wants to frighten the reader and to make him realize that things may go either right or wrong, depending on the moral, social and civic respon-sibility of the citizens. A descendant of satirical utopia and of anti-utopia, dystopia rejects the idea that man can reach perfection. But although the writers of dystopias present very negative images of the future, they expect a very positive reaction on the part of their readers: on the one hand, the readers are led to realize that all human beings have (and will always have) flaws, and so social improvement – rather than individual improvement – is the only way to ensure social and political happiness; on the other hand, the readers are to understand that the depicted future is not a reality but only a possibility that they have to learn to avoid. If dystopias provoke despair on the part of the readers, it is because their writers want their readers to take them as a serious menace; they differ, though, in intent, from apocalyptic writings that confront man with the horror of the end of society and human-ity. Dystopias that leave no room for hope do in fact fail in their mission. Their true vocation is to make man realize that, since it is impossible for him to build an ideal society, then he must be committed to the construction of a better one. The writers of dystopias that have been published in the last three decades, in particular, have tried to make it very clear to their readers that there is still a chance for humanity to escape, normally offering a glim-mer of hope at the very end of the narrative; because of this, these utopias have often been called critical dystopias. They are, in fact, a variant of the same social dreaming that gives impetus to utopian literature.[17]

The optimistic view of the future that fed nineteenth-century euchronias met its end at the beginning of the twentieth century, and set the tone, with a few exceptions, for the whole century. It is true that there was a very brief moment of confidence, at the very end of the 1960s and in the 1970s, which was clearly linked to the students' movement of May 1968.

During those few years, utopia was fed by the hope of change put forward by ecologist, feminist and New Left thinkers. Still, those euchronic writings already revealed a different attitude towards utopian thinking, presenting views of a better future, but by no means a perfect future. The awareness of the existing flaws in imagined societies had a positive intent, though: they aimed at making the readers keep looking for alternatives. Because of this, they came to be called critical utopias. But apart from these years, the twentieth century was predominantly characterized by man's disappointment – and even incredulity – at the perception of his own nature, mostly when his terrifying deeds throughout the two World Wars were considered. In this context, utopian ideals seemed absurd; and the floor was inevitably left to dystopian discourse. In the second half of the twentieth century, in particular, dystopias became the predominant genre in the United States.

Two ideas, which are intimately connected, have fed dystopian discourse: on the one hand, the idea of totalitarianism; on the other hand, the idea of scientific and technological progress which, instead of impelling humanity to prosper, has sometimes been instrumental in the establishment of dictatorships. The first images of a future where the results of scientific and technological progress were misused are to be found in the canonical dystopias of the Russian writer Yevgeny Zamyatin (*We,* 1921), Aldous Huxley (*Brave New World*, 1932), and George Orwell (*Nineteen Eighty-Four*, 1949), and have, in fact, inspired generations of authors.[18] Mainly from the 1970s until the present, dystopias, nourished by projective images of scientific and technological advancement, have in fact been frequently confused with science fiction (which, as we have seen above, has also acquired a more acute political vocation).

Heterotopia is another neologism which is frequently used regarding dystopia. This neologism is of a different kind from the ones that we mentioned above. In fact, it was created as a medical term to refer to a misplacement of organs in the human body. When the French theorist Michel Foucault used the term heterotopia out of the context of medical usage, it had already been deneologized in that field; as it was new only insofar as it was being used in a different context, the word heterotopia can be classified as a diaphasic neologism. Heterotopian spaces are spaces that present an order which is completely different – even opposite – to that of real spaces. Within the context of dystopian literature, heterotopias represent a kind of a haven for the protagonists, and are very often to be found in their memories, in their dreams, or in places which, for some reason, are out of the reach of the invigilation system which normally prevails in those societies.[19]

The death of utopia? Political and philosophic utopias

In recent years, several anti-utopian authors have declared that utopia is on the verge of disappearing – if it is not dead already. These authors have grounded their claims on the idea that we are now witnessing a moment of cultural retreat, as well as of a vanishing of real political convictions, and envisage the fact that contemporary writers seem to be capable of writing dystopias only as a very clear sign of man's incapacity to put forward positive images of the future. The topic of the death of utopia is by no means new, and it dominated the intellectual discussion of the 1950s and the 1960s.[20] The prediction of such a death has been mainly grounded on three reasons.

The first reason – which is really the most common – is related to utopia as a literary genre; this is, however, a false reason. In fact, what we have witnessed, since the creation of utopia by Thomas More in 1516, is the history of an amazing survival of the literary genre, which has indeed been capable of adapting itself to the demands of new times. Actually, to each historical moment, utopian literature put forward made-to-measure solutions; and when those solutions seemed to be no longer suited to the problems posited by new historical circumstances, the announcement of the death of utopias seemed to be inevitable. This announcement was based, though, on confusion between the form (the literary genre) and content (the message). We can no doubt accept the idea of the death of the utopias of the Renaissance, of the utopias of the Enlightenment or of socialist utopias, in the sense that the solutions that they put forward had short-term relevance and ceased to be applicable to subsequent historical moments. The idea of the death of utopia as a literary genre is absurd, though. In effect, utopia has in the last two decades proved once more to be versatile and capable of adapting itself to the demands of the new world and to the technological interests of the younger generations. By adopting the logic of the narrative construction of hyperfiction,[21] utopia has in fact transformed itself into something that can best be described by a derivation neologism: hyperutopia. Posted on the Internet and relying on an assemblage of texts connected by Internet links, hyperutopia forces its reader to deal with the problems of multilinear reading, of the abolition of the idea of centre and margins, as well as of all forms of hierarchies. In fact, it is for the reader to decide which links are to be activated, each reading of the texts corresponding to a different interpretation. In the virtual space of the Internet, hyperutopia is the actual proof of utopia's capacity for change and will certainly ensure the survival of literary utopias – until the day the development of some new technologies leads us to more utopian (re)inventions.[22]

The second reason which has led anti-utopian thinkers to proclaim the death of utopia has to do with its identification with Marxist ideology, which dominated intellectual discussion throughout the second half of the twentieth century. It was first asserted by Karl Popper, in his famous book *The Open Society and its Enemies* (1945), where in a rather abusive way the philosopher put utopian and Marxist thought at the same level, denouncing both for being fed by a wish to construct a radically new, beautiful world at the cost of the sacrifice of good things that exist in the present.[23] The same reasoning was employed by a considerable number of authors of the 1950s and the 1960s. In fact, at that time, the theme of the death of utopia was intimately related to the ideas of the end of philosophy, the end of ideology and the end of history.

The third reason for the announcement of the death of utopia is, paradoxically, connected with a very positive view of the possibilities of changing society, and was the result of the revival of utopian spirit that took place in the late 1960s and 1970s. Representing this optimistic trend, Herbert Marcuse announced, in 1967, that the end of utopia was finally possible because all the material and intellectual forces that would enable change were already within the reach of man, who would only have to find a way to overcome the difficulties posed by the productive forces.[24]

Having looked at these reasons for the possible death of utopia, it is easy to see that this feeling has arisen due to the misconception that utopia must have a political agenda, which is to be fulfilled. This situation forces us to think about the nature of utopia: is it not possible for utopia to exist without an underlying political plan?

In order to answer this question, we first have to consider the very nature of utopia. As we have seen, utopian thought, defined as the tendency for man to think of an alternative when he lives in unfavourable circumstances, clearly preceded the invention of the word by Thomas More at the beginning of the sixteenth century. In fact, it could not have been otherwise, as utopian thought has an anthropological dimension, and must be seen as a manifestation of the wishing nature of man. This nature reveals itself in times when man is particularly discontent; in this way, the act of imagining, of creating what does not exist yet (to use Ernst Bloch's idea), is justified, on the one hand, by the very disposition of man towards utopia, and is aroused, on the other hand, by his dissatisfaction with the circumstances in which he lives.[25]

Actually, the idea of the death of utopia derives from a very common confusion of the concepts of utopia, project and ideology: utopia is innate to man and has a perennial and immeasurable nature; by contrast, ideological projects are provisional solutions to transitory problems. Utopia may well be nourished by a project, but its strength is not totally exhausted by it; it has an energy of its own, which outlives the blueprint. We can certainly understand this better if we bear in mind the distinction, suggested by Ernst Bloch, between ideal and idealization.[26] Utopia belongs to the realm of the ideal, whereas the project belongs to the realm of idealization. Political–ideological utopia derives from the coincidence of the ideal with the idealization; and if it seems to have a short lifetime, this is because the idealization cannot, by nature, overcome the frontiers of the problems it tries to solve. The utopian ideal, however, is nourished by an immeasurable and perennial desire – a surplus of desire – which not only ensures the survival of utopia, but also its dynamic nature.

The distinction between the concepts of ideal and idealization provides us with a basis for the understanding of the difference between the political utopia and the philosophical utopia, as well as with an explanation for the fact that only sometimes is utopia capable of fulfilling its catalytic function, that is, of inspiring man to take action.[27] The political vocation of utopia was particularly apparent in the seventeenth century in England, in the works of Winstanley and Harrington, for example, and even more systematically promoted in the nineteenth century in the works of utopists such as the British designer and writer William Morris or the American writer Edward Bellamy, where the entanglement of utopia and socialist thought was more obvious.

However, as we have seen, the twentieth century was mostly nourished by dystopian (if not completely disenchanted) images of the future. Actually, in spite of the very inspiring critical works of thinkers such as Ernst Bloch (1885–1977) and Karl Mannheim (1893–1947), the catalytic function of utopia was only revealed in the late 1960s and in the 1970s, cherished by the hope of feminist, ecological and New Left thinkers. But what has become of utopia at the dawn of the new millennium?

Utopia today

The world is experiencing a grave crisis; the nature of our predicament is economic, environmental, social and political, but it is certainly also philosophical. Throughout history, utopia has been subject to similar pressures – will it not have a role to play this time? Looking around, it seems that utopia has been replaced by images of a very unsatisfactory present, or, in the case of utopian literature, by images of a dystopian future. Has man lost his capacity to think of alternatives? Is utopia, in fact, finally on the verge of death?

Neither utopia as a concept nor as a literary genre is moribund; on the contrary, it is alive and well. We may have some difficulty in recognizing it because, once more, it has given proof of its extraordinary capacity to survive by reinventing itself. This process of reinvention has been dictated by the common confusion we mentioned above between utopia and political blueprints. At the end of the nineteenth century and in the first half of the twentieth century, utopia was too easily identified with socialist-communist projects, as well as with the idea of totalitarianism. The two World Wars, Hitler's utopian aspiration to 'purify the human race' and the collapse of the communist regimes all over the world led people to retreat from dreaming and forced them to adopt a very realistic perspective. Stigmatized by the ideas of impossibility and totalitarianism, utopian thought underwent an expressive change, and redefined its scope of action.

Although it did not abandon the idea of the future, utopian thought began to face it in a more short-term way. In fact, the vision of a completely different future, based on the annihilation of the present, which had been put forward by the political utopias of the nineteenth century, was replaced by a focus on a slower but effective change of the present. Utopia has then reshaped its nature and, by emphasizing its pragmatic features, it came to be associated with the idea of social betterment. Actually, the more usual formula promoted by an increasing number of authors would some decades ago have been considered a paradox – the idea of pragmatic utopianism. Abandoning the idea of blueprints and the need to define ambitious targets to be reached, utopia is now asserted as a process, and is incorporated in the daily construction of life in society.[28] There has no doubt been a significant shift: utopia no longer aspires to change the world at a macro-level, and is focused now on operating at a micro-level.[29] Inevitably, a new set of concepts has become part of utopian discourse: being envisaged mainly as a process of transformation, utopia incorporated the idea of possibilitism, and the thought of a sustainable utopianism took shape.

However, the concept of a pragmatic utopia must not be seen as a betrayal of the utopian visions of old times. Utopia has certainly not lost its critical perspective of the present; instead, it has become more relevant to the transformation of society: it continues to question, and the desire to accomplish effective change is still alive. However, the idea of a blueprint has been replaced by the idea of vaguer guidelines, indicating a direction for man to follow, but never a point to be reached. Contemporary utopianism is in fact dynamic, as it is nourished by the Blochian concept of a surplus of desire.

From this perspective, we can clearly see the functions that contemporary utopian thought has to fulfil. If it is true that its compensatory function has been rendered more visible, it is also true that its critical function has been reinforced, since the present is now seen not as a reality that has to be destroyed and replaced by a totally different society, but as a time-space from which we need to depart. By establishing horizons of expectations (with the inevitable awareness that they will never be reached), utopias guide man to the reinvention and the reconstruction of humanity, and thus lead him to his emancipation. By this process, utopia also performs an expressive catalytic function.

Utopia is thus to be seen essentially as a strategy. By imagining another reality, in a virtual present or in a hypothetical future, utopia is set as a strategy for the questioning of reality and of the present. Taking mainly the shape of a process, refusing the label of an 'impossible dream', utopia is a programme for change and for a gradual betterment of the present; in that sense, it operates at different levels, as a means towards political, economic, social, moral and pedagogical reorientation. At last, utopia has become a strategy of creativity, clearing the way for the only path that man can possibly follow: the path of creation. By incorporating into its logic the dynamic of dreams and using creativity as its very driving force, utopia reveals itself as the (only possible?) sustainable scheme for overcoming the contemporary crisis.

NOTES

1 There are several moments in the creation of a neologism: (1) the moment when it is created; (2) the moment when it is received and starts being used by a given group; (3) the moment when it is *deneologized*, in other words when it ceases to sound unusual and is incorporated into the lexicon of that group.

2 On the importance of the idea of otherness for the definition of utopia, see Louis Marin, 'Frontiers of Utopia: Past and Present', *Critical Inquiry* 19:3 (1993), 403–11, and Darko Suvin, 'Theses on Dystopia 2001', in Tom Moylan and Raffaella Baccolini (eds.), *Dark Horizons: Science Fiction and the Dystopian Imagination* (New York: Routledge, 2003), pp. 187–201.

3 For a thorough analysis of these characteristics see Ruth Levitas, *The Concept of Utopia* (New York: Philip Allan, 1990).

4 Raymond Ruyer famously described these possible alternatives as *the possible laterals* in *L'Utopie et les utopies* (Paris: P.U.F., 1950). The concept of *not-yet*, which forms the ontological structure of Ernst Bloch's thought, is very important for the understanding of utopia as the principle of hope, since it presents the universe as an open system where nothing is static and where everything is in a constant process of formation. *Not-yet* is in fact the driving force of the idea of possibility for the future.

5 On the need for a distinction between utopianism and utopia as a literary genre, see Raymond Trousson, *Voyages aux Pays de Nulle Part: Histoire de la Pensée Utopique* (Brussels: Éditions de l'Université de Bruxelles, 1979) and Vita Fortunati, 'Utopia as a Literary Genre', in Vita Fortunati and Raymond Trousson (eds.), *Dictionary of Literary Utopias* (Paris: Honoré Champion, 2000), pp. 634–43. Lyman Sargent suggests utopianism has been expressed in three different forms: utopian literature, communitarianism and utopian social theory in 'The Three Faces of Utopianism Revisited', *Utopian Studies* 5:1 (1994), 1–37.

6   For a description of the utopian motifs (tempests, shipwrecks …) and of recurrent characters in utopian literature, see Vita Fortunati, 'Fictional Strategies and Political Messages in Utopias', in Nadia Minerva (ed.), *Per una definizione dell'utopia: Atti del Convegno Internazionale di Bagni di Lucca, 12–14 settembre 1990* (Ravenna: Longo, 1992). On the importance of the voyage in utopia, see Marin, 'Frontiers of Utopia'.

7   Several authors, such as Darko Suvin in *Metamorphoses of Science Fiction: On the Poetics and History of a Literary Genre* (New Haven: Yale University Press, 1979) and Lyman Tower Sargent, 'The Problem of the Flawed Utopia', in Moylan and Baccolini (eds.), *Dark Horizons*, pp. 225–31, have refused to integrate the idea of perfection into the notion of utopia. On the argument that the idea of flaw is closer to utopia than the idea of perfection, see Sargent, 'The Problem'.

8   Louis-Sébastien Mercier, *L'An 2440: Un rêve s'il en fut jamais* (translated into English as *Memoirs of the Year Two Thousand Five Hundred*) (1771).

9   The publication of *Utopias of the British Enlightenment* by Gregory Claeys (Cambridge University Press, 1994) was very important in that sense, as it shed light on utopias that had literally been forgotten and that put forward constructive views of positive societies. Such is the case of 'Ideal of a Perfect Commonwealth', by David Hume, and 'Description of "New Athens"', by Ambrose Philips, included in that volume.

10 Thomas Paine, *Rights of Man*, Part I (J. S. Jordan: London, 1791), Part II (1792).

11 William Godwin, *Enquiry Concerning Political Justice* (London: G. G. J. and J. Robinson, 1793).

12 Karl Marx and Friedrich Engels, *The German Ideology* (1845) (Moscow: Marx-Engels Institute, 1932).

13 Karl Mannheim, *Ideology and Utopia* (1929) (London: Routledge & Kegan Paul, 1936).

14 William Morris, *News from Nowhere* (London: Kelmscott Press, 1892).

15 The background to satirical utopia is Greek satire. The latter is in fact a *prefiguration* of the former, just as the myth of the Golden Age is a prefiguration of utopia itself.

16 John Stuart Mill, *The Collected Works of John Stuart Mill: Public and Parliamentary Speeches Part I November 1850–November 1868*, ed. John M. Robson and Bruce L. Kinzer (Toronto and London: University of Toronto Press and Routledge & Kegan Paul, 1988), vol. 28, ch. 88, 'The State of Ireland 12 March, 1868'.

17 On the idea of critical utopias and dystopias, see Tom Moylan, *Demand the Impossible: Science Fiction and the Utopian Imagination* (New York: Methuen, 1987) and Moylan and Baccolini (eds.), *Dark Horizons*.

18 Yevgeny Zamyatin, *We* (1921) (London: Jonathan Cape, 1970); Aldous Huxley, *Brave New World* (London: Chatto & Windus, 1932); George Orwell, *Nineteen Eighty-Four* (London: Secker & Warburg, 1949).

19 For a thorough analysis of the ways the word heterotopia has been used, see Kevin Hetherington, *The Badlands of Modernity: Heterotopia and Social Ordering* (London: Routledge, 1997).

20 Some good examples of this attitude can be found in Judith Shklar, *After Utopia: The Decline of Political Faith* (Princeton University Press, 1957), Seymour Martin Lipset, *Political Man* (London: Heinemann, 1960), Daniel Bell, *The End of Ideology* (Glencoe, IL: Free Press, 1960) and Raymond Aron, *Eighteen Lectures on Industrial Society* (New York: Free Press, 1962).

21 The concept of hyperfiction results from the conjugation of two notions: hypertext and fiction. Hypertext opened up the possibility of non-sequential reading and thus a different reading on the part of the reader, according to his/her interest in the information conveyed.

22 Hyperutopias differ from both micronations and virtual communities in that they describe imaginary countries, reporting with careful detail the invented political, economic, social and religious systems. Relying on cyborg aesthetics, hyperutopias are 'open texts' and must be seen as pieces of literature that materialize the experiment in hypertextual literature. For a good example of a hyperutopia, see the country of Bergonia (www.bergonia.org).

23 Karl Popper, *The Open Society and its Enemies* (1945) rev. edn (Princeton University Press, 1950).

24 Herbert Marcuse, *La Fin de l'Utopie* (Paris: Éditions du Seuil, 1967). In fact Marcuse gave voice to an optimistic view of the future which characterized the 1970s, when, as Raffaella Baccolini and Tom Moylan have pointed out in *Dark Horizons* (2003), ecological, feminist and New Left thought gave shape to a utopian revival.

25 On the anthropological disposition of the human being towards utopia, see Frank and Fritzie Manuel, *Utopian Thought in the Western World* (Cambridge, MA: The Belknap Press of Harvard University Press, 1979), Vincent Geoghegan, *Utopianism and Marxism* (Oxford: Peter Lang, 2008) and Cosimo Quarta, 'Homo Utopicus: On the Need for Utopia', *Utopian Studies* 7:2 (1996), 153–66. For a contrary view see Levitas, *The Concept of Utopia* and Krishnan Kumar, *Utopia and Anti-Utopia in Modern Times* (Oxford: Basil Blackwell, 1987).

26 For an elaboration on the distinction between the concepts of *ideal* and *idealization*, see Henri Maler, *Convoiter l'Impossible* (Paris: Albin Michel, 1995).

27 On the discussion of the need for a distinction between philosophical and political utopias, see Adalberto Dias de Carvalho, 'From Contemporary Utopias to Contemporaneity as a Utopia', in Fátima Vieira and Marinela Freitas (eds.), *Utopia Matters: Theory, Politics, Literature and the Arts* (Porto: Editora University Press, 2005), pp. 63–80.

28 Good examples of this shift can be found in Lucy Sargisson, *Utopian Bodies and the Politics of Transgression* (London: Routledge, 2000), Arrigo Colombo, 'The New Sense of Utopia: The Construction of a Society Based on Justice', *Utopian Studies* 11:2 (2000), 181–97, Eric McKenna, *The Task of Utopia: Politics and Culture in an Age of Apathy* (New York: Basic Books, 2001) and Michael Marien, 'Utopia Revisited: New Thinking on Social Betterment', *The Futurist* 36:2 (March/April, 2002), 37–43.

29 Recent literary utopias reflect this new utopian attitude. See Fredric Jameson, *Archaeologies of the Future: The Desire Called Utopia and Other Science Fictions* (London: Verso, 2007) for a description of the way utopias have become auto-referential and meta-utopian.

BIBLIOGRAPHY

Aron, Raymond, *Eighteen Lectures on Industrial Society* (New York: Free Press, 1962).
Baccolini, Raffaella and Tom Moylan, 'Dystopia and Histories', in Tom Moylan and Raffaella Baccolini (eds.), *Dark Horizons: Science Fiction and the Dystopian Imagination* (New York: Routledge, 2003), pp. 1–12.
Bell, Daniel, *The End of Ideology* (Glencoe, IL: Free Press, 1960).
Carvalho, Adalberto Dias de, 'From Contemporary Utopias to Contemporaneity as a Utopia', in Fátima Vieira and Marinela Freitas (eds.), *Utopia Matters: Theory, Politics, Literature and the Arts* (Porto: Editora University Press, 2005), pp. 63–80.
Claeys, Gregory (ed.), *Utopias of the British Enlightenment* (Cambridge University Press, 1994).
Colombo, Arrigo, 'The New Sense of Utopia: The Construction of a Society Based on Justice', *Utopian Studies* 11:2 (2000), 181–97.
Fortunati, Vita, 'Fictional Strategies and Political Messages in Utopias', in Nadia Minerva (ed.), *Per una definizione dell'utopia: Atti del Convegno Internazionale di Bagni di Lucca, 12–14 settembre 1990* (Ravenna: Longo, 1992).
  'Utopia as a Literary Genre', in Vita Fortunati and Raymond Trousson (eds.), *Dictionary of Literary Utopias* (Paris: Honoré Champion, 2000), pp. 634–43.
Geoghegan, Vincent, *Utopianism and Marxism* (Oxford: Peter Lang, 2008).
Godwin, William, *Enquiry Concerning Political Justice* (London: G. G. J. & J. Robinson, 1793).
Hetherington, Kevin, *The Badlands of Modernity: Heterotopia and Social Ordering* (London: Routledge, 1997).
Huxley, Aldous, *Brave New World* (London: Chatto & Windus, 1932).
Jameson, Fredric, *Archaeologies of the Future: The Desire Called Utopia and Other Science Fictions* (London: Verso, 2007).
Kumar, Krishan, *Utopia and Anti-Utopia in Modern Times* (Oxford and New York: Basil Blackwell, 1987).
Levitas, Ruth, *The Concept of Utopia* (New York: Philip Allan, 1990).
Lipset, Seymour Martin, *Political Man* (London: Heinemann, 1960).
Maler, Henri, *Convoiter l'Impossible* (Paris: Albin Michel, 1995).
Mannheim, Karl, *Ideology and Utopia* (1929) (London: Routledge & Kegan Paul, 1936).
Manuel, Frank and Fritzie Manuel, *Utopian Thought in the Western World* (Cambridge, MA: The Belknap Press of Harvard University Press, 1979).
Marcuse, Herbert, *La Fin de l'Utopie* (Paris: Éditions du Seuil, 1967).
Marien, Michael, 'Utopia Revisited: New Thinking on Social Betterment', *The Futurist* 36:2 (March/April, 2002), 37–43.
Marin, Louis, 'Frontiers of Utopia: Past and Present', *Critical Inquiry* 19:3 (1993), 403–11.
Marx, Karl and Friedrich Engels, *The German Ideology* (1845) (Moscow: Marx-Engels Institute, 1932).
Mercier, Louis-Sébastien, *L'An 2440: Un rêve s'il en fut jamais* (1771; translated into English as *Memoirs of the Year Two Thousand Five Hundred*).

McKenna, Erin, *The Task of Utopia: Politics and Culture in an Age of Apathy* (New York: Basic Books, 2001).

Mill, John Stuart, *The Collected Works of John Stuart Mill: Public and Parliamentary Speeches Part I November 1850–November 1868*, ed. John M. Robson and Bruce L. Kinzer (Toronto and London: University of Toronto Press and Routledge & Kegan Paul, 1988), vol. 28, ch. 88, 'The State of Ireland 12 March, 1868'.

Morris, William, *News from Nowhere* (London: Kelmscott Press, 1892).

Moylan, Tom, *Demand the Impossible: Science Fiction and the Utopian Imagination* (New York: Methuen, 1987).

Moylan, Tom and Raffaella Baccolini (eds.), *Dark Horizons: Science Fictions and the Dystopian Impulse* (New York: Routledge, 2003).

Orwell, George, *Nineteen Eighty-Four* (London: Secker & Warburg, 1949).

Paine, Thomas, *Rights of Man* (J. S. Jordan: London, 1791 and 1792).

Popper, Karl, *The Open Society and its Enemies* (1945) rev. edn (Princeton University Press, 1950).

Quarta, Cosimo, 'Homo Utopicus: On the Need for Utopia', *Utopian Studies* 7:2 (1996), 153–66.

Ruyer, Raymond, *L'Utopie et les utopies* (Paris: P.U.F., 1950).

Sargent, Lyman T., 'The Three Faces of Utopianism Revisited', *Utopian Studies* 5:1 (1994), 1–37.

'The Problem of the Flawed Utopia', in Tom Moylan and Raffaella Baccolini (eds.), *Dark Horizons: Science Fiction and the Dystopian Imagination* (New York: Routledge, 2003), pp. 225–31.

Sargisson, Lucy, *Utopian Bodies and the Politics of Transgression* (London: Routledge, 2000).

Shklar, Judith, *After Utopia: The Decline of Political Faith* (Princeton University Press, 1957).

Suvin, Darko, *Metamorphoses of Science Fiction: On the Poetics and History of a Literary Genre* (New Haven: Yale University Press, 1979).

'Theses on Dystopia 2001', in Tom Moylan and Raffaella Baccolini (eds.), *Dark Horizons: Science Fiction and the Dystopian Imagination* (New York: Routledge, 2003), pp. 187–201.

Swift, Jonathan, *Travels into Several Remote Nations of the World. In Four Parts. By Lemuel Gulliver…* (London: Benjamin Motte, 1726 [revised 1735]).

Trousson, Raymond, *Voyages aux Pays de Nulle Part: Histoire de la Pensée Utopique* (Brussels: Éditions de l'Université de Bruxelles, 1979).

'Utopia as a Literary Genre', in Vita Fortunati and Raymond Trousson (eds.), *Dictionary of Literary Utopias* (Paris: Honoré Champion, 2000), pp. 634–43.

Zamyatin, Yevgeny, *We* (1921) (London: Jonathan Cape, 1970).

2

J. C. DAVIS

Thomas More's *Utopia*: sources, legacy and interpretation

Towards the end of his discussion of the good life, happiness and unhappiness in Plato's *Republic* (591a–592b), Socrates stresses the importance of self-rule or self-discipline as a key to producing 'attunement and harmony' within each individual. To become involved in the vexed business, turmoil and conflict of governing flawed communities, might make such interior harmony or peace of mind unattainable. The good, having struggled to achieve attunement and harmony, should seriously consider jeopardizing it before entering the fray of politics in an imperfect world. Only in the ideal society which Socrates and Glaucon, earlier in their dialogue, had 'just been founding and describing' but 'which can't be accommodated anywhere in the world, and therefore rests at the level of ideas', might it be possible to be socially and politically active without corruption and self-destruction. Nevertheless, that ideal society 'is retained in heaven as a paradigm for those who desire to see it and *through seeing it, to return from exile*'. Whether it actually exists or not is of no matter, since it remains the only community in whose government the good and happy person could participate without ceasing to be good or happy. It remained their only true home; their return from exile.

There are multiple tensions at work here. The dilemma of the good citizen confronting the disquieting, even corrupting, influence of politics in a dysfunctional world is paralleled by the choice between the inescapable turmoil of political participation and the possible 'attunement and harmony' of contemplative detachment. But the twist of the knife was that detaching oneself from the life and problems of the community induced a sense of alienation, failure of duty and compromised goodness, of exile. Contemplating a society in which these tensions could not arise, however fictitious that society was, might be the only source of relief.

This dilemma, Plato's dual approach to it and the general precedent of his *Republic*, haunt, without ever dominating, More's *Utopia*. Plato's justification for utopian thinking is replicated there as are the tensions exposed in his discussion of the good life. More's masterpiece is, however, both a more eclectic work than this might suggest and one in which the question of human goodness, and its confrontation with social deficiency, is made even more intractable by the underlying context of Christian ethics.

Thomas More's *Utopia* was the collaborative product of an early sixteenth-century European intellectual elite, in Latin but engaging with the classical Greek of which they were advocates. This linguistic complexity has not prevented it enjoying worldwide popularity, being translated into numerous vernaculars and scarcely ever out of print in the 500 years since its first publication in 1516. It is at once jocular and serious, seeking both to profit and delight the reader. One of its jokes is inherent in the word which came to be its title, 'Utopia'. More coined this word from Greek roots, eu-topia (the place where things are well) and u-topia (no place) but it is a word which, overcoming its Latinized-Greek origins, has taken on a life of its own. Versions of it exist in all major languages. It has become a term of common parlance, its linguistic complexity lost to most of its users. More is often credited with re-establishing as well as naming, a tradition, the modern utopian, and by extension dystopian, tradition. Yet some see *Utopia* as a profoundly anti-utopian work. In its early editions the principal text accumulated supporting letters, poems, artwork, an alphabet and a map (the *parerga*) by More's collaborators, all designed to clarify what the work meant to them, how it was written and how it should be read. Despite this, controversy has raged unabated about the correct interpretation of the text and, for many, *Utopia* has come to seem a question without an answer. It was More's first extended prose publication and yet it is a masterpiece of European literature. Where did it come from: a moment when More confronted the option of state service or from a long intellectual gestation?

The interpretative debate begins within the text itself and in a manner which signals interpretative complexity. The story begins with Thomas More (a real person and author) meeting Peter Giles (a real person and friend) outside the church of Notre Dame, 'the most beautiful and popular church in Antwerp' (possibly a real encounter). Giles introduces More to Raphael Hythloday, a Portuguese traveller and intellectual. The fictional status of Hythloday would be immediately obvious to More's scholarly readers by his names. 'Raphael' was both an angelic messenger and responsible for curing Tobit's blindness in the Apocryphal Book of Tobit. In counterpoint, 'Hythloday' suggested to humanist grammarians an idle talker, a dealer in nonsense or an expert in trifles. Once this move was made, the name 'Thomas More' became fair game: 'Thomas', the sceptical, doubting apostle, and 'Morus', the fool – a particularly relevant inference given the publication of *Moriae Encomium* (*Praise of Folly*) by Erasmus in 1511. So learned

readers were immediately being asked to decide whether to attach credibil-
ity to an account by the most disinterested and experienced of travellers, a
healer and divine messenger, but also perhaps a purveyor of nonsense, or to
the reaction of a sceptic who might also be a fool. Responses to those char-
acterizations continue to play a central part in the interpretative debate.

The issue is complicated by textual uncertainties. The first five (1516–19)
Latin editions of the work all differed. The three earliest translations (German
(1524), Italian (1548), French (1550)) all omitted Book I entirely, thus producing a work of a completely different character and, to cap it all, *Utopia* was
not the original title of the book. The first Latin edition published in England
did not appear until 1663, almost a century and a half after the first edition
and after numerous Latin editions had been published in Louvain (six), Paris,
Basel (three), Florence, Cologne (two), Wittenberg, Frankfurt, Hanover (two),
Milan and Amsterdam (two). By the time an English translation was first in
print (1551), *Utopia* was already available in German, Italian and French.
It is important therefore to recognize that it was pre-eminently a work of
European, not English, literature. More's Latin was compressed but lucid,
vigorous, elegant and allusive in complex ways. Translating it remains a challenge and one never satisfactorily met to all tastes.[1] Addressing his patron,
William Cecil, Ralph Robynson, translator of the first English edition (1551),
noted that, as a Catholic martyr, More had remained blind to the true light
of the Gospel. The adoption of a post-Reformation prism through which to
view the work and its author was but the first of many adjustments of interpretation to changing times and contexts. Bishop Gilbert Burnet, translating
Utopia in the 1680s, when Catholicism was resurgent, to dissociate More
from that process presented him as 'a Protestant reformer *avant la lettre*'.[2]
In Enlightenment Scotland an edition of Burnet's translation published in
1743 was subtitled 'A Philosophical Romance'. By the mid-nineteenth and
early twentieth centuries, *Utopia* was often seen as a foundation document
of modern socialism. The most extreme manifestation of this was the inclusion of More's name on an obelisk commemorating the eighteen founders
of communism, erected on Lenin's orders in post-revolutionary Moscow.
Utopia continues to be hailed as one of the harbingers of modernity.[3] But a
text for which such weighty importance was claimed could also be read as a
jeu d'esprit, an exhibition of Renaissance versatility, or, as C. S. Lewis put it,
'a holiday work'.[4]

The publication of the most elaborate English/Latin edition of *Utopia* in
1965, in the Yale University Press edition of More's complete works, was
an attempt to escape anachronism and refine the contextualization of the
work.[5] This goal of establishing a more precise historical contextualization
has dominated serious discussion of the work in the last half century. Debate

has been engaged on two fronts: what is the appropriate context into which the work should be placed and what keys to the work's meaning can be derived from that context? An ancillary debate has been over More's seriousness about the utopian model presented in Book II. Was it meant, even if not as a blueprint for social change, then as a Platonic model to console and guide the good and wise political actor? Or, does it suggest the folly, the nowhere, of rigid idealism in the real world and is it, perhaps, a profoundly anti-utopian work? Or yet again, is it a witty but serious exploration of the problem of accommodating ideals to political realities, of the price the good and wise may have to pay to perform their civic duties, a work which raises questions that, in the end, it challenges the reader to answer? All of these issues have a moral dimension and for More and his collaborators, whether we call them Christian humanists or not, this raised the problem of the efficacy of Christian ethics. All of them are questions with a wider relevance for our general approach to modern utopian literature.

The conundrums of More's great fiction continue to generate a rich and remarkable literature.[6] This chapter will focus on where the contextual consensus has settled in the last two decades and where major differences remain. It suggests that there may be sufficient clues, both in the text itself and in other contemporary works, to guide us towards a closer approximation to More's intentions.

In an influential series of essays, Quentin Skinner established the centrality to More's text of the 'best state' exercise inaugurated by Plato and continuing to preoccupy his readers thereafter. Linked to these concerns was a divergence of views on 'true nobility' – merit only (Plato) or partially a function of lineage, leisure and wealth (Aristotle) – and to the relative merits of political engagement (*vita activa*) compared with political detachment (*vita contemplativa*).[7] To this, David Wootton has added the notion of *Utopia* as a meditation on friendship, the ideal of a community of friends versus the reality of a society of enemies or, at least, rivals.[8] Here More was influenced by Erasmus, himself building on ideas expressed by Pythagoras, Plato and Cicero. In the 1515 edition of his *Adages*, Erasmus began with two proverbs which seem to inform More's utopian design: 'Between friends all is common' and 'Friendship is equality. A friend is another self.' In its equality of goods, labour and leisure, Utopia then looks like a Pythagorean society of friends. But Erasmus, discussing the two proverbs, had also been at pains to point out that 'nothing that was said by a pagan philosopher comes closer to the mind of Christ'.[9]

Most scholars working on *Utopia* would accept Skinner's and Wootton's findings but the reference to Erasmus points us to a further debate. To what extent was *Utopia* building on the work of Erasmus and the 'Christian humanists' or was it, in effect, a critique of their views? For George M. Logan, *Utopia* rejects the view that politics is a matter of personal morality rather than of institutional and conventional constraints. In other words, it brushes aside the assumptions underpinning *The Education of a Christian Prince* which Erasmus wrote in the year that *Utopia* was first published.[10] More recently, it has been suggested that More's argument, rather than challenging, may have rested on Erasmus's work, in particular the latter's edition of Seneca on which he was working at the time that More was writing *Utopia*. In this view, the dialogue of Book I sets Seneca's advocacy of the *vita contemplativa* against Cicero's urging of the *vita activa*.[11] Also attempting to locate More's book in the context of Erasmian debates, Eric Nelson has argued that, in its willingness to embrace communism, its preference for happiness over glory and contemplation over participation, its values are Greek rather than Roman.[12]

A problem with these interpretations is that they tend to polarize debates, within Erasmian circles, where an exploration of many positions was in process. It is also misleading to reduce the political thought of classical Greece and Rome to monolithic entities, readily opposed one to another. There are differences but writers like Cicero, Sallust, Augustine and Jerome – all admired by More and his friends – were self-conscious transmitters of a Greek heritage. Above all, *Utopia* is an enormously eclectic work, a bravura display of humanist learning and wit. It is this, allied with its playfulness, its Lucianic, ludic and serio-comic tone which has led to a growing emphasis on its interpretative indeterminacy. John Ruskin described it as 'perhaps the most really mischievous book ever written'. Recent commentators have seen More's intention in *Utopia* as to provoke a reader response rather than to give a definitive authorial direction. Two of the most probing and illuminating exponents of this view have been Dominic Baker-Smith and Elizabeth McCutcheon. The latter's study of one item in the extensive *parerga*, More's letter to Giles, stresses the destabilizing effect of paradox in *Utopia* typified by the 'inexhaustible paradoxicality' of this letter.[13] Likewise, Baker-Smith concluded that 'the function of the book is not to establish a preferred viewpoint but to convey through its literary form a complex interplay of ideas which lie at the very roots of Western political discussion'. In the end the reader was obliged 'to shoulder the burden of interpretation' but definitive meanings ran counter to the careful balance of More's dialogue.[14] Perhaps the extremes of interpretative indeterminacy are reached in Marina Leslie's depiction of *Utopia* as a Foucaultian 'heterotopia' on the basis that, while most utopias run with the grain of language, and therefore of meaning, More's work undermines both, so that the reader is ultimately left in a no place between cynical pragmatism and unyielding idealism.[15]

There is a case for caution in reaching for any definitive interpretation of a work which has all the playfulness of a puzzle, teasing with both words and ideas. More's intention is, in part, to present multiple perspectives, to open and reopen the question from many directions and to deepen our engagement with the problem. But, as always, indeterminacy has its limits. More chose to problematize some issues and not others. What do his choices tell us about his intentions in this work? There are limits to the questions *Utopia* sets. Can we discern any limitations on what he saw as the possible range of answers? Can we track down any reliable interpretative meaning – or does the modern utopian tradition begin in a blur of questions without answers?

The openness to interpretation of *Utopia* may in part be attributed to the fact that the work draws on a number of hotly debated issues which More's friends encountered in their studies of classical authors.[16] The most obvious of these is that of the state most conducive to the good life. The Platonic formula, that only the collaboration of philosophers and kings could be the basis for such an outcome, raised the problem of political counsel. On what terms could philosophy and wisdom inform politics? From Plato onwards, it was recognized that the good and wise (the philosopher) confronted a choice between the risk of corruption attendant on political engagement, and the sense of exile, or neglect of duty, inherent in a retreat to the contemplative life. While the much-admired Cicero chose the former, Pico della Mirandola (whose biography, translated by More, was published in 1510) had deliberately chosen the latter.

Introducing a Christian dimension at a time of serious religious renewal, heightened the urgency of these problems. In a fallen world how much could the moral heroics of devout individuals be expected to achieve? Augustine, on whose *City of God* More had lectured in 1501, had suggested that the most we could achieve in the earthly city was a kind of second best. How then should we engage with that city so as not to find ourselves slipping from that already compromised standard? Might we be able to restructure the earthly city to make engagement with it more morally satisfactory? Central to this cluster of questions for More, as a man strenuously committed to lay Christian piety, was how the optimum state of a commonwealth (*De Optimo Republicae Statu*) could be built around deficient human beings. Erasmus, in his *Education of a Christian Prince,* advised sinful human beings to act as if they had never fallen, to re-engage in the pursuit of moral standards which they had proven incapable of in the most favourable of circumstances, pre-lapsarian Eden. In this sense, *Utopia* is a critique, not only of 'Erasmian humanism', but of the whole perfect moral commonwealth, mirror-of-princes' tradition.

Achieving the optimum – even if this was the optimum second best – was accordingly dependent on institutional and social restructuring, on envisaging an alternative world, not one mired in the flawed customs of the contemporary *polis*, nor one which assumed the transformation of nature, human or material. In imagining an alternative world, More could draw on three kinds of resources. The first were the examples of predecessors like Plato. Their fictions generally functioned at a high level of abstraction and *Utopia* was to take a different course, vigorously embracing the specific. Secondly, there were the exciting and recently published accounts of the 'New World'. More's brother-in-law, John Rastell, himself embarked, six months after the publication of *Utopia*, on a voyage to the 'New Found Lands'. Since Hythloday was said to have accompanied Amerigo Vespucci on the last three of his four voyages, More may well have known the latter's sensational accounts of his adventures. Equally, Pietro Martire d'Anghiera's *De orbe novo* (1511) may have been a source of some inspiration. Both accounts alluded to communism, female involvement in warfare and contempt for gold – all features of utopian society. But arguably as important, if not more so, was the theatre, an alternative world following alternative scripts and conventions.

As a youth, in the household of Cardinal Morton, More had both witnessed and taken part in domestic theatrical performances. Henry Medwall, Morton's chaplain at that time, was also a dramatist. More's brother-in-law, John Rastell, had his own stage on his estate and Erasmus claimed that More not only performed but wrote plays for such private productions. But the theatre was also important to him as a metaphor, an alternative way of looking at the world. The trope of the world as a stage was conspicuous in works like Lucian's *Necromantia*, Erasmus's *Praise of Folly* and More's own *Richard III* (where kings' games were compared to stage plays on a scaffold, a political theatre which consumed its actors). Cicero used the drama metaphor repeatedly in *De Officiis* and in his political speeches. As well as in the *Praise of Folly*, Erasmus used it in his *Copia*, the *Adages* and *The Ciceronian*. Seeing the world as a stage suggested a social environment of illusion, where actors persuaded themselves that they were other than they were and conspired in the self-delusion of their audience. Players acted and responded to the particular conventions and scripts they were given. It might, nevertheless, be possible to see through the illusion and to adopt different scripts and conventions. Ultimately, the theatrical trope implied social and political plasticity, the possibility of conceiving alternative worlds.

'Is that the King? I think you are fooling me. He seems to be a man in an embroidered garment.'[17] More's epigram on monarchy as a form of political dissimulation typifies a strain which runs powerfully through his work as a whole. Human life could seem 'like a long pageant' organized by Fortune, who allocated and changed roles. But when the pageant was over and death removed the costumes, the illusion collapsed. Everyone was the same.[18] Should we accommodate ourselves to the play in hand, and the self-delusion that involved, or risk alienation (exile) by refusing to play our part? It is a question debated, in precisely these terms, by 'More' and Hythloday in *Utopia*. But it also raised the issue of whether the same actors could perform 'better' in a different theatre, with different conventions and scripts. In Book I of *Utopia* we are presented with one such theatre, with its own codes of dissimulation, its own fictions, and in Book II with another. In his contribution to the *parerga*, a letter to Peter Giles, More quotes a character from Terence's play *The Lady of Andros* to establish the legitimacy of his fictional exercise (113–14). The theatre was, Stephen Greenblatt suggested, More's favourite metaphor and while many have noted the theatrical element in *Utopia* – the conversation in the garden, the dramatic episodes, the flashbacks – the parallel has been drawn more in relation to form than substance.[19] The argument here is that the theatre metaphor, like the references to the New World, opened a gateway to alternative possibilities and so is part of the substance of the book's argument. Society is a theatre whose conventions and scripts constrain and circumscribe our roles and even our intentions. Might these scripts be rewritten, conventions be adapted so that our roles, intentions and behaviour are transformed? In particular, can we move from a stage (described in Book I) where self-interest rules against the common interest to one (Book II) where the common interest rules and subsumes self-interest, where wisdom and goodness prevail?

Renaissance humanism was not a narrowly philological enterprise. Certainly, grammar and rhetoric were central to it but poetry, history, moral philosophy, biblical studies, political thought, art, science and philosophy were also important. Such a range of activities gave scope for debates and controversies. A central feature of the 'Christian humanists'' work was the self-conscious appropriation of classical learning for Christian purposes. They saw no innovation in this. What was new was their exploitation of the technology of print and the involvement of pious and learned laymen. More and Erasmus had been friends since 1499. They jointly published their translation of Lucian in 1506. *The Praise of Folly* was written in 1511 while Erasmus was a guest in More's home and its title punned on the Latin version of his host's surname, *Morus*. It was often read as a companion piece to *Utopia*. Erasmus and Giles were heavily involved and intervened textually in the production of the early editions of *Utopia*. The letters of the Erasmian network constantly evoke a sense of friendship, common endeavour and mutual support. What is striking is the number of lay intellectuals, men of business – More, Budé, Busleyden and Giles – who were active participants in the group's activities.

They and others furnished the *parerga* in which the main text came to be embedded. In all, these products of other hands amounted to just under a quarter of the total text. *Utopia* was emphatically a collaborative work and the nature of that collaboration may set some limits to the indeterminacy of its interpretation. The *parerga* are vital to the sense of a many-sided conversation rather than a two-sided dialogue. They add to the interpretative openness of the book while circumscribing the book's intentions and immediate reception. They bring out, first, the international character and importance of the work as the product of a European intellectual milieu. Furthermore, they associate it with a particular strand of that milieu, the Erasmian humanist one with its agenda of classically assisted Christian renewal. They play on the overlap of fiction and reality, the blurring of illusion, self-delusion and dissimulation, on the theatrical, performative qualities of social, political and cultural life. Beyond this, the *parerga* provide a guide to the major preoccupations of the work itself.

The first of these – signalled in the book's title – is the combination of profit and delight. As a truly golden handbook, *Utopia* is 'No less beneficial than Entertaining'. Horace, Lucian and Erasmus had all emphasized that the combination of delight and profit could draw in and move readers. Repeatedly, the letters and poems emphasize that this is a work which will entertain but which it will also be in our interest to read. But where did real profit lie? More and Budé both use their letters to raise this question, the first in relation to writing the work, the second in relation to reading it. More excuses his delay in completing *Utopia* on the grounds of his distraction by worldly and family business, his pursuit of advantage for himself, his kin, his clients. Was this truly a more profitable busy-ness than writing the book? Likewise, Budé, on receiving his copy, was preoccupied with the business of his estate and legal affairs: the 'nonsense' of 'getting and saving', of 'accumulating more and more'. The language of profit, interest, advantage runs, like a *leit-motif*, through More's great work. Men's pursuit of their own interests was a fact of nature which political calculation must recognize. In his Latin epigrams, More had noted that the only safe king was one perceived to rule in his subjects' interests (*utiliorem*).[20] Commenting on the adage 'What is one's own is beautiful', Erasmus had observed, citing Cicero, that 'Everyone is most influenced by his own particular interest.'[21] In Utopia, subject to the observance of properly ratified laws, 'to pursue your interests is prudence' (70). At the same time, following Aristotle, they recognized that the unreflective pursuit of self-interest could jeopardize the community which it was in our interests to preserve.

The questions which then arose were: what were our true interests and were we capable of identifying them?

A powerful claim made by Hythloday for Utopia as an ideal is that 'every man's perception of where his true interest lies, along with the authority of Christ our Saviour (whose wisdom could not fail to recognise the best, and whose goodness could not fail to counsel it) would long ago have brought the whole world to adopt utopian laws, were it not for one single monster, the prime plague and begetter of all others – I mean Pride' (109). Here perception of our interests and the authority, wisdom and goodness of Christ converge to underwrite the claim of Utopia to be an optimal state. But it is, of course, the recognition of our true interest rather than the pursuit of perverse interest, driven by pride, which can lead us to this happy, and apparently sanctified, outcome.

How then are we to accurately and consistently discriminate between true and perverse interests? One answer was to accept the view of More's favourite Roman historian Sallust, that the fundamental underpinning of political community, its *concordia*, was in friendship between equals.[22] Or, as Cicero put it, 'the whole human race should co-exist as a single fellowship cemented by reason and common speech' adding the identification of such fellowship with the friendship between those who hold all things in common.[23] As we have seen, Erasmus gave this motif the prominence of priority in his *Adages*. Not only was 'nothing more wholesome' but it was astonishing that 'this common ownership of Plato's' was distasteful to Christians when 'nothing was ever said by a pagan philosopher which comes closer to the mind of Christ'. This Pythagorean friendship, a 'sharing of life and property', was 'the very thing Christ wants to happen among Christians'. So community of property was in our true interest as was the equal obligation to labour.[24] As William Budé wrote in the letter to Thomas Lupset for which the third edition of *Utopia* was held up, Christ not only 'left his followers a Pythagorean rule of mutual charity and community property' but, in doing so, undermined the legitimacy of both civil and canon law which were devoted to the protection of false private interests. It was Utopia which maintained 'the truly Christian customs and the authentic wisdom' by adhering to the three 'divine institutions' of equality, love of peace and contempt for gold and silver (118–19). Generally the *parerga* breathe the spirit of friendship which may have been the subject regarded as the key to *Utopia* by Thomas More himself.[25]

If friendship and the community of equals associated with it was in our true interest as human beings and Christians, could the wise and good engage in politics unscathed without the establishment of such a community and the redefinition of true nobility which it represented? The debates on counsel, true nobility and friendship thus interlocked. Erasmus, meditating on the maxim 'To be a slave to your theatre', again anticipated the discussion in *Utopia* by asking how adaptable we can be, how accommodating to circumstances, without loss of integrity. In the world as it is and because of human variability, having many friends depended on a protean adaptability. On the one hand, as Horace had shown in his *Satires*, there was 'a disgusting type of flattery which assents to everything in everybody'. In Holy Scripture we were told that 'the fool is as inconstant as the moon; the wise man like the sun is always himself'. And yet, some accommodation to prevent danger to oneself or one's household might be sensible. St Paul 'became all things to all men, that he might win all for Christ'. Then again, the ambitious man, risking honour, conscience and peace of mind, might win the friendship of his prince, only to fall away from the friendship of Christ.[26]

Most commentators would agree that this balancing of integrity and accommodation to circumstance, nobility and its perversion, true and false interests and pleasures form powerful and consistent themes traversing the two books of *Utopia* and cementing their unity. They would also agree that Book I offers a devastating indictment of early sixteenth-century government and society. There, the pursuit of false pleasure and false interests is the norm. Friendship is negated in favour of competitive emulation, community eroded by gross inequality. Folly shuts out wisdom along with Christian precept in all areas of policy – fiscal, military, economic and penal. Wisdom is at such a disadvantage that Hythloday can mount a strong case for detachment from public life. As Budé points out, a society of emulative and destructive competition is sustained and operated by legally trained mediators and 'fixers' such as Budé and Thomas More himself (16–17). It relentlessly shapes its members' expectations, aspirations and standards of behaviour. The discussion moves on to explore how the good and wise should operate in such a context – accepting corruption or appearing as idealistic fools – and whether it is possible to envisage an alternative world, another theatre in which friendship might flourish, wisdom be sustained, learning be valued and true pleasure be pursued; a theatre in which the truly good, noble and wise would not have to accommodate themselves to a context premised on the surrender of principle.

When 'Thomas More' is introduced to Raphael Hythloday by Peter Giles outside the church of Notre Dame in Antwerp he is encountering the perfectly equipped counsellor, a man designed to make a difference in politics. Having dispersed his patrimony, Raphael has no personal or familial interest in the acquisition of power and influence. He is without ambition and values his liberty more highly than the trappings of power. He is, moreover, vastly experienced and a shrewd analyst, a man who has not only ranged across the face of the globe but one whose experiences have been refined by his deep learning, especially in philosophy and particularly in the Greeks. 'More' urges him to set aside his personal distaste for power since, devoid of ambition, Raphael is especially well equipped to guide and incite a great prince to do good things. Raphael responds by shifting the debate from the issue of ability to that of effectiveness. What hope would he have of being heard? His answer is 'Very little' and his reasons are given added impact by some case studies.

To begin with, Raphael insists that he would confront the predilection of princes for *gloria*, for war over peace, for the emulative struggle which equips them to triumph over their rivals. Secondly, in courts composed of 'people who envy everyone else and admire only themselves', he would confront minds closed by a similar emulative competition. He illustrates this with an account of a discussion in the court, familiar to More, of Archbishop John Morton. The debate is over a more rational and Christian penal practice than the harsh one already failing to reduce offending in a society where inequity and deprivation generate ever more crime. The portrait of Morton is deeply ambiguous and his court represented as fawning, competitive and closed-minded. The conclusion is that, in such a context, the philosopher and his counsel are barely relevant (15–28).

More's riposte is to advise persistence: to 'overcome your aversion' (28). Otherwise, what hope was there for Plato's desired collaboration between philosophers and kings? Perhaps alluding to Erasmus, Raphael pointed out that philosophers had already written books of advice for princes and that Plato's own experience as royal counsellor had been miserable and fruitless. To underline the point he cited two further examples. The first was a discussion of aggressive foreign policy at the court of the King of France. To preach the curtailment of territorial ambition, to urge concentration on ruling well what you have, would be laughed out of a court where *gloria* and dynastic competition were the norm. Similarly, faced with the fiscal rapacity of dynastic state builders, to advise the limitation of royal treasuries would be to be dismissed (28–34). 'More' sees the validity of these points but complains that Raphael is behaving as if he were an actor in one theatre when the curial context is quite another. The philosophy to be used is one 'better suited for the political arena, that takes its cue, adapts itself to the drama in hand, and acts its part neatly and appropriately' (35–6). Not only behaviour but counsel, and the philosophy underpinning it, must be accommodated to the theatre of contemporary politics. Raphael's rejoinder is extensive and vigorous. To adopt an accommodational mode would be like the healer attempting to cure madness by becoming mad himself. He rejects the lie involved in such practice and his radicalism is suddenly revealed in his first reference to Utopia. The shaping force behind contemporary political culture, he alleges, is private property. In that context, to evoke the communism of the Utopians (and here More anticipated a common reader response to *Utopia*) 'would seem inappropriate'. Yet to follow the politics of accommodation would be to set aside Christ's rule and His injunction against dissembling. Those, who have accommodated Christ's teachings to the world as it is, have only made men's consciences secure in doing evil. For Raphael, the wise man's choice is stark indeed. Either one maintains one's integrity and remains different, aloof and ignored, or one adopts the mores of a distorted and distorting political culture and becomes as guilty as the others. There can be no just or happy government without the community of goods advocated by Plato and practised by the Utopians. The implication is that, if 'More' is right in his advocacy of political 'realism', Christ and Plato are wrong (35–9).

Yet, in a final vital move, Raphael suggests that *even if good advice were listened to and resulted in desirable legislation* it could never be fully effective. The indictment moves from the flaws of courts to those of society in general. 'The social evils I mentioned may be alleviated and their effects mitigated for a while, but so long as private property remains, there is no hope at all of effecting a cure and restoring society to good health' (39). Not only does wise counsel face an intimidating uphill struggle; even when it results in law-making it will be ineffective in society as it is, in the present theatre of politics. The culmination of the debate on counsel is, then, the issue of the limiting and constraining force of social and political structures, customs and conventions. Private property limits the possibilities in a damaging way. Utopia, based on communal property, offers, in Raphael's view, an ideal alternative. 'More' rehearses the well-known Aristotelian objections to a society based on communal property: the absence of private incentives to effort, disorder and the collapse of all authority. To demonstrate the invalidity of these objections, Raphael offers to give a full account of Utopia. It will be a society in which the barriers to wisdom have collapsed and where minds are open to the philosophers' teachings.

In his indictment of sixteenth-century society, More identifies the key source of its dysfunctionality as pride, but it is important to recognize that it is a particular kind of pride which causes such devastating damage. It is not simply pride in possessions, lineage, power or reputation, misguided though such a pride may be, but a pride in that these things enable us to triumph over others, an emulative pride. 'Pride measures her advantages not by what she has but by what other people lack. Pride would not deign even to be made a goddess if there were no wretched for her to sneer at and domineer over. Her good fortune is dazzling only by contrast with the miseries of others, her riches are valuable only as they torment and tantalise the poverty of others.' The *sine qua non* of such pride is inequality and the grosser that is the more corrosive it becomes. It glories 'in putting down others by superfluous display' (109, 56–7). As Jerome Busleyden pointed out, in his contribution to the *parerga,* the pride of competitive emulation pits everyone against everyone else, creating a society of enemies rather than a community of friends (128).

More's emphasis on what Budé called 'idiot competition' (119) is not unique to *Utopia*. His translations from Lucian contained the observation that 'surely to deem another's good fortune one's own misfortune, to rage at the success of others, to be vexed by praise of others, to be tormented by another's happiness – is not this the greatest misery, is it not the most extreme madness?'[27] And, in *Richard III*, More has King Edward IV, on his deathbed, condemn at length the destructiveness of emulative competition.[28] In the *Life of Pico* an envious man demanded to receive twice whatever his neighbour had. When the neighbour lost one eye, the man had both of his own put out.[29] In his later work, More was still hammering on this theme of emulous madness. *A Dialogue of Comfort* warned his readers that prosperity all too easily nurtured pride and self-regard, which in turn fed emulative disdain for others. About the same time, in *A Treatise on the Passion*, they were urged to identify the pride which brought down Satan with those emulative qualities of aspiring to raise ourselves while being eager to demean others. Erasmus, in his book most closely associated with *Utopia*, *The Praise of Folly*, suggested that almost all relationships in existing society were dependent on illusions, self-satisfaction and self-delusion; that is, on folly. Such folly was common to all, at once a social glue, but in its emulative dimension poisoning all social relationships.[30] What Augustine had called the *libido domandi*, the lust to assert ourselves over others, needed the illusion that it was compatible with the 'happiness', glory and nobility of the 'real' world while denigrating the 'unrealism' of a society based on the Platonic-Pythagorean-Christian-Erasmian ideal of equality and friendship, where the common good and private interest were become one in a culture of mutual support.

It followed that, in order to nourish that source of pride – the *libido domandi* – and the emulative triumph associated with it, dissimulation was essential. To protect the claim to superior wisdom, minds must be closed to the possible validity of the arguments of others. We indulge the fantasy of being wiser than anyone else, just as, to protect status and position, we amass superfluous possessions, assuring ourselves that they are the key to the good life when they clearly are not. The display of excess in food, housing, clothing, horses, retainers, servants, wives, lineage, 'nobility' and glory transcended the limitations of others' lives. But these markers of social discrimination only worked when subscription to the illusion sustaining them was universal or near-universal and that depended on the wisdom of philosophy being shut out. To protect the Emperor's new clothes, the small boy had to be kept away from the parade.

'Pride is a serpent from hell that twists itself around the hearts of men acting like a suckfish to hold them back from choosing a better way of life' (109–10). Ultimately, we must deceive ourselves as well as others, pretending that our bogus superiority is true nobility, true magnificence, true virtue and true pleasure when, on the contrary, it is both an expression of 'the great emptiness lying concealed at the heart of things'[31] and a catalyst for our fear, suspicion and enmity towards others. If the good society was a community of friends, contemporary society had become a collection of enemies, bound together by little more than emulative competition. Piercing its self-delusion, we might, admittedly somewhat anachronistically, call it a dystopia, the dystopian reality which evokes Raphael's, 'More''s and the readers' sustained moral outrage.

Utopia's claim to ideality, then, rests on overcoming or containing competitive emulation. It achieves this not by moral exhortation but by recontextualizing the natural propensity of almost everyone to calculate and pursue their own interests. 'In other places men talk very liberally of the commonwealth but what they mean is simply their own wealth; in Utopia, where there is no private business, every man zealously pursues the public business. *And in both cases men are right to act as they do*' (107; my emphasis). Rationality and interest, though not morality, become relative to the circumstances in which they have to operate. To use a metaphor familiar to More and his collaborators, society can either be a theatre of competitive emulation or a theatre of equality and friendship. Both, in radically different ways, are theatres which shape what is perceived as rational and/or in their members' interests.

How does Utopia achieve this shift in political culture, this redefinition of interests and rationality? A large part of that transformation rests on the detailed removal of every occasion for emulative triumph. Most critically, communal property eliminates all opportunities for displays of superfluous private wealth. In Utopia dress is almost entirely uniform, as is housing, which is regularly reallocated: 'there is nothing private or exclusive' (47). Dining is communal and all are equally free to draw upon the communal store. Jewels, gold and silver are demeaned. Cosmetic enhancement is detested. Travel is controlled. The household is made as uniform, in size and personnel, as possible. All have equal access to health care and education. The obligation to work hard for uniformly restricted hours is common to all and all are obliged to work in both agriculture and trade. Everyone's day conforms to a uniform pattern. Just as all must work equally, so all have equal leisure and use it to pursue those true pleasures which they associate with the mind. All have access to learning and public lectures. 'The chief aim of their constitution is that, as far as public needs permit, all citizens should be free to withdraw as much time as possible from the service of the body and devote themselves to the freedom and culture of the mind. For that, they think, is the real happiness of life' (55).

The markers commonly associated with elite culture or aristocratic prestige are absent. Horses are few and oxen, because of their usefulness, are preferred. Hunting and gambling are regarded as illusory pastimes, 'unworthy of free men' (73). Sexual promiscuity, or the attempt to practise it, is regarded as a crime. Surplus produce is either stored against future need or exported. There are, then, minimal markers of status: no prescriptive or inherited rights to authority over others, no legal exemptions or privileges, and canvassing for political preferment is proscribed. Women have the same entitlement to leisure and education as men. There is a representative form of government in which all households share equally. Faction and conspiracy, the emulative competition of rival political groups, are prevented by the proscription of political discussion outside of the senate or popular assembly. The only deviations from equality of status, privileges and esteem relate to those licensed from work, state officials, bondsmen and a general deferring to older over younger. The first of these categories includes those officers charged with supervising the work of others, although they tend not to take advantage of the exemption (51, 53). Slavery is reserved for those convicted of a crime, prisoners of war, foreigners condemned to death in their own country, and the overworked poor of foreign countries who voluntarily choose slavery in Utopia. These bondsmen are distinguished in their physical appearance and by being assigned the most demeaning work. Utopian citizens who have been sentenced to slavery are treated the most harshly since 'they had an excellent education and the best of moral training, yet still couldn't be restrained from wrongdoing' (47, 80). Those most fitted for the pursuit of knowledge are exempted from manual work. If they are productive and excel, their exemption continues. Otherwise, they revert to physical labour. But equally those labourers who excel in their studies may be released from work for intellectual pursuits. The operative standard is merit and value to society, not privilege. Even the elected prince is not distinguished by dress or regalia: 'he is known only by a sheaf of grain carried before him' (84). Fear of want and pride 'which glories in putting down others by superfluous display of possession' may be common to Europe. 'But this sort of vice has no place whatever in the Utopian way of life' (56–7).

When these bases of emulative competition were eliminated, many of those things perversely regarded as pleasures went with them. The self-delusion of those who 'act as if they were set apart by nature herself, rather than their own fantasies' was punctured (71). Spurious pleasures were unobtainable in Utopia because the means of their satisfaction were unavailable. What then remained to be said about the pleasures of Utopian life? Raphael's answer sounds so bold as to suggest a hedonism verging on a crudely understood Epicureanism: '… no kind of pleasure is forbidden, provided harm does not come of it' (60). The qualification is vital for, as we have seen, the pursuit of false pleasure does enormous harm. They may 'seem rather too much inclined to the view that all or the most important part of human happiness consists of pleasure' (67–8). Two things off-set that perception. The first is their religion which is serious, strict, stern and forbidding and to the principles of which they always relate considerations of true happiness. The second is their view of pleasure. Happiness is only found, they believe, in virtuous pleasure. Indeed, some of them, like St Augustine, claim that 'virtue is itself happiness' (68–9). The two rules of virtuous happiness are to love God, to whom we owe our existence and all happiness, and to live as free of anxiety and as full of joy as possible while helping others to do the same. True pleasure therefore does not injure others, is not followed by pain and does not preclude a greater pleasure. Amongst true pleasures they give priority to those of the mind. 'Tireless in intellectual pursuits', they include in these: knowledge, delight in contemplating truth and in looking back on a life well spent and in looking forward to the hope of happiness to come. The lesser pleasures of the body fall into two categories. Sensory pleasures remain true pleasures only as long as they bring no pain to ourselves or others. More valued than them is a 'calm and harmonious state of the body' (74–5). The concern for the welfare and happiness of others which is built into these principles is in itself anti-emulative. The same can be said of their attitude to religion.

Three basic religious truths are insisted upon: the beliefs that the soul is immortal, that we are born for happiness, and that, after death, we will be judged and rewarded according to the true virtue of our living.[32] Without these 'rational' principles men would maximize pleasure and minimize pain *without regard to virtue*. No one would pursue hard and painful virtues or give up any pleasure, however vicious, or suffer pain, when the advantage was only to others and not to themselves.

Beyond these minimal fundamentals, Utopians may adopt whatever form of religious beliefs they choose, provided they do no harm to others. The vast majority believe in an unknown God: 'a single power, unknown, eternal, infinite, inexplicable, far beyond the grasp of the human mind, and diffused throughout the universe, not physically, but in influence'. Those who proselytize, slighting other religions and asserting the superiority of their own, are, however, sentenced to exile. The Utopians are impressed by Christianity, to which Raphael and his comrades introduce them, and some of them are baptized. What they find most impressive is Christ's encouragement to community of goods and the persistence of this practice 'among the truest groups of Christians'. In religion, as in other things, the Utopians are able to show an openness of mind which is unfettered by emulative pride. They may only preach 'quietly, modestly, rationally and without bitterness towards others'. Resort to abuse or violence is punished by exile or slavery (96–7).

The emulative capacities associated with possessions, display, leisure, access to learning, food and housing, travel, work and religious superiority have been removed. Accordingly, they make war, emulative violence, in a way which robs it of all glory. Subterfuge, assassination, the encouragement of treachery, the exploitation of neighbours and hiring of mercenaries are amongst their first recourse. They despise war as 'an activity fit only for beasts' and treat it with contempt. So they hire 'the worst possible men' for the improper use of mercenary slaughter. War is an ignoble, not an ennobling, activity and when Utopians themselves fight it is always in defence of their own territory and a collective responsibility and burden. On no account would they allow foreign auxiliaries to fight on their land (92, 95).

The contrast with a Europe in which inequality and the triumphant exploitation of it in all conceivable forms were normal was indeed stark and shocking: 'empty, ceremonial honours', absent in Utopia, were the stock in trade of early modern Europe. The false nobility of slaughtering animals and humans, in hunting and war, was regarded as contemptible in Utopia, even if, in the last resort, war could become a necessity. But More would not concede that this meant that in Utopia people were more rational or, in essence, better than Europeans: 'in both cases men are right to act as they do' (107). 'These and the like attitudes the Utopians have picked up partly from their upbringing, since the institutions of their community are completely opposed to such folly, partly from instruction and the reading of good books' (65). 'Different customs, different feelings' (63). The visit to Utopia of the Anemolian ambassadors, accoutred in the full panoply of a display of superiority in dress, gold chains and jewels, illustrates the point. To the Utopians their finery looks clownish and the ambassadors are deeply embarrassed by this reaction. But, perhaps the significant point is that after a few days the Anemolians, realizing their mistake, leave off their display and adopt Utopian ways (63–5). The theatre in which we are called upon to act our part informs the rationality and good sense, the appropriateness of our behaviour. In Europe the theatre of convention has gone badly and destructively wrong. *Utopia* raises the question of whether it is possible to conceive a better theatre in which it would be in our interests to act with true nobility, to pursue true happiness and to relate to others as equal friends not enemies, a theatre in which justice would prevail and the wise be able to return from exile to be listened to by open minds.

The final paragraphs of *Utopia* bring the conversation to a close with 'More''s own reflections on what he had heard. The note struck is one of indeterminacy, even scepticism, and some commentators have taken this to indicate the real More's final attitude to Utopia – at best hesitation, at worst scepticism. 'More' reflects on the 'absurdity' of some Utopian customs and laws: those relating to war, religion but above all 'their communal living and their moneyless economy' (110). But, observing Raphael's weariness and knowing his objection to those who 'might not appear knowing enough unless they found something to criticise in other men's ideas', he ended by praising the Utopian way of life which in so many fundamental respects he found absurd. There is no finality here; no resolution of the prolonged dialogue we have been witness to. Yet we should note that this indeterminacy is powerfully charged with irony in two principal respects. The first is the preference of *Thomas Morus* – the sceptical fool – for the 'nobility, magnificence, splendour and majesty, which (in the popular view) are the true ornaments and glory of any commonwealth' but which are rejected by the Utopians as false, illusory and destructive. In other words, 'More' remains (realistically or is it tragically?) in the theatre of contemporary European society, an actor on its stage, his perceptions conditioned by its conventions and scripts. Secondly, Raphael has condemned the fawning condescension, the appeasement of evil, the accommodation with the world as it is, the desire to win favour rather than speak the truth and risk offending which he found so characteristic of European courts (14) and so alien to the open-minded culture of the Utopians. 'This readiness to learn is, I think, the really important reason for their being better governed and living more happily than we do, though we are not inferior to them in brains or resources' (41). 'More' remains silent about his objections and 'with praise for the Utopian way of life and his account of it' takes Raphael in to supper. The theatre of interests, in which 'More' continues to play his part, retains its hold. The question is whether the reader's response will be governed by the same grip of convention and self-delusion.

Utopia is then unambiguously engaged with the issue of true interest/true pleasure and their necessary universality in a society which has eradicated emulative pride, a society embodying friendship and the 'folly' of Christian charity. But, however we look at it, the work leaves us with urgent and, in some cases, disturbing questions. How can justice and law/custom be made convergent? How can goodness be given force in a society already distorted by pride and managed by legal chicanery (117)? How can the destructive consequences of an emulative and acquisitive social and political culture be eliminated and can this be done without removing the inequities of riches and poverty, without the 'absurdity' and 'folly' of communism? Perhaps the final unanswered question, the nub of the work's interpretative indeterminacy, is whether wisdom and power can ever be reconciled or is power doomed to mistake wisdom and folly?

Like so many of the poets, novelists and satirists who came after him, More seems to be saying that we need fiction to see reality afresh: in particular, we need utopian fiction to see the reality of our own society and the costs of putting it right. Inevitably, for a humanist like More, such a project draws on the Platonic 'best state' exercise just as, for its inverse, it draws on the Socratic image of the cave.[33] Plato, pursuing the logical path or dialectic of reason, produced limited fictions veiling an engagement with ideas on the level of abstraction. In order to engage reason with imagination and emotion, Thomas More had to embrace a richer but more elusive fiction. Raphael described his ideal society 'as if he had walked its streets and sat in its gardens'.[34] The challenge of the ideal society of More's aspiration was how to reasonably manage imagination and emotion without crushing both under the imperative of reshaping the human will,[35] without replicating the great emptiness at the heart of things. One of his tools was an elusive, teasing humour. Whether he succeeded is perhaps the most open of all the open questions.

NOTES

1 I have preferred the translation in G. M. Logan and R. M. Adams (eds.), *Thomas More: Utopia* (Cambridge University Press, 1989). References will be to this edition and will appear in brackets in the text (with one exception which is noted below).

2 John Guy, *Thomas More* (London: Arnold, 2000), p. 14.

3 Krishan Kumar, *Utopianism* (Buckingham: Open University Press, 1991), p. 42.

4 C. S. Lewis, *English Literature in the Sixteenth Century, Oxford History of English Literature*, vol. 3 (Oxford University Press, 1954), pp. 167–71.

5 E. Surtz and J. H. Hexter (eds.), *Thomas More: Utopia, The Complete Works of St Thomas More*, vol. 4 (New Haven: Yale University Press, 1965). An even more elaborate French edition with the same objective appeared in 1978: A. Prévost (ed.), *L'Utopie de Thomas More* (Paris: MAME, 1978).

6 The best quick introduction to that debate is in Guy, *Thomas More*, chapter 5. The best sustained interpretative surveys are G. M. Logan, *The Meaning of More's Utopia* (Princeton University Press, 1983) and D. Baker-Smith, *More's Utopia* (University of Toronto Press, 1991).

7 Quentin Skinner, 'Political Philosophy', in C. B. Schmitt, Q. Skinner, E. Kessler and J. Kraye (eds.), *The Cambridge History of Renaissance Philosophy* (Cambridge University Press, 1988), pp. 389–452; and Quentin Skinner, 'Sir Thomas More's *Utopia* and the Language of Renaissance Humanism', in Anthony Pagden (ed.), *The Languages of Political Theory in Early Modern Europe* (Cambridge University Press, 1997), pp. 123–57.

8 See David Wootton, 'Friendship Portrayed: A New Account of Utopia', *History Workshop Journal* 45 (1998), 30–47; Wootton (ed. and trans.), *Thomas More's 'Utopia' with Erasmus's 'The Sileni of Alcibiades'* (Indianopolis: Hackett, 1999), Introduction.

9 D. Erasmus, *Adages*, trans. M. M. Phillips, annotated by R. A. B. Mynors, *Collected Works of Erasmus*, vol. 34 (University of Toronto Press, 1982), pp. 29–30.

10 Logan, *Meaning of More's Utopia*, pp. 38–9, 60. Logan and Adams (eds.), *Thomas More: Utopia*, pp. xi–xii, xx–xxvi.

11 J. M. Parrish, 'A New Source for More's *Utopia*', *The Historical Journal* 40:2 (1997), 493–5.

12 E. Nelson, 'Greek Nonsense in More's *Utopia*', *The Historical Journal* 44:4 (2001), 889–917; *The Greek Tradition in Republican Thought* (Cambridge University Press, 2004).

13 E. McCutcheon, *My Dear Peter: The Ars Poetica and Hermeneutics for More's Utopia* (Angers: Moreana, 1983).

14 Baker-Smith, *More's Utopia*, pp. 225, 243, xii.

15 M. Leslie, *Renaissance Utopias and the Problem of History* (Ithaca and London: Cornell University Press, 1998), pp. 72–3, 80.

16 The principal classical sources More draws on in *Utopia* include, as well as Plato, Aristotle and Pythagoras, Cicero, Augustine, Aquinas, Anselm, Plutarch and Lucian.

17 L. Bradner and C. L. Lynch (eds.), The *Latin Epigrams of Thomas More* (University of Chicago Press, 1953), pp. 205–6.

18 C. R. Thompson (ed.), *Thomas More: Translations of Lucian*, The *Complete Works of St Thomas More*, vol. 3:1 (New Haven: Yale University Press, 1974), pp. 176–7.

19 S. Greenblatt, *Renaissance Self-Fashioning: From More to Shakespeare* (University of Chicago Press, 1980), pp. 27–9.

20 Bradner and Lynch (eds.), *Latin Epigrams*, p. 174.

21 Erasmus, *Adages*, p. 158. A sharper version of this is to be found in Aristotle, *Politics*, II.3.1161b35.

22 D. C. Earl, *The Political Thought of Sallust* (Amsterdam: Hakkert, 1966), p. 11.

23 Cicero, *On Moral Obligation*, trans. J. Higginbotham (London: Faber, 1967), p. 57.

24 Erasmus, *Adages*, pp. 30, 32 and 34 citing Paul, Thessalonians 3:10.

25 Wootton, 'Friendship Portrayed', pp. 33–45.

26 Erasmus, *Adages*, 134–5, 146.

27 Thompson (ed.), *Translations of Lucian*, p. 97.

28 R. S. Sylvester (ed.), *Thomas More: The History of King Richard III*, *Complete Works of St Thomas More*, vol. 2 (New Haven: Yale University Press, 1963), pp. 12–13.

29 A. G. Edwards, K. G. Rogers and C. H. Miller (eds.), *Thomas More: English Poems, Life of Pico, The Last Things, The Complete Works of St Thomas More*, vol. 1 (New Haven: Yale University Press, 1997), pp. 159–60.
30 Erasmus, *Praise of Folly*, trans. B. Radice, ed. A. H. T. Levi (Harmondsworth: Penguin, 1971), pp. 7–8, 93–4.
31 Cornelis de Schrijver to the Reader, in Surtz and Hexter (eds.), *Utopia*, p. 31. I have preferred the Yale translation here but see Logan and Adams, *Thomas More*, p. 129.
32 See Logan, *Meaning of More's Utopia*, p. 143 for the influence of Epicurus via Cicero on this position.
33 Plato, *Republic*, trans. R. Waterfield (Oxford University Press, 1993), pp. 514–18.
34 Wootton, 'Friendship Portrayed', p. 45.
35 D. Baker-Smith and C. C. Barfoot (eds.), *Between Dream and Nature: Essays on Utopia and Dystopia* (Amsterdam: Rodopi, 1987), p. 4.

BIBLIOGRAPHY

Aristotle, *The Politics*, trans. with notes by E. Barker (Oxford University Press, 1988).
Baker-Smith, D., *More's Utopia* (University of Toronto Press, 1991).
Baker-Smith, D. and C. C. Barfoot (eds.), *Between Dream and Nature: Essays on Utopia and Dystopia* (Amsterdam: Rodopi, 1987).
Bradner, L. and C. L. Lynch (eds.), *The Latin Epigrams of Thomas More* (University of Chicago Press, 1953).
Brown, P., *Augustine of Hippo: A Biography* (London: Faber & Faber, 1967).
Cicero, *On Moral Obligation*, trans. J. Higginbotham (London: Faber & Faber, 1967). *Selected Works*, trans. M. Grant (Harmondsworth: Penguin, 1971).
Earl, D. C., *The Political Thought of Sallust* (Amsterdam: Hakkert, 1966).
Edwards, A. G., K. G. Rodgers and C. H. Miller (eds.), *Thomas More: English Poems, Life of Pico, The Last Things, The Complete Works of St Thomas More*, vol. 1 (New Haven: Yale University Press, 1997).
Erasmus, D., *Adages*, trans. M. M. Phillips, annotated by R. A. B. Mynors, *Collected Works of Erasmus*, vol. 34 (University of Toronto Press, 1982). *The Education of a Christian Prince*, ed. L. Jardine, trans. N. M. Cheshire and M. J. Heath (Cambridge University Press, 1997). *Praise of Folly and Letter to Martin Dorp*, trans. B. Radice, ed. A. H. T. Levi (Harmondsworth: Penguin, 1971).
Greenblatt, S., *Renaissance Self-Fashioning: From More to Shakespeare* (University of Chicago Press, 1980).
Guy, J., *Thomas More* (London: Arnold, 2000).
Hexter, J. H., *More's Utopia: The Biography of an Idea* (Princeton University Press, 1952).
Kraye, J., *The Cambridge Companion to Renaissance Humanism* (Cambridge University Press, 1996/2007).
Kumar, K., *Utopianism* (Buckingham: Open University Press, 1991).
Leslie, M., *Renaissance Utopias and the Problem of History* (Ithaca and London: Cornell University Press, 1998).

Lewis, C. S., *English Literature in the Sixteenth Century*, Oxford History of English Literature, vol. 3 (Oxford University Press, 1954).

Logan, G. M., *The Meaning of More's Utopia* (Princeton University Press, 1983).

Logan, G.M. and R. M. Adams (eds.), *Thomas More: Utopia* (Cambridge University Press, 1989).

Marius, R., *Thomas More: A Biography* (Cambridge, MA: Harvard University Press, 1984).

McCutcheon, E., *My Dear Peter: The Ars Poetica and Hermeneutics for More's Utopia* (Angers: Moreana, 1983).

'Thomas More at Epigrams: Humanism or Humanisms?', in T. Hoenselaars and A. F. Kinney (eds.), *Challenging Humanism* (Newark: University of Delaware Press, 2005), pp. 75–89.

Nelson, E., 'Greek Nonsense in More's Utopia', *Historical Journal* 44:4 (2001), 889–917.

The Greek Tradition in Republican Thought (Cambridge University Press, 2004).

Pagden, A. (ed.), *The Languages of Political Theory in Early-Modern Europe* (Cambridge University Press, 1997).

Parrish, J. M., 'A New Source for More's Utopia', *Historical Journal* 40:2 (1997), 493–5.

Plato, *Republic*, trans. R. Waterfield (Oxford University Press, 1993).

Prévost, A., *L'Utopie de Thomas More* (Paris: MAME, 1978).

Sacks, D. H. (ed.), *Utopia by Sir Thomas More*, trans. Ralph Robynson, 1556 (Boston: Bedford/St Martins, 1999).

Schmitt, C. B., Q. Skinner, E. Kessler and J. Kraye (eds.), *The Cambridge History of Renaissance Philosophy* (Cambridge University Press, 1988).

Skinner, Quentin, 'Political Philosophy', in C. B. Schmitt, Q. Skinner, E. Kessler and J. Kraye (eds.), *The Cambridge History of Renaissance Philosophy* (Cambridge University Press, 1988), pp. 389–452.

'Sir Thomas More's *Utopia* and the Language of Renaissance Humanism', in Anthony Pagden (ed.), *The Language of Political Theory in Early Modern Europe* (Cambridge University Press, 1997), pp. 123–57.

Stump, E. and N. Kretzmann (eds.), *The Cambridge Companion to Augustine* (Cambridge University Press, 2001).

Surtz, E. and J. H. Hexter (eds.), *Thomas More: Utopia, The Complete Works of St Thomas More*, vol. 4 (New Haven: Yale University Press, 1965).

Sylvester, R. S. (ed.), *Thomas More: The History of King Richard III, The Complete Works of St Thomas More*, vol. 2 (New Haven: Yale University Press, 1963).

Sylvester, R. S. and G. P. Marc'hadour (eds.), *Essential Articles for the Study of Thomas More* (Hamden, CT: Archon, 1977).

Thompson, C. R. (ed.), *Thomas More: Translations of Lucian, The Complete Works of St Thomas More*, vol. 3:1 (New Haven: Yale University Press, 1974).

Wootton, D., 'Friendship Portrayed: A New Account of Utopia', *History Workshop Journal* 45 (1998), 29–47.

Wootton, D. (ed. and trans.), *Thomas More's 'Utopia' with Erasmus's 'The Sileni of Alcibiades'* (Indianapolis: Hackett, 1999).

3

NICOLE POHL

Utopianism after More: the Renaissance and Enlightenment

A map of the world that does not include Utopia is not worth even glancing at, for it leaves out the one country at which Humanity is always landing. And when Humanity lands there, it looks out, and, seeing a better country, sets sail. Progress is the realisation of Utopias. (Oscar Wilde, *The Soul of Man under Socialism*, 1891)[1]

Oscar Wilde's poignant analysis suggests that three important aspects of Utopia are evident in the Renaissance and the Enlightenment. Firstly, Wilde recognizes the persistent ubiquity of utopian desire in human history. Utopia springs from the same impulse as the myth or the eschatological desire for a better afterlife and thus yearns to realize a condition of happiness, well-being and social harmony. Indeed, myths of the Island of the Blessed, the Land of Cockaygne, Elysium, Shangri-La and the Garden of Eden haunted philosophers, writers and travellers for centuries and paved the way for the geographical utopia of the Renaissance period and the voyage utopia of the eighteenth century which believed in the transformative quality of alterity.

Wilde's aphorism also indicates that neither the genre's founder, Thomas More, nor seventeenth- and eighteenth-century followers could claim perfection and universality as invariable principles. What we therefore see, mostly later in the period, is recognition of the human restlessness that renders the classical idea of human nature and thus the ideal of static utopianism futile. Utopias are discourses on change itself rather than simply blueprints.

Generically, too, utopias of the period are hybrid, integrating the 'literary' and 'political' into a polygeneric and polymodal literary genre. Primitivist and nostalgic utopias, sentimental individualist utopias, voyage utopias, satires, anti-utopias, pornographic utopias (somatopias), feminist utopias (feminotopias), micro-utopias, philosophical tales and utopias with mixed legislative systems document this diversity. Two main paradigms of utopias of the period however can be identified: utopias that are strictly regulated by the state/government in all aspects of human life and society ('archistic') and utopias which are based on the idea of maximizing freedom and self-regulation ('anarchistic'). Thus, while utopia's form, function and content are historically variable, its defining characteristics remain constant: the desire to recognize, mobilize and transform.

In 1516 Thomas More (1478–1535), advisor to King Henry VIII, Catholic martyr and saint, published his most controversial book, *De optimo reipublicae statu deque nova insula Utopia Libellus vere aureus, nec minus salutaris quam festivus (Of the best state law and of the new island Utopia, truly a golden booklet, as beneficial as it is cheerful)*, now known as *Utopia*. Whilst More's *Utopia* was unique in its 'atopic' quality, that is without one singular and certain meaning, it also reignited classical utopianism and adapted it to the early modern context.[2]

The term 'utopia', however allegorical its meaning, has always carried a spatial dimension that created imaginary geographies. Renaissance and early modern utopias displaced their ideal and other worlds by locating them in faraway, undiscovered countries and remote uncharted islands and planets. Texts such as More's *Utopia*, Francis Bacon's *New Atlantis* (1627), Francis Godwin's *The Man in the Moone; or, A Discourse of A Voyage Thither* (1638) and Gabriel Plattes's *A Description of the Famous Kingdome of Macaria* (1641) were clearly influenced by contemporary quests of discovery and colonization. Utopia exists because Abraxa (the original name of the country) and its people were forcefully colonized by King Utopus. Francis Bacon's *New Atlantis* echoes Richard Hakluyt's *Principal Navigations, Voyages and Discoveries of the English Nation* (1589) and reflects Walter Raleigh's journey to and disastrous colonization of Guiana. Gonzalo's famous micro-Utopia in *The Tempest*, 'Had I plantation of this isle, my lord,/And were the king on't, what would I do?', borrows from the 1609 Bermuda pamphlets[3] but also paraphrases Michel Montaigne's primitivist argument on natural justice and virtue made in his essay 'On Cannibals' (1580). Michael Drayton's poem 'Ode to the Virginian Voyage' (1606), borrows from Hakluyt, projects 'Earth's onely Paradise' onto the New World but at the same time calls upon 'You brave heroic minds,/Worthy your country's name' to refuel England's eminence in the colonization of America. The extensive appropriation and settlement of the 'New World' is justified by a model of progressive socialization: such narratives use the displacement of fantastic voyages, Robinsonades and Utopia, to define society and civilization as progressive alienation from barbarism to civilization. The narrator in Book II of *Utopia* emphasizes that the original inhabitants of Abraxa, 'rude and uncivilized inhabitants' were brought 'into such a good government, and to that measure of politeness, that they now far excel all the rest of mankind'.[4]

Paradoxically, More's *Utopia* also resonated with or inspired utopian projects that attempted to reverse the colonial process or at least create peaceful relations between colonizers and colonized. In 1520, initially supported by Charles I, Bartolomé de Las Casas (1484–1566) tried to establish a network of farm communities in present-day Venezuela inhabited by both Spanish and free Indians, but had to abort his plans in 1522. Vasco de Quiroga (c. 1470–1565), translator and passionate disciple of *Utopia*, attempted on several occasions to realize More's blueprint in Mexico. His hospital-pueblos of Santa Fe and the free Indian communities in Lake Pátzcuaro were highly successful until the prohibition of slavery was lifted by Charles V in 1534. Quiroga's book *Información en derecho* (*Information on the Law*, 1535) projects the utopian vision of a Christian state onto the New World. Like More and Montaigne, who were disenchanted by some aspects of European society, Quiroga hails the native justice and virtue of Mexican Indians as exemplary, and sketches out the scheme of an elective Christian monarchy to govern the Mexican Indians freely and peacefully without colonial force and intervention. Both de Las Casas and Quiroga pre-empted the eighteenth-century Jesuit utopian colonies ('Reductiones') in Paraguay which sought to reconcile primitive Christianity and aboriginal primitivism.

> Campanella wrote a City of the Sun. What about my writing a 'City of the Moon?' Would it not be excellent to describe the cyclopic mores of our time in vivid colors, but in doing so – to be on the safe side – to leave this Earth and go to the Moon? (Johannes Kepler)[5]

Utopia is inseparable from the imaginary voyage. Prester John's Indian kingdom, the voyage of St Brendan and St Brendan's Isle, *terra australis* and the icy north of the kingdom of Thule, voyages within the earth and beyond the stars are all expressions of utopian desire. Medieval and Renaissance maps (*mappae mundi*) inserted the speculative geographies of Eden, the Island of the Blessed, St Brendan's Isle and the mythical island of Brazil (Hy-Brazil) into their navigational charts, destabilizing the boundaries of the world. The lunar voyage challenged the boundaries of the cosmos. The tradition of the lunar voyages popular since Lucian and Plutarch's *The Face of the Moon* was reignited both by the geographical discoveries of the age of Columbus and by the heliocentric discourse of the Copernican revolution. In that sense, imagining a world on the moon was perhaps a response to the Renaissance world in which systems of hierarchy, authority, religion, as well as planetary revolutions, were called into question. Reflecting on the consequences of Copernicus, John Donne concludes that 'new philosophy calls all in doubt' (*An Anatomy of the World: The First Anniversary*, 1611).

Literature on moon travel was also fundamentally satirical, providing a safe medium to criticize contemporary society.

The mathematician, astronomer and disciple of Tycho Brahe, Johannes Kepler, wrote his lunar dream, *Somnium* (posth. 1634) partly as a defence of the non-geocentric solar system but also to speculate on the possibilities of interplanetary travel and life. Kepler's endeavour to promote Copernican science and challenge his contemporaries' scientific view by providing a 'lunar' perspective on planetary science would have clashed with a detailed utopian blueprint of an idealized lunar society. His *Somnium*, however, paved the way for subsequent lunar utopias and science fiction.[6]

In 1638, Bishop Francis Godwin published the first English lunar novel, *The Man in the Moone: or a Discourse of a Voyage Thither by Domingo Gonsales the Speedy Messenger*. The book takes the form of a travel account, combining elements of adventure narration and literary utopia with scientific description. What makes Godwin's voyage utopia so interesting is that the picaresque wanderings of the main character take him to different worlds that all function as a critical contrast to his own, not so utopian world. Gonsales's voyage starts in Spain, brings him to St Helena and then to the moon. Godwin accepted the notion that air filled the space between worlds and that the moon was inhabited by intelligent human beings. Thus, after a successful flight that followed the scientific principle that the earth's gravitation diminishes with distance, Domingo Gonsales meets a 'Man in the Moon' who acts as his liaison to the Lunarians. Their conversations include the fundamentals of the lunar society, science, the Lunarian language, religion in contrast to the nature of politics, and religious conflict on earth. Though earthly society seems inferior, Gonsales returns home to spend the rest of his days with the Jesuits in China. Thus pre-empting the critical voyage utopia of the eighteenth century, Godwin does not propose one simple utopian blueprint, but uses the picaresque, Robinsonade and the lunar voyage to reflect critically on his own society and world.

Godwin's work influenced John Wilkins to revise his *The Discovery of a World in the Moone; or, A Discourse Tending to Prove, That 'Tis Probable There May Be Another Habitable World in That Planet* (1638) and *A Discourse Concerning a New World & Another Planet* (1640). Both Godwin's and Wilkins's works were imitated in several important ways in Cyrano de Bergerac's *Histoire comique contenant les États et Empires de la Lune* (1657). The lunar voyage persisted in the eighteenth century with David Russen's *Iter lunare* (1703), Diego de Torres Villarroel's *Viaje fantástico* (1723), Eberhard Kindermann's *Die geschwinde Reise auf dem Luftschiff nach der obern Welt* (1744), Robert Paltock's *The Life and Adventures of Peter Wilkins* (1751) and Voltaire's *Micromegas* (1752). Subterranean voyages such as *Lamékis ou les voyages extraordinaires d'un Egyptien dans la terre intérieure; avec la découverte de l'Isle des Sylphides* (1735–8), Baron Holberg's *Journey of Niels Klim to the World Underground* (1741) and Casanova's *L'Icosameron* (1788) further extended the boundaries of the imaginary geography of utopia in the eighteenth century.

Although geographical utopias/voyage utopias of this period are akin to contemporary narratives of explorers, conquerors and merchants, they also projected archaic ideals of Paradise onto new worlds. If Paradise or the Golden Age had been lost, then surely it could be found and thus become a utopian paradigm. The Irish monk, St Brendan, documented his seven-year search for the earthly Paradise in the *Navigatio of Saint Brendan*. The settlement of America was recorded as the discovery of Eden, Paradise, Canaan and a chiliastic 'new Heaven and a new Earth'. Even the later Cotton Mather's *Magnalia Christi Americana* (1720) and the writings by the Shaker Ann Lee described America as Eden. This quest for Paradise, embodied in the iconographic tropes of the Golden Age and Arcadia, was shaped by either a nostalgic grief for the lapsarian loss or, in the case of Thomas More, a dynamic utopian impulse that sought to recreate the terrestrial Paradise. Arcadia's yearning for containment forges an 'artful' harmony (Philip Sidney) that reassures the individual in an immediate natural environment but at the same time alludes to the conflicts in the 'non-pastoral' world. Instead of merely harking back to the memory of a long-lost Golden Age, the pastoral juxtaposes an idea of moral economy with the historical disturbances of war, feudal exploitation and the increasing split between country and court. Arcadia thus has always been a classical literary trope and appears in different guises and cultures. The Chinese myth *The Peach Blossom Spring*, recorded in a poem by Tao Yuanming (365–427) describes a peaceful peasant society, inaccessible and irretrievable. The early Irish *Tír nan Óg* ('The Land of the Ever-Young'), recorded in Micheál Coimín's poem *Laoi Oisín i dTír na nÓg* (1750), mythologizes the simple Arcadian existence. In 1502 the Italian poet and humanist Jacopo Sannazaro published his poem *Arcadia*, which fixed the early modern perception of Arcadia as a lost world of idyllic bliss, remembered in regretful laments in the manner of the Idylls of Theocritus. Edmund Spenser, in his *Letter to Sir Walter Raleigh*, places *The Faerie Queene* (1590–6) in the tradition of a Morean utopianism, depicting 'a Commune welth such as it should be'.[7] Thomas Traherne's 'The Third Century' in the posthumously discovered and published *Centuries of Meditation* (1908) marries visions of blissful prelapsarian childhood with *arcadia utopica* and in many ways pre-empts the Romantic utopian celebration of childhood innocence.

The most striking example of an anarchistic pastoral text is the medieval *Land of Cockaygne* (Land of 'small cakes'). Merging the classical myths and fantasies of Lucian's *True History* and Hesiod's Golden Age of Kronos and the chiliastic yearning for Heaven and Eden, it adds to the history of early modern utopianism the element of the carnivalesque. Addressing similar issues to More's preoccupation in Book I with rural poverty, land migration and agrarian capitalism, the *Land of Cockaygne* tells of a prelapsarian land of plenty where peaceful peasants once lived in abundance and well-being with no restrictions of private property or laws, juxtaposing the ideal of plenty with the reality of feudal serfdom and rural poverty. In the same vein, the Spanish novelists Antonio de Guevara in his *Libro Llamado Menosprecio de Corte y Alabança de Aldea* (1591) and Miguel de Cervantes in *Don Quixote de La Mancha* (1605) use the utopian fantasy of a rural Arcadia to comment on the conflict between rural migrants (*jornaleros*) and farmers.

We have thus seen so far that any consideration of the legacy of Thomas More's text needs to consider cross-over influences by other genres and ideal-society writings. The texts and projects considered above are part of a larger and European-wide conversation about the 'best state of a commonwealth'.

The question remains what the generic and modal matrix is within which utopia operates. Whilst indebted to classical utopianism, early-modern travel writing, the pastoral/Arcadian tradition and finally Christian Chiliasm, *Utopia* borrowed its generic make-up from classical literature, particularly Menippean and Lucian satire, travel writing and the romance novel. The Platonic dialogue is prominent in More's *Utopia* and doubled-up by the dialogue between Books I and II. It offers a systematic and detailed description of Utopian society and contrasts historical reality with the alternative history/society. Through this 'cognitive estrangement' (Darko Suvin) or the imagination of strange worlds, the reader learns to see his/her own world from a new perspective.[8]

Utopia's literariness and didacticism spring from Renaissance poetics. In particular, Philip Sidney's *Defence of Poesy* (1595) provides a useful model for *Utopia*'s commitment to verisimilitude but also rhetorical ambivalence. His central premise is that poetry is an art of imitation, that is a 'representing, counterfeiting, or figuring forth' not unlike a 'speaking picture'.[9] More's thought-experiment to resolve early-modern Europe's problems is thus a literary counterfeit, an imaginary history of a 'Not-Yet' better world (Ernst Bloch).[10] With the emergence of new literary genres, especially the early novel, the generic make-up of utopias diversifies.

Thomas More's *Utopia* provides the model for the archistic Utopia, a strand of utopianism that believes in strong governmental control to achieve the common good. Underlying More's *Utopia* is the idea of (original) sin. Certainly, 'the chief and progenitor of all plagues', Pride, is sought to be eradicated in the utopian environment where strict social control, education and the threat of the death penalty replace self-interest with the idea of common good and true friendship. The absence of privacy, private property and the idea of self-interest in an isolated social environment forces pride to fade. In *La Città del Sole* by Tommaso Campanella (1623) and Johann Valentin Andreae's *Reipublicae Christopolitanae Descriptio* (1619), the sins that are targeted are Tyranny, Sophistry and Hypocrisy, variations on Pride and self-interest. Again, social engineering and education are proposed to eradicate these great evils. However, the danger of sin is not overcome in these Renaissance utopias. Instead human nature is reprogrammed and disciplined (often through the threat of the death penalty). The primarily monastic make-up of the archistic utopias functions to subdue sin in favour of the common good.

In opposition to the geometry of the archistic utopia, the anarchistic utopia is ruled by an Arcadian primitivism that determines the constructed environment, social relations and organization of private/domestic relations. Especially, the liberation of human sexuality (strictly regulated in the archistic utopia) is the main reason for the success of these utopian societies. Rabelais's *Abbey of Thélème* (1534), which foreshadowed the libertarian utopianism of de Sade, declares the absolute authority of the individual, governed only by his or her wishes and desires. 'Do as thou wouldst' is the motto of the Abbey. However, the strand of archistic utopianism remained dominant, if expressed through different religious denominations and reform principles, for the two centuries after More produced his 'Golden Handbook'.

Utopia's initial critical reception is contained within the prefatory letters (*per-arga*) of the volume: the letters from More's own friends and contemporaries endorse the text. Six reprints of the Latin text in the sixteenth century and translations into German and English document the popularity of *Utopia*. By 1611 the word 'Utopia' was entered into an English dictionary and inspired writers throughout Europe to imagine idealized communities which were situated in the distant reaches beyond the known world. The most prominent ones are predominately Christian utopias of different denominations. The utopias by Andreae, Stiblin, Campanella and More propose ideal states that seek 'to lessen the burden of our mortality' (Johann Andreae) by making religion, education and science their utopian handmaidens.[11]

More's *Utopia* was closely followed by Johann Eberlin von Günzburg's pamphlet series *Die fünfzehn Bundesgenossen* (1521).[12] Embedded in the series is Eberlin's ideal city state, *Wolfaria*, today acknowledged as the first Protestant utopia. Eberlin's social and political reform programme derives from the principles of the Lutheran Reformation and the Peasants' uprisings between 1502 and 1517. Eberlin's utopia was not as radical as More's work, but certainly its commitment to social equality and justice and the appraisal of technology and science for the common good were uncompromising and, as Eberlin thought, necessary reforms. Eberlin's fellow Swabian Kaspar Stiblin published his Counter-Reformation Utopia *Commentariolus de Eudaemonnensium Republica* in 1555.[13] The frame narrative follows *Utopia* and describes the Catholic plutocracy of Macaria, the neighbouring island of Utopia. The capital city Eudaimon is radial and built on principles of hygiene and transparency. Physical labour, science, liberal arts and technological advancement are elevated to the guiding principles of the society, but the ultimate focus is on the afterlife; in opposition to More, Stiblin's Utopia is fundamentally chiliastic.

La Città del Sole (*The City of the Sun*), by Tommaso Campanella (1568–1639), was originally written in Italian in 1602, just after Campanella was condemned to life imprisonment for sedition and heresy in Naples. *The City of the Sun* is very much a result of Campanella's active role in the Calabrian rebellion against the Spanish in 1599. Convinced that great political and social changes were imminent and that he was both a prophet and a leader of the millennium, Campanella wanted to replace the existing form of the Spanish rule with a utopian commonwealth. His *City of the Sun*, written in prison, took the archistic principles of *Utopia* to the next level as every institution of the state is geared towards the education of the community spirit (*bonum commune*) in the Solarians. Set within a short frame narrative, the bulk of the text is the 'poetical dialogue' between a Genoese sailor who had accompanied Columbus on his voyage to America and a Knight Hospitaller. The City of the Sun was devised as a 'body politic' with its individual parts integrated so as to form a unitary organism and its various limbs, specialized on definite functions, entirely coordinated to serve the communal well-being. In that way, Campanella anticipated Thomas Hobbes's metaphorical use of the biblical figure of the Leviathan. Campanella's city state is a theocracy, governed by twenty-four priests and the head of the state, Sol. There is no division between the state, church and judiciary. Three priests are responsible for the government of private/social issues such as love and sexual relations; indeed, the community of goods extends to women and children. Social control is again exemplified in the urban structure. The city is radial, divided into seven large circuits, named after the seven planets. The city walls carry educational murals, time lines and samples of metals, stones, minerals, fluids, specimens of trees, herbs and other objects, moving from the representation of mathematics on the inner wall of the first (inner) circuit, to geography, social anthropology, geology, medicine, evolutionary biology and mechanical arts, and culminating in a portrayal of Jesus Christ, the twelve Apostles, Caesar, Alexander and other famous historical and religious figures. These murals are used for the elementary education of the children but also for the continuous and indeed subliminal instruction of the adults. The end of knowledge is to know God, the centre of the radial city is Sol. But despite these elaborate technologies of the self, the 'Utopian Paradox' appears in the *City of the Sun*, too. Crime is not eradicated and dissent from the communal good occurs. Similarly to More's *Utopia*, the commonwealth relies on agriculture and some minor trade with the outside world. However, in opposition to More, agricultural technology is, as the murals suggest, advanced and used to maximize yield on a minimum of work.

A Lutheran version of the perfect commonwealth was proposed by the German theologian Johann Valentin Andreae. In his *Reipublicae Christianopolitanae Descriptio* (*Christianopolis*) (1619), Andreae sought to renew 'the inner life of the Lutheran church' and society. The pattern of Andreae's fictitious community is succinctly described in the text as a 'republic of workers, living in equality, desiring peace, and renouncing riches'. It is based on principles of rationality, order and complete social control, underpinned again by a geometric city plan with a College in its centre. Christianopolis's motto is: 'We have come from freedom to doing good.' The political relationship between government and governed is patriarchal, and based on the relationship between God and man. Education is the principal political and social tool in Christianopolis. It is the basis of a superior society, consisting of intellectually and morally exceptional citizens. This basic theme is reflected in the spatial and symbolic placement of the main institution, the College. It is the heart of this utopian enterprise and, accordingly, occupies the most prominent position in Christianopolis. However, academic and moral instruction is not confined solely to the academy. The complex curriculum is expanded to the city itself with a range of visual materials, exhibits and libraries. The city of Christianopolis thus is not only a massive proto-industrial and self-sufficient workshop, but also a large-scale educational institution with a very distinctive political agenda: the education of the utopian subject.

Campanella and Stiblin in many ways prefigured science fiction, not by using imaginary science to reach other places and planets (like the vast body of moon voyages), but by their preoccupation with using science and technology to create an ideal, or at least better, world.

The period between 1620 and 1638, at least in England, is characterized by a distinct shift in ideal politics due to changes in the political arena, an increasing global trade and a historicized consciousness of time. What we can identify is the gradual shift from geographical utopias (*utopias*) to chronological utopias (*uchronias*), and more importantly, a period of paradigmatic overlap where the ideal commonwealth is located in an imaginary, undiscovered, isolated place and at the same time, reforms are revealed as utopian hope and utopian possibilities. This becomes particularly apparent in the utopian experiments of the New England Puritans (and generally millenarian groups), where utopian mastery is exercised not in an imaginary but an actual utopia.

The rhetoric of ideal politics in the writings of King James I transcends the brief of a mere royal proclamation. The justification of his absolute reign by divine right provided a discourse of ideal politics and its utopian implications, analogous to the utopian impetus in Bacon's *The Advancement of Learning* (1605) but also in contemporary utopias as discussed above. What unites James I and the utopian writers is not the genre of utopia but an expression of an anticipatory hope that transcends mere political ideology, and, at the same time, invests in early modern colonialism, mercantilism and the scientific revolution.

Francis Bacon's fragment, *New Atlantis: A Worke Unfinished written by the Right Honourable Francis Lord Verulam, Viscount St Alban*, posthumously published as part of *Sylva Sylvarum* in 1627, is perhaps the first true scientific utopia. Following the now familiar pattern, it describes the accidental discovery of a fortified city state, Bensalem, located in the Pacific Ocean. The main body of the text consists of conversations between the unnamed narrator and different officials and citizens. These reveal, if insufficiently, the social and political structure of this utopian society as well as its complex foundation history. The centre of the city is Salomon's House or the College of the Six Days' Work, a fictional precursor to the philosophical college founded in London in 1645 and the Royal Society of 1660. It unites a scientific community composed of different disciplines with a defined hierarchical structure of fellows, novices and apprentices. Salomon's house, 'dedicated to the study of the Works and Creatures of God', institutes faith and social order through scientific knowledge. Economically, Bensalem is, by choice, isolated and self-sufficient. Family life is hierarchical and regulated by fundamentally Christian principles. Whilst the scientists do not have any direct political power, they exercise a greater and sanctified moral authority. They are indeed the true rulers of the Atlantan society. Although 'the end of our Foundation is the knowledge of Causes, and secret motions of things; and the enlarging of the bounds of the Human Empire, the effecting of all things possible', the scientists withhold that 'which we think fit to keep secret'. Thus, the utopian subject is the subjected *object* of Atlantan utopian principles.

What defined the utopianism of the 1640s was a steadfast evolution towards concrete political and social reform. The circle around Samuel Hartlib, Jan Amos Comenius and Gabriel Plattes, the Pansophists, pre-empted the rise of a revolutionary idealism that resulted in later constitutional changes. What characterized their language and that of later Parliamentarians and pamphleteers and writers was a novel and radical political leverage, a practical, social approach to political discourse and an element of millenarian chiliasm. Pansophy's ultimate goal was salvation, but salvation for the Pansophists meant deliverance from ignorance, tyranny and conflict. Thus their reform programmes focused on politics, education and religion to recover the original wisdom that mankind lost with the expulsion from Eden.

Jan Amos Comenius's *The Labyrinth of the World and the Paradise of the Heart* (1623) is a spiritual allegory on utopian hope and sets out more general and cosmopolitan principles for the transformation of human society through education and Enlightenment. Ultimately, though, for Comenius, salvation can only be found in the soul, in the acceptance of Christ. Gabriel Plattes's *A Description of the Famous Kingdome of Macaria. Shewing its Excellent Government* (1641) and Samuel Gott's *Nova Solyma* (1648) targeted directly the Long Parliament (1640–53), where a special select committee was set up to frame 'a remonstrance on the deplorable estate of the kingdom'. Given the political context, it is not surprising that Gott and Plattes were proposing institutional reform and an educational system that would promote the creation of the best possible society in advance of the coming millennium.

They were not the only utopians. James Harrington's *The Commonwealth of Oceana* (1656), dedicated to Oliver Cromwell, and William Cavendish's *Advice* to Charles II, revised the *Speculum Principis* tradition for the mid-seventeenth century. Gerrard Winstanley's Digger pamphlets of 1648 and *The Law of Freedom* (1652) were perhaps the most radical readings of Scripture to challenge private ownership of land. In 1649 Digger communities squatted on common land on St George's Hill in Surrey, Cox Hill in Kent and Iver in Buckinghamshire to sow 'the ground with parsnips, carrots and beans'.

The outbreak of the Civil War in 1642, the death of Charles I, and the Protectorate document the radical changes that different religious and political groups wanted to implement. Utopianism spread throughout the whole nation through public debates, petitions and millenarianist reform proposals. These now also provided a space for women writers. Mary Cary's visionary text, *A New and More Exact Mappe; or, Description of New Jerusalems Glory* (1651), brings together the millennial ideal of a just society with the pragmatic political questions surrounding the establishment of the English Republic. According to Cary, the millennial society will be truly just and egalitarian – a society based on the 'holy use' of reason which makes no distinction of class or gender.

On the other side of the political spectrum is Margaret Cavendish's *The Description of a New World, Called the Blazing World* (1666). *The Blazing World* is a fictional utopia of an absolute monarchy ruled by an enlightened Empress and her alter-ego, Margaret, Duchess of Newcastle. As its basic guiding principles – one monarch, one language, one religion – attest, it is clearly a reaction to the disruptions of the Civil War in England at the time. However, *The Blazing World* is far from being a conventional aristocratic plea for monarchy. It raises questions about women's education and intellectual perfectibility, scientific paradigms and gender and genre in such a progressive and modern way that Margaret Cavendish was labelled 'Mad Madge' by contemporaries.

Indeed women's education became one of the rallying points and common denominators of female utopian writing in the seventeenth century. Margaret Cavendish, Bathsua Makin and Mary Astell built upon the ground cleared by Descartes and his philosophical adherents. Descartes and other authors advocated the development of woman's intellect, and claimed not only that education was in the interest of and even a natural right of the individual, but also that women's education would ultimately benefit society. Arguments for female education converge with the concept of 'perfectibility' to underpin utopian projects and fiction in the late seventeenth century. Mary Astell's *A Serious Proposal to the Ladies for the Advancement of their True and Greatest Interest* (1694) with a sequel of 1697, Part II: *Wherein a Method is Offer'd for the Improvements of their Minds*, is the best-known publication in this debate. Astell envisaged a community founded on the sole pleasures of 'Noble Vertuous and Disinteress'd Friendship' of women which was informed by a specific understanding of intellectual and spiritual perfectibility – a concern that has forged the post-Reformation link between convents and female academies. Secular and religious aspirations for women's education such as Astell's scheme prompted a nascent utopian tradition that envisaged secular or Anglican convents and, quickly, the 'female academy'.

But utopian hope was not universally embraced. Bishop Joseph Hall's *Mundus Alter et Idem* ('The Other and the Same World', *c.* 1605) initiated the tradition of the anti-utopia later perfected by Jonathan Swift. Set in *Terra Australis incognita*, *Mundus* is a carnivalesque satire on the futility of utopian hope. There is indeed nothing worth discovering in the *Terra Australis* and the narrator is finally asked: 'What other age are you dreaming of, what other land?' What Hall's anti-utopia indicates, however, is an increasing widening of the generic and typological spectrum of utopia throughout the seventeenth and eighteenth centuries.

In the eighteenth century, the geographical utopia evolved into different models. Eighteenth-century utopias made use of Enlightenment discourses on progress, perfectibility, reason, sociability and reform. Utopian writers formulated a range of alternative possibilities in their stances against absolutism, against the sycophantic existence of the aristocracy and, in the case of French writers, at least, the dogmas of the Catholic Church.

Ethnological utopias speculated on diverse models of progressive socialization from a 'state of nature' culminating in an 'Age of Commerce' (Adam Smith), or in modern civil society (Samuel Pufendorf). Natural histories of civil society developed an idea of a gradual progression of at least a portion of humanity through comparisons between European and non-western societies. Such narratives served to demarcate western achievements in science and technology, the arts and culture, in short, civilization. This conjectural historiography not only reinforced the superiority of the 'Old World' but justified and naturalized the extensive appropriation and colonization of the 'New World' – as we have seen in Thomas More. A more relativist representation of human nature and human values drew attention to fundamental geographical, climatic and historical differences between peoples and cultures. Within this framework, progress and the concept of civilization itself were redefined as relative, not absolute. This is also where utopia intersected with non-utopian historiographies of civil society and political economy and literary genres such as the pastoral, and indeed became another stepping stone for contemporary anthropology and political science. Historical pessimism created utopias that idealized the 'state of nature' and defined society and civilization as progressive alienation from an original good – they thus opposed Hobbes's anti-social notion of the 'natural' man. Here utopia promised the regeneration of society to its original state of innocence and peace. Utopias such as Denis Vairasse's *History of the Sevarites* (1675) or Gabriel de Foigny's *La Terre Australe connue* (The Southern Land Known) (1676) document simple, virtuous and self-sufficient communities and thus offer their own contribution to the contemporary debate on luxury. Aphra Behn's rather conventional description of the Indians in Surinam in *Oroonoko* (1688) anticipates Jean-Jacques Rousseau's apparent paean to the innocence, simplicity and peaceableness of the 'noble savage'.

The projection of utopian hopes and desires onto the New World continued in the eighteenth century. These utopias promoted domestic, self-sufficient economies of production, based on Native American economies, accompanied by the abolition of private property and money within the utopian society. Frances Brooke in *The History of Emily Montagu* (1769) set her micro-utopia on the American continent where the narrator's remarks on the Canadian Indians combine primitivist anthropology with an explicit social critique of European gender inequality. Brooke's celebration of the native utopian model however is ambivalent. Henry Mackenzie in *The Man of the World* (1773), Lesage's *Les Aventures de M. Robert Chevalier, dit de Beauchêne, capitaine de flibustiers dans la Nouvelle-France* (1732), and Abbé Prévost's great philosophical novel, *Le Philosophe anglais, ou histoire de Monsieur Cleveland* (1731–9) idealized the simplicity of the Native American societies. This idealization also became a notable trope in German literature of the time. Sophie von La Roche's *Erscheinungen am See Oneida* (1798) is an interesting reworking of Rousseau's novel *Julie*, which outlines a conjectural history of society from the Edenic union of Adam and Eve (the Wattines) in the American wilderness to the creation of a city with other European immigrants. Sophie Mereau's *Das Blüthenalter der Empfindung* and Henriette Frölich's *Virginia, oder die Republik von Kentucky* provide similar blueprints.

A variation on the primitivist theme was proposed by Smith and Priber. Reverend William Smith of Philadelphia's utopian tract, 'A General Idea of the College of Mirania' (1753), offers an account of a fictitious college of learning in an imaginary American colony which instructs youth 'in the liberal arts and sciences'. What is interesting and novel is the curriculum of non-denominational religious teaching, government, basic reading and writing, husbandry and agricultural studies, mathematics, astronomy and navigation, ethics, history and metaphysics and, finally, conversation and public speaking. Smith sought to include the Native American nations (as suitable British allies) and German immigrants (again as necessary allies) in the educational and cultural assimilation of the community.

Another, more conspicuous but real-life community was founded by Christian Gottlieb Priber, who left Germany in 1735 to found a city state named Paradise, for prisoners, criminals and slaves amongst the Cherokee nation. Priber sought, if unsuccessfully, to imitate the simple and more 'natural' lifestyle of the North American Indians, a lifestyle he encountered as a former captive of Indians himself.

The fast-expanding geographical knowledge of the New World located an important sub-genre of eighteenth-century fantastic voyage and utopias onto the still-unknown Antipodes. As the essential world upside down, early representations of the Antipodes projected the monstrous and the grotesque onto the continent and provided, in the eighteenth century, an important new *locus* for the anti-utopian satire. By the second half of the eighteenth century, Pacific explorations forced authors to review their dystopian projection. Denis Diderot's *Supplement to Bougainville's 'Voyage'* (1772) made a case for the simple, natural ways of a South Sea Island culture as reported by Bougainville, a French explorer. The European lifestyle is discredited in comparison. Communal property and complete sexual freedom are the mainstays of their philosophy, although few details of government, law and the economy are given.

The continent of Africa was less used in eighteenth-century utopian writings than in the utopias of the nineteenth century. This was partially due to the lack of geographical knowledge and exploration. However, Gabriel de Foigny's *La Terre Australe connue* (1676) locates two of his four utopian episodes in the kingdoms of Congo and Madagascar, Simon Berington's *The Adventures of Sig. Gaudentio di Lucca* (1737) sets his utopian city state in the centre of the continent and the Pirate Commonwealth in the *General History of the Pirates* (1728, attributed to Daniel Defoe) is located in Madagascar. A perhaps more ambivalent utopian re-colonization project was the relocation of former African slaves by the Sierra Leone Company in 1792. Three colonies in Sierra Leone, Bulama and Port Jackson were devised as quasi-utopian 'Provinces of Freedom' for former slaves. Furthermore, 'the Blessings of Industry and Civilisation' were to be introduced into Africa, with a focus on profit and economics, and Freetown was eventually renamed 'A Town of Slavery'.

But it was not only the New World or the Antipodes but the Orient too that served as a site of utopian desire and imagination. Male fantasies of 'oriental sapphism' dominated the travel literature of the seventeenth and eighteenth centuries and opened the doors for a wide range of pornographic (somatopian) literature set in the Orient. Women writers such as Lady Mary Wortley Montagu in her posthumous *Turkish Embassy Letters* created Orientalist utopias by contrasting their (liberating) experiences of the Orient with an experience of eighteenth-century England that was patriotic, expansionist, eurocentric and patriarchal. Paradoxically, it is the despotic Orient and in particular, the harem, that provided the space for their imaginative geography.

Eighteenth-century utopias might be collectively identified as offering a 'poly-utopia' or 'critical utopia'. These texts contrast a plurality of social models in one text without offering one satisfactory utopian solution. These poly-utopias are indeed critical utopias; that it to say, they are aware of the limitations of the classical utopian model and at the same time strive for a dynamic utopia. Their structure is episodic and moves from philosophical *exemplum* to *exemplum* to juxtapose and debate contrasting arguments about visions of utopia and human happiness. In Gabriel de Foigny's *La Terre Australe connue* (1676), the protagonist Sadeur – very much a Robinsonian figure who was conceived 'in America and born on the ocean', is taken on a voyage of discovery and self-discovery via the East Indies, Zaire, Congo and Madagascar to Australia. He encounters the Congo and Zaire as versions of the classical utopia distinguished by an artificial harmony and order through splendid isolation. Consequently, he suffers from boredom and inactivity. Sadeur ends up in Australia in a homogenized paradise of hermaphrodites only to discover that he does not belong. In Samuel Johnson's Oriental tale, *Rasselas* (1759), Rasselas and his companions reflect on their sojourn in the Happy Valley only to confirm that 'such ... is the state of life, that none are happy but by the anticipation of change: the change itself is nothing; when we have made it, the next wish is to change again'.[14] Abbé Prévost's *Monsieur Cleveland* (1731–9) also traces a range of utopian spaces and societies from the paradisiacal Caribbean island of Sainte-Hélène, the island of Madeira to the native society of the Abaquis and the Nopandes in North America and the commune of Fanny in Cuba. All utopian models, even the one created by Cleveland himself as the legislator of the Abaquis, are flawed, and based on an artificial and thus fragile model of harmony and order. And Voltaire's own sceptical *Candide* (1759) takes us from the 'terrestrial Paradise' Thunder-Ten-Tronckh to El Dorado to Candide's garden where utopia is actively created, indeed cultivated.

More pessimistic and openly anti-utopian is Swift's satire *Gulliver's Travels* (1726, revised 1735), which echoes in some ways the formal characteristics of More's *Utopia*. Indeed, what *Utopia* and *Gulliver's Travels* share is the technique of distortion (*reductio ad absurdum*) as corrective in its aim. In a letter to Charles Ford on 14 August 1725, Swift wrote about the first draft of his book: 'I have finished my Travells, and am now transcribing them: they are admirable Things, and will wonderfully mend the world.'[15] Structured as an imaginary voyage with elements of the Robinsonade, the first-person narrator travels through imaginary geographies and encounters very different societies and people. The fast-expanding geographical knowledge of the New World located *Gulliver's Travels* onto the, by then still relatively unknown, Antipodes. As the essential 'world upside down', seventeenth-century representations of the Antipodes/Australasia projected the monstrous and the grotesque onto the continent and provided the ideal locus for his anti-utopian satire for Swift.

Gulliver's Travels sets up a complex paradox between Gulliver, the reader and eighteenth-century Europe. Although Swift's book was a great and immediate success with contemporaries who particularly relished the unforgiving but witty political satire (thus revealing 'Keys' to *Gulliver's Travels* were very popular), its careful and sustained parody on Enlightenment philosophy and religion is perhaps more significant. Ultimately, though, Swift's construction of Gulliver as a myopic and unreliable narrator has its greatest satirical design on the reader himself. *Gulliver's Travels* raises questions about the fault lines that developed during the eighteenth century on ideas of language, history, perfectibility and, indeed, utopianism itself. Whilst Gulliver finds near-utopias in the Brobdingnagian and Houyhnhnm societies, Swift concluded that human nature itself (including Gulliver's) thwarts the realization of any utopian society. This becomes particularly apparent in Book IV, often interpreted as the only true utopia that Gulliver encountered. The society of the Houyhnhnms is based on the immutable principles of 'Temperance, Industry, Exercise, and Cleanliness'. But – and we have a similar critique of static utopianism in the contemporary voyage utopia – this homogenized, prelapsarian paradise reveals itself ultimately as a system of mental and political slavery. The Houyhnhnms' insistence on 'the Perfection of Nature' (which is indeed the etymology of their name) was to parody and perhaps question the possibility of perfectibility in an Anglican or philosophical sense.[16] Insisting that 'I do not hate mankind', Swift resigned himself to the fact that human beings 'degenerate every day, merely by the folly, the perverseness, the avarice, the tyranny, the pride, the treachery, or inhumanity of their own kind'.[17] Like the critical utopia, *Gulliver's Travels* identifies the paradoxical complexity of the Enlightenment project and its fundamentally utopian nature.

Swift's satire established a long tradition of sequels, often termed Gulliveriana. The first response was by Abbé Pierre Desfontaines, the French translator of *Gulliver's Travels*, who published *Le Nouveau Gulliver ou Voyages de Jean Gulliver, fils du capitaine Lemuel Gulliver* in 1730. Bernard Mandeville's *Fable of the Bees: or, Private Vices, Publick Benefits* (1714), the anonymous *Les songes du Chevalier de La Marmotte* (1745) and *L'Isle des Philosophes* (1790) all echo Swift's anti-utopian stance. Whilst Thomas More started an influential conversation about Utopia as *De optimo reipublicae statu* – as 'a very good, or excellent, state of the commonwealth', eighteenth-century utopian satires declared this conversation to be over.

Another strand of geographical utopias contains the 'individualistic' utopias, the Robinsonades, that pre-empted the critical voyage utopias in their celebration of the self-imposed exile or involuntary retreat from the world as the only place where true happiness, contentment and self-fulfilment can be ensured. It is thus not surprising that Jean-Jacques Rousseau celebrated Robinson Crusoe as a man in a 'state of nature' who lived a solitary life of simple virtue. The Robinsonade is related to the utopian satire and the imaginary voyage but is essentially a genre in its own right. The main difference is that the 'worldview implicit in the English Robinsonade does not envisage the construction of a perfect world beginning from the zero-point of history (the state of nature)'.[18] Whilst Daniel Defoe's *Robinson Crusoe* defined the genre in 1719, other texts such as Grimmelshausen's *Der Abentheuerliche Simplicissimus Teutsch und Continuatio des abentheuer-lichen Simplicissimi* (1668), Henry Neville's *The Isle of Pines* (1668), *Les Aventures de Télémaque* by François de Salignac de la Mothe Fénelon (1699) and Hendrik Smeeks's *The Mighty Kingdom of Krinke Kesmes* (1708) provided prior models. Defoe's novel was likely influenced by the real-life castaway Alexander Selkirk, who was stranded for four years on the Pacific island Más a Tierra, Chile.

Robinsonades participated in the eighteenth-century discourse of colonization, bourgeois individualism and unfettered capitalist accumulation. In *Das Kapital* (1867, 1885, 1894) Karl Marx read Crusoe's experiences on the island as representing the inherent economic value of labour over capital. What Marx failed to see is that Robinsonades also complicated and in some ways questioned the paradigm of conquest, adventure and colonial capitalism. Grimmelshausen's Simplicissimus declines returning to Europe after fifteen years of solitary living, preferring his individualist utopia to his homeland. Like Robinson Crusoe, Peter Wilkins in Robert Paltock's *The Life and Adventures of Peter Wilkins* (1751) forces a flawed replica of Georgian England onto the society of Saas Doorpt Swangeanti only to realize his great misjudgment when leaving it. Indeed, Hendrik Smeeks's *The Mighty Kingdom of Krinke Kesmes* (1708), Neville's *The Isle of Pines* (1668), J. G. Schnabel's *Die Insel Felsenburg* (1731–43) and again Defoe's Robinson Crusoe in his *Farther Adventures* (1719) all came to distance themselves from the providential enthusiasm invested in colonial utopianism. Certainly, *Robinson Crusoe* and the *Farther Adventures of Robinson Crusoe* and *The History of the Pirates* (1734) (though Defoe's authorship is disputed here) suggest that colonial utopias as experiments of racial hybridity were likely to fail.

Half a century later, Thomas Spence used the Robinsonade again as a form to advocate a cooperative commonwealth with majority rule and a citizen militia. In the *Supplement to the History of Robinson Crusoe* (1780), Spence returns to Crusoe's Island, and establishes a democratic utopia in 'Crusonia'. The *Description of Spensonia* (1795) and the *Constitution of*

Spensonia (1803), modelled on the French Constitution of 1793, complemented Spence's thorough attack on the institutions of English society at the time. Spence's particular interest lay in ownership of land, legislative reform, education of the labouring poor and female suffrage.

At first sight, Robinsonades are masculinist in their celebration of possessive individualism and colonial triumph. The female characters in Grimmelshausen, Neville, Schnabel and Paltock were framed merely in terms of their sexual and social usefulness. However, the female Robinson promotes the utopian rather than the colonist conceit of the Robinsonade tradition, and added particularly proto-feminist concerns to the genre. Perhaps the first English example of a (lunar) female Robinsonade was *The Description of a New World, Called the Blazing World*, by Margaret Cavendish (1666), where the heroine actively conquers and organizes the New World. In a similar vein to women's domestic utopias of the time, the eighteenth-century female Robinsonade advanced female friendship (if there are more shipwrecked travellers), peace, equality and harmony. The island experience, for instance, in *Die beglückte Inseln, oder die Geschichte der Fräulein von Jalling, von ihr selbst aufgezeichnet* (1777), is one of harmonious government by a female matriarchy, and pre-empts modern separatist utopias by writers such as Charlotte Perkins Gilman (*Herland*, 1915). Rescue in this context then meant a forced return to the patriarchal European society, and like some of their male counterparts, not all female Robinsons welcomed their return home.

The eighteenth-century novel also offered to the utopian mode a formal innovation within which utopian explorations could be extended and reconfigured – the utopian novel *per se* and the 'micro-utopias' or 'petites sociétés'.[19] Delarivier Manley's *Atalantis* (1709), Sarah Scott's *Millenium Hall* (1762) and Lady Mary Hamilton's *Munster Village* (1778), utopian novels in their entirety, serve as examples of the former; Sarah Fielding's *David Simple* (1744) presents one good example of the latter.

In 1709, Manley published her notorious *roman-à-clef, Secret Memoirs and Manners of Several Persons of Quality, of both Sexes. From the New Atalantis, An Island in the Mediterranean. Written Originally in Italian.* The book is a satire on contemporary society – the first edition even had a separately printed key that revealed the true identities of the protagonists. Within it, however, is embedded a separatist *locus amoenus*, a country retreat based on shared property, friendship and pleasure that echoes Astell's female Paradise. Like Astell and subsequently Sarah Scott, Manley creates a community that emancipates women from patriarchal oppression and sexual exploitation.

The eighteenth-century reverence of sensibility results in two paradoxically antithetical stances. On the one hand, 'sympathy' bound feeling human beings in a community of affectionate responsiveness to one another's joys and sorrows; the identification of the witness with the pain of the sufferer extended and consolidated the human community of which both are a part by directing the immediate feelings of the responsive witness into sympathetic action, the requirements of moral duty. On the other hand, sentimentalism, a novelistic outgrowth of the cult of sensibility, leads to the 'individualist utopia' – the private return to nature or the retreat of the like-minded few, the alternative micro-societies of Scott's *Millenium Hall*, Rousseau's *Julie: ou, La nouvelle Héloïse* (1761) and Sarah Fielding's *David Simple*. Scott's vision of an economy based on social capital is representative of these writings. Although carefully couched in the context of decorous behaviour, apparent support of the institution of marriage, chaste living and genteel good works, *Millenium Hall* represents a major challenge to patriarchy, mercantilism and colonialism. Scott's utopian world is made up of women who are remaking their environment through the exchange of individual fortune and power for feminist solidarity and community. It is important to note that Sarah Fielding's *The Adventures of David Simple* and more specifically *Volume the Last* (1753) are, on the one hand, a radical critique of patriarchal capitalism, but on the other, also a reflection on the futility of utopian hope based on feminine and sentimental values.

More optimistic was Olympe de Gouges, a playwright of some note in France at the time of the French Revolution. After the French National Assembly adopted the Declaration of the Rights of Man in 1789, de Gouges rewrote the document to include women in her 1791 *Declaration of the Rights of Woman and of the Citizen*. Unfortunately, her proposal for professional and educational equality and freedom of speech was not welcome. Article 10 declares that 'If ... woman has the right to mount the scaffold; she must equally have the right to mount the rostrum.' She was herself guillotined in 1793.

Whilst eighteenth-century women writers clearly address the position of women and their rights in marriage in their utopian writings, male authors, too, defended universal human rights and civil liberties for women. James Lawrence's *Empire of the Nairs, or The Rights of Women* (1793, trans. into English in 1811) based his progressive ideas on Mary Wollstonecraft's *Vindication of the Rights of Woman* (1792) and William Godwin's *Enquiry Concerning Political Justice* (1793). *The Travels of Hildebrand Bowman* (1778), *An Essay on Civil Government, or, Society Restored* (1793) and William Hodgson, *A Treatise Called the Female Citizen: or, A Historical,*

Political, and Philosophical Enquiry into the Rights of Women (1796) were also particularly forthright in their claims for women's equality.

At the other end of the utopian spectrum, writers such as Bernard le Bovier de Fontenelle and Morelly, following Plato's and More's models of statism, sought to rehabilitate the institutions of the state, and devised, in strikingly different ways, interventionist political systems. These texts were motivated by the threat of poverty and social turmoil that could be resolved only by radically new forms of economic and social organization. In the case of Morelly, his philosophical treatise *Code of Nature* (1755) and the epic poem *Basiliad* advanced the remedy of communism to eliminate poverty and social exploitation. Seventeenth-century English agrarian republicanism represented by Winstanley's *Law of Freedom* inspired a surge of political utopian pamphlets at the time and was reconceptualized into eighteenth-century radical politics in the writings of John Clare, Thomas Spence, John Thelwall, Richard 'Citizen' Lee and the Pantisocratists.

The middle ground, so to speak, of utopian schemes, was occupied by reform programmes deriving from a partial fusion of utopianism and the tradition of seventeenth-century commonwealth writings. Mixed legislative models such as the enlightened or benevolent monarchy were devised; these either envisioned the transformation of a whole civic state (Johann Gottfried Schnabel, *Insel Felsenburg* (1731–43)) or tribal associations (La Mothe-Fénelon, *Les Aventures de Télémaque*). William Hodgson's *The Commonwealth of Reason* (1795) and Elihu Hubbard Smith's deist 'Pansophia', *The Institutions of the Republic of Utopia* (written in 1796–7), successfully marry the characteristics of the classical utopia (geometrical town plans, strict division of electoral districts, republican government, state-enforced system of moral education) with Enlightenment principles of universal education and, if in moderation, women's liberation. Both utopias are essentially statist, a reaction not only to the Terror of the French Revolution but also, in the case of Smith, to a keen interest in the intersection between physical and moral health (Smith wrote extensively on epidemiology and the nation's health).

> Bliss was it in that dawn to be alive
> But to be young was very heaven!
>
> William Wordsworth[20]

The French Revolution's slogan, *Liberté, Egalité, Fraternité*, stands in dialectical relation to the Enlightenment's epistemological projects and utopian philosophy of history. Utopian thought was integrated into the multiple levels of Enlightenment political debates, and utopian elements were evident in various combinations in much Enlightenment political writing. This also meant an amalgam of genres and literary modes.

In 1790 Edmund Burke published his *Reflections on the Revolution in France*, which set off a pamphlet war between Burke and English radicals such as Thomas Paine, Mary Wollstonecraft and William Godwin. Despite his fervent support of the American Revolution, Burke turned in his *Reflections* to defend 'antient principles' of 'virtue, honour, courage, patriotism and loyalty'.[21] The French Revolution for him was an expression of horrific barbarism and the violent overthrow of a legitimate government confirmed by history and tradition. His antagonists argued for and promoted principles of republicanism, agrarianism, civic virtue and liberty, and understood British (and French) history as the history of naturalized oppression.

Mary Wollstonecraft's *Vindication of the Rights of Men* (1790) was published in response to Burke. Hers was the first response in a pamphlet war in which Thomas Paine's *Rights of Man* (1792) became the centrepiece for reformers and radicals. Wollstonecraft not only attacked monarchy and hereditary privilege but also the language that Burke used to defend and elevate it. *A Vindication of the Rights of Woman* (1792) continued Wollstonecraft's plea for civic virtue and equality with a special focus on women's rights and education. Her political philosophy was based on principles of reason and perfectibility, though her novels drew heavily on the language of sensibility to promote women's rights.

William Godwin's *An Enquiry Concerning Political Justice and Its Influence on General Virtue and Happiness* (1793) and his novel *Things as They Are; or, The Adventures of Caleb Williams* (1794) equally advocated the rule of reason and personal freedom.[22] In opposition to Burke, Godwin believed that existing political systems failed to produce happiness, equality or freedom. *Political Justice* and *Caleb Williams* are thus penetrating enquiries into the ways in which private property, aristocracy and monarchical government impose themselves upon individuals and limit the political development of society as a whole. Developing his philosophy from Rousseau, Godwin argued that the pursuit of perfectibility, reason and universal benevolence would eventually abolish the need for governments and institutions. Godwin's philosophical anarchism had a profound influence on Robert Owen, Robert Bage, William Thompson and other utopians in the nineteenth century as well as the Romantic poets.

The poetry of Romanticism was governed by a form of utopian displacement where the goal of liberation from hierarchy, oppression and poverty and the political struggle to achieve a just and egalitarian society were resituated in a variety of visions such as the pastoral, agrarian utopias, prophetic art/creativity, and onto the 'New World'.

William Blake's *America: A Prophecy* (1793) and *Europe: A Prophecy* (1794) serve as models for utopian reform in the light of the utopian hopes that the American and French Revolutions generated (and disappointed). Joseph Priestley, a staunch but persecuted English supporter of the French Revolution, sent his son Joseph, Jr, and son-in-law Thomas Cooper to America to start a community of 'English friends of freedom'. Mary Wollstonecraft's partner Gilbert Imlay also wrote a tract, *A Topographical Description of the Western Territory of North America* (1792), that sought to inspire the foundation of utopian communities. Both Cooper's and Imlay's writings may have influenced Southey and Coleridge, whose own 'Pantisocratic' society was to be located, like Priestley's community, on the banks of the Susquehanna. The 'Pantisocracy' was framed in principle in Coleridge's *Lectures on Revealed Religion* (1795) and was to be a utopian, noble and philosophical project where the tenet of equal rule by all prevailed. After grave disagreements and quarrels about the final location (the plans were for Susquehanna or Wales) the project was aborted in 1795.

The Romantics' interest in childhood and education led to another strand of perhaps more practical utopianism. Robert Bage's novels were particularly shaped by Rousseau and Wollstonecraft and their idea of the education of the utopian subject. *Hermsprong: Or, Man As He Is not* (1796) outlines the childhood of an American boy raised entirely by American Indians, without either formal education or religion. Thomas Day's children's book *The History of Sandford and Merton* (1783–9) also promoted the utopian educational ideals set out by Rousseau in his controversial *Emile, or, On Education* (1762) and complements a range of contemporary pamphlets and novels on the importance of education of future (utopian) generations ranging from Mary Astell, Daniel Defoe, Edward Chamberlayne, Clara Reeve to Mary Wollstonecraft.

> ... 'Twas in truth an hour
> Of universal ferment; mildest men
> Were agitated; and commotions, strife
> Of passion and opinion fill'd the walls
> Of peaceful houses with unquiet sounds.
> The soil of common life was at that time
> Too hot to tread upon; oft said I then,
> And not then only, 'what a mockery this
> Of history; the past and that to come!
> Now do I feel how I have been deceived,
> Reading of Nations and their works, in faith,
> Faith given to vanity and emptiness;

Oh! laughter for the Page that would reflect
To future times the face of what now is!'

William Wordsworth[23]

The new emphasis on history-as-progress had a profound impact on the genre. What determines this shift are successive epistemological paradigms, a philosophy of history and the emergence of a public sphere that makes (political) satire redundant. The period between 1750 and 1800 is marked by a canon of conjectural and philosophical histories that include utopian elements or are indeed utopias. But these conjectural histories differ greatly in their understanding of history and progress. Enlightenment, understood by Kant as 'man's emergence from his self-incurred immaturity', is a desirable end to the achievement of which thinking should construct history in order that 'we might by our own rational powers accelerate the coming of this period which will be so welcome to our descendants' (*What is the Enlightenment?*). Reason in history thus will produce progress.

Rousseau's *Discourses* (*Discours sur les sciences et les arts*, 1750, and *Discours sur l'origine et inégalité parmi les hommes*, 1754 on the other hand are histories which refer nostalgically to pre-modern or primitive cultures and reject the notion of history as perfectibility. However, rather than being simply primitivist, Rousseau suggests in his conjectural anthropology that society corrupts men only insofar as the Social Contract has not *de facto* succeeded. A new and egalitarian Social Contract is needed to ennoble man and modern society.

Voltaire and Condorcet did not share Rousseau's nostalgic pessimism and presented more dialogic views of possible futures, implying, as was the case with Condorcet and Mercier, that a better future required a break with the imperfections of the past. The latter laid the path for the temporalization of the early modern 'geographical' utopia culminating in the futuristic visions of Louis-Sébastien Mercier (*L'An 2440: Un rêve s'il en fut jamais/Memoirs of the Year Two Thousand Five Hundred*, 1771) and Julius von Voß (*Ini: Ein Roman aus dem Ein und Zwanzigsten Jahrhundert*, 1810).

Mercier's utopia provided a detailed and harsh critique of the *ancien régime*. Consequently, it was immediately banned upon its initial publication but went on to become a bestseller. It follows the classical utopia paradigm in proposing order based on reason, moderation and work. For Mercier, the path towards a better society lay in the triumph of reason over passion and the sacrifice of individual desires for the common good.

Voß's now rather neglected novel *Ini* and his later play *Berlin im Jahre 1924* complement his visionary non-fiction, such as *Hohe Aussichten der Menschheit oder Der Christenstaat* (1808). In opposition to Mercier, Voß has clear ideas about the development of a futurist society from the late nineteenth century to the twenty-first century, outlining the necessary paradigms for reform and perfectibility. *Ini* fuses the scientific utopianism of Francis Bacon with the idea of the enlightened monarch in his blueprint for a 'monarchical republic'. The formation of the utopian subject in *Ini* can be traced back to Campanella, Bacon and Andreae with a strict scientific approach to human behaviour and moral education. Voß set the scene for a German tradition of futuristic writing and was followed by August von Kotzebue's *Die hundertjährigen Eichen oder das Jahr 1914* (1821) and later in the century, Rudolf Greinz's *Der Jüngste Tag* (1893), while the French tradition was successfully continued by Jules Verne.

Not all visions of a future world, though, were positive. Mary Shelley's apocalyptic *The Last Man* (1826), a document of the post-French revolutionary disillusionment, mourns the corrosion of revolutionary ideals by flaws of human nature. The novel clearly questions the Enlightenment faith in the inevitability of progress through individual and collective perfectibility.

Historians still dispute the extent to which the *philosophes* and utopians directly influenced the events of the American and French Revolutions and vice versa. If nothing else, Kant's article, *What is the Enlightenment?* (1784), promoted an emancipatory commitment to critique and reflection, 'a concept of reason that is sceptical and post-metaphysical, yet not defeatist'.[24] Eighteenth-century utopianism reflected this mandate and in 'some instances, too, utopian tracts led liberal and humanitarian thinking about individual rights, at least a century and sometimes two in advance of their times'.[25] In the nineteenth century, the utopian tradition continued to prosper in the guise of utopian socialism, communitarianism and the cooperative movement. The nineteenth-century novel and utopian romance became an established medium to popularize utopian political and economic principles. Similarly, a number of communal ventures were undertaken by Owen, Fourier and Saint-Simon in the form of contained, usually short-lived, utopian communities intended to test the feasibility of a fully cooperative society (as a converse to the Industrial Revolution). What the nineteenth century learnt from its utopian predecessors was that, in the words of H. G. Wells, the 'Modern Utopia must be not static but kinetic, must shape not as a permanent state but as a hopeful stage leading to a long ascent of stages.'[26]

NOTES

1   Oscar Wilde, *The Soul of Man Under Socialism and Selected Critical Prose*, ed. Linda Dowling (Harmondsworth: Penguin, 2001).

2 Michèle Le Dœuff, *The Philosophical Imaginary*, trans. Colin Gordon (Stanford University Press, 1989).

3 The so-called Bermuda Pamphlets were accounts of a shipwreck that occurred in the summer of 1609. News reached England in 1610 and the earliest account by William Strachey, *True Reportory* (1625), possibly circulated in manuscript form in 1610. See Alden T. Vaughan, 'William Strachey's *True Reportory* and Shakespeare: A Closer Look at the Evidence', *Shakespeare Quarterly* 59:3 (Fall 2008), 245–73.

4 More, *Utopia* (London: Everyman, 1992), p. 56.

5 Carola Baumgardt, *Johannes Kepler: Life and Letters* (New York: Philosophical Library, 1951), pp. 155–6.

6 See as the most recent one, Kim Stanley Robinson, *Galileo's Dream* (London: HarperCollins, 2009).

7 Edmund Spenser, 'Letter to Sir Walter Raleigh', *The Faerie Queene*, ed. A. C. Hamilton (London: Longman, 1977), pp. 737–8, 737.

8 Darko Suvin, 'Defining the Literary Genre of Utopia: Some Historical Semantics, some Genology, a Proposal and a Plea', *Studies in the Literary Imagination* 6 (Fall 1975), 121–45.

9 Philip Sidney, 'Defence of Poetry', in *Selected Writings*, ed. Richard Dutton (London: Carcanet Press, 1987), pp. 102–48, 114.

10 Ernst Bloch, *The Principle of Hope*, trans. Neville Plaice, Stephen Plaice and Paul Knight (3 vols., Cambridge, MA: MIT Press, 1995).

11 Johann Valentin Andreae, *Christianopolis*, trans. Edward H. Thompson (Dordrecht: Kluwer, 1999), p. 281.

12 Johann Eberlin von Günzburg, *Die fünfzehn Bundesgenossen* (Basel: Pamphilus Gengenbach, 1521).

13 Kaspar Stiblin, *Commentariolus de Eudaemonnensium Republica* (Basel: J. Oporinus, 1555).

14 Samuel Johnson, *The History of Rasselas, Prince of Abissinia: A Tale* (Dublin: G. & A. Ewing, 1759).

15 Jonathan Swift to Charles Ford, 14 August 1725, in Jonathan Swift, *Gulliver's Travels*, ed. Robert A. Greenberg (London: Norton, 1970), p. 263.

16 David Womersley, 'Dean Swift hears a Sermon: Robert Howard's Ash Wednesday homily of 1725 and *Gulliver's Travels*', *Times Literary Supplement* (20 February 2009), 14–15.

17 Jonathan Swift, 'Further Thoughts on Religion', in Herbert Davis (ed.), *The Prose Works of Jonathan Swift* (14 vols., Oxford: Basil Blackwell, 1939–74), vol. 3.

18 Artur Blaim, *Failed Dynamics: The English Robinsonade of the Eighteenth Century* (Lublin: Uniwersytet Marii Curie-Slktodowskiej, Wydział Humanistyczny, 1987), p. 134.

19 Jean-Michel Racault, *L'Utopie narrative en France et en Angleterre 1675–1761* (Oxford: The Voltaire Foundation, 1991).

20 William Wordsworth, 'French Revolution: As it appeared to Enthusiasts at its Commencement. Reprinted from 'The Friend',' *Prelude* (1805), Book xi.

21 Edmund Burke, *Reflections on the Revolution in France* (London: J. Dodsley, 1791), pp. 312, 202.

22 The book went through three editions within five years and each edition was changed significantly from the previous one.

23 William Wordsworth, 'Residence in France', *Prelude*, Book ix.
24 Jürgen Habermas, 'The Unity of Reason in the Diversity of its Voices', in James Schmidt (ed.), *What is Enlightenment? Eighteenth-Century Answers and Twentieth-Century Questions* (Berkeley, CA: University of California Press, 1996), pp. 399–425, 400.
25 Gregory Claeys (ed.), *Utopias of the British Enlightenment* (Cambridge University Press, 1994), p. xi.
26 H. G. Wells, *A Modern Utopia* (1908) (London: J. M. Dent, 1998), p. 5.

BIBLIOGRAPHY

Andreae, Johann Valentin, *Reipublicae Christianopolitanae Descriptio* (1619), trans. Edward H. Thompson (Dordrecht: Kluwer, 1999).
Baumgardt, Carola, *Johannes Kepler: Life and Letters* (New York: Philosophical Library, 1951).
Blaim, Artur, *Failed Dynamics: The English Robinsonade of the Eighteenth Century* (Lublin: Uniwersytet Marii Curie-Slktodowskiej, Wydział Humanistyczny, 1987).
Bloch, Ernst, *The Principle of Hope*, trans. Neville Plaice, Stephen Plaice and Paul Knight, (3 vols., Cambridge, MA: MIT Press, 1995).
Burke, Edmund, *Reflections on the Revolution in France* (London: J. Dodsley, 1791).
Claeys, Gregory (ed.), *Utopias of the British Enlightenment* (Cambridge University Press, 1994).
Eberlin von Günzburg, Johann, *Die fünfzehn Bundesgenossen* (Basel: Pamphilus Gengenbach, 1521).
Habermas, Jürgen, 'The Unity of Reason in the Diversity of its Voices', in James Schmidt (ed.), *What is Enlightenment? Eighteenth-Century Answers and Twentieth-Century Questions* (Berkeley, CA: University of California Press, 1996), pp. 399–425.
Johnson, Samuel, *The History of Rasselas, Prince of Abissinia: A Tale* (Dublin: G. & A. Ewing, 1759).
More, Thomas, *Utopia* (London: Everyman, 1992).
Le Dœuff, Michèle, *The Philosophical Imaginary*, trans. Colin Gordon (Stanford University Press, 1989).
Racault, Jean-Michel, *L'Utopie narrative en France et en Angleterre 1675–1761* (Oxford: The Voltaire Foundation, 1991).
Robinson, Kim Stanley, *Galileo's Dream* (London: HarperCollins, 2009).
Sidney, Philip, 'Defence of Poetry', in *Selected Writings*, ed. Richard Dutton (London: Carcanet Press, 1987), pp. 102–48.
Spenser, Edmund, 'Letter to Sir Walter Raleigh', *The Faerie Queene*, ed. A. C. Hamilton (London: Longman, 1977).
Stiblin, Kaspar, *Commentariolus de Eudaemonnensium Republica* (Basel: J. Oporinus, 1555).
Suvin, Darko, 'Defining the Literary Genre of Utopia: Some Historical Semantics, some Genology, a Proposal and a Plea', *Studies in the Literary Imagination* 6 (Fall 1975), 121–45.

Swift, Jonathan, 'Further Thoughts on Religion', in Herbert Davis (ed.), *The Prose Works of Jonathan Swift* (14 vols., Oxford: Basil Blackwell, 1939–74), vol. 3.

Gulliver's Travels, ed. Robert A. Greenberg (London: Norton, 1970).

Vaughan, Alden T., 'William Strachey's True Reportory and Shakespeare: A Closer Look at the Evidence', *Shakespeare Quarterly* 59:3 (Fall 2008), 245–73.

Wells, H. G., *A Modern Utopia* (1908) (London: J. M. Dent, 1998).

Wilde, Oscar, *The Soul of Man Under Socialism and Selected Critical Prose*, ed. Linda Dowling (Harmondsworth: Penguin, 2001).

Womersley, David, 'Dean Swift hears a Sermon: Robert Howard's Ash Wednesday homily of 1725 and *Gulliver's Travels*', *Times Literary Supplement* (20 February 2009), 14–15.

4

KENNETH M. ROEMER

Paradise transformed: varieties of nineteenth-century utopias

If the nineteenth century was not *the* Golden Age of utopianism, it was certainly *a* golden age. All three major 'faces of utopia', to borrow Lyman Tower Sargent's phrase, flourished: literary utopias, non-fictional utopian social theory, and intentional communities. This Cambridge Companion highlights one of the 'three faces' – the literary utopia. My working definition of a literary utopia is a fairly detailed narrative description of an imaginary culture – a fiction that invites readers to experience vicariously an alternative reality that critiques theirs by opening intellectual and emotional spaces that encourage readers to perceive the realities and potentialities of their cultures in new ways. If the author and/or readers perceive the imaginary culture as being significantly better than their 'present' reality, then the work is a literary eutopia (or more commonly, a utopia); if significantly worse, it is a dystopia.

Within this definitional framework, an overview of the nineteenth century could have an especially narrow chronological focus, since there is a general consensus that for most of the century utopian social theory and communal experiments thrived, but only in the final years of the century did literary utopias flourish.[1] There is ample evidence to support this claim from North America to Great Britain, Europe, Australia, New Zealand and Asia.[2]

As tempting and as logical as it might be to focus primarily on the late nineteenth-century rebirth of the literary utopia, this approach would gravely distort the origins and contributions of nineteenth-century utopian writing, for obvious reasons. First, a significant number of well-known and popular writers made important contributions to the literary utopia before the end of the nineteenth century. These include the French socialist, Étienne Cabet – whose *Voyage en Icarie* (1840,[3] 1842) inspired egalitarian readers and communitarians on both sides of the Atlantic – as well as writers as different as the popular American writer, Elizabeth Stuart Phelps (Ward), the Russian, Fyodor Dostoevsky, the British satirist, Samuel Butler and the Americans Nathaniel Hawthorne and Herman Melville. Second, at least since Aristophanes responded satirically to the utopian visions of Plato, utopian literature has been a dialogic literature. In order to understand the rebirth of utopian literature in the late nineteenth century, we must be aware of early and mid-nineteenth-century utopian literary conventions, as well as the broad social and intellectual constructions of human nature mapped out in the writings of earlier utopian social theorists.

The next section of this essay will begin to address these contexts by offering brief comments on the intellectual, social and historical trends and events that inspired and frustrated the authors of nineteenth-century utopian social theory and literary utopias. This section will be followed by discussion of how several major early to mid-nineteenth-century European and British social thinkers – notably Saint-Simon, Fourier, Owen and Marx – responded to the trends shaping the industrial world. The interrelated purposes of the fourth section are to demonstrate the importance of the early to mid-nineteenth-century literary utopias and dystopias and to suggest the diversity of these genres throughout the nineteenth century. Because of the tremendous impact of Edward Bellamy's *Looking Backward* (1888) and its many imitators, scholars typically characterize nineteenth-century literary utopias as didactic guide-visitor narratives that are heavy on long socio-economic dialogues, lightened by touches of romance and travel-adventure episodes and firmly grounded in cooperative or socialistic ideologies. This portrait is appealing, since it highlights the transformation of utopian literature from an emphasis on thought experiments in many pre-nineteenth-century utopias to an emphasis on blueprint utopias during the end of the century. But this portrait also obscures the significance of other important forms of nineteenth-century utopian literature: for example, the hierarchical, conservative vision of James Fenimore Cooper; a best-selling 'primitivist' utopia by Herman Melville; the widely read pearly-gates utopias by Elizabeth Stuart Phelps (Ward); later a popular social-gospel utopia by the American minister Charles M. Sheldon; the complex precursors of the modern critical utopias and dystopias by Nathaniel Hawthorne and Fyodor Dostoevsky; and the vibrant and complex satiric utopias by Samuel Butler and, later in the century, Mark Twain.

The final section examines the multi-level rebirth of the literary utopia in the late nineteenth century, especially the tremendous popularity of *Looking Backward* and the importance of the hundreds of literary responses to Bellamy, including William Morris's *News from Nowhere* (1890), the responses by key arbiters of culture and literature, like William Dean Howells, and the lesser-known but intriguing responses by women authors and dystopias by Ignatius Donnelly and Will N. Harben. In this section I will also examine the American political reactions to *Looking Backward* and its impact around the world, as well as the influence of the print culture, socio-economic forces and cultural values that fostered the rebirth of the genre and nurtured its reception. I conclude by considering the degree to which the late nineteenth-century literary utopias represent a restatement or a departure from the concepts of human nature and human development professed by early nineteenth-century utopian theorists, and by speculating about whether the popularity and nature of the late nineteenth-century literary utopia set the stage for the predominantly dystopian tenor of twentieth-century utopian literature.

Imagining utopia is a suspect enterprise. Trying to convince readers that a concept of utopia is a valid guide to understanding the realities and potentialities of their world is even more suspect. In order to make this strange form of literature convincing, whether the imaginings take the form of a social theory or a literary utopia, the readers' culture has to provide perceptual tools in the forms of shared worldviews, ideologies and values that invite readers to 'see' utopia as an important and even inspirational guide to the past, present and future. These perceptual tools must be grounded in historical and contemporary evidence that convinces readers of the significant correlations between the utopists' imaginings and the reader's realities. The perceptual tools help them to see the correlations, but there still needs to be enough evidence to correlate. Nineteenth-century readers had ample access to the tools and the evidence.

Some of the perceptual tools had origins in centuries-old Millennial desires for a Kingdom of God on earth and in the eighteenth-century Enlightenment. The latter's emphasis on human reason did not signal abandonment of belief in divine agency, but it did emphasize the powers of human reason to examine religion, politics and social structures and, thus, did signal a shift towards the importance of human agency.

Near the end of the eighteenth century two history-altering revolutions in the American colonies and France proclaimed a concept of utopia that celebrated democracy and equality and maintained that the pursuit of a better life was the natural goal of human history. Thus, it is not surprising that the United States Declaration of Independence enshrines democracy and equality as *natural* human *rights*. Of course, the revolutions themselves provided powerful evidence that utopian ideals could change history and be put into practice on earth, though the French Reign of Terror convinced major early nineteenth-century British and French utopian theorists, including Cabet, that evolution, not violent revolution was the hoped-for method of pursuing the happiness of an egalitarian, democratic utopia.

The positive elements of the revolutions provided evidence that could be used to bolster the believability of millennial and Enlightenment world-views and, of course, in democracy and equality. The industrial revolution and urbanization both supported and undermined belief in another crucial perceptual tool: history viewed as progress. Laurent Portes's observation about nineteenth-century French utopias helps us to understand the impact of this perception on utopian literature: 'the alternative worlds proposed were less and less "*elsewhere*" and increasingly "*time to come*"'.[4] Eutopia became euchronia. True, there were earlier 'good times' utopias, notably Louis-Sébastien Mercier's *Memoirs of the Year Two Thousand Five Hundred* (1771),[5] and true, there were still a significant number of utopias set in distant places. But the belief that under the right conditions improvement was not only possible, but also natural, invited readers to assume that progress was as self-evident as the laws of nature that promised democracy, equality and happiness in the Declaration of Independence.

The primary socio-economic evidence for the perception of progress was the industrial revolution. Finally it seemed as if the basic goals of traditional utopias could be met: science, technology, mass production and improved distribution systems ensured that all humanity could be fed, clothed and sheltered. The industrial revolution did indeed create great wealth – and great poverty. In fiction and non-fiction, from Charles Dickens's early nineteenth-century novels to Karl Marx and Friedrich Engels's *The Manifesto of the Communist Party* (1848) to Henry George's *Progress and Poverty* (1879), influential works decried the suffering, especially of the urban poor. The use of Gatling guns by Union soldiers in the American Civil War also demonstrated how science, technology and industry could combine to destroy human life on a scale rarely witnessed thus far in human history.

The destructive effects of the industrial revolution undermined belief in the inevitability of progress. But this dystopian challenge to progress also set up a tension that created fertile grounds for utopian theory and literature. Few forms of writing depend so heavily upon stark contrasts between what is and what could/should be. The positive elements of recent late eighteenth-century history-altering revolutions combined with great scientific, technological and industrial progress seemed to demonstrate that it was reasonable, ethical, possible, even natural to create the 'good time' of democracy and an equality of abundance in 'real places'. But this grand opportunity for a secular millennium could be lost and engulfed in a dystopian future unless someone could offer inspirational and reasonable plans to achieve utopia rather than oblivion. Enter the utopians.

The three utopian social theorists most frequently associated with the early nineteenth century – Henri de Saint-Simon (1760–1825), Charles Fourier (1772–1837) and Robert Owen (1771–1858) – would most likely prefer not to respond to the call, 'Enter the utopians.' They considered their responses to their era to be rational and scientific, not speculative and imaginative. But even before Friedrich Engels (1820–95) and Karl Marx (1818–83) labelled these three as 'unscientific' thinkers, there were grounds for questioning their legitimacy as prophets of euchronia. In *Utopian Thought in the Western World* (1979), Frank and Fritzie Manuel acknowledge elements of Saint-Simon, Fourier and Owen's writings and lives that set them up for criticism and ridicule. But they also examine the important contributions they made.[6] For example, Saint-Simon predicted that in an industrial age, scientists and industrialists, rather than philosopher-kings or religious leaders, would initiate and administer progress; Owen developed one of the most important industrial complexes in Great Britain (the textile plant at New Lanark, Scotland) and pioneered a successful form of regimented paternalism that transformed unskilled workers into efficient factory hands; and Fourier predicted the benefits of massive reforestation long before 'global warming' became a household phrase. But the concepts of human nature developed by each of the three may well be their most important contributions to utopian thought.

Saint-Simon's theories about different components of human nature culminated in his essay 'L'Artiste, le savant, et l'industriel' in a collection published during the last year of his life: *Opinions littéraires, philosophiques, et industrielles* (1825).[7] Drawing heavily upon another French thinker, Marie-François Xavier Bichat, Saint-Simon argued that there were three primary capacities of human nature with corresponding social functions: the emotive (feeling), e.g., writers and artists who could initiate ideas and inspire actions; the rational (thinking), e.g., scientists who could evaluate ideas; and the motor (implementing), e.g., administrators, industrialists and workers who could put to use the evaluated ideas. In a radically improved society everyone would be educated in all three areas until teachers and mentors could determine which of the three human capacities dominated an individual's character. Thereafter the individual's particular strengths could be developed more intensely. The imagined end result was a balanced society: in this case an interrelated and synergistic dynamic of initiating, evaluating and implementing rather than Plato's hierarchy of guardians/philosopher-kings, soldiers and workers.

Like Saint-Simon, Fourier claimed discovery of the fundamental elements of human nature and, like Saint-Simon and the eighteenth-century philosopher, Jean-Jacques Rousseau, he believed that modern civilization stifled development of natural human qualities and that progress should be gauged in terms of society's ability to foster these qualities. But Fourier's concept of human nature was more complex than Saint-Simon's and more like the needs hierarchies of the twentieth-century American psychologist Abraham Maslow than it was like Plato's hierarchy of citizens. In early and later works – for instance, *Théorie des quatre mouvements et destinées générales* (1808) and *Le Nouveau Monde industriel* (1827) – Fourier built a complex concept of human nature represented by twelve types of 'passions': five 'luxurious passions' corresponding to the needs of the five senses; four 'affective passions', oriented towards group associations (honour/respect, friendship, love, parenthood); and three 'serial' or 'distributive' passions that represented socialization mechanisms relating to 'making arrangements' and creating 'intrigue' and 'variety' (here I am using the Manuels' translations of the terms).[8] Fulfilment of the serial passions would create the multiple associations that fostered the first nine passions. Fourier calculated that there were 810 different types of configurations of these passions; hence 810 different types of people. The ideal environment for humans was a community (a phalanstery) with a bit more than twice the number of human types (1,700 to 1,800). Psychological directors would screen members to ensure variety, and job rotation would enhance the variety of associations. Unlike Cabet's utopian environment, Fourier's was not a utopia of economic equality. It was a joint stock association; the joys of the fulfilment of the natural passions would render economic inequalities much less important than in the unreformed world. This utopian state of 'harmony' would evolve slowly, but once networks of phalansteries existed, they would foster the grand 'industrial armies' whose reforestation and other public works would transform the world.

Owen also envisioned grand civic armies that grew out of smaller communities. But equality grounded his imaginary communal-ownership communities, and the unemployed populated the communities and armies. Owen's concept of human nature reveals another striking difference. Saint-Simon and Fourier defined inherent human qualities and needs. Owen's concept was closer to B. F. Skinner's than to theirs. In *The Revolution in the Mind and Practice of the Human Race* (1849) he proclaimed that human nature was infinitely malleable and that humans have no free will. Their environment shapes them. Another dimension of Owen's concept of human nature both supports and contradicts his claims of human malleability.[9] In *The Book of the New Moral World* (1836–44) he offered an elaborate age taxonomy that stressed the importance of the ideal environment for human development, but also implied that certain age brackets (typically five-, ten-, or twenty-year increments) inherently qualified people for particular functions. For example, from birth to five years old, proper diet and exercise, exposure to acts of charity and affection, access to accurate information and an absence of false information would lead to the creation of the healthy, rational and caring person. Owen assumed that people from age thirty to forty should govern and that those aged forty to sixty should be in charge of external relations.[10] To some these rigid age designations suggest a biological essentialism – an inherent rather than a malleable human nature; to others they represent a variety of more traditional paternalism or patriarchalism.

Saint-Simon, Fourier and Owen would baulk at the label 'utopian'. The German social theorists Karl Marx and Friedrich Engels would be outraged. They believed that social theorists should not be fantasizing distracting 'pictures' of phalansteries, or imaginary balanced states of artists, scientists and industrialist/administrators, or even Étienne Cabet's envisioned centralized, egalitarian utopia. Instead reformers should be organizing workers and exposing the evils of capitalism that alienated labourers from their work in factories, created horrendous class inequalities and stifled natural tendencies in human nature towards developing 'species being' – the foundation of a communal identity.

Despite their objections to utopian imagining, there are obvious connections between Engels and Marx and the earlier French and British utopian socialists. Owen's followers in Manchester directly influenced Engels. Marx and Engels's promotion of job rotation, in *The German Ideology* (1845–6), as a means of alleviating alienating labour, reflected Fourier's concepts of work; and their advocacy of redistributing urban labourers to rural workers' communities in *The Manifesto of the Communist Party* (1848) echoed Fourier and Owen's faith in intentional communities. On a broader level they agreed that the current social system oppressed the natural and good tendencies in human nature and they even indulged in a bit of imaginary picture making when they envisioned the ultimate goal of a communist reality – the withering away of the state in a classless society.

There was, nevertheless, a major difference on the journey from capitalism to classless socialism. The outrageous flaws of capitalism, according to Marx and Engels, would sow the seeds of a workers' revolution that would clear the way for a rational, just and efficient centralized state before the coming of the classless utopian society. Small-scale changes, such as job rotations and communal experiments, would not be enough to counter the tremendous forces of capitalism described in *Das Kapital* (1867–94). But after the workers' revolution and the abolition of private property, the technological and scientific might of the industrial revolution could be nationalized and administered for the good of the people.

The logical transition from Marx and Engels to the rebirth of the literary utopia in the late nineteenth century is an easy one to imagine. Despite the tendency of utopists like Bellamy to avoid using the terms 'socialism' and 'communism', it is clear that the tremendous impact of Marx and Engels's responses to the industrial revolution directly or indirectly shaped much of the utopian literature that ushered in the rebirth of the literary utopia in the United States, Britain, the British Commonwealth, Europe and Asia. But as indicated previously, over-emphasis on the late nineteenth century and the utopias of cooperation and socialism, distorts the history of nineteenth-century utopian literature by obscuring the importance of earlier works and the variety of the century's literary utopias. In an introductory essay it is impossible to examine thoroughly this significance and diversity. I can, nevertheless, suggest both by offering examples of a range of literary utopias, including a critique of popular democratic ideologies; a sophisticated rendering of the exotic 'primitivist' utopia; a pair of works expressing popular religious visions of utopia; and three texts that foreshadow the complexities of twentieth- and twenty-first-century dystopias, satires, critical utopias and critical dystopias.

Three years after Owen's *Book of the New Moral World* appeared and one year before Marx and Engels's *Manifesto*, James Fenimore Cooper (1789–1851) published *The Crater; or, Vulcan's Peak* (1847).[11] Like many of the early nineteenth-century American utopias, *The Crater* critiqued the 'modern absurdities' of Jacksonian Democracy, in particular the popular advocacy of expanded suffrage and equality. To express this critique in fictional form, Cooper borrowed liberally from the shipwreck narratives popularized by Daniel Defoe's *Robinson Crusoe* (1719), J. R. Wyss's *Swiss Family Robinson* (1812), and his own maritime adventures, *The Pilot* (1824) and *Red Rover* (1827).

Cooper's is the only utopia founded upon decayed seaweed and guano. After a South Seas shipwreck, Woolston and Betts survive on the ship's cargo and plants grown in volcanic island soil enhanced by seaweed and guano. The community that arises from these humble beginnings values individual initiative, private property, constructive self-interest and a natural and divinely ordained concept of hierarchy that echoes the ideology of John Winthrop's 'City Upon a Hill' sermon (1630). Cooper's city upon a volcano thrives until a wave of immigrants – fractious ministers, lawyers and newspaper editors demanding power for the people – disrupts Woolston's utopia. Woolston and his followers leave. By the time he returns, the community has vanished: a volcanic convulsion has destroyed the chaotic and corrupt community. This allegory of divine retribution goes beyond warnings about the extremes of democracy, especially since Woolston himself had arrogantly forgotten his debt to Divine Providence before the outsiders arrived. Even with just and natural hierarchies the inherent flaws of humans ensure that utopia will never be found in human history.

Many mid-nineteenth-century British and American readers would dis-agree, pointing out that a year before *The Crater* appeared, Herman Melville (1819–91) had discovered a Polynesian paradise and described it in almost anthropological detail in his best-selling, semi-autobiographical travel adventure *Typee* (1846). Two young sailors jump ship at Nukuhiva, take a wrong turn, and end up among the Typee, who are rumoured to be can-nibals. But Tommo, the narrator and one of the two sailors, realizes that in many ways these people are healthier, freer, happier and more human than 'civilized' people. Of course, celebrating an exotic paradise was nothing new. Rousseau, Montaigne and before them the mythical Isles of the Blest and the vision of Cockaigne had celebrated the 'body utopia' of distant places. But *Typee* created what was probably the most popular nineteenth-century English language version of the exotic paradise, especially the bachelor's paradise, whose '[l]uxurious provisions' included the enchanting Fayaway and 'the girls of the house [who] gathered about me ... [to] anoint my whole body with a fragrant oil ... [called] "aka" ... applied to the limbs by the soft palms of sweet nymphs ... '.[12]

But *Typee*'s paradise is not a one-dimensional, masculinist, escapist nar-rative. Tommo's enjoyment of paradise is conflicted by a strange leg wound that heals under the influence of the 'luxurious provisions' and freedoms as he enjoys them and festers when he ruminates on many of the alien ways of the Typee. For a non-native this is at best a temporary utopia. Like Henry David Thoreau's Walden pond retreat – which noticeably, lacked 'aka' and nymph palms – the Typee paradise is a moratorium stage, a temporary ven-ture into an alternative realm that enables the visitor to perceive his more familiar world in new ways that undermine his racist concepts of 'civiliza-tion' and 'savagery'.

Another popular utopian vision definitely did not envision a bachelor's paradise. Elizabeth Stuart Phelps (Ward)'s (1844–1911) *The Gates Ajar* (1868) and its sequels – *Beyond the Gates* (1883) and *The Gates Between* (1887), which was recast as a drama, *Within the Gates* (1901) – depict heavenly domestic paradises that eliminate fears of want, purify the home and reform errant husband/fathers.[13] *The Gates Ajar* reaffirms the import-ance of religion in nineteenth-century utopias. Phelps claimed that an angel inspired her to write the book, and the Christian heaven is her utopia. In heaven utopia is an idealized home life, complete with family and friends and plenty of gingersnaps in the cookie jar for the kids. But this heaven is more than a Victorian domesticated Cockaigne. In *Beyond the Gates* the protagonist discovers that her deceased father performs household chores; the inconsiderate husband in *The Gates Between* abandons derogatory labels like 'hysteric' for women, recognizes their intelligence and cares for his ill son in ways women would on earth. A potential advantage of Phelps's 'Gates' utopias is that, after the readers' vicarious voyage to heaven, they might view the reality and potentiality of family relationships differently in ways that would promote enhanced respect for women and more sharing of domestic responsibilities among men and women. Of course, one obvious disadvantage of Phelps's and other nineteenth-century utopists' heavenly utopias is that their emphasis on the anticipated joys of the afterlife could lessen readers' motivation to address injustices on earth, thus confirming Marx's famous proclamation that 'Religion ... is the opium of the people.'

For Charles M. Sheldon (1857–1946) religion was not an escapist drug; it was an everyday encounter. Sheldon, a Congregationalist minister from Topeka, Kansas, did not write the first popular Social Gospel novel. British works by Mrs Humphrey Ward (*Robert Elsmere*, 1888) and William Stead (*If Christ Came to Chicago*, 1894) preceded Sheldon's *In His Steps: 'What Would Jesus Do?'* (serialized, 1896, book publication, 1897).[14] But *In His Steps* is the most widely read Social Gospel utopia ever written. Sheldon's method of narrative estrangement was simple and direct. A minister is stunned during a service by the appearance of an ill and unemployed printer who dies chastising the congregation for their hypocrisy. The minister and a small group respond by pledging not to make decisions without asking first 'What would Jesus do?' A singer spurns high-paying jobs in favour of performing for poor churches. An editor risks financial ruin by refusing liquor and boxing ads. This applied Christianity spreads, and by the end of the novel a personalized Social Gospel movement is influencing Chicago, suggesting that a down-to-earth Christian utopia could spread throughout America.

Cooper's critique of a democratic ideology that shuns 'natural' leaders and uncritically embraces change and the immense popularity of Melville's Polynesian utopia and the pearly gates and down-to-earth Christian utopias of British and American authors demonstrate that there were important forms of nineteenth-century literary utopias that do not fit the Bellamy paradigm of utopia. Still, it could be argued that readers had to wait until the early to mid-twentieth century to experience complex dystopias and until the late twentieth century to read 'ambiguous' or 'critical' utopias that questioned the whole process of utopian speculation while sympathetically participating in that very process. Among many possible complex nine-teenth-century works, two American, one Russian and one British, in particular suggest that readers did not have to wait to experience sophisticated utopian speculations worthy of the 'complex', 'ambiguous' and 'critical' labels.

As with Melville's writings,[15] several of Fyodor Mikhailovich Dostoevsky's (1821–81) works have been associated with dystopian and utopian literature, including *Crime and Punishment* (1866), 'The Dream of a Ridiculous Man' (1877) and *Diary of a Writer* (1873, 1876–7, 1880–1), which Gary Saul Morson analyses thoroughly in *The Boundaries of Genre* (1981).[16] *Notes from Underground* (1864) is especially interesting for its attack on the assumptions that humans should desire a rational, orderly humanistic utopia and that this state of well-being will result from an improved environment. The narrator argues, in monologue form, that this goal and means are impossible and undesirable because humans are deeply flawed, 'morally oblique', 'ungrateful bipeds'. His claim of the undesirability of a rational and ordered utopia in part stems from an Enlightenment desire for individuality. But it also reflects complex tensions and desires: an acknowledgement of the fear of completion (and thus an ensuing state of stasis) and an enjoyment of process, irrationality, suffering and smashing things up (which prolongs process). The narrator's worldview is thus comparable to later provocative writings by Freud, Yevgeny Zamyatin and even the late twentieth-century American writer Thomas Pynchon.

If Dostoevsky's *Notes from Underground* demonstrates that the nineteenth century produced dystopian visions worthy of comparison to great twentieth-century dystopias, Samuel Butler's (1835–1902) *Erewhon* (1872) demonstrates that the nineteenth century produced utopian satire comparable to *Gulliver's Travels* (1726) and to critical utopias and dystopias written a century later.[17] Despite its disunities – its mix of adventure, romance and non-fiction genres – *Erewhon* ranks as one of the most important utopian satires because of the rich variety of targeted topics, the diversity of forms of satire employed and the sophistication of the satiric critiques. The targets are as specific as the urban clutter of public statues, vegetarian fads and the irrelevancies of higher education and as broad as colonial exploitation, institutionalized religion, scientific and technological progress and how humans comprehend their natures. Butler's techniques include exaggeration (in shame a man commits suicide for sneaking meat to improve his health) and defamiliarization (institutionalized religion is represented by monumental musical banks attended by those seeking the appearance of respectability). As in the cases of the banks, some of Butler's most poignant satire distances readers with unfamiliar absurdity only to invite them to see parallels to their own worlds; for example, an absurd proposal to save Erewhonians by forcing them to move and work sugar plantations while living with Christian families precedes a note describing an actual plan to exploit Polynesian natives.

This technique is especially effective when Butler dramatizes how humans judge each other and the value of progress. The visitor to Erewhon soon discovers that illness, ugliness and even bad luck are criminal acts – a woman feigns alcoholism to avoid revealing her indigestion; on a more tragic level, a 23-year-old consumptive is condemned to death for his illness. The visitor eventually concludes that it is not unfair to punish bad luck and reward good luck. After all, in his home country the well-born, healthy and rich are often rewarded and the downtrodden and ill frequently neglected and/or punished. Obviously Butler invites readers to see the parallels that critique the real world. Almost as absurd as the Erewhonian system of punishments and rewards is their extreme distaste for technological progress. At a turning point in their history, a 'prophet' inspired them to abandon all machines created in the preceding 271 years. Erewhonians view the visitor's wristwatch as a 'heinous crime'. As ludicrous as their Luddite-like revolution seems, modern readers are likely to see, not only a critique of a nineteenth-century unexamined love affair with the machine, but also a perceptive critique of our own time. The prophet foresaw a time when the sophisticated evolving minds of machines would blur the boundaries between human and machine, and people would become (as Thoreau would say) servants of technology: the appeal of technological advance and our subservience to the machine – 'our bondage' – would overcome us silently. Butler's satire of anti- and pro-technological development represents one of the most sophisticated and perceptive foreshadowings of the twenty-first-century 'post-human' dilemma.

If Butler's *Erewhon* is one of the most complex and sophisticated utopian satires of the nineteenth century, Mark Twain's (1835–1910) *A Connecticut Yankee in King Arthur's Court* (1889) is one of the most hilarious, prophetic and terrifying complex satires.[18] By the time Twain completed his manuscript, the burlesque that he initially imagined (contrasting the unsanitary and unjust age of King Arthur with the technologically advanced democracy of the United States) became overburdened with the negative implications of technological progress (in a climactic scene Hank Morgan, the American time traveller, utilizes electric wires, Gatling guns and dynamite to massacre 25,000 knights), the impossibility of altering human nature (the combined forces of decades of conditioning and the depravity of humanity undermine improvement) and the frightening possibilities that come with a self-righteous imposition of cultural values. True, Hank's inventiveness and showmanship improve the health (and body odour) of the Arthurians and usher in a brief period of radical technological and industrial advance. But his technological know-how also enables him to extend, on a grand and tragic scale, his reform agendas, making him a frightening anticipation of twentieth-century dictators and nineteenth- and twentieth-century imperialists.

Twain's *Connecticut Yankee* represents utopian satire gone awry prophetically. Nathaniel Hawthorne (1804–64) did not predict technological holocausts or twentieth-century dictators, but his *The Blithedale Romance* (1852) does foreshadow the complexities of twentieth- and twenty-first-century utopian literature.[19] *Blithedale* is much more than a fictionalized account of a famous intentional community (in 1841 Hawthorne lived at Brook Farm). It presents readers with dynamic characters, notably Zenobia and Hollingsworth. Zenobia is a complex, ambivalent figure – a passionate advocate of women's rights who falls passionately and fatally in love with the dominating Hollingsworth who loves Zenobia's submissive younger sister. Hollingsworth is a landlocked Captain Ahab who longs to use the members of this tiny community as tools in his obsessive prison-reform plans. But, also like Ahab, he is 'madness maddened' (he is aware of his madness) and he has his 'humanities'. In private he admits his flaws, his inflexibilities; and by the end of the novel, he has become flexible enough to abandon his fixation on prison reform so that he can reform himself.

As in modern critical utopias, ambiguity and self-reflexivity characterize the narrative and authorial voices of *Blithedale*. Coverdale, a poet and the narrator (with a rather ironic name for a writer), is disillusioned. The unpleasant physical labour and the flaws of human nature, represented most clearly in the love triangle, undermine his ability to believe in utopian possibilities. And yet in his concluding chapter he proclaims that 'More and more, I feel that we had struck upon what ought to be a truth',[20] though the conditional 'ought' complicates any explicit confirmation of utopian impulses.

The authorial voice expresses the most profound self-reflexivity. What begins as a conventional Preface disclaimer about fiction becomes a fascinating comment on the role of utopists and functions of utopian literature. The author declares that Brook Farm was only a catalyst for his imagination, a 'theatre' for the 'creatures of his brain' – what Ursula K. Le Guin might call a 'thought experiment', or Fredric Jameson might define as an arena for examining the possibility (more likely impossibility) of imagining utopia. But that view of the authorial and narrative voices is complicated by the unfavourable light cast upon the cold intellectualizing performed by Coverdale and criticized by Coverdale himself, who, in the conclusion, pairs himself with Hollingsworth – too much single-minded dedication vs. too little commitment. The complex characters and the ambiguities of the authorial and narrative voices raise questions about the functions of utopia and the teller of the tale as old as the ambiguities of More's persona and Hythloday in *Utopia* and as new as the perplexed worrying of the fictional editor/compiler, Pandora, in Ursula Le Guin's critical utopia *Always Coming Home* (1985).[21]

Hawthorne defines his recollections of Brook Farm, and by implication utopian literature, as a 'theatre' for his imagination. Edward Bellamy (1850–98), who was compared to Hawthorne by the influential American editor and novelist, William Dean Howells, began writing the most famous nineteenth-century literary utopia, *Looking Backward 2000–1887* (1888), using a similar concept of utopian literature.[22] At first he envisioned the book as 'literary fantasy', even a 'fairy tale'. But while writing an episode about an organization not unlike Owen's grand civil armies and Fourier's industrial armies, Bellamy's concept of utopia changed from fairy tale to blueprint.

Bellamy presented this blueprint in narratives of estrangement, romance and conversion with arguments presented in guide–visitor dialogues and a sermon. Time travel (the narrator's 113-year sleep) creates the initial sense of estrangement from the 'present'; the evolving love between Julian West, the estranged visitor and the utopian guide's daughter, Edith Leete (the great-granddaughter of Julian's nineteenth-century lover), creates the love interest; and the conversion dramatizes the transformation of a rather selfish wealthy individual (Julian) into a supporter of a centralized, socialized, egalitarian economy and a concept of self that merges the individual and humanity. The guide–visitor dialogues provide most of the explicit intellectual arguments that convince the visitor to convert, though a long sermon by the Reverend Barton near the conclusion of the book helps Julian to comprehend the concept of the social self. Edith's nurturing sympathies are the primary forces behind his emotional and psychological conversion process, which is often plagued by severe bouts of physiological (burning eyes, crying and nausea) and psychological suffering (split identity and guilt). Even at the conclusion of the narrative, after Julian has awakened from a horrible nightmare that placed his converted self back in 1887, he is tortured by a guilt that drives him to confess to Edith, while sobbing, that he is an unworthy presence in her twentieth-century utopia.

Except for a visual overview of Boston from Dr Leete's rooftop, visits to an enormous distribution centre and a public dining facility with separate family rooms and a brief and traumatic street-level walk, Julian's visual confirmation of the new world is limited to the Leete's home, where he listens to long explanations offered by Dr Leete and to the Reverend Barton's electronically transmitted sermon. Hence, Julian's experience of the 'outside' utopian world is almost exclusively a verbal-construct experience. One of the key elements of this construction is the historical transformation to utopia as a natural and peaceful evolution. Huge separate corporations gradually grew into one Great Trust, which, without revolution by the people or great antagonism from the capitalists, became an enormous people's trust – a nationalized public system of production and distribution (the industrial army) administered by ten national departments. This economic engine is the real government. There are no state governments and Congress rarely meets. All basic issues are settled. There is little for legislators to do. Groups of three judges try the few court cases; most of the accused plead guilty. The many ranks of the industrial army (a meritocracy of skill and effort that would please Twain's Hank Morgan) encompass the entire labour-management force, which is headed by a president elected by the retired members of the industrial army.

As in Cabet's *Voyage*, economic equality is a crucial element of this utopia. Everyone receives a life-long (and quite generous) annual credit allowance (credit cards are the means of exchange; each year each citizen receives an equal allotment of the national product). After a free and excellent public education (with a few exceptions) everyone serves in the industrial army from the age of twenty-one to forty-five. The first three years require unskilled labour work; the rest are for further education, training and careers. Citizens choose their careers; a sliding work-hour scale (more hours for popular work, fewer for less popular) ensures an even distribution of the labour force. Exceptions to the time served include mothers (but not fathers) who opt to raise their children for several years (they still receive a full annual allotment for this essential work). Dr Leete also indicates several forceful restrictions: only wives and mothers can achieve the highest ranks in the women's branch of the industrial army, and any able person who refuses to serve leads a solitary, bread-and-water existence. Approximately half of one's life – the retirement period – is stimulating. This can mean travel and entertainment, but Leete stresses the freedom to pursue intellectual and spiritual interests, especially one identified by the Reverend Barton: a profound desire to associate individual achievement with the improvement of humanity – a utopian desire not unlike Christian brotherhood, Ralph Waldo Emerson's Transcendental unity and Marx's 'species being'.

Of nineteenth-century American books, only *Uncle Tom's Cabin* and possibly *Ben Hur* outsold *Looking Backward*. The book's popularity inspired several reform journals (e.g., *The Nationalist* and *The New Nation*) and numerous book-length fictional responses, the most famous being William Morris's *News from Nowhere* (1890). Between 1888 and the early years of the twentieth century, at least 200 literary utopias appeared in the United States alone, including Bellamy's sequel to *Looking Backward*, *Equality* (1897).[23] Literary, social, labour and reform leaders as different as William Dean Howells, Mark Twain, Upton Sinclair, Samuel Gompers, Eugene Debs, Charlotte Perkins Gilman and Elizabeth Cady Stanton voiced public support; and at least 165 Nationalist or Bellamy Clubs appeared in America and grew into the Nationalist Party that influenced the national Populist Party.

Translations of *Looking Backward* inspired reform movements around the world with especially strong impacts in England, Europe, Russia, Canada, Australia and New Zealand, where a minister of education and a prime minister reviewed *Looking Backward*. During the twentieth century many Socialist, Progressive and New Deal politicians cited Bellamy as an important influence. It is not surprising that in 1935 the philosopher John Dewey, the historian Charles Beard and the editor of *Atlantic Monthly*, Edward Weeks, contended that of books published since 1885 only Marx's *Das Kapital* had done more to shape the thought and action of the world.[24]

To return to the questions posed previously about early nineteenth-century utopian social theory, what was the contemporary 'evidence' that called for utopias and what perceptual tools made literary utopias convincing responses to the evidence? The evidence was abundant: for instance, the financial panic of 1873 and the depression of 1893, the Haymarket riot of 1886 and numerous strikes and labour disturbances; and trends such as political corruption, unrest among women and farmers, new immigration from southeastern Europe, rapid urban sprawl, challenges to traditional intellectual and religious beliefs and an unequal distribution of wealth. Before the publication of *Looking Backward*, Henry George's popular *Progress and Poverty* (1879) offered perceptual tools that helped readers to see the contradictions of this unequal distribution of wealth.[25] When placed within the contexts of many familiar American attitudes and expectations (including the Millennial and Enlightenment worldviews noted previously), the above-mentioned events and trends highlighted economic and numerous other contrasts: thousands of men and women unable to find work or even refusing to work (strikers) in the land of opportunity that celebrated the work ethic; the loss of influence by the farmer and rural America in Nature's Nation; and the swelling numbers of urban immigrants who declined to dissolve into the Protestant melting pot. Few forms of writing depend so heavily upon explicit and implicit contrasts, particularly between what is and what should be, to the degree found in utopian fiction. Hence, historical circumstances were important catalysts for the writing and enthusiastic reception of literary utopias, not only because they provided familiar topics that would both ground and energize utopian narratives and because they helped readers to desire a better world, but also because they sensitized readers to the meaningfulness and usefulness of a literature that viewed the world as a collage of cruel contrasts in need of fixing.

This sensitivity was heightened and the utopias rendered more believable by technological advances and improvements in distribution systems (especially the railroad) that made it possible to feed, clothe and shelter populations of industrialized countries. Also significant were the successes of nineteenth-century reform organizations as localized as temperance movements and as national as abolitionism (though the latter took a war to succeed). The faith in reform organizations reflected a broader faith in large organizations and the concept of national identity and power. The highly centralized bureaucracy of Bellamy's industrial army frequently repulses modern readers. But many of Bellamy's American, British and European contemporaries perceived the industrial army through their idealized visions of 'the nation' and of the successful (from a Northern United States view-point) Civil War machine that combined large-scale industrial and military forces. The most pronounced expression of this faith was a series of fictional and non-fictional utopian projections written by King Camp Gillette, inventor of the safety razor, who was in part inspired by Bellamy. In books such as *The Human Drift* (1894) and '*World Corporation*' (1910) Gillette imagined a gigantic people's corporation and the concentration of most of the American population in an enormous national city near Niagara Falls, which would supply a practically limitless source of energy.[26]

An awareness of significant historical events and perceptions is crucial to understanding the popularity and impact of utopian literature. It is also important to remember that this era was the golden era of print media – the ideal moment for the utopian book. Important economic, educational and technological advances (e.g., electricity and improved eyeglasses, printing processes and distribution systems) led to dramatic increases in production, distribution, circulation and literacy from 1880 to 1920. True, print media were not the only communication forces available. The telegraph, the tele-phone (less frequently) and (in rare cases) the phonograph carried messages across rooms, towns and regions. But the 1890s 'was the "Golden Age" of the book in the West: the first generation which acceded to mass literacy was also the last to see the book unchallenged as a communication medium'.[27] Books were plentiful, accessible (via cheap editions, libraries and literacy) and powerful. Cultural leaders proclaimed that the best books were books that transformed lives for the better. Literary utopias could claim to offer the ultimate transformative reading experience.

William Morris (1837–96) believed that *Looking Backward* would trans-form lives in devastating ways. For him Bellamy's Boston of AD 2000 was a corruption of the aims of socialism, one that sacrificed creativity for secur-ity and emphasized a middle-class mentality that wasted human energy on unnecessary and unattractive material objects. In *News from Nowhere: Or, an Epoch of Rest* (1890) he envisioned a very different world at the open-ing of the twentieth century in and around London.[28] There was no waste, no spoilage, no pollution (the Thames was clear) and much green space. Like Bellamy, he imagined an efficient world with abundant parks, but in

Morris's AD 2003, trees and meadows replaced railroad tracks, factories and crowded cities. It was difficult for the nineteenth-century dream traveller, William Guest, to tell where the town ended and the country began and his guide, Dick (Richard Hammond) revealed that rather than identifying with city, nation or humankind, citizens of this utopia defined their identities in terms of communities, parishes and small groups of workers. Everywhere around him Guest saw, heard and tasted beauty, from the colours and sounds of nature to the smells and tastes of communal feasts to the details of his guide's tooled buckle and the tile roofs and mosaic marble floors of the buildings. He also learned that this beautiful world did not come about without pain. Unlike the peaceful evolution of the Great Trust and then the people's industrial army forecast by Bellamy, Morris's beautiful world was built upon widespread class unrest and violence (much of the United States was destroyed) followed by state socialism, which led to the withering of the state and his decentralized utopia.

Beneath the surface of Morris's beautifully crafted world fundamental questions challenge assumptions that guided the majority of the late nineteenth- and early twentieth-century literary utopias of the western world. Obviously Morris's utopia questions a faith in a peaceful evolution. The thriving parishes and villages challenge the faith in big organization. Progress, the ideological god of the industrial revolution, is dethroned. Nowhere's citizens haven't destroyed machines as enthusiastically as Butler's Erewhonians did (in Morris's Nowhere machines that eliminate drudgery still operate), but they got rid of factory machinery that produced crude materials that corrupted people by making them desire unnecessary and wasteful goods. The celebration of late medieval guilds also questions the narrowness of the forward-looking orientation of progress ideology. On the most fundamental level Morris's utopia raised questions about human motivation, in particular the motivation to work. Bellamy replaced the Original Sin explanation of the necessity of work with a commitment to duty and individual identification with human brotherhood. In Morris's Nowhere, after the inequalities and ugliness of mass-produced capitalism had been vanquished by the revolutions, a tremendous craving for beauty arose in the people. The great pleasure in creating something of beauty, reminiscent of the joys of Fourier's passions, became the prime human motivator.

Women's role in society was another point of difference between Morris and Bellamy. Although the citizens of Nowhere experienced a much more flexible form of adult relationships (marriage was not bound by law), they assumed that what women 'do best' is done in the home – managing the household and raising children. Bellamy's Bostonians certainly honour motherhood. The nuclear family is the norm, and if a mother wants a leave from the industrial army to raise her children, she is granted those years at full pay. But Bellamy's twentieth-century women have the same education benefits and career opportunities as men and they can rise through the ranks to become General in the woman's industrial army, though Bellamy qualifies these progressive women's roles by indicating that they don't include strenuous physical occupations and only mothers need apply to be General. In response to criticism of Edith Leete's conventional demeanour and apparent lack of an occupation, Bellamy's narrator reveals in *Equality*, *Looking Backward*'s sequel, that Edith works on a high-tech farm operating machinery. Most of the American utopists didn't go that far in liberating their female characters, but approximately 90 per cent of them created imaginary worlds in which women were not economically dependent upon men.[29]

Matthew Beaumont and Darby Lewes have demonstrated convincingly the importance of late nineteenth-century utopias written by British women who addressed many of the issues reflected in Bellamy's and Morris's utopias.[30] These utopias responded to the hopes and failures of suffragette movements, discussion of the New Woman and fierce anti-feminist attacks. Beaumont singles out Elizabeth Corbett's *New Amazonia* (1889) for particular comment. The narrative mixes feminism, imperialism and eugenics. After a momentous victory of the suffragists, many of these progressive women colonize Ireland; by AD 2472 a rigid eugenic agenda favouring the healthy, the intelligent and the moral creates a utopia of socialistic cooperation and peace with women controlling crucial leadership positions. (An underlying essentialist assumption is that women are more ethical than men.) As Beaumont observes, of particular interest is the nineteenth-century visitor's role as a professional writer. The women of the future ask her to write a history of the nineteenth century. This request within the narrative would make her real Victorian readers the 'point of origin for her history of the future'.[31] This narrative strategy is similar to Bellamy's, since Julian West, who has become a writer (an historian) in AD 2000, grounds his narrative in nineteenth-century beginnings. But the fact that Corbett identifies her narrator as a woman who was a professional writer *before* her arrival in utopia, especially emphasizes the importance of the power of the written word to transform the world and the contribution that women can make to that transformation.

As Carol Kessler's bibliographies demonstrate, a significant number of American women answered the call to make transformative contributions.[32] Although many of these writers agreed with Bellamy's emphases on problems with nineteenth-century gender roles, one of the striking characteristics of the post-1888 utopias written by women in the United States was their diversity. There were Bellamy spin-offs. Frances H. Clarke's *The Co-opolitan*

(1898) envisioned Nationalist communities spreading throughout Western states. C. H. Stone's *One of 'Berrian's' Novels* (1890) revealed the contents of a romance written by a novelist mentioned in *Looking Backward*.[33] Other utopias were markedly different from Bellamy's. M. A. Pittock offered a shipwreck adventure (*The God of Civilization*, 1890), while M. Louise Moore utilized an inner-earth narrative to plunge her readers beneath the North Pole where they discovered a cooperative civilization (*Al-Modad*, 1892).[34] Two of the most interesting feminist utopias stay above ground: one near the North Pole, the other far from it. In the former, Mary E. Bradley Lane's *Mizora* (serialized 1880–1, book form 1889), we find a single-sex utopia appearing decades before Gilman's *Herland* (1915).[35] Scientific discoveries by women chemists eliminated men's role in procreation; men, war and poverty are things of the distant past. Eugenics has created a superior form of blonde Aryan women; like Gilman, Lane succumbed to her era's racial attitudes. The other intriguing feminist utopia foreshadows Ursula K. Le Guin's and Doris Lessing's technique of offering co-existing alternative worlds. Alice Ilgenfritz Jones and Ella Merchant's *Unveiling a Parallel* (1893) is a utopian satire set on Mars.[36] In one society gender equality means that women can do anything that men can – all the good and the bad (for instance, boxing and substance abuse). In the preferable society men and women are still equal, but the vulgar and destructive qualities of both sexes have been eliminated and replaced by a brotherly and sisterly love that guides the citizens' secular and spiritual lives.

Forecasting the focus on small-scale interpersonal relations found in many twentieth-century utopias written by women, the intentional community became a dominant setting for these women utopists. But again there was great variety. As mentioned previously, Frances H. Clarke offered a futuristic Nationalist community that spread. Eva Wilder McGlasson's historical fiction, *Diana's Livery* (1890), described a failed (imaginary) Kentucky Shaker community.[37] There were failed secular rural communities (Adel Orpen's *Perfection City*, 1897) and successful urban communities (Katherine Pearson Woods's *Metzerot, Shoemaker*, 1889). And there were varieties of Christian communities: a dystopian view of a stern fundamentalist evangelist's reign over a North Carolina community (Caroline A. Mason's *A Woman of Yesterday*, 1900); a secret and successful Christian community hidden in a mountainous region of Italy where, as in *News from Nowhere*, citizens value beautiful handicrafts (Mary Agnes Tinckner's *San Salvador*, 1892); and a Christian profit-sharing community founded by an aristocrat inspired by his fiancée (*A New Aristocracy*, 1891). The diversity of utopian genres and viewpoints reflected in these utopias make them fascinating reflections of attitudes about American women at the turn of the century.

The diversity of the utopias written by women reflects the overall variety of the outpouring of literary utopias in the United States during the closing years of the nineteenth century. True, the majority of the authors, like Bellamy, indeed inspired by Bellamy, criticized the unjust inequalities spawned by the industrial revolution and exacerbated by capitalism; in response they imagined technologically advanced cooperative or socialistic cultures. But there were counter-currents. For example, one of the three cultures imagined by the multi-millionaire John Jacob Astor in *A Journey to Other Worlds* (1894) was an AD 2000 haven for technologists, expansionists and strong competitors. David H. Wheeler was even more explicit in his enthusiasm for capitalism. In a series of speculative essays entitled *Our Industrial Utopia and Its Unhappy Citizens* (1895), he proclaimed that America was utopia and that people didn't perceive this because they lacked character and desired 'superfluities'; as for the poverty, it was caused by laziness, though it could inspire character building.[38]

As my previous discussions of *Connecticut Yankee* and *In His Steps* demonstrate, the diversity went beyond debate over socioeconomic systems. William Dean Howells's Altrurian Romances presented an appealing middle ground between Bellamy and Morris that advocated a national socialistic system of production and distribution but celebrated a small village-pastoral lifestyle. There were also varieties of dystopias. In Paul Haedicke's heavy-handed dystopian satire *The Equalities of Para-Para* (1895), after a fiercely competitive period (the 'Man Chest' era), authorities enforce equality with imposed mental norms and selective mutilation.[39] Ignatius Donnelly, a well-known Populist leader, imagined a more conventional near-future dystopian scenario in *Caesar's Column* (1890): beneath the 'gorgeous shell' of industrialized America in 1988 lies a 'rotten' core of oppressed classes waiting to ignite.[40] The core does ignite led by the brutish leader of a secret brotherhood that wreaks apocalyptic destruction. Hope only comes from glimpses of an alternative 1988 future: a pastoral utopia colonized by whites in Africa. Though it lacks the graphic drama of *Caesar's Column*, Will N. Harben's *The Land of the Changing Sun* (1894) is the most insightful American prediction of the powerful dystopias of the twentieth century, especially Orwell's and Huxley's.[41] Another gorgeous shell opens the narrative: a marvellous, sub-oceanic world created by brilliant scientists and technicians. Slavery is the rotten core in this case; the people are slaves to the scientists, who are experts in psychological torture, banish those deemed unfit and maintain a powerful police force equipped with sophisticated video scanners. It takes a devastating flood to convince the ruler that it is blasphemous to misuse scientific and technological means to gain god-like powers.

It is important to stress the diversity of late nineteenth-century American utopian literature and to indicate the attempts, however limited, of these mostly middle- to upper-middle-class male authors to address problems of the poor and women, as well as the elderly and disabled. (Bellamy's concept of suffrage only for retired members of the industrial army certainly empowers citizens over forty-five and his emphasis on including the disabled, at full pay, in the industrial army recognizes their importance.) But especially in the United States, and also in England and Europe, utopia turned a blind eye on the existence and value of racial diversity. In his utopian fiction, only once does Bellamy explicitly draw attention to African Americans, and that is in *Equality*. He indicates that blacks, like everyone else, shared in utopia's economic equality, but that they were thoroughly segregated from the white population. Only one pre-1900 American utopia, *Imperium in Imperio* (1899), focused on African Americans and it was written by the only late nineteenth-century black utopist, Sutton Griggs, a respected Baptist minister.[42] The narrative takes the form of two fictional biographies of black leaders, during the Jim Crow era, who organize a secret society inspired by visions of freedom and a perfect form of government. The society is torn between two factions: one supports peaceful co-existence and plans to establish a separatist colony in Texas; the other advocates revolution. The revolutionaries triumph and the book ends with warnings for the future of America.

African Americans were typically ignored, but the real invisible men and women of American utopias were the first Americans. If they were mentioned at all, Indians were included in brief derogatory allusions to savagery (for example in *Connecticut Yankee*), in an occasional racist tirade, as in the 'Lo! The poor Indian' chapter in Thomas and Anna M. Fitch's *Better Days* (1892), or in 'vanishing American' scenarios – in Walter McDougall's *The Hidden City* (1891). In McDougall's opinion Indians are dying off because the draw of 'civilization' is too powerful, but they are too weak to acquire civilized ways.[43] At the turn of the century the native population in the United States was at its low point and the remaining Indian population was perceived as a part of the past. Their cultures, numbers and association with the past did not fit into either the bleak portraits of the oppressive present or the grand visions of the future of (white) America as utopia. Readers would have to wait until the twentieth century when authors including Samuel R. Delany, Gerald Vizenor, Ursula K. Le Guin and Octavia Butler made utopia a truly multi-cultural reading experience.

At the beginning of this essay I promised to conclude with speculations looking backward and forward – speculations that compared the concepts of human nature articulated by the early nineteenth-century social thinkers to the concepts implied by the fictions at the end of the century; and speculations about how the worldwide popularity of Bellamy and his respondents influenced the development of twentieth-century utopian literature. From Saint-Simon, Fourier and Owen to Bellamy and after, there is a continuation, indeed a grand enhancement, of the assumption that the present reality stifled admirable human characteristics and that planned environments (physical, social and cultural) could cultivate the admirable traits. By the end of the nineteenth century Paradise had indeed been transformed. Technological advances made more credible the construction of environments that could transform humanity. And the transformative power of books during their golden era, made them ideal vehicles for communicating plans for radically improved environments.

Besides enhanced book power and an increased emphasis on the believability of environmental reconstruction of humans, another difference was a de-emphasizing of Saint-Simon's emotive qualities and Fourier's five 'luxurious passions' (passions of the senses) and an increased stress on Saint-Simon's evaluative and administrative traits and Fourier's and Owen's emphasis on group associations and social mechanisms. It would be tempting to explain these shifts by pointing to Victorian prudery, a tendency to avoid controversial 'personal' topics and attempts to make proposals seem rational plans rather than fairy tales. But it is also crucial to acknowledge the deep fear of the perceived disorder and chaos of the late nineteenth century and a sincere desire to tame the chaos with humane orderliness.

Although Marx and Engels would agree with the emphasis on social and economic environments and the shift away from the emotive to the rational or even 'scientific' orientations, there were powerful dissenters throughout the century. The satirists and dystopians objected. Butler piercingly questioned whether or not reason (and ethics) could overcome a human tendency to conform to social norms even if those norms were ridiculous; Dostoevsky forcefully challenged the possibility and desirability of a wellness formed by a rational, humane environment; and Twain imagined the horrific consequences of forcing a practical and humane worldview on a population. Hawthorne and several of the women authors, who imagined intentional communities, emphasized the constructive and destructive power of interpersonal relations/emotions even in planned communities. Actually Hawthorne stressed the power of the extremes: having too much or too little emotion as primary determinants of human interactions. On the positive side of dissention, Melville and especially Morris preserved, even enhanced, the importance of cultivating emotive and sensory capacities.

Today the dissenters, especially Morris, rather than the popular 'mainstream' utopists, often entrance readers. But it is important to remember that it was Bellamy's vision of utopia that captivated late nineteenth-century readers around the world, and that captivation certainly helped to prolong interest in utopian literature in the twentieth century and laid the ground-work for different forms of modern utopianism. But ironically, *Looking Backward*'s popularity and the transformations it implied – thought experi-ment to practical blueprint, imagined possibility to expected probabilities, and a personal and the sensuous longing to an impersonal merging with organizations and humanity – also set up a backlash against utopian specu-lation by raising expectations so high and so near that it was quite easy for detractors to discredit utopianism by pointing to events as 'small' as the demise of Bellamy's Nationalist Party and as large as world wars and attempts by the likes of Hitler and Stalin to impose their large-organization-anti-sensuous utopian visions. But, under attack, utopia did not die. Instead, once again, it transformed to meet the needs of twentieth- and twenty-first-century worlds that would no doubt have sometimes delighted, sometimes horrified, and frequently baffled the likes of nineteenth-century utopists from Saint-Simon to Bellamy.

NOTES

1 Krishan Kumar, *Utopianism* (Minneapolis: University of Minnesota Press, 1991), p. 47.
2 See for example, Matthew Beaumont, *Utopia Ltd.: Ideologies of Social Dreaming in England 1870–1900* (Leiden: Brill, 2005); Sylvia Bowman *et al.*, *Bellamy Abroad: An American Prophet's Influence* (New York: Twayne, 1962); Darby Lewes, *Dream Revisionaries: Gender and Genre in Women's Utopian Fiction 1870–1920* (Tuscaloosa: University of Alabama Press, 1995); Vernon Louis Parrington, Jr, *American Dreams: A Study of American Utopias* (1947) (New York: Russell & Russell, 1964); Jean Pfaelzer, *The Utopian Novel in America, 1886–1896: The Politics of Form* (University of Pittsburgh Press, 1984); Kenneth M. Roemer, *The Obsolete Necessity: America in Utopian Writings, 1888–1900* (Kent, OH: Kent State University Press, 1976), *Utopian Audiences: How Readers Locate Nowhere* (Amherst: University of Massachusetts Press, 2003) and (ed.), *America as Utopia* (New York: Burt Franklin, 1981); Howard Segal, *Technological Utopianism in American Culture* (1984) (Syracuse, NY: Syracuse University Press, 2005). See also Yoriko Moichi, 'Japanese Utopian Literature from the 1870s to the Present and the Influence of Western Utopianism', *Utopian Studies* 10:2 (1999), 89–97, and Laurent Portes, 'Utopia and Nineteenth-century French Literature', in Roland Schaer, Gregory Claeys and Lyman Tower Sargent (eds.), *Utopia: The Search for the Ideal Society in the Western World* (New York: Oxford University Press, 2000), pp. 241–7. See also the bibliographies by Arthur O. Lewis, *Utopian Literature in the Pennsylvania State University Libraries: A Selected Bibliography* (University Park: Pennsylvania State University Libraries, 1984) and Lyman Tower Sargent, 'Australian Utopian Literature: An Annotated Chronological Bibliography, 1667–1999', *Utopian Studies* 10:2 (1999), 138–73 and 'Utopian

Literature in English Canada: An Annotated Chronological Bibliography', *Utopian Studies* 10:2 (1999), 174–206.

3   Étienne Cabet, *Voyage en Icarie* (Paris: Au Bureau du Populaire, 1840).

4   Portes, 'Utopia and Nineteenth-century French Literature', p. 241.

5   Louis-Sébastian Mercier, *L'An 2440: Un rêve s'il en fut jamais* (Amsterdam: 1771; translated into English as *Memoirs of the Year Two Thousand Five Hundred*).

6   Frank E. Manuel and Fritzie P. Manuel, *Utopian Thought in the Western World* (Cambridge, MA: The Belknap Press of Harvard University Press, 1979), pp. 581–693. I have drawn heavily upon the Manuels' excellent discussions.

7   *Ibid.*, p. 600.

8   *Ibid.*, pp. 642–9.

9   *Ibid.*, pp. 684–5, 686–92.

10 See Gregory Claeys and Lyman Tower Sargent (eds.), *The Utopia Reader* (New York University Press, 1999), pp. 207–19.

11 James Fenimore Cooper, *The Crater; or, Vulcan's Peak: A Tale of the Pacific* (2 vols., New York: Burgess, Stringer and Company, 1847).

12 Herman Melville, *Typee: A Peep at Polynesian Life* (1846) (Evanston: Northwestern University Press-Newberry Library, 1968), pp. 111, 124.

13 Elizabeth Stuart Phelps (Ward), *Three Spiritualist Novels* [*The Gates Ajar* (1868), *Beyond the Gates* (1883), *The Gates Between* (1887)], ed. Nina Baym (Champaign, IL: University of Illinois Press, 2000).

14 Charles M. Sheldon, *In His Steps: 'What Would Jesus Do?'* (serialized, 1896, book form Chicago: Advance, 1897).

15 Other works by Melville that have been associated with utopian literature are *Omoo* (1847), *Mardi* (1848), and *Moby-Dick* (1852).

16 Gary Saul Morson, *The Boundaries of Genre: Dostoevsky's 'Diary of a Writer' and the Traditions of Literary Utopia* (Austin: University of Texas Press, 1981).

17 Samuel Butler, *Erewhon* (London: Trübner & Co., 1872).

18 Mark Twain, *A Connecticut Yankee in King Arthur's Court* (London: Chatto & Windus, 1889).

19 Nathaniel Hawthorne, *The Blithedale Romance* (1852), ed. Seymour Gross and Rosalie Murphy (New York: Norton Critical Edition, 1978).

20 Hawthorne, *The Blithedale Romance*, p. 226.

21 Ursula K. Le Guin, *Always Coming Home* (London: Gollancz, 1985).

22 Edward Bellamy, *Looking Backward 2000–1887* (1888), ed. John Thomas (Cambridge, MA: Harvard University Press, 1967).

23 Edward Bellamy, *Equality* (London: William Heinemann, 1897).

24 Roemer, *Utopian Audiences*, pp. 9–10. See also Carl J. Guarneri, 'An American Utopia and Its Global Audiences', *Utopian Studies* 19:2 (2008), 147–87.

25 Henry George, *Progress and Poverty* (New York: D. Appleton & Co., 1880).

26 King Camp Gillette, *The Human Drift* (Boston: New Era Publishing Co., 1894); 'World Corporation' (Boston: New England News, 1910).

27 Martyn Lyons, 'New Readers in the Nineteenth Century', in Guglielmo Cavallo and Roger Cartier (eds.), *A History of Reading in the West* (Amherst: University of Massachusetts Press, 1999), pp. 313–44, p. 313.

28 William Morris, *News from Nowhere; Or, an Epoch of Rest* (London: Reeves & Turner, 1891).

29 Roemer, *The Obsolete Necessity*, pp. 127–8.

30 Beaumont, *Utopia Ltd*; Lewes, *Dream Revisionaries*.
31 Beaumont, *Utopia Ltd.*, p. 126.
32 See Carol Farley Kessler (ed.), *Daring to Dream: Utopian Stories by United States Women, 1836–1919*, revised edn (Syracuse University Press, 1995).
33 Frances H. Clarke [Zebina Forbush], *The Co-opolitan: A Story of the Co-operative Commonwealth of Idaho* (Chicago: Charles H. Kerr, 1898); C. H. Stone, *One of 'Berrian's' Novels* (New York: Welch, Fracker Co., 1890).
34 M. A. Pittock, *The God of Civilization: A Romance* (Chicago: Eureka, 1890); M. Louise Moore, *Al-Modad; Life Scenes Beyond the Polar Circumflex: A Religio-Scientific Solution to the Problems of Present and Future Life* (Shell Bank, Cameron Parish, LA.: M. Louise Moore and M. Beauchamp, 1892).
35 Mary E. Bradley Lane, *Mizora: A Prophecy* (serialized 1880–1; book form 1889]) (Boston: Gregg Press, 1975).
36 Alice Ilgenfritz Jones and Ella Merchant, *Unveiling a Parallel: A Romance* (Boston: Arena, 1893).
37 Eva Wilder McGlasson, *Diana's Livery* (New York: Harper, 1891).
38 John Jacob Astor, *A Journey to Other Worlds: A Romance of the Future* (New York: Appleton, 1894); David H. Wheeler, *Our Industrial Utopia and Its Unhappy Citizens* (Chicago: A. C. McClurg & Co., 1895).
39 Paul Haedicke, *The Equalities of Para-Para* (Chicago: Schuldt-Gathmann, 1895).
40 Ignatius Donnelly, *Caesar's Column: A Story of the Twentieth Century. By Edmund Boisgilbert* (Chicago: F. J. Schulte & Co., 1890).
41 Will N. Harben, *The Land of the Changing Sun* (New York: Merriam, 1894).
42 Sutton Griggs, *Imperium in Imperio* (Cincinnati, OH: Editor Publishing Co., 1899).
43 Thomas and Anna M. Fitch, *Better Days: or A Millionaire of Tomorrow* (San Francisco: Better Days, 1891); Walter McDougall, *The Hidden City* (New York: Cassell Publishing Co., 1891).

BIBLIOGRAPHY

Astor, John Jacob, *A Journey to Other Worlds: A Romance of the Future* (New York: Appleton, 1894).
Beaumont, Matthew, *Utopia Ltd.: Ideologies of Social Dreaming in England 1870–1900* (Leiden: Brill, 2005).
Bellamy, Edward, *Equality* (London, William Heinemann, 1897).
    Looking Backward 2000–1887 (1888), ed. John Thomas (Cambridge, MA: Harvard University Press, 1967).
Bowman, Sylvia, *et al.*, *Bellamy Abroad: An American Prophet's Influence* (New York: Twayne, 1962).
Butler, Samuel, *Erewhon* (London: Trübner & Co., 1872).
Cabet, Étienne, *Voyage en Icarie* (Paris: Au Bureau du Populaire, 1840).
Claeys, Gregory (ed.), *Modern British Utopias, c. 1700–1850* (8 vols., London: Pickering and Chatto, 1997).
Claeys, Gregory and Lyman Tower Sargent (eds.), *The Utopia Reader* (New York University Press, 1999).
Clarke, Frances H. [Zebina Forbush], *The Co-opolitan: A Story of the Co-operative Commonwealth of Idaho* (Chicago: Charles H. Kerr, 1898).

Cooper, James Fenimore, *The Crater; or, Vulcan's Peak: A Tale of the Pacific* (2 vols., New York: Burgess, Stringer and Company, 1847).

[Donnelly, Ignatius], *Caesar's Column: A Story of the Twentieth Century. By Edmund Boisgilbert* (Chicago: F. J. Schulte & Co., 1890).

Fitch, Thomas and Anna M. Fitch, *Better Days: or A Millionaire of Tomorrow* (San Francisco: Better Days, 1891).

George, Henry, *Progress and Poverty* (New York: D. Appleton & Co., 1880).

Gillette, King Camp, *The Human Drift* (Boston: New Era Publishing Co., 1894).

'World Corporation' (Boston: New England News, 1910).

Griggs, Sutton, *Imperium in Imperio* (Cincinnati, OH: Editor Publishing Co., 1899).

Guarneri, Carl J., 'An American Utopia and Its Global Audiences', *Utopian Studies* 19:2 (2008), 147–87.

Haedicke, Paul, *The Equalities of Para-Para* (Chicago: Schuldt-Gathmann, 1895).

Harben, Will N., *The Land of the Changing Sun* (New York: Merriam, 1894).

Hawthorne, Nathaniel, *The Blithedale Romance* (1852), ed. Seymour Gross and Rosalie Murphy (New York: Norton Critical Edition, 1978).

Jones, Alice Ilgenfritz and Ella Merchant, *Unveiling a Parallel: A Romance* (Boston: Arena, 1893).

Kessler, Carol Farley (ed.), *Daring to Dream: Utopian Stories by United States Women, 1836–1919*, revised edn (Syracuse, NY: Syracuse University Press, 1995).

Kumar, Krishan, *Utopianism* (Minneapolis: University of Minnesota Press, 1991).

Lane, Mary E. Bradley, *Mizora: A Prophecy* (serialized 1880–1; book form 1889) (Boston: Gregg Press, 1975).

Le Guin, Ursula K., *Always Coming Home* (London: Gollancz, 1985).

Lewes, Darby, *Dream Revisionaries: Gender and Genre in Women's Utopian Fiction 1870–1920* (Tuscaloosa: University of Alabama Press, 1995).

Lewis, Arthur O., *Utopian Literature in the Pennsylvania State University Libraries: A Selected Bibliography* (University Park: Pennsylvania State University Libraries, 1984).

Lyons, Martyn, 'New Readers in the Nineteenth Century', in Guglielmo Cavallo and Roger Cartier (eds.), *A History of Reading in the West* (Amherst: University of Massachusetts Press, 1999), pp. 313–44.

Manuel, Frank E. and Fritzie P. Manuel, *Utopian Thought in the Western World* (Cambridge, MA: The Belknap Press of Harvard University Press, 1979).

McDougall, Walter, *The Hidden City* (New York: Cassell Publishing Co., 1891).

McGlasson, Eva Wilder, *Diana's Livery* (New York: Harper, 1891).

Melville, Herman, *Typee: A Peep at Polynesian Life* (1846) (Evanston, IL: Northwestern University Press-Newberry Library, 1968).

Mercier, Louis-Sébastian, *L'An 2440: Un rêve s'il en fut jamais* (Amsterdam 1771; translated into English as *Memoirs of the Year Two Thousand Five Hundred*).

Moichi, Yoriko, 'Japanese Utopian Literature from the 1870s to the Present and the Influence of Western Utopianism', *Utopian Studies* 10:2 (1999), 89–97.

Moore, M. Louise, *Al-Modad; Life Scenes Beyond the Polar Circumflex: A Religio-Scientific Solution to the Problems of Present and Future Life* (Shell Bank, Cameron Parish, LA.: M. Louise Moore and M. Beauchamp, 1892).

Morris, William, *News from Nowhere; Or, an Epoch of Rest* (London: Reeves & Turner, 1891).

Morson, Gary Saul, *The Boundaries of Genre: Dostoevsky's 'Diary of a Writer' and the Traditions of Literary Utopia* (Austin: University of Texas Press, 1981).

Parrington, Vernon Louis, Jr, *American Dreams: A Study of American Utopias* (1947) (New York: Russell & Russell, 1964).

Pfaelzer, Jean, *The Utopian Novel in America, 1886–1896: The Politics of Form* (University of Pittsburgh Press, 1984).

Phelps (Ward), Elizabeth Stuart, *Three Spiritualist Novels [The Gates Ajar* (1868), *Beyond the Gates* (1883), *The Gates Between* (1887)], ed. Nina Baym (Champaign, IL: University of Illinois Press, 2000).

Pittock, M. A., *The God of Civilization: A Romance* (Chicago: Eureka, 1890).

Portes, Laurent, 'Utopia and Nineteenth-century French Literature', in Roland Schaer, Gregory Claeys and Lyman Tower Sargent (eds.), *Utopia: The Search for the Ideal Society in the Western World* (New York: Oxford University Press, 2000), pp. 241–7.

Roemer, Kenneth M., *The Obsolete Necessity: America in Utopian Writings, 1888–1900* (Kent, OH: Kent State University Press, 1976).

Utopian Audiences: How Readers Locate Nowhere (Amherst: University of Massachusetts Press, 2003).

Roemer, Kenneth M. (ed.), *America as Utopia* (New York: Burt Franklin, 1981).

Sargent, Lyman Tower, 'Australian Utopian Literature: An Annotated Chronological Bibliography, 1667–1999', *Utopian Studies* 10:2 (1999), 138–73.

British and American Utopian Literature, 1516–1985 (New York: Garland, 1988).

'Utopian Literature in English Canada: An Annotated Chronological Bibliography', *Utopian Studies* 10:2 (1999), 174–206.

Schaer, Roland, Gregory Claeys and Lyman Tower Sargent (eds.), *Utopia: The Search for the Ideal Society in the Western World* (New York: Oxford University Press, 2000).

Segal, Howard, *Technological Utopianism in American Culture* (1984) (Syracuse, NY: Syracuse University Press, 2005).

Sheldon, Charles M., *In His Steps: 'What Would Jesus Do?'* (serialized 1896, book form Chicago: Advance, 1897).

Stone, C. H., *One of 'Berrian's' Novels* (New York: Welch, Fracker Co., 1890).

Twain, Mark, *A Connecticut Yankee in King Arthur's Court* (London: Chatto & Windus, 1889).

Wegner, Phillip E., *Imaginary Communities: Utopia, the Nation, and Spatial Histories of Modernity* (Berkeley: University of California Press, 2002).

Wheeler, David H., *Our Industrial Utopia and Its Unhappy Citizens* (Chicago: A. C. McClurg & Co., 1895).

5

GREGORY CLAEYS

The origins of dystopia: Wells, Huxley and Orwell

Introduction: Malice in Wonderland – concepts and theory

Where did it all go wrong? When did the vision of heaven on earth become an anticipation of hell? In many accounts we emerge from the hopeful, dream-like state of Victorian optimism to pass through what H. G. Wells called the age of confusion into a nightmarish twentieth century, soon powerfully symbolized by the grotesque slaughter of the First World War. Enlightenment optimism respecting the progress of reason and science was now displaced by a sense of the incapacity of humanity to restrain its newly created destructive powers. From that time ideal societies have accordingly been more commonly portrayed negatively in dystopian rather than utopian form. Like most other parts of *terra utopus*, however, the concept of dystopia has been much contested, many eutopias or ideal societies having dystopic elements and vice versa. Dystopias are often described as 'conservative', though they may in fact be sharply critical of the societies they reflect, as we will see. 'Dystopia' is often used interchangeably with 'anti-utopia' or 'negative utopia', by contrast to utopia or 'eutopia' (good place), to describe a fictional portrayal of a society in which evil, or negative social and political developments, have the upper hand, or as a satire of utopian aspirations which attempts to show up their fallacies, or which demonstrate, in B. F. Skinner's words, 'ways of life we must be sure to avoid' – in the unlikely event that we can agree on particulars.[1] Yet as we will see, the most famous exemplar of the genre, Orwell's *Nineteen Eighty-Four*, was not intended to be anti-utopian as such.

The term 'dystopia' enters common currency only in the twentieth century, though it appears intermittently beforehand (dys-topia or 'cacotopia', bad place, having been used by John Stuart Mill in an 1868 parliamentary debate). The flowering of the dystopian genre was preceded by a variety of satirical tropes. Francis Bacon's scientific ambitions were brought down several notches in Swift's famous parody in book three of *Gulliver's Travels* (1726). The dystopian ideal has also been linked both historically and logically to proclamations of the 'end of utopia' (for instance in Marcuse, *Five Lectures*, 1970)[2], and has sometimes also been wedded to the now-debunked hypothesis of the 'end of history'. In the wake of totalitarianism it was also suggested, in the works of Karl Popper (see *The Open Society and its Enemies*, 1950),[3] Jacob Talmon, and others, that the utopian impulse was itself inherently dystopian. That is to say, the desire to create a much improved society in which human behaviour was dramatically superior to the norm implies an intrinsic drift towards punitive methods of controlling behaviour which inexorably results in some form of police state.

This contention, effectively a *reductio ad absurdam*, was anticipated decades earlier in the suggestion by the Italian psychologist Cesare Lombroso that all socialists were 'lunatics', or deviant personalities, as well as in the sociologist Herbert Spencer's allegation that all forms of socialism implied 'slavery' or some variation on the 'servile state'. It is flawed for two main reasons. On the one hand, logically, it assumes that utopianism seeks perfectibility, and thus, incapable of accepting less, must punish whatever falls below this standard. Most utopias however do not demand or anticipate *perfection* as such, but accept considerably *improved* behaviour as an attainable norm. On the other, historically, it fails to acknowledge that many forms of utopian practice, such as monasticism, intentional communities of various kinds, and many other variants on 'ideal' societies, have not proven 'totalitarian'. Thus while we may continue to debate the ambiguity of, for instance, the fourth voyage to the land of the Houyhnhnms in Swift's *Gulliver's Travels*, the broad implication that all forms of theorizing which aim at a vast improvement in human society are 'totalitarian' or 'dystopian' has itself been disproven by history. Many of us indeed live today in the utopias of the past, in circumstances vastly better than those most of our ancestors even dreamt of. Thus the liberal paradigm of universal opulence and stable democracy is itself also a utopian ideal, and itself susceptible to dystopian failure, both economically and environmentally. There is of course something in the argument that, just as one person's terrorist is another's freedom-fighter, so is one person's utopia another's dystopia. Indisputably, thus, whether a given text can be described as a dystopia or utopia will depend on one's perspective of the narrative outcome. Such ambiguity should, however, be a provocative source of discussion, rather than a rationale for dismissing the genre as such.

Nonetheless it is generally conceded that in the twentieth century dystopia becomes the predominant expression of the utopian ideal, mirroring the colossal failures of totalitarian collectivism. This chapter will focus on the 'turn' towards dystopia from the late nineteenth until the mid-twentieth century, which is here portrayed as foreshadowed by two preceding movements of a similar type. It concentrates on British utopian literature, the richest such tradition, and that which has produced its two best-known examples. It is suggested that this 'turn' was inherently ambiguous from the start; that is to say, that its two major features, the socialist engineering of human behaviour via the reconstitution of society; and the eugenic engineering of human behaviour via biological manipulation, were viewed widely as both positive and negative developments. This is illustrated by offering a brief introduction to the key texts which define the genre, initially by H. G. Wells, but more especially Aldous Huxley's *Brave New World* and George Orwell's *Nineteen Eighty-Four*, as well as some lesser texts which define its range and breadth. Their common theme is the quasi-omnipotence of a monolithic, totalitarian state demanding and normally exacting complete obedience from its citizens, challenged occasionally but usually ineffectually by vestigial individualism or systemic flaws, and relying upon scientific and technological advances to ensure social control.

Before commencing, two notes, one theoretical, one historical. Firstly, we should briefly consider demarcating the boundaries of the 'dystopian' concept. The term is used here in the broad sense of portraying feasible negative visions of social and political development, cast principally in fictional form. By 'feasible' we imply that no extraordinary or utterly unrealistic features dominate the narrative. Much of the domain of science fiction is thus excluded from this definition: Wells's *The War of the Worlds* (1898), for instance, is not based on the extrapolation of some existing trend as such, and is thus not a dystopia; 'Martians' belong not to the realm of dystopia but to that of science fiction, or fantasy *pur et simple*. (Jules Verne thought Wells too unrealistic, as a consequence.) If of course there had been evidence of extra-terrestrial life either in 1898 or now, these boundaries would necessarily shift; they are fluid by definition, or to use Wells's own formula, *kinetic*. By this definition, totalitarian dystopias are clearly dystopias, that is, mirrored if refracted realities. A voyage in a balloon in 1863 thus is not science fiction; a journey to the moon is. A voyage to another planet was science fiction in 1850, but will probably not be in 2020. Eugenic dystopias remain within the bounds of possibility. Conquest by alien beings, or robots, or the final calling of time by God at Judgment Day, may portray dystopic elements (as well as utopic, or both simultaneously). But texts portraying such events are not 'dystopias' as such.

The first dystopian turn

Secondly, we should note that just as the seminal political moment definitive of modernity was the French Revolution, so we witness in this period the first evidence of a theoretical and fictional 'dystopian turn' of the type more commonly associated with the later nineteenth and early twentieth centuries. Satires upon Enlightenment conceptions of a life lived according to the principles of reason appear in the preceding period, notably in Swift and in Burke's *Vindication of Natural Society* (1756); indeed much utopian writing in this period can be read as a discourse upon corruption and degeneration. Fantasies of the 'Last Man' and of the Apocalypse occur intermittently in the eighteenth and nineteenth centuries. But it is only with the French Revolution that we witness a dialectical relationship emerging between three elements: utopian thought, here some of the underlying principles of the Revolution; the creation of fictional utopias; and a fictional anti- or dystopian response. In this case, on the one hand we witness fictional works inspired by leading trends in utopian thought, notably by Thomas Spence (*The Constitution of Spensonia*, 1801), and by acolytes of William Godwin, particularly Thomas Northmore's *Memoirs of Planetes* (1795).[4] On the other, these texts were met with a barrage of fictional satires of the 'new philosophy', loosely defined as 'perfectibility', which portrayed Godwinian invocations of a society governed by reason as inducing disaster, such as Hannah More's *The History of Mr Fantom* (1797). This is also the point at which both major strands of the later dystopian turn, population control and socialism, are addressed by the most famous anti-utopian text of the nineteenth century, and a key source for Darwin's *Origin of Species* (1859), T. R. Malthus's *Essay on Population* (1798).[5] This in its first edition targeted Condorcet and William Godwin, and in its second, substituted the founder of British socialism, Robert Owen, for Godwin.

At the very end of this cycle of texts appeared Mary Shelley's gothic masterpiece, *Frankenstein* (1818), often held to be the founding text of the genre of science fiction, but also partly a satire on the failed aspirations of the Revolution, heralding one of the key themes of late dystopian writings.[6] Subtitled 'or the Modern Prometheus', the work explores the perils of usurping the divine monopoly on creation, the creature standing in part for the 'new man' of the revolutionary ideal, and also centrally focuses on the Godwinian (or Rousseauesque) theme of naturally virtuous individuals being corrupted by society. For many, the theme of science- (or scientist) gone-wild, then, first heralds dystopia, from Swift onwards. Thereafter science, technology, utopia and dystopia move forward increasingly in tandem, and after 1900 the characteristic form of the imaginary society would be both dystopian and often formally cast in the genre of science fiction, set normally in the future rather than the past or elsewhere in the here-and-now.

The second dystopian turn

Owenism produced little in the way of literary utopianism, and correspondingly little by way of anti- or dystopian satire. Two developments shape the clearer and more traditionally identified 'turn' towards dystopia in the closing decades of the nineteenth century: eugenics and socialism. Utopian thought in both Europe and North America had been strongly affected by Owenism, Fourierism and Saint-Simonism from the 1820s through mid-century. From the early 1880s, however, the fictional genre becomes dominated by the promises of these two, often interwoven, ideals of social and individual improvement, both positively and negatively. Many writers were keen to urge the compatibility of socialism and Darwinism, notably Karl Pearson, who saw socialism as the 'logical outcome of the law of Malthus'.[7] In Britain, Samuel Butler's *Erewhon* (1872) discussed the new Darwinian creed, while Edward Bulwer-Lytton's *The Coming Race* (1871) described a society in which Darwinian competition had been eliminated. On the socialist side, William Morris's *News from Nowhere* (1890) espoused a proto-environmentalist socialist ideal wedded to Ruskinian aestheticism. Many works united these themes seamlessly, such as Walter Besant's *The Inner House* (1888), in which physical decay is arrested by scientific advance, and socialism is the only accepted form of organization. Eugenics might well be described as the 'Darwinian utopia', and the theme of racial war recurs frequently in later nineteenth-century utopias, sometimes with the 'Anglo-Saxons' winning (e.g., Robert William Cole, *The Struggle for Empire: A Story of the Year 2236*, 1900), and sometimes other races, such as the Japanese (e.g., [Ernest George Henham], John Trevena, *The Reign of the Saints*, 1911). In some 'utopias' black peoples have been entirely eliminated (e.g., William Hay, *Three Hundred Years Hence*, 1881, p. 256) – but for non-whites this would be a dystopia. From the 1890s onwards the appearance of an increasing number of dystopian texts thus seemingly indicates a negative trend in the wider utopian genre as a whole. I have argued elsewhere, however, that this is not the case.[8] A large number of texts do portray the socialist revolution gone awry, and the destruction of individualism at the hands of socialist revolutionaries, such as Charles Fairchild's *The Socialist Revolution of 1888* (1884). Commonly national collapse has been instigated by such revolutions, with widespread poverty resulting, as in *A Radical Nightmare: Or, England Forty Years Hence* (1885). One of the earliest is Percy Clarke's *The Valley Council; or, Leaves from the Journal of Thomas Bateman of Canbelego Station, N.S.W.* (1891), where a dictatorship results from a socialist revolution. Not uncommonly socialist and eugenicist themes are combined in dystopian form, as in *Red England: A Tale of the Socialist Horror* (1909), where after the revolution three doctors must approve all marriages, and children are removed from their parents' care and raised by the state.[10]

Eugenic themes, however, were also capable of being portrayed positively in many works, to such a degree, indeed, as to prevent us from positing a negative 'turn' in the genre as such generated from this source. Sometimes this is as simple as a reduction in family size and reorientation of society towards greater productivity and efficiency, as in Frank Perry Coste's *Towards Utopia (Being Speculations in Social Evolution)* (1894). But more overtly positive eugenics endorsements appear in many works. In *Pyrna: A Commune; or, Under the Ice* (1875), a society beneath a Swiss glacier is encountered where there is perfect equality, fraternal love and community of property and children. But no unhealthy children are permitted to survive. Similarly, in *Posterity: Its Verdicts and Its Methods; or Democracy A.D. 2100* (1897), medical examinations for organic diseases are a precondition of citizenship, and the 'morally unsound and the mentally diseased' are prohibited offspring. In G. Read Murphy's *Beyond the Ice* (1894) a marriage bureau regulates pairing, while in Andrew Acworth's *A New Eden* (1896) family size is restricted to two children, and euthanasia is the norm. In *Quintura: Its Singular People and Remarkable Customs* (1886) all children are raised by the state, and priority is given to hygienic improvement.

Other themes helped to nourish the dystopian flavour of the epoch, including the threat of a Prussian invasion of Britain. In G. T. Chesney's *The Battle of Dorking* (1871), for instance, written during the Franco-Prussian War, poorly trained English volunteers are swiftly routed by a technologically superior force. In *Cromwell the Third: Or, the Jubilee of Liberty* (1886), Britain is annexed by Germany. 'Alien' invasions would merely extend such fears into an ever more fantastic domain. Ecological catastrophe was firstly portrayed strikingly in Richard Jefferies's *After London; or, Wild England* (1885), one of the sources of Morris's *News from Nowhere*.[9] Yet the yearning for primitivism, the simpler life, was not uniformly a dystopian theme, either; Morris himself famously confessed to feeling consoled that barbarism might again flood the world. And there are arcadian elements in many other socialist utopias of the period, including some usually termed dystopias, such as Robert Blatchford's *The Sorcery Shop* (1909), as well as in utopian thought (Edward Carpenter, for instance, mentioned Melville's *Typee* as a model for future socialist emulation).[10]

H. G. Wells's dystopian *entrée*

Herbert George Wells is a writer famous for, amongst other things, commencing his career amidst an aura of *fin de siècle* pessimism, by writing a number of dystopian works, and then embracing utopia and exchanging degeneration for regeneration.[11] Wells thus initially epitomizes what we have here termed the 'second dystopian turn', but also the outpouring of late nineteenth-century utopian sentiment, often in taking up the very same themes, notably authority, leadership and the advancement (or threat) of science and technology. Many of his early works go beyond dystopia, as defined here, into science fiction, often, instigated by his scientific training under T. H. Huxley, by moving beyond short-term to long-term evolution. That is to say, they breach our expectations of the genuinely possible within the social and especially the scientific constraints of the day, while offering a moral tale or prescient warning which clearly has contemporary application.

Whether evolution was controllable by a species manifestly often not up to the task of the utopian 'taking hold' of evolution, as *Men Like Gods* insisted, was indeed to become perhaps *the* quintessentially Wellsian theme. As defined here, *The Time Machine* (1895), *The Invisible Man* (1897) and *The First Men in the Moon* (1901), are works of science fiction, while *The Island of Doctor Moreau* (1896) is a dystopia. Yet all are extrapolations of present trends of one form or another, varying in their degree of plausibility. In *The Time Machine*, perhaps his most pessimistic work, Wells recounts the discovery of a world of AD 802,701 which is divided into two great groups, a master-race, the Eloi, 'a real aristocracy, armed with a perfected science and working to a logical conclusion the industrial system of to-day', and an underground slave race, the Morlocks. The satire here is upon both communism and schemes of selective breeding. *The Island of Doctor Moreau* – in which Wells acknowledged that Swift (notably book four of *Gulliver's Travels*) loomed large – focuses more narrowly on scientific control of genetic development. With the creation of 'beast-men' or 'quasi-human monsters' – a prospect Wells thought plausible enough – man becomes 'at last as remorseless as Nature', and Promethean themes again abound: we are near enough to *Frankenstein* to appreciate the parallels. In *When the Sleeper Awakes* (1899), set 200 years in the future, a slave-state is ruled by a quasi-Nietzschean usurper named Ostrog (a Russian word for prison); this is 'no Utopia, no Socialistic state' of a Bellamy, Morris or Hudson type (all are mentioned). Why? What went wrong? Corrosive urbanization, the creation of 'this great machine of the city', concentration of wealth, and an incessant economic struggle, compared to the 'idyllic easy-going life' of the nineteenth century. Satirized here are Carlyle's hero-worship ideal and Plato, and there are echoes yet again of Swift. Disease has been virtually abolished, but the common man, gulled by 'the world-wide falsehoods of the news-tellers,' remains 'helpless in the hands of demagogue and organiser, individually cowardly, individually swayed by appetite, collectively incalculable'.[12] The great aim? Simply to retain property in the hands of the rich.

While not properly a dystopia, though it satirizes human folly, *The First Men in the Moon* (1901) is a much less theoretically significant work. Written during the Boer War, it portrays the export of imperial violence, with humans killing the Selenite lunarians as they had slain savages on earth. Wells here took up the analogy of Columbus and the Americas.[13] From 1901, however, he began to devote himself to the life-long pursuit of creating the world-state, sometimes called socialism, sometimes republicanism or 'cosmopolis'. His last moment of hesitation was expressed in the 'social imaginings' of *Anticipations* (1901), in which eugenic themes continue, and the dying out of the less efficient races is regarded as seemingly inevitable. But Wells had now firmly turned to both prophecy and advocacy. Thereafter he would regard a world-state as mankind's only solution to its gravest social and scientific problems, though his idea of what this would entail would in turn feed other dystopian visions. He remained certain that a superior caste or class had to guide this movement, exploring their role in so doing in elaborate detail in *A Modern Utopia* (1905), and practically in the Fabian Society. Like many of his generation, he had faith in the capacity of scientists and engineers to bring happiness to the masses, even if the creation of the world-state had to be instigated by planetary catastrophe, as in *In the Days of the Comet* (1906) or nuclear war (in *The World Set Free*, 1914). But as the new century advanced Wells also became ever less certain as to how to create, maintain and motivate this elite. By his death in 1946 he was deeply pessimistic about historical developments, his growing sense of dismay fed by a Gibbonian sense of recurrence.

A further writer worthy of note from this period is Yevgeny Zamyatin (1884–1927), who was influenced by Wells, and was in turn a key source later for Orwell. Zamyatin's *We* (written 1921, published in English in 1924) was anticipated by Jerome K. Jerome's story, 'The New Utopia' (1891), in which post-revolutionary individuals are assigned numbers rather than names, are forced to dress similarly, and lead highly regimented lives supervised by 'guardians'. Zamyatin describes the One State, in which people live in glass houses, and where the 'Benefactor', constantly elected unanimously, is the ruling figure, and sex is freely available if strictly controlled. Seemingly futile human resistance to this (by the 'enemies of happiness'),[14] their discovery, torture and 'cure' unite Zamyatin's and Orwell's portrayals. Orwell wrote in 1946 that *We* satirized 'not any particular country but the implied aims of industrial civilisation'.[15] This remains an important clue to his own aims in *Nineteen Eighty-Four*.

Huxley's *Brave New World* (1932)

In its outlines Huxley's text is familiar to most readers.[16] The world described, some 600 years 'After Ford', is one in which institutionalized eugenic engineering underpins a rigidly stratified class society, the World State, based upon breeding both intelligent rulership and complacent subservience, and governed by a privileged group of controllers. Huxley later termed this 'the completely controlled, collectivised society'.[17] 'Fordism' represents the subordination of humanity to the machine and to the scientific ideal as such. Children are raised in common, behavioural manipulation is elevated to a highly refined science, and, all books and monuments relating to the former society having been destroyed, the past has been erased. There is no need for mass brutality. With the exception of a few 'savages' left to their own devices, science has tamed society, and produced what Huxley termed 'a really efficient totalitarian state' in which the population of slaves 'love their servitude'.[18] They do so because sexual promiscuity is the norm, and anxiety-alleviating drugs, notably the 'perfect drug', the euphoric *soma*, guarantee a 'holiday from reality'. Hedonism, in short, is the predominant ethos. Everyone is happy, and endlessly reminds themselves of the fact: psychobabble rules, in consequence.

There are many targets here: utilitarianism, 'the horrors' of Wells's World State (*Men Like Gods* is often seen as the satirical object; Huxley once described its author as 'a rather horrid, vulgar little man'), totalitarianism, utopia itself, historical fatalism and, above all thought- and mind-control. There is, however, an alternative worldview presented. From the Savage Reservation comes an uncorrupted specimen of the former state of humanity, John, to challenge the assumptions of the established order. He represents art, science, humanity, individuality, religion and the folly of humankind. What, then, was Huxley's point? Did he really think such a society might emerge from the present? Is this a celebration of some variation on the Noble Savage, a romantic rebellion against conformity and materialistic hedonism? Was this a *realistic* dystopia, or does the point lie elsewhere? The 'whole idea' of *Brave New World*, Huxley once said, was that if you could iron people 'into a kind of uniformity, if you were able to manipulate their genetic background ... if you had a government sufficiently unscrupulous you could do these things without any doubt'.[19] Where then does Huxley wish our sympathies to lie? Not, certainly, with the hapless rulers of the future world, who reach for soma at the slightest anxiety. Even the Controller admits that the state of happiness achieved in the new society appears 'pretty squalid in comparison with the over-compensations for misery'. Yet in 1932, after the millions of deaths of the First World War, the stability achieved here was no mean outcome. Even at the cost of unbelief? 'If you allowed yourselves to think of God, you wouldn't allow yourselves to be degraded by pleasant vices', says the savage, God being 'the reason for everything noble and fine and heroic', to be met by the riposte that 'civilization has absolutely no need of nobility or heroism', that there is no 'right to be unhappy'. Are we then to identify with the old-fashioned savage, still wedded to ideas of love, monogamy, marriage, 'freedom', in short, first expressed by throwing away the soma boxes? And does Huxley wish us to see the assertion of such ideals as contingent upon religious belief, with no discernible secular alternative to mindless hedonism? The answer is apparently yes. The satire, in other words, is as much upon contemporary materialism and consumerism as upon the eugenic super-state; it is upon the threads which connect America with the Germany of Hitler and the Russia of Stalin, the human willingness to renounce a more diverse life in favour of certainty and stability, the 'primal and the ultimate need'.[20] Critics have accused Huxley of anti-American snobbism. Yet this is somewhat beside the point: Huxley is a critic of modernity as such, and America is only a leading instance of its definitive characteristics. His characters are named after Russians, French, British, Italians and Americans. The problem is not nationality, and it is not ideology.

Huxley's chief concern, then, is much more with how servitude becomes attractive than it is with science or technology as such. In response to his critics he proposed in a 1946 preface to *Brave New World* that a better world might be imagined in which science and technology were 'made for man, not ... as though man were to be adapted and enslaved to them'. The economics were to be decentralized and Henry-Georgian, the politics Kropotkinesque and cooperative, and a quasi-religious knowledge of the Godhead or 'Final End' was posited to which utilitarianism was subordinated, bringing a 'philosophical completeness' to the original novel. But Huxley was in fact growing more, not less, pessimistic, particularly about overpopulation; he worried in 1950 that the world might reach three billion before commencing to diminish.[21] *Ape and Essence* (1949) again raised fears of both science and leaders, particularly in combination, gone awry, with 'progress' portrayed like an uncontrollable genie released from the bottle. In *Brave New World Revisited* (1958) he returned to consider the issue of 'freedom and its enemies'. Critics had accused *Brave New World* of moral failure in a time of crisis. But nearly thirty years of reflection had proven to Huxley how successful the techniques of mind-control could be. He admitted that the very desire for freedom seemed to be 'on the wane'. While paying homage to Orwell, Huxley insisted that behavioural engineering in both Soviet-style and western regimes was enormously threatening. Yet he was much more explicit now that the greatest danger promoting such trends was world overpopulation, the probability of which 'leading through unrest to dictatorship becomes a virtual certainty'.[22] Degeneration into uniformity through loss of the sense of freedom is thus still a key theme. But is religion still an antidote? To an impressive degree, Huxley now opted for freedom of information as the key to withstanding mass manipulation and an explicitly capitalist ethos of conditioned consumption. 'Democracy', in the sense of collective, conscious self-government, was now more specifically pitted against capitalist hedonism. Huxley still worried about drugs, and about communism. He was not an egalitarian, and doubted whether the modern world exhibited any 'improvements in individual virtue and intelligence'.[23] But the most insidious enemy lay in the application of the techniques of mind control to advertising, to politics, to undermining the sense of reality and reinforcing egotism and hedonism. Democracy was to drown in popcorn and toothpaste, with citizenship debased to a mere commodity, not to be stomped under the Hitlerian jackboot. Huxley proposed limiting political campaign spending, and even banning 'anti-rational propaganda' in election campaigns.[24] The answer, then, was not religion: it was birth control – requiring an attack on some religions – and rationalism in politics.

Huxley's later novel, *Island* (1962), is usually described as a Buddhist- and drug-inspired utopia whose engagement with spirituality was an effort to compensate for the apparent moral impasse of *Brave New World*. Huxley himself termed it 'a kind of reverse *Brave New World* ... a Topian rather than a Utopian phantasy, a phantasy dealing with a place, a *real* place and *time*, rather than a phantasy dealing with *no* place and time'.[25] In both instances society has conquered violence, crime, hunger and inhumanity. However, if it reveals Huxley's search for more humane religious principles, *Island* lacks the degree of confrontation with the problems of hedonism and mass manipulation which mark his chief work. Pavlov makes an appearance; the problem is still collective somnambulism.[26] But the response is not on a scale sufficient to answer the questions left begging in *Brave New World*. The religious answer, too, is private and individual, the product of inner self-mastery, at best bounded by a small community like John Humphrey Noyes's Oneida, which Huxley admired, not a mass collective bond of public worship. Yet this at least lay within the bounds of possibility. For Huxley had no faith in utopias where people were portrayed 'radically unlike human beings ... quite different from what they are and from what, throughout recorded history, they have always been'.[27] (He condemned Swift's obsessive reluctance to acknowledge the realistic humanity of the Yahoos in *Gulliver's Travels*.) The answer, then, lay in a more 'rational mode' of democracy, one in which 'a ruling aristocracy of mind' – but not one based upon eugenics – was given a much more prominent role, in order to balance self-interest, demagoguery and corruption. Here a crucial role was to be played by those capable of practising the 'disinterested virtues', and it was this that religion, itself aiming at 'non-attachment', sought as its secular end. Here too Huxley worried that the worship of man, with 'all the virtues and perfections of God have been lodged in humanity', posed a significant danger, as did equivalent devotion to party, state, nation or race. It permitted immersion in 'the sub-human world of crowd emotion', which was the most effective totalitarian tool. Yet Huxley was not opposed to intelligent planning for the future. He may have lacked Orwell's commitment to a socialist variation on collectivism, but he praised Roosevelt's and other attempts to anticipate the results of technological developments and similar reforms so long as they were 'carried out by the right sort of means and in the right sort of governmental, administrative and educational contexts', that is to say, in an ethically sound manner, and through 'decentralization and responsible self-government'. And he retained an enduring interest in whether small-scale communities of intelligent, like-minded individuals could further such ends.[28]

Orwell's *Nineteen Eighty-Four* (1949)

Unlike *Brave New World*, George Orwell's *Nineteen Eighty-Four* was written after much of the scale and enormity of totalitarian brutality had been revealed.[29] Orwell's dystopian world-state is blunt, stark and pitiless. Consent rests upon punishment and fear rather than the manipulation of pleasure. Conformity is instilled by routine practice rather than eugenic conditioning; the abuse of science is Huxley's great theme, that of power, Orwell's.[30] Here too individuality has been eradicated, but much less comfortably, at a much higher price. Less secure, the regime has to work harder to maintain order. History to Ford is merely 'bunk'; here it must be continuously rewritten. Many readers see both novels as pitting the hapless individual against society in an unwinnable contest. Yet if Huxley's target was the agreeable self-deceptive conformity of capitalist society, and the obsessive, infantile grasping for happiness of the moderns, Orwell's was less distant from this than is often recognized. Huxley's work is often described as anti-materialistic, Orwell's rarely so, Huxley as a man engaged in permanent religious crisis, Orwell not. And while Orwell's great work was at one level intensely political, Huxley's has often been described as having few political overtones at all.

This section examines George Orwell's novel in the light of four issues. Firstly, it asks the 'realist' question as to how the work mirrored or distorted the totalitarian world Orwell satirized. Secondly, it argues that *Nineteen Eighty-Four* represented for Orwell not merely a satire of totalitarianism, but the rejection of many other aspects of modernity. Thirdly, it contends that an illumination of a number of preceding texts assists in our interpretation of the main text here. And finally, it suggests that one of the major themes which emerges in our interpretation of *Nineteen Eighty-Four* is Orwell's fear, evident from the mid-1930s onwards, that intellectuals in the socialist movement had been corrupted by power-worship, and hence would not function as capable or morally honest leaders in any new socialist society. Like Wells, Huxley (who also detested the *trahison des clercs*) and other writers of the period, Orwell thus recognized the problem of leadership to be central to the design of any viable future society.

The term 'totalitarianism', first introduced in 1928, but central to thinking during the Cold War period (1947–91), purports to define the common core of both dictatorships in terms of a militantly anti-liberal, anti-bourgeois philosophy hostile to most ideas of individualism and individual rights in particular. Unlike previous ideas of tyranny, including monarchical absolutism and military dictatorship, the key aspect of the new ideal was held to be the desire for complete control over the hearts and bodies, minds and souls, of the citizens of the nation. Totalitarian regimes assumed seven main features:

(1) a one-party state with hegemony over the secret police, and a monopoly over economic, cultural and informational sources; fascists see this state as the focus of the spiritual unity of the nation, possessing a will of its own, and having nothing existing outside it, while communists view the state as an extension of proletarian power during an interim 'dictatorship of the proletariat';

(2) a technological basis to centralized power, e.g., especially through the use of the media and surveillance techniques;

(3) the willingness to destroy large numbers of domestic 'enemies' in the name of the goals of the regime; such as the Jews under the Nazis, the kulaks (rich peasants) by Stalin; or the intellectuals by Pol Pot;

(4) the use of 'total terror' (an emphasis particularly associated with the work of Hannah Arendt) to intimidate the population and ensure complete loyalty;

(5) the willingness of the regime to annihilate all boundaries between the individual and the party/state, by destroying most intermediary organizations and politicizing any which remain, such as youth organizations;

(6) a 'totalist' philosophy or ideology which demands absolute loyalty and sacrifice, and the absolute submission of the citizen to the party/state,

leaving no part of private life unpoliticized; for fascists this was based more on the idea of necessary myths for the masses, for Stalinists, it rested upon a true account of necessary historical development based on Marx's materialist conception of history; in both instances society becomes extremely militarized;

(7) a cult of leadership: in fascism, the leader embodies the spirit, will and virtues of the people, and is identified with the nation; in communism, despite the fact that Marx offered no theory of leadership as such, an equally strong cult emerged around Lenin, Stalin and later leaders like Mao Zedong and Kim Il-Sung.

In order to see how this analysis of totalitarianism meshed with other criticisms of those aspects of modernity which Orwell found most disturbing we must first consider the development of Orwell's thought prior to *Nineteen Eighty-Four.* Orwell was born as Eric Blair in Bengal in 1903, to a 'lower-upper-middle class' family with a history of colonial service. He early and long possessed a strong sense of his own inferiority as well as the hypocrisy, drudgery and soullessness of his class. His earliest memories of St Cyprian's school (described in 'Such, Such Were the Joys') were of 'a continuous triumph of the strong over the weak'.[31] After a period at Britain's leading public school, Eton, in which he underwent a 'Tory anarchist' or individualist phase[32] and demonstrated a strong love of nature and a pronounced sense of the Graeco-Roman ideal of citizenship, Orwell showed his 'natural hatred of authority'[33] by going to Burma as a colonial policeman between 1922 and 1927. Here he became overtly anti-imperialist. His first major novel, *Burmese Days*, describes the British Empire as 'simply a device for giving trade monopolies to the English'. But we here also encounter Orwell's earliest criticisms of modern 'progress' as such. At one point, for instance, the narrator gazes out upon the jungle, and envisions that in 200 years 'All this will be gone – forests, monasteries, pagodas all vanished. And instead, pink villas fifty yards apart ... with all the gramophones playing the same tune. And all the forests shaved flat, chewed into wood pulp for the News of the World, or sawn up into gramophone cases.' And here, too, Orwell offers his first insights into a world dominated by officialdom and the administrative mentality, describing the colonial atmosphere as 'a stifling, stultifying world in which to live ... a world in which every word and every thought is censored'.[34]

During the middle 1930s Orwell rapidly established his reputation as a novelist, writing *Down and Out in Paris & London* (1933), which dealt with poverty and unemployment; *A Clergyman's Daughter* (1935), which linked the themes of poverty and the question of how to live a meaningful life after the loss of religious faith; and *Keep the Aspidistra Flying* (1936), which dwelt on the motif of individual failure in the face of a system of degrading work. We here also encounter Orwell's first view of socialism, which he parodied as 'Some kind of Aldous Huxley Brave New World: only not so amusing. Four hours a day in a model factory, tightening up bolt number 6003. Rations served out in grease-proof paper at the communal kitchen. Community-hikes from Marx Hostel to Lenin Hostel and back. Free abortion-clinics on all corners.'[35]

This view was to change dramatically swiftly. At the end of 1936 Orwell went to Spain to join Republican resistance to Franco's coup. In *Homage to Catalonia* (1938) he condemned not only fascism but also Moscow's subversion of the Republican cause. As importantly, he wrote that in Spain he had 'seen wonderful things, and at last really believe in Socialism, which I never did before'.[36] On his return to Britain this commitment was exemplified in *The Road to Wigan Pier* (1937). But this account of the life of the poor in the industrial north of Britain also included the observation that the physique of the people was declining because of 'the modern industrial technique which provides you with cheap substitutes for everything', adding that it might be found 'in the long run that tinned food is a deadlier weapon than the machine gun'. Orwell now argued that socialism, 'wholeheartedly applied, is a way out', because it would at least give the world enough to eat. But he also condemned socialist intellectuals, who included too many fruit juice drinkers, nudists and sandal-wearers, as being out of touch with the common people. Many socialists he feared also had an overly enlarged sense of order, and tended to see mechanical progress as an end-in-itself, 'almost as a kind of religion', or cult of order and efficiency. But, protested Orwell, 'we can actually feel the tendency of the machine to make a fully human life impossible', for machinery tended 'to frustrate the human need for effort and creation'. The logical end of mechanical progress was 'to reduce the human being to something resembling a brain in a bottle', even if 'the machine has got to be accepted … grudgingly and suspiciously'.[37] In the last and best of his pre-war novels, *Coming Up For Air* (1939), this hostility to modernity as such is again a key theme. At one point the narrator enters a milk-bar, then one of the great novelties of the period. He exclaims:

> There's a kind of atmosphere about these places that gets me down. Everything slick and shiny and streamlined; mirrors, enamel, and chromium plate whichever direction you look in. Everything spent on the decorations and nothing on the food. No real food at all. Just lists of stuff with American names, sort of phantom stuff that you can't taste and can hardly believe in the existence of … A sort of propaganda floating around, mixed up with the noise of the radio, to the effect that food doesn't matter, comfort doesn't matter, nothing matters except slickness and shininess and streamlining.[38]

This resistance to what Bernard Crick has referred to as 'Fordification',[39] a combination of mass-production techniques with a technocentric aesthetic, was to remain an enduring theme. Orwell's growing concern was particularly with the totalitarian disregard for historical truth, as well as the possibility that mass propaganda could produce a population who no longer loved liberty. Increasingly he feared the destruction of the ideal of the 'autonomous individual', and the belief that socialists might so blindly worship at the altar of industrial progress that they would forgo democracy and any other but mass-produced goods.

In the early 1940s Orwell's critique shifted in several ways. He began to pay greater heed to the dangers of technocrats and bureaucrats in general. During the Second World War he warned of the dangers of what he termed at one point 'the falsity of the hedonistic attitude to life', which he claimed Hitler had recognized.[40] He now increasingly believed, too, that both fascism and communism were 'moving towards a form of oligarchical collectivism'.[41] Orwell however clearly retained his socialist commitment during the wartime period as well as after. In *The Lion and the Unicorn* (1941) he attempted to define a unique brand of British socialism which could reconcile the need to centralize the economy with a sense of the value of freedom, privacy, the dislike of regimentation and an incorruptible belief in law. He hoped that working-class culture, which he believed did not encourage power-worship, and retained instead a vital measure of moral integrity, might help sustain these values. But he still warned of 'the persistent effort to chip away English morale and spread a hedonistic, what-do-I-get-out-of-it attitude to life'.[42] Thus, as he put it later, England might provide 'the much needed alternative to Russian authoritarianism on the one hand and American materialism on the other'.[43] Little of this optimism, however, was evident in his wartime satire, *Animal Farm* (1945), though this work, in which the pigs who lead the revolution against human exploitation eventually come to resemble their former masters, foreshadows perhaps the chief theme of Orwell's greatest work, the betrayal of the revolution by intellectuals.

Nineteen Eighty-Four (1949)

While *Nineteen Eighty-Four* has commonly been interpreted as an anti-Stalinist tract, it has been suggested here that Orwell combined certain anti-modernist and anti-capitalist themes with a hostility to Stalinism and Fascism. Others have taken a similar view. Richard Rees, for instance, has seen the main thrust of the work as being 'simply that our industrial civilisation is tending to deracinate and debilitate us', while John Mander describes the novel as 'an anthology of all the things he hated most; this explains why many of its horrors are capitalist rather than Stalinist horrors'.[44] Despite the prominence of the anti-communist interpretation of the work, Orwell himself wrote that it was

> NOT intended as an attack on Socialism or on the British Labour Party (of which I am a supporter) but as a show-up of the perversions to which a centralised economy is liable and which have already partly been realised in Communism and Fascism. I do not believe that the kind of society I describe necessarily *will* arrive, but I believe (allowing of course for the fact that the book is a satire) that something resembling it *could* arrive. I believe also that totalitarian ideas have taken root in the minds of intellectuals everywhere, and I have tried to draw these ideas out to their logical consequences.[45]

Nineteen Eighty-Four is set in Oceania, Airstrip One, which has become an American province.[46] As explained in Emmanuel Goldstein's *Theory and Practice of Oligarchical Collectivism*, the book within the book, which turns out to be written by Inner Party leaders, the existing world system is one of three great states engaged in permanent warfare both for labour-power and as a means of ruling their own populations.[47] These wars expend the results of machine production without actually raising the standard of living, which Orwell implies would threaten their power and legitimacy because greater equality would threaten hierarchy. The three states share the same set of values, variously defined as Ingsoc, Neo-Bolshevism and the Obliteration of the Self. The object of war is thus to maintain the ruling structures of the three regimes, hence the truthfulness of the apparent paradox, 'War is Peace.' In Oceania the Party is an oligarchy, though 'not a class in the old sense of the word'. In keeping with a Nietzschean gloss on Social Darwinism, Inner Party members seek power for its own sake: 'power is not a means, it is an end', a leading Inner Party member insists. Ultimately the Party's power rests upon its ability to manipulate the past: 'Who controls the past controls the future; who controls the present controls the past.' The Party even insists that 'Reality exists in the human mind, and nowhere else.'[48]

If imperfect, the system nonetheless functions adequately. Amidst an atmosphere of drabness, shortages and monotony, the novel recounts the clumsy rebellion of Winston Smith, an anti-heroic lower-level Outer Party member, whose crimes are writing a diary and having an affair with Julia, Orwell's crudely drawn female character, who is 'corrupt to the bones'. Winston is of course caught, tortured and then rehabilitated. At the end 'He loved Big Brother.' As a satire or caricature of totalitarianism the novel focuses on two dominant themes. The first is the totalitarian demand for complete loyalty, which requires slavish submission by the intellectuals, the debasement of logic and language ('doublethink' and 'newspeak'), the evocation of the worst popular passions ('Hate Week'), and hostility to individualism ('ownlife'), with even eroticism suppressed in the name of war-fever and leader-worship. Secondly, there is the omnipresence of state power: the telescreen, the posters of Big Brother (who may or may not actually exist), the ubiquitous Thought Police, the continuous rewriting of the past. The grotesquely simple and blatantly unapologetic dishonesty of the regime stands out for many commentators as the grand theme of the work; one of Orwell's greatest concerns about totalitarianism was that it attacked the concept of objective truth. We are not led by Orwell to believe that this regime is likely to collapse from internal pressures, for the Party stifles its own dissent easily. Winston reflects, thus, that 'if there was hope, it must lie in the proles'.[49] But they are kept from rebelling by a diet of mass literature, heavy physical work, films, football, beer and gambling. No one cares what they say, and Winston is informed, in a crude paraphrasing of Marxist theory, that they could not rebel until they were conscious, and vice versa. Nonetheless the proles retain a moral honesty and authenticity which Orwell clearly believed they possessed in real life. They, crucially, have not been corrupted by power-worship. Neither, at least not completely, has Winston, left pondering his fate at the Chestnut Tree café. But then his rebellion never stood much chance of success anyway.

The corruption of the intelligentsia by the lust for power, then, remains the central and most compelling theme of Orwell's chief work, and one which we have seen was clearly foreshadowed in his major writings from the mid-1930s onwards. The nineteenth-century faith in the guiding role to be played in a post-aristocratic society by a Coleridgian clerisy or Carlylean man of letters had thus been utterly misplaced. As Richard Rees has written, Orwell's main conclusion respecting contemporary politics was that the working class lacked 'any power to counteract the decadence of the intellectuals and the bestiality of the hate-mongering political fanatics'.[50] Orwell himself, in his final years, and despite chronic poor health, clearly attempted some reckoning with this increasingly pessimistic assessment. In a book review published in 1945 he proclaimed the necessity of restoring what he termed 'the religious attitude of life' in order to counteract 'the disastrous consequences of worshipping man instead of God'. He became convinced (perhaps quite erroneously) that 'the modern cult of power worship is bound up with the modern man's feeling that life here and now is the only life there is'.[51] Yet at the same time he had himself lost his religious faith, and could propose no secular alternative to either religion or power-worship. Re-establishing a sense of moral certainty eluded him to the end, though it remained crucial to his hope for the future. For capitalism, he proclaimed, in reviewing Friedrich Hayek's *The Road to Serfdom*, produced only 'dole queues, the scramble for markets, and war', while collectivism led 'to concentration camps, leader worship, and war'. There seemed to be no alternative to this dismal choice between possible human fates, 'unless a planned economy can be somehow combined with freedom of the individual, which can only happen if the concept of right and wrong is restored to politics'.[52] Orwell did not know how this plea for decency, which some have seen as his central and abiding concern, might be realized. But he still believed in (what many Cold War readers failed to acknowledge) democratic socialism of a non-Marxian and peculiarly English type to be a step in the right direction, if somehow 'the religious attitude of life' could be wedded to it.

There are thus major differences as well as similarities between Huxley's and Orwell's visions of the future nightmare. Huxley's is clean, efficient, complacent, defined by pleasure, Orwell's clumsy, crude, brutal and focused on pain. Huxley penetrated much further into the behavioural psychology of consumer society. Yet Orwell captured the true horrors of the twentieth century far more accurately, and the manipulative nature of popular, mass culture is an essential ingredient in his description of it: what stood between Huxley and the world of *Nineteen Eighty-Four* was Hitler. Huxley had foreseen what Wells seemingly had not, the dark side of machine civilization, that progress was 'a swindle' (and Wells, Orwell too would allege, was incapable of appreciating the real threat of totalitarianism). Rees has argued that 'Aldous Huxley's theory is equally plausible: that people can be reduced to a servile condition by means of mass-suggestion, hypnopaedia and drugs, without any overt brutality or cruelty and without any conscious suffering.'[53] Orwell did not agree with Huxley and other 'neo-pessimists', or with a religious reckoning which was not essentially geared to the improvement of public morals. (It has been contended that Orwell was moving back towards Christianity. But evidence for this is slight; Orwell would reiterate the need to 'reinstate the belief in human brotherhood without the need of a "next world" to give it meaning'.[54]) With Huxley he agreed that truth-telling, history-writing, was essential to keeping society in balance. And he shared with Huxley, but in a much deeper and intense way, a sense of the betrayal of the intellectuals as a class, of their descent into the mental preoccupation with a 'struggle for power'. It was this *voluntary* betrayal, not instigated by breeding, which produced Orwell's dictatorship, though it did not touch the essential humanity of the working classes, whose decency was epitomized by their behaviour in Barcelona in 1937. Huxley continued to maintain that control based upon reward was likely to be more effective, in the long run, than that based upon violence. But Orwell came to see Huxley's 'completely materialistic vulgar civilization based on hedonism' as 'a danger past', and vastly less threatening than totalitarianism, contending that instead:

> we are in danger of quite a different kind of world, the centralised slave state, ruled over by a small clique who are in effect a new ruling class, though they might be adoptive rather than hereditary. Such a state would not be hedonistic, on the contrary its dynamic would come from some kind of rabid nationalism and leader-worship.[55]

Hence he condemned *Brave New World* for not providing an account of the motive of this ruling class, for not providing a reason 'why society should be stratified in the elaborate way that is described', particularly in terms of 'power-hunger'.[56] And Huxley was satirizing the desire for equality, which Orwell essentially admired and supported. Critics thus agree that Zamyatin's *We* was much closer in intent and design to *Nineteen Eighty-Four*; indeed Orwell thought Huxley owed an unacknowledged debt to it. For Zamyatin, with Arthur Koestler in *Darkness at Noon* and Jack London in *The Iron Heel*, possessed 'an intuitive grasp of the irrational side of totalitarianism – human sacrifice, cruelty as an end in itself, the worship of a Leader who is credited with divine attributes',[57] and it was this which in Orwell's view made Zamyatin's book superior to Huxley's.

Conclusion: Some other dystopian trends after 1900

Besides the major texts assessed so far here, a number of other twentieth-century dystopias merit mention. In some cases apparent dystopias were vehicles for socialist propaganda and aimed at capitalism, as in London's *The Iron Heel* (1907), where an 'Oligarchy' of 'trusts' or capitalist dictatorship is orchestrated from Wall Street, and opposed by socialist revolutionaries.[58] Feminist writers also contributed a variety of other dystopian visions in this period, including Charlotte Perkins Gilman's *With Her in Ourland* (1916), a response in part to her own utopian *Herland* (1915).[59] Extremely long-term evolutionary themes prevail in Olaf Stapledon's *Last and First Men* (1930), in which many existing dystopian ideas – American predominance, an emergent American World State which collapses, eugenic manipulation – are explored. In Stapledon it is the most vulgar American traits which triumph.[60] The rise of fascism provoked a number of fictional satires. In the best-known of these, Katharine Burdekin's *Swastika Night* (1937), a pioneering feminist critique, it is the triumph of the 'soldierly virtues' of bloodshed, brutality and ruthlessness against the Christian virtues of gentleness, mercy and love which mark modern degeneracy.[61] Many subsequent works would portray a damning indictment of hedonism as a central and possibly fatal moral weakness of western liberal societies, such as Ray Bradbury's famous *Fahrenheit 451* (1953). Other notable contributions after the Second World War include William Golding's *The Lord of the Flies* (1954), Ayn Rand's *Atlas Shrugged* (1957), Anthony Burgess's *A Clockwork Orange* (1962), Pierre Boulle's *Planet of the Apes* (1963), Robert Rimmer's *The Harrad Experiment* (1966), Ira Levin's *This Perfect Day* (1970) and Ernest Callenbach's *Ecotopia* (1975). Notable later feminist dystopias include Margaret Atwood's *The Handmaid's Tale* (1986), which is set in the United States in the near future. A number of these are discussed in later essays in this volume.

NOTES

1 See Lyman Tower Sargent, 'The Three Faces of Utopianism Revisited', *Utopian Studies* 5:1 (1994), 1–37. On dystopia, see Mark Hillegas, *The Future as Nightmare: H. G. Wells and the Anti-Utopians* (Carbondale: Southern Illinois University Press, 1967); W. Warren Wagar, *Terminal Visions: The Literature of Last Things* (Bloomington: Indiana University Press, 1982); M. Keith Booker, *The Dystopian Impulse in Modern Literature* (Westport, CT: Greenwood Press, 1994); Erika Gottlieb, *Utopian Fiction East and West* (Montreal: McGill-Queen's University Press, 2001).
2 Herbert Marcuse, *Five Lectures: Psychoanalysis, Politics, and Utopia* (Harmondsworth: Penguin, 1970).
3 Karl Popper, *The Open Society and its Enemies*, rev. edn (Princeton University Press, 1950).
4 Reprinted in Gregory Claeys (ed.), *Utopias of the British Enlightenment* (Cambridge University Press, 1994).
5 T. R. Malthus, *An Essay on the Principle of Population; or, a View of its Past and Present Effects on Human Happiness; with an Inquiry into our Prospects Respecting the Future Removal or Mitigation of the Effects which it Occasions. A New Edition, very much Enlarged* (1798) (London: Printed for J. Johnson by T. Bensley, 1803).
6 Mary Shelley, *Frankenstein, or the Modern Prometheus* (London: n.p., 1818).
7 Karl Pearson, *The Ethic of Freethought and Other Addresses and Essays* (London: T. Fisher Unwin, 1888), p. 319.
8 On these texts see Gregory Claeys (ed.), *Late Victorian Utopias* (6 vols., London: Pickering and Chatto, 2008), introduction.
9 Richard Jefferies, *After London; or, Wild England* (London: Cassell & Co, 1885).
10 Edward Carpenter, *Ioläus: An Anthology of Friendship* (1908) (New York: Mitchell Kennerley, 1917).
11 On Wells's dystopian writings, see in particular Bernard Bergonzi, *The Early H. G. Wells: A Study of the Scientific Romances* (Manchester University Press, 1961); John Huntington, *The Logic of Fantasy: H. G. Wells and Science Fiction* (New York: Columbia University Press, 1962); Frank McConnell, *The Science Fiction of H. G. Wells* (Oxford University Press, 1981); Patrick Parrinder, *Shadows of the Future: H. G. Wells, Science Fiction, and Prophecy* (Syracuse University Press, 1995). A good overview of Wells's writings is J. R. Hammond, *An*

H. G. Wells Companion (London: Macmillan, 1979). Wells's attitudes towards science are particularly explored in Roslynn D. Haynes, *H. G. Wells: Discoverer of the Future* (London: Macmillan, 1980).

12 H. G. Wells, *The Sleeper Awakes and Men Like Gods* (London: Odham's Press, n.d.), p. 249; *The Time Machine* (London: Heinemann, 1937), p. 84; *The Island of Doctor Moreau* (London: William Heinemann, 1896), p. 116; *When the Sleeper Awakes* (London: Harper, 1899), pp. 69, 169, 236.

13 H. G. Wells, *The First Men in the Moon* (London: G. Newnes, 1901), p. 129.

14 Yevgeny Zamyatin, *We* (1921) (London: Jonathan Cape, 1970), p. 186.

15 George Orwell, *The Complete Works*, ed. Peter Davison (20 vols., London: Secker & Warburg, 1998), vol. 18, p. 15.

16 A good introduction is Katie de Koster (ed.), *Readings on Brave New World* (San Diego: Greenhaven Press, 1999).

17 George Orwell, *The Collected Essays, Journalism and Letters of George Orwell* (4 vols., London: Secker & Warburg, 1968), p. 295.

18 Aldous Huxley, *Brave New World* (Harmondsworth: Penguin, 1955), p. 12.

19 Sybille Bedford, *Aldous Huxley: A Biography* (2 vols., London: Chatto & Windus, 1973), vol. 1, p. 244.

20 Huxley, *Brave New World*, pp. 174, 184–5, 167, 44.

21 Aldous Huxley, *Themes and Variations* (London: Chatto & Windus, 1950), p. 247.

22 Aldous Huxley, *Brave New World Revisited* (London: Harper and Row, 1965), pp. 4, 13.

23 Aldous Huxley, *Proper Studies* (London: Chatto & Windus, 1929), p. 13.

24 Huxley, *Brave New World Revisited*, p. 110.

25 Bedford, *Aldous Huxley*, vol. 2, p. 241.

26 Aldous Huxley, *Island* (London: Chatto & Windus, 1962), p. 210.

27 Huxley, *Proper Studies*, p. ix.

28 Huxley, *Proper Studies*, pp. 157, 215; *Ends and Means. An Enquiry into the Nature of Ideals and into the Methods Employed for their Realization* (London: Chatto & Windus, 1937), pp. 3, 59, 62; *Collected Essays* (London: Harper & Row, 1958), p. 257; *Ends and Means*, pp. 59, 62.

29 George Orwell, *Nineteen Eighty-Four* (London: Secker & Warburg, 1949).

30 For a contrast of the texts, see Peter Firchow, *The End of Utopia: A Study of Aldous Huxley's 'Brave New World'* (Cranbury, NJ: Associated University Presses, 1984) and Jenni Calder, *Huxley and Orwell, 'Brave New World' and 'Nineteen Eighty-Four'* (London: Edward Arnold, 1976). The literature on Orwell is now large. A good introduction is John Rodden (ed.), *The Cambridge Companion to George Orwell* (Cambridge University Press, 2007). The standard biography is Bernard Crick, *George Orwell: A Life* (Harmondsworth: Penguin, 1980).

31 Orwell, *Collected Essays*, vol. 4, p. 359.

32 Crick, *George Orwell*, p. 16.

33 Orwell, *Collected Essays*, vol. 1, p. 26.

34 George Orwell, *The Complete Novels of George Orwell* (Harmondsworth: Penguin, 1983), pp. 96, 113.

35 *Ibid.*, p. 632.

36 Orwell, *Complete Works*, vol. 11, p. 28.

37 George Orwell, *The Road to Wigan Pier* (1937) (London: Secker & Warburg, 1959), pp. 99, 202.

38 Orwell, *Complete Novels*, pp. 442–3.
39 Crick, *George Orwell*, p. 239.
40 Orwell, *Collected Essays*, vol. 2, p. 29.
41 *Ibid.*, vol. 2, pp. 40–2.
42 *Ibid.*, vol. 2, p. 103.
43 *Ibid.*, vol. 3, p. 47.
44 Richard Rees, *George Orwell: Fugitive from the Camp of Victory* (London: Secker & Warburg, 1961), p. 116; John Mander, 'George Orwell's Politics', *Contemporary Review* (1960), 118.
45 Orwell, *Collected Essays*, vol. 4, p. 564.
46 Studies of the text include: William Steinhoff, *The Road to 1984* (London: Weidenfeld & Nicolson, 1975); Irving Howe (ed.), *1984 Revisited: Totalitarianism in Our Century* (London: Harper & Row, 1983); Peter Stansky (ed.), *On Nineteen Eighty-Four* (New York: W. H. Freeman & Co., 1983); Ejner J. Jensen (ed.), *On the Future of Nineteen Eighty-Four* (Ann Arbor: University of Michigan Press, 1984); Paul Chilton and Crispin Aubrey (eds.), *Nineteen Eighty-Four in 1984* (London: Comedia Publishing Group, 1983).
47 James Burnham, *The Managerial Revolution* (London: Putnam, 1942), p. 69. Orwell wrote no less than five times between 1944 and 1947 on this book. Burnham in turn summarized the views of various writers, notably Mosca, Michels, Ostrogorski, Pareto and Sorel.
48 Orwell, *Complete Novels*, pp. 863, 886.
49 *Ibid.*, p. 783.
50 Rees, *George Orwell*, p. 84.
51 Orwell, *Collected Essays*, vol. 3, p. 126.
52 *Ibid.*, vol. 3, p. 144.
53 Rees, *George Orwell*, p. 116.
54 Orwell, *Complete Works*, vol. 12, p. 126.
55 *Ibid.*, vol. 15, p. 310.
56 *Ibid.*, vol. 18, p. 15.
57 Orwell, *Collected Essays*, vol. 4, p. 75.
58 Jack London, *The Iron Heel* (New York: Macmillan, 1907).
59 Charlotte Perkins Gilman, *With Her in Ourland* (1916) (Westport, CT: Greenwood Press, 1997); *Herland* (1915) (New York: Panther, 1979).
60 Olaf Stapledon, *Last and First Men: A Story of the Near and Far Future* (London: Methuen & Co., 1930), p. 30.
61 Katharine Burdekin, *Swastika Night* (1937) (London: Lawrence & Wishart, 1985).

BIBLIOGRAPHY

Bedford, Sybille, *Aldous Huxley: A Biography* (2 vols., London: Chatto & Windus, 1973).
Bergonzi, Bernard, *The Early H. G. Wells: A Study of the Scientific Romances* (Manchester University Press, 1961).
Blatchford, Robert, *The Sorcery Shop* (London: Clarion Press, 1907).
Booker, M. Keith, *The Dystopian Impulse in Modern Literature* (Westport, CT: Greenwood Press, 1994).
Burdekin, Katharine, *Swastika Night* (1937) (London: Lawrence & Wishart, 1985).

Burnham, James, *The Managerial Revolution* (London: Putnam, 1942).

Calder, Jenni, *Huxley and Orwell: 'Brave New World' and 'Nineteen Eighty-Four'* (London: Edward Arnold, 1976).

Carpenter, Edward, *Ioläus: An Anthology of Friendship* (1908) (New York: Mitchell Kennerley, 1917).

Chilton, Paul and Crispin Aubrey (eds.), *Nineteen Eighty-Four in 1984* (London: Comedia Publishing Group, 1983).

Claeys, Gregory, *The French Revolution Debate in Britain* (Basingstoke: Palgrave, 2007).

Claeys, Gregory (ed.), *Late Victorian Utopias* (6 vols., London: Pickering and Chatto, 2008).

   (ed.) *Modern British Utopias 1700–1850* (8 vols., London: Pickering and Chatto, 1997).

   (ed.) *Utopias of the British Enlightenment* (Cambridge University Press, 1994).

Crick, Bernard, *George Orwell: A Life* (Harmondsworth: Penguin, 1980).

de Koster, Katie (ed.), *Readings on Brave New World* (San Diego: Greenhaven Press, 1999).

Firchow, Peter, *The End of Utopia: A Study of Aldous Huxley's 'Brave New World'* (Cranbury, NJ: Associated University Presses, 1984).

Gilman, Charlotte Perkins, *Herland* (1915) (New York: Panther, 1979).

   With Her in Ourland (1916) (Westport, CT: Greenwood Press, 1997).

Gottlieb, Erika, *Utopian Fiction East and West* (Montreal: McGill-Queen's University Press, 2001).

Hammond, J. R., *An H. G. Wells Companion* (London: Macmillan, 1979).

Hay, William, *Three Hundred Years Hence* (London: Newman & Co., 1881).

Haynes, Roslynn D., *H. G. Wells: Discoverer of the Future* (London: Macmillan, 1980).

Hillegas, Mark, *The Future as Nightmare: H. G. Wells and the Anti-Utopians* (Carbondale: Southern Illinois University Press, 1967).

Howe, Irving (ed.), *1984 Revisited: Totalitarianism in Our Century* (London: Harper & Row, 1983).

Huntington, John, *The Logic of Fantasy: H. G. Wells and Science Fiction* (New York: Columbia University Press, 1962).

Huxley, Aldous, *Brave New World* (1932) (Harmondsworth: Penguin, 1955).

   Brave New World Revisited (1958) (New York: Harper & Row, 1965).

   Collected Essays (New York: Harper & Row, 1958).

   Ends and Means: An Enquiry into the Nature of Ideals and into the Methods Employed for their Realization (London: Chatto & Windus, 1937).

   Island (London, Chatto & Windus, 1962).

   Proper Studies (London: Chatto & Windus, 1929).

   Themes and Variations (London: Chatto & Windus, 1950).

Jefferies, Richard, *After London; or, Wild England* (London: Cassell & Co, 1885).

Jensen, Ejner J. (ed.), *On the Future of Nineteen Eighty-Four* (Ann Arbor: University of Michigan Press, 1984).

London, Jack, *The Iron Heel* (New York: Macmillan, 1907).

Malthus, T. R., *An Essay on the Principle of Population; or, a View of its Past and Present Effects on Human Happiness; with an Inquiry into our Prospects Respecting the Future Removal or Mitigation of the Effects which it Occasions.*

A New Edition, very much Enlarged (1798) (London: Printed for J. Johnson by T. Bensley, 1803).

Mander, John, 'George Orwell's Politics', *Contemporary Review* (1960).

Marcuse, Herbert, *Five Lectures: Psychoanalysis, Politics, and Utopia* (Harmondsworth, Penguin, 1970).

McConnell, Frank, *The Science Fiction of H. G. Wells* (Oxford University Press, 1981).

Morris, William, *The Collected Letters of William Morris*, ed. Norman Kelvin (4 vols., Princeton University Press, 1987).

Orwell, George, *The Collected Essays, Journalism and Letters of George Orwell* (4 vols., London: Secker & Warburg, 1968).

The Complete Novels of George Orwell (Harmondsworth: Penguin, 1983).

The Complete Works, ed. *Peter Davison* (20 vols., London: Secker & Warburg, 1998).

Nineteen Eighty-Four (London: Secker & Warburg, 1949).

The Road to Wigan Pier (1937) (London: Secker & Warburg, 1959).

Parrinder, Patrick, *Shadows of the Future: H. G. Wells, Science Fiction, and Prophecy* (Syracuse, NY: Syracuse University Press, 1995).

Pearson, Karl, *The Ethic of Freethought and Other Addresses and Essays* (London: T. Fisher Unwin, 1888).

Popper, Karl, *The Open Society and its Enemies*, rev. edn (Princeton University Press, 1950).

Rees, Richard, *George Orwell: Fugitive from the Camp of Victory* (London: Secker & Warburg, 1961).

Rodden, John (ed.), *The Cambridge Companion to George Orwell* (Cambridge University Press, 2007).

Sargent, Lyman Tower, 'The Three Faces of Utopianism Revisited', *Utopian Studies* 5:1 (1994), 1–37.

Shelley, Mary, *Frankenstein, or the Modern Prometheus* (London: n.p., 1818).

Stansky, Peter (ed.), *On Nineteen Eighty-Four* (New York: W. H. Freeman & Co., 1983).

Stapledon, Olaf, *Last and First Men* (London: Methuen & Co., 1930).

Steinhoff, William, *The Road to 1984* (London: Weidenfeld & Nicolson, 1975).

Wagar, W. Warren, *Terminal Visions: The Literature of Last Things* (Bloomington: Indiana University Press, 1982).

Wells, H. G., *The First Men in the Moon* (London: G. Newnes, 1901).

The Island of Doctor Moreau (London: William Heinemann, 1896).

The Sleeper Awakes and Men Like Gods (London: Odham's Press, n.d.).

When the Sleeper Awakes (London: Harper, 1899).

The Time Machine (London: Heinemann, 1937).

Zamyatin, Yevgeny, *We* (1921) (London: Jonathan Cape, 1970).

PART II

Literature

6

PETER FITTING

Utopia, dystopia and science fiction

The once and often suggestive field of utopian fantasy has been exploited, perhaps under the comic-book definition, into a bastard literary device known as 'science fiction.' This product bears about the same resemblance to utopian speculation that the tales of Horatio Alger bore to the economic theories of Adam Smith.[1]

[Literary] forms are the common property ... of writers and audiences or readers, before any communicative composition can occur.[2]

Despite some dismissals of science fiction's significance for utopian writing, it is impossible to study the utopias and dystopias of the past fifty years or more without acknowledging the central role of science fiction. Darko Suvin and Lyman Tower Sargent (among others) have reviewed and clarified the existing definitions of utopia and – unlike science fiction – there is little disagreement today about the boundaries and characteristics of the genre.[3] Sargent writes that utopia is 'a non-existent society described in considerable detail and normally located in time and space'.[4] This definition includes the positive utopia (eutopia) as well as its negative manifestations – the dystopia and the anti-utopia.[5] Suvin, on the other hand, restricts his definition to the positive utopia: 'the verbal construction of a particular quasi human community where sociopolitical institutions, norms, and individual relationships are organized according to a *more perfect principle* than in the author's community ...'.[6]

Science fiction, on the other hand, has proved much harder to define and there is still no single accepted definition of the genre: 'There is no good reason to expect', the editors of the *Encyclopedia of Science Fiction* tell us, 'that a workable definition of SF will ever be established.'[7] Darko Suvin's celebrated characterization of science fiction as the 'literature of cognitive estrangement' has been important in forcing critics to look beyond definitions that relied primarily on a work's contents – however crucial themes and motifs like robots or space travel may be to the genre – and his definition refocused critical efforts on how science fiction functions: '*SF is, then, a literary genre whose necessary and sufficient conditions are the presence and interaction of estrangement and cognition, and whose main formal device is an imaginative framework alternative to the author's empirical environment.'*[8]

Suvin goes on to describe utopia as a sub-genre of science fiction,[9] a dubious categorization which complicates our understanding of the relationship between the two genres. To do this, Suvin grounds this definition in a division of all prose literature into either 'naturalistic' or 'estranged' narratives; and he also argues that modern science fiction is but the latest manifestation of a genre which is several thousand years old. Finally, Suvin's definition of science fiction includes a normative dimension, something which is generally absent from definitions of utopia. Either a work meets the formal criteria of the utopian genre or it does not. There are certainly utopias whose alternative society I do not like or which many readers may find abhorrent (B. F. Skinner's 1948 *Walden Two* is a well-known example[10]), but this does not mean that such works are not utopias. Other different utopias contain varying degrees of aesthetic qualities, and some are recognized for their literary values while others are studied primarily for their depiction of an alternative society. Lyman Tower Sargent's authoritative bibliography of *British and American Utopian Literature*, for instance, does not exclude works based on literary merit.[11] In the case of science fiction, the concepts of 'cognitive' and 'estrangement' introduce a normative element into the definition, since such judgments are ultimately subjective; and Suvin goes on to exclude or dismiss much twentieth-century science fiction as inadequately cognitive.

There is an equivalent problem if one considers the effect or function of the utopia in terms of estrangement. First of all, despite Suvin's protests, there is a science fiction which continues to claim for itself some predictive or extrapolative function, from the discussions of space travel in the science-fiction magazines of the 1940s to the dystopian forecasts of writers as diverse as John Brunner and Margaret Atwood. (That these predictions or blueprints have not been realized does not really change their status.) To an even greater degree, the effect or function of a utopia is for many readers that of a blueprint or representation of a better society, an attitude that was certainly shared by the many readers of Edward Bellamy who went on to found Bellamy Clubs to discuss the implementation of his ideas; as well as by those who wrote to warn about the dangers of Bellamy's socialism. This practical or modelling use of the utopian form can be seen as recently as Ernest Callenbach's 1975 *Ecotopia* (and its sequel describing the transition to utopia in *Ecotopia Emerging* in 1981). Even the 'critical utopias' of the 1970s were often perceived as outlining the essential components of a better society and of having been designed to encourage the reader to work towards those goals; or at a minimum, to give the reader an indication of what needed to be changed in her own society (to make the world a better place).

While the utopian form – particularly as prose narrative – stretches back at least to More's 1516 *Utopia*, what today's readers recognize as science fiction with its familiar icons of the alien and the spaceship, its manifestations in a multiplicity of media – from stories and novels to comics, television and film – is a phenomenon which is at best 200 years old. Arguments have been made for including some of the works of Lucian or of Cyrano de Bergerac and Kepler in the science-fiction canon, but today's readers might not recognize or consider such work as science fiction, and to discuss them here would obscure the specificity of modern science fiction as a response to the effects of the scientific transformation of the world beginning around the end of the eighteenth century: in the European awareness of history and the future, and in the increasing impact of the scientific method and of technological change on people's lives. Accordingly many critics set the birth of modern science fiction in the nineteenth century, some arguing for Mary Shelley's *Frankenstein* (1818) or H. G. Wells's *The Time Machine* (1895) – or Jules Verne's third novel, *Journey to the Centre of the Earth* (*Voyage au centre de la terre*), 1864; or *From the Earth to the Moon* the following year (*De la Terre à la Lune*); while others identify it with Hugo Gernsback's *Ralph 124C 41+* (1925),[12] or with his launching of *Amazing Stories: The Magazine of Scientifiction* in April 1926 (he only coined the term 'science fiction' a few years later). Gernsback is a significant figure in the understanding of modern science fiction (at least in the United States) insofar as he epitomizes the enthusiasm for the possibilities of science and technology. He was in fact an amateur inventor and before *Amazing Stories* he had published magazines like *Electrical Experimenter*, *Modern Electrics*, *Science & Invention* and *Radio News* (and many others).

The stories published in the US magazines in the 1930s and 1940s are different from earlier estranged narratives (like those of Lucian or Kepler) – first of all, because of the enormous growth and change in readership in the late nineteenth and early twentieth centuries. Indeed, science fiction is almost from the beginning a popular form and, with a bit of editing, the works of Verne and Wells were easily recognizable to Gernsback's readers as science fiction. In fact, the construction of a science-fiction canon is an important component of the early issues of *Amazing Stories*, where Gernsback published (and often shortened) works by Edgar Alan Poe, Jules Verne and H. G. Wells alongside original stories.[13] Another aspect of the construction of modern science fiction as a recognizable form and body of work can be seen in its immediate connection to the new medium of the cinema: one of the first film narratives is in fact science fiction, Georges Méliès's *Voyage to the Moon* (*Voyage dans la Lune*, 1902), a 14-minute version of the Jules Verne story. Indeed, all three of the nineteenth-century texts in contention as the 'first' science-fiction novel – *Frankenstein, Journey to the Centre of the Earth* and *The Time Machine* – have been filmed several times, although the film versions of the oldest of these novels – *Frankenstein* – are perceived more as horror films than as science fiction.[14] This close relationship with film underlines the modernity of science fiction when juxtaposed to the centuries-old tradition of the utopian narrative – whose basic structure has not changed (the voyage to the alternative society followed by the description of a better society) and, because of the focus on description, has little affinity with film. While there are literally thousands of science-fiction films (and hundreds of books about science-fiction film), most people would have trouble naming more than one or two utopian films.

The intersection of modern science fiction and utopia begins with what I consider the foundational characteristic of science fiction, namely its ability to reflect or express our hopes and fears about the future, and more specifically to link those hopes and fears to science and technology. Rather than being set in the future, most utopias before the nineteenth century were set *elsewhere* – on some imaginary island or unexplored region of the earth – a narrative strategy which continues to appear in utopian fiction well into the twentieth century: from the interior of South America in *Herland* (1915) to the setting of utopias in outer space. This last development can already be found, of course, in Cyrano de Bergerac's seventeenth-century voyages to the Moon and the Sun, or much earlier, in Lucian's *True History* (second century CE); and this setting can still be found in many contemporary science-fiction utopias (e.g., Ursula K. Le Guin's Anarres or Kim Stanley Robinson's Mars). The awareness of the future and of the possibility of social change is often seen as emerging in Europe in the late eighteenth century, particularly following the French Revolution, and it brings a new dimension to utopian writing. The history of science fiction and utopia takes an important first step in this sense with the birth of the *uchronia* – specifically Louis-Sébastien Mercier's 1771 *Memoirs of the Year Two Thousand Five Hundred* (*L'An 2440: Un rêve s'il en fut jamais*).[15] In this inaugural time-travel utopia, the narrator falls asleep and wakes up 700 years later in a futuristic and transformed Paris. For utopian fiction the uchronia opened a new range of possibilities. Alternative societies could now be set in the future rather than simply depicted as already existing somewhere else; by extension an alternative society could be designed and planned and not just dreamed about: the present could be changed. Moreover, the uchronia allows the possibility of showing how the utopian society evolves out of the author's own world, and in many cases the transition to the new social order is specifically addressed, and often serves as the principal intrigue.

This leads to the second element that science fiction brings to the utopian genre, namely an awareness of the effects and importance of science and technology. By this I do not mean technology as a means for transporting the visitor to the new society, but the role of technology as a tool for social transformation. To visit unknown countries in the seventeenth and eighteenth centuries often involved a sea journey, while in the twentieth century this becomes a spaceship, which is hardly a significant change. Getting to the future can be a little more complicated. The most obvious means of time travel, as we have just seen in Mercier, is through the device of a character's falling asleep and awaking years later (better known in the English-speaking world through Washington Irving's 1819 'Rip van Winkle'). In English-language utopian fiction, the model is Edward Bellamy's *Looking Backward 2000–1887* (1888) where the protagonist awakens more than 100 years in the future to discover that there has been a peaceful transition to socialism in the United States.[16] Science fiction does of course offer the possibility of using technology to go to the future, a method introduced in H. G. Wells's *The Time Machine*. But again, like the transition from sailing vessel to spaceship, Wells's introduction of a machine to travel through time is not that different from falling asleep, for the time machine does not in any way change the future. Wells uses the time machine simply as a means of transportation. The novel is not about the impact of technology, although it certainly could be called a dystopia – it is a vision of the future in which class division and conflict have led to a degraded society in which the underground Morlocks feed on the degenerate remnants of the aristocracy whom they raise as cattle.[17]

While there were certainly dystopias and anti-utopias written prior to the twentieth century, the positive utopia was the prevailing manifestation of the genre until the first half of the century when these bleaker forms came to dominate (at least until the late 1960s). Social upheaval and the negative reactions to the prospect of socialism at the dawn of the twentieth century played an important role in the turn from utopia, as can be seen in the many hostile responses to Bellamy's work. Similar to Bellamy's provocative influence, Mark Hillegas has argued for the central role of Wells in the development of the anti-utopia, as a lightning rod for the critics of reason and progress:

> To an extraordinary degree the great anti-utopias are both continuations of the imagination of H. G. Wells and reactions against that imagination. At the same time they often attack ideas that Wells championed, in many cases ideas

which were in turn a protest against the decaying Victorian order of things. Altogether, it is doubtful that without Wells the anti-utopian phenomenon would ever have taken the shape it has.[18]

Of perhaps more consequence in this regard, however, was the Russian Revolution of 1917, which produced a living and breathing alternative to capitalism. The reality of the Soviet Union certainly contributed to the rise of the anti-utopia, beginning with Yevgeny Zamyatin's *We* (1921), followed by Aldous Huxley's 1932 *Brave New World* and George Orwell's 1949 *Nineteen Eighty-Four* (to cite the three best-known examples of the genre). For the epigraph to *Brave New World* Huxley cites the Russian philosopher Nikolai Berdyaev:

> Utopias seem very much more realizable than we had formerly supposed. Now we find ourselves facing a question which is painful in a new kind of way: how to avoid their actual realization.[19]

This attitude aptly sums up the rise of anti-utopianism in the twentieth century.

In contrast to these fears, the growth of science fiction as seen in the pulp magazines of the 1920s and 1930s in the United States was resolutely optimistic and increasingly convinced of the role of technology in the making of a better world (particularly in the years following the Great Depression). The optimism about the possibilities of science and technology are summed up, for instance, in the glowing images of the future as presented at the 1933/34 Chicago World's Fair and especially at the 1939/40 New York World's Fair (which was entitled 'Building The World of Tomorrow'). However, with the decision to use the atom bomb against civilian targets in Japan (in 1945), science fiction lost much of its optimism as the greatest invention of the twentieth century was used not to improve the world but to almost instantly kill some 200,000 people.

This dystopian mood, the sense of a threatened near future, can be seen in the titles of some of the studies of science fiction written as the genre began to grow in popularity and importance in the 1960s, beginning with Kingsley Amis's *New Maps of Hell* (which was first given as a series of lectures at Princeton in 1960). As the study of science fiction began to interest the academy, there was a strong focus on its dystopian characteristics, an attitude summed up by H. Bruce Franklin in 1966:

> Today the capitalist world's literary visions of the future are almost all nightmares. Anti-utopia seems to have triumphed ... The most widely-read survey of the science fiction of the 'free world' bears an apt title: *New Maps of Hell*. In this slough of despondency the dominant nineteenth-century American views of the future may seem laughably quaint and naive.[20]

Furthermore, in early studies like those of Chad Walsh, *From Utopia to Nightmare* (1962)[21] and Mark Hillegas, *The Future as Nightmare: H. G. Wells and the Anti-Utopians* (1967) there is also a tendency to conflate anti-utopia and dystopia, describing science fiction as predominantly pessimistic.

This is not to say that most utopias are entirely positive. Following More's example, most literary utopias in fact juxtapose a critique of the author's existing society (Book I of More's *Utopia*) with the description of the better society (Book II). However, unlike the rather even balance of the two books of More's *Utopia*, the proportion of social critique and the positive description of a new social system can vary greatly from work to work; some utopias only critique the author's existing social order implicitly; while at the other end of this spectrum, there are utopian works that focus almost entirely on social critique, leaving it up to the reader to imagine what a world without these injustices and inequalities would look like. But social critique and the critique of utopianism are not the same thing, and there is a clear distinction between dystopian social critique and the critique of the very idea of wanting to imagine a better world, whether the latter sort of criticism is aimed at a political system (as in Zamyatin's *We*) or because dreams of a better world here below are, in Thomas Molnar's words, a 'defiance of God'.[22] The critique of contemporary society expressed in the dystopia implies (or asserts) the need for change; the anti-utopia is, on the other hand, explicitly or implicitly a defence of the status quo.

Science fiction, accordingly, is more dystopian than anti-utopian. Nonetheless, as a literary genre grounded in the Enlightenment and the prospect of scientific and technological solutions to social problems, the use of the atom bomb against Japan posed a crucial dilemma for the science-fiction community. But science fiction's innate optimism and hope for change continued to manifest themselves in the 1950s even as some writers wrote of nuclear devastation, continuing war and/or some form of a future police state (e.g., Ray Bradbury's *Fahrenheit 451*); or presented more substantial critiques of the utopian dream as in the science fiction of Arthur C. Clarke (the ridiculing of the utopian experiment of New Athens in *Childhood's End*). While technological optimism was muted, some writers turned to non-technological solutions and visions. Interestingly enough, in a kind of dialectical reversal, it is the very menace of radioactive fallout and the resultant mutations which produce glimpses of a transformed future during this period, as in the utopian 'Zeeland' (New Zealand) glimpsed at the end of John Wyndham's *The Chrysalids* (1955) where radioactive fallout has produced a generation of mutated children, many of whom are telepathic; or Theodore Sturgeon's new collective form of humanity in his 1953

More than Human.[23] Moreover, during the darkest days of the McCarthy witch hunts, science fiction was one of the few places where social criticism flourished. Nowhere is this more evident than in Frederik Pohl and C. M. Kornbluth's 1952 'Gravy Planet' (republished in novel form as *The Space Merchants* in 1953). The novel is a satirical critique of capitalist consumerism through the eyes of an advertising executive. However faintly, it concludes with the utopian escape to Venus where some enlightened humans who question the validity of capitalism will start again: 'The human race needs Venus. It needs an unspoiled, unwrecked, unexploited, unlooted ... unpirated, undevastated [planet] that the race can expand into.'[24] The novels of Sturgeon and Wyndham underline the shift in 1950s science fiction away from an emphasis on technological progress to themes of some more generalized human transformation. In short, despite the dystopian fears generated by fears about nuclear war, I would argue that US science fiction is fundamentally optimistic.

Indeed the United States had emerged from the Second World War as the most powerful and prosperous nation on Earth, and in the 1950s various pundits proclaimed that the United States was in fact an achieved utopia (as in Morris Ernst's now forgotten novel *Utopia 1976* or in Clare Booth Luce's declaration that the twentieth century would be 'The American Century'). In 1956, for instance, the editors of *Fortune* magazine published a special edition outlining America's glowing prospects entitled 'The Fabulous Future: America in the Sixties'. Yet what was triumphantly hailed as a new era of prosperity was to some extent an illusion as many citizens were excluded from the American Dream: African Americans of course, as well as women and the poor. Rosa Park's refusal to move to the back of the bus happened in 1955, a year after the US Supreme Court had declared segregated schools 'inherently unequal and therefore unconstitutional', and Michael Harrington's *The Other America: Poverty in the United States* was published in 1962. By the early 1960s, then, these increasing tensions within US society led to various forms of resistance and struggle – in the Civil Rights Movement and the demonstrations against the war in Vietnam, and in the Women's Movement and the 'Counter Culture' – all of which challenged the smooth functioning of what had triumphantly been dubbed 'people's capitalism'. As the American consensus was torn apart the quest for alternatives had begun. This is the beginning of modern utopianism.

In the 1960s, under the impact of larger social trends, a new generation of writers brought new ideas and interests to the genre (the harbinger: Robert Heinlein's 1961 *Stranger in a Strange Land*) – attitudes summed up in the 21-year-old Samuel Delany's 1967 novel *The Einstein Intersection* with its theme of the necessity of change in a post-nuclear holocaust world filled with strange mutants.[25] This dystopian tendency ended definitively in the early 1970s with the publication of works like Ursula K. Le Guin's *The Dispossessed* (1974), which was quickly followed by a number of utopian novels by some of the most important of the younger generation of science-fiction writers, in particular Samuel Delany's *Triton* (1976) and Joanna Russ's *The Female Man* (1975) – in addition to Suzy McKee Charnas's 'science fantasy' *Motherlines* (1978).[26]

One way of understanding the particular affinity between science fiction and utopia in the 1970s is to look again at the rise of utopias in the seventeenth and eighteenth centuries, many of which were written as imaginary voyages. It was (precisely) the European voyages of discovery which contributed to the growing popularity of travel narratives and they in turn led to narratives of imaginary voyages: the accounts of real lands and peoples were followed by accounts of invented lands and peoples. Of course travel narratives and fantastic voyages have existed at least since the Greeks, as have voyages to the Moon and the Sun, but the moment of the European voyages of discovery corresponded to a flood of literary utopias. Insofar as these voyages of discovery made possible, as it were, their imaginary cousins, so something similar happened, I would argue, which accounts for the flourishing of utopia in the science fiction of the 1970s. The existence of science fiction, a genre which specialized in imaginary worlds and the future of our own planet (as much as the genre's innate optimism) provided a perfect narrative home for utopian speculation. Let me explain by turning to Ursula K. Le Guin's *The Left Hand of Darkness* (1969), which is not a utopia, but which can be seen as opening the utopian possibilities of science fiction.[27]

This prize-winning science-fiction novel grows out of arguments about sex and gender and the role of women in American society, a debate which had entered public consciousness in 1963 with Betty Friedan's *The Feminine Mystique*. A woman's choices in life seemed to be determined by her biology (a position championed by conservative and fundamentalist representatives of most traditional religions and seemingly sanctioned by common sense). In reply, Second Wave feminists argued the importance of distinguishing biological sex from the historical and social construction of gender. Le Guin's novel can be seen as an intervention in this debate, one that science fiction was more suited to make than many traditional forms of argument. Le Guin's story of an emissary from a future federation of intelligent worlds to the planet Gethen is the discovery of a world where this distinction has been made flesh: for most of the time the humans on this planet have no biological sexual characteristics and no sexual drives or desires; and then for about a week of every month, they develop male or female sexual characteristics and become sexually active. Whether they become male or female happens more or less randomly: a person can be a female one month and male the next; the same person can become pregnant and bear a child, and then when sexual activity resumes, perhaps be a father. Without the constraints of gender, 'anyone [the novel tells us] can turn his hand to anything'.[28]

Science fiction's specific ability is not so much to predict the future, then, but to show our own present through a particularly effective distorting lens – here the distant alien world and its inhabitants. In this way Le Guin's novel can be seen as the first step in the reawakening of utopian fiction. For with the planet Gethen, she had imagined a different world, but not an alternative or one meant to be seen as better than our own. But the realization quickly spread that science fiction's capacity to picture *other* worlds (while indirectly showing our own) held the possibility for being able to imagine *better* worlds; and her novel was shortly followed by a wave of utopian fiction – mostly science fiction, mostly influenced by feminism – that began to try and imagine what a world beyond private property and without sexual exploitation and domination would actually look and feel like, and how men and women might live together according to new social and sexual relationships.

There were a number of utopian science-fiction novels published in the 1970s, but four in particular are at the centre of most discussions: Samuel Delany's *Triton* (1976), Ursula K. Le Guin's *The Dispossessed* (1974), Marge Piercy's *Woman on the Edge of Time* (1976)[29] and Joanna Russ's *The Female Man* (1975). Of these, three were written by science-fiction writers active within the genre – Le Guin's novel received both the Hugo and Nebula awards as best science-fiction novel of the year while Joanna Russ's short story 'When it Changed', on which *The Female Man* was based, was nominated for the Nebula award; Samuel Delany's *Triton* was not so recognized although he has won the Nebula on other occasions. Only Piercy might be considered as coming from 'outside' the science-fiction community (and she has written two other novels with a utopian dimension; *Body of Glass*, 1991, is a science-fiction novel). This points to another difference between science fiction and utopia: the fact that there is no utopian community as there is with science fiction – no fan conventions, awards or magazines devoted to utopian writing. Furthermore, many science-fiction writers work within the boundaries of the genre on a more or less regular basis, while authors of utopias usually only write one utopia, although there are examples of clarifications and additions, as was the case with Edward Bellamy's *Equality*, published a decade after *Looking Backward*, or Ernest Callenbach's 'prequel' to *Ecotopia* – *Ecotopia Emerging* (1981) – which explains how the ecotopian society came about. But there are few examples of writers like H. G. Wells who could be said to have written a number of utopias and dystopias throughout his long career, for he wrote both science fiction (what he called 'scientific romances') with dystopian overtones (*The Time Machine* (1895), *The First Men in the Moon* (1901), *The War of the Worlds* (1898), *The Island of Doctor Moreau* (1896)) as well as more classic utopias including *A Modern Utopia* (1905), *Men Like Gods* (1923) and *The Shape of Things to Come* (1933).

Turning to the science-fiction utopias of the 1970s, Samuel Delany's *Triton* (1976) is set some 150 years in the future, in an enclosed city on a moon of Neptune. (There is a war in the background, between the colonies on the 'Outer Satellites' and the two inner worlds, Earth and Mars, which seek to impose full economic control in the Solar System.) Through the minimal narrative, we follow Bron, who, despite the freedoms and economic guarantees provided by his society, is unhappy, and whose distress calls into question the universal happiness that traditional utopias take for granted.

Delany's novel is subtitled 'An Ambiguous Heterotopia' as a reply to the 'ambiguous utopia' of Ursula K. Le Guin's *The Dispossessed*. Moreover Delany's world of an unhappy character in a world of comfort is in stark contrast to the hardship world that Le Guin creates in *The Dispossessed*, where she juxtaposes the home world of Urras to its desolate and near desert moon, Anarres, to which the followers of Odo emigrated some 150 years before the story opens to set up an egalitarian society. Through the device of the protagonist's return to the mother world, the novel alternates between the depiction of the utopian society of Anarres and that of the older world, whose three major countries present a simplified sketch of the 'three worlds' model of our own major socio-political systems. In the counterpoising of the abusive and exploitative capitalist patriarchy of A-Io on Anarres with the gradual reemergence of hierarchy and privilege and the increasing bureaucratization of the utopian experiment there, Le Guin shows many of the failings of today's world while pointing to some of the difficulties of the utopian project itself. Such doubts, however, give way to – indeed, strengthen – Shevek's renewed commitment to the ideal of 'permanent revolution' at the end of the novel when he returns to Anarres: 'that the Odonian society on Anarres had fallen short of the ideal did not, in his eyes, lessen his responsibility to it'.[30]

The next two novels present more fully utopian societies, as the novelists juxtapose the utopian future with the present and with a call for help in bringing the future world into existence. Communitarian, ecological and feminist ideals are prominent in Marge Piercy's *Woman on the Edge of Time* (1976), which is set in New York City in the present. Connie, a Mexican-American woman unjustly confined to a mental hospital, is contacted telepathically from the future, which she is then able to visit in the same way.

In the Mattapoisett of 2137, the people of Earth live in an interlocking network of self-sufficient regions. They have achieved a utopian future through a long struggle against the exploitative forces of multinational capitalism – a fight which is still being waged in the future by the 'multis' from bases in Antarctica and in space. This fight reaches back to our present as well, and Connie has been contacted to join in the struggle for a better future. As she gradually comes to appreciate the utopian future, she also realizes that her own situation in the hospital, as the unwilling subject in a psycho-surgical experiment designed to control 'anti-social behavior', is a part of the war to control the future. In a desperate act of defiance and as her own conscious declaration of war against the increasing repression and exploitation of our present system, she poisons the doctors' coffee: she cannot remain in utopia; she will not be saved by a happy ending. But, the novel tells us, if we also begin to fight in the present, we may yet win the battle for the future.

Joanna Russ's *The Female Man* (1975) is a remarkable and controversial novel which has sometimes been dismissed because of its polemical aspects and unconventional formal features. Set in an 'alternate' United States in the late 1960s, the novel overlays four versions or 'other selves' of the narrator. Jeannine, a 1950s' woman who tries desperately to meet social expectations about correct feminine behaviour, and Joanna, the 'female man' of the title who has understood and rejected patriarchal conventions, are juxtaposed with two visitors from the future: Janet and Jael. The former is from an alternate Earth 900 years in the future where, after a plague killed all the men, the women have learned to fend for themselves and have developed, in the process, a more human, satisfying and nurturing world than that of the present. However, as we learn late in the novel, the 'natural' emergence of the utopian society is itself a myth. This utopian world without men is not accidental but instead the result of a choice, for there was an interim stage between the present and the utopian future in which our world split into two warring camps – men against women – from which the women emerged victorious. Jael is a warrior-woman, sent from that interim future to recruit help in the present. In Russ's pastoral Earth of the future there are no 'true cities' left, and life is organized cooperatively and collectively around families of women. Although they live in a respectful and harmonious way with the environment, however, this novel does not resemble the anti-scientific pastoral utopias of the nineteenth century: the women have a pronounced reliance on technology – which includes not only reproductive technology, but also time travel, mining colonies in space, and, more immediately, mind-computer link-ups, portable power sources, food factories and so on.

There are two ways to measure how these utopias differ from the utopian tradition, by asking if they are different from (a) utopias written by non-science-fiction authors, and (b) how they differ from earlier utopias. Although technology may facilitate or make possible conditions for a utopian society, as in the comforts and guaranteed income of the lunar society in Samuel Delany's *Triton*, or in the computer which assigns work in Ursula K. Le Guin's *The Dispossessed* (*divlab*), the introduction of technology is not an essential factor in the emergence of utopia in either of these novels, although it does make these worlds possible. Both Delany and Le Guin focus on questions about the limits and shortcomings of utopia more than they do on the role of technology in bringing it about. (This is even more developed in Kim Stanley Robinson's *Mars Trilogy*, 1993–6,[31] where arguments about politics and new forms of self-governance are very much tied to discussion about technologies for making possible and enhancing life on Mars.)

What is different in these novels does not lie in their science-fiction characteristics or how the familiar science-fiction motifs and devices contributed to the making of the utopia, but as I have suggested, in a critical examination of the utopian ideal itself. According to the critic Tom Moylan these science-fiction utopias of the 1970s should be seen as 'critical utopias': the 'negation of the negation' of earlier reactions against utopia in the twentieth century, one which preserves the fundamental utopian dream of human emancipation while acknowledging the 'limitations of the utopian tradition'.[32]

This more wary and critical stance towards the utopian tradition can already be seen in the subtitles of the novels of Le Guin ('An Ambiguous Utopia') and Delany (following Foucault, 'An Ambiguous Heterotopia'). Earlier utopias often depicted worlds in which the better society has already been achieved and which offered a blueprint for the better society, one which is inscribed in terms of laws and institutions, architecture and the like. On the other hand these more recent utopias are often 'in process', societies which are somehow imperfect, as in Delany and Le Guin; or have not yet come into being, struggling to emerge or to survive, as in the novels of Piercy and Russ. At the same time, the four works under discussion are clearly utopias, and they do evoke in some detail a better society. But again there is a difference. While these utopias remain strongly influenced by socialism (or anarchism in Le Guin's case), particularly in terms of the pre-eminence of collective values as well as by the rejection of private property (in the context of the perceived failure of the Soviet model), for the most part they are reluctant to imagine a better society that imposes its values on its citizens and they reject government control (*The Female Man* is an exception here).

Earlier moments of utopian writing were influenced by historical events; eighteenth-century utopias imagined alternatives to French Absolutism while late nineteenth-century utopias reacted to the struggles of workers. Similarly the struggles of the 1960s, the counter-culture and especially 'Second Wave' feminism have strongly influenced the utopian writing of the 1970s. Like the classics of the tradition, these recent works also invented societies which were grounded in the economic and political reorganization of society and which emphasized communitarian goals and ideals. But instead of describing at length the new society's institutions or laws, greater stress is given to decentralization and cooperation: for the most part, these recent works leave the political and economic structures in the background and concentrate on the lived reality of the characters. Whereas older utopias were usually plotted as a kind of guided tour of the new society, recent utopian writing has tried to involve the reader on a different level, by means of the thoughts and feelings of the characters in that new society who are involved in the daily struggle to build a world of human freedom and self-fulfilment.

This emphasis on daily life is an application of the feminist slogan 'the personal is political' and a recognition that the purpose of any social transformation is to produce genuine changes in our daily lives. Consequently these novels address as central to the new society such 'personal' issues as living arrangements, in opposition to the hegemony of the nuclear family; sexuality, as against the norms of heterosexuality and procreative sexuality; and more generally, the ideological, psychological and economic structures of gender division under capitalism. In calling attention to the centrality of the everyday to any project of human liberation, these works attempt to imagine new societies in which all forms of human behaviour are valorized and in which the older dichotomies which inform our lives have been transformed: work versus play, intellectual versus manual labour, creative versus non-creative, the home versus the workplace, productive versus non-productive work, and so on.

Thus the valorization of all forms of human activity begins with a fundamental transformation of work itself, from an 'obligation enforced by poverty and external goals' (wage labour) to more rewarding and largely self-determining activities. The availability of work according to individual inclinations marks the end of the sexual division of labour in these novels. Moreover, to ensure that individuals can vary tasks according to ability and inclination, and to balance those inclinations with social needs, these novels propose a variety of work-posting schemes. Disagreeable work is shared more equitably, or in some cases reduced through technology, while in all these worlds there is a reduction in the socially necessary labour each individual must perform.

Although socialists have usually focused on the workplace as the primary site of contestation, this is no longer the case in these utopian novels, which go beyond issues of economic exploitation to show that alienation and domination are embedded in the patriarchal structures of everyday existence – structures which, however, would not of themselves disappear following the collectivization of the means of production. These works develop new social forms based on equality of the sexes and on alternative forms of love relationships, living patterns, and parenting. Women are in full control of their reproductive functions, and there is an acceptance of diverse forms of sexual expression, most particularly of homosexuality.

In contrast to many earlier utopias, here the emphasis on everyday life extends to the biosphere as well. These works all reject the earlier utopian commitments to growth and the domination of nature. In varying ways and to varying degrees, they espouse rather the development of an integrative and non-exploitative attitude towards nature. In the attention given to everyday life, then, these works blend the practical description of new social and human relations with the vision of an alternative society and with the images of an emancipated human nature in which playfulness, spontaneity, creativity and eroticism are no longer sublimated to the demands of capitalism and patriarchy.

I have been trying to show that there is not a necessary connection between utopia and science fiction, and in recent years the two have drifted apart. First of all, it is important to remember that not all US utopias written in the past fifty years are science fiction. I have already mentioned B. F. Skinner's 1948 *Walden Two* which describes a small community set up according to his analysis of human behaviour. This novel is clearly a utopia, but it cannot in any way be considered science fiction. Similarly, during the revival of utopian writing in the 1970s, there were utopias that fell outside the confines of science fiction, beginning with Ernest Callenbach's *Ecotopia* (1975).[33] The novel is set in the near future, after Northern California, Oregon and Washington have seceded from the United States. This novel is not really science fiction, and the visitor's sector-by-sector discovery and account of the new society owes more to the utopias of the eighteenth and nineteen centuries than it does to science fiction. Moreover the author (who came from outside the science-fiction field) clearly intended his vision to be taken seriously, as a model for a more ecologically aware society. Indeed, his concern with the novel's being taken seriously led him to write a 'prequel' – *Ecotopia Emerging* (1981) – explaining just how the new society would come about. If Callenbach's utopia proceeds to give a realistic and plausible description of a new society (and certainly not an estranged vision of an alternative), Sally Gearhart's 1979 *The Wanderground* is at the other end of the spectrum: it portrays a near-future in which Mother Earth has rebelled against patriarchy and its destructive tendencies (industrialization, militarism etc) – an anti-technological utopia akin to the pastoral utopias of the eighteenth and nineteenth centuries. This is no longer an attempt at offering a literal vision of the future (as with Callenbach), but a utopian fantasy – and a manifesto for a kind of feminist separatism: again a recent utopia which falls outside the boundaries of science fiction.[34]

By the mid-1980s this utopian moment in English-language science fiction had come to an end, however, as that earlier euphoria faded, a casualty of the rise of neo-liberalism (as marked by the elections of Reagan and Thatcher), and by the collapse of the Soviet Union and the socialist alternative a few years later. While the study of utopias and utopianism is flourishing (as can be seen by this volume), and there are still some utopias being written, the utopian moment of the 1960s and 1970s has passed.

But if utopian writing has waned in the past twenty-five years, science fiction has boomed; it is more successful than ever, omnipresent across the full range of cultural forms, from advertising and music to its more traditional home in films and novels. And this is significant, for it points to the fundamental difference between science fiction and utopia and should help lay to rest the notion that somehow the two have merged. Utopia by definition opposes the dominant culture: as Suvin put it, 'where sociopolitical institutions, norms, and individual relationships are organized according to a *more perfect principle* than in the author's community ...'.[35] The moments of convergence between the two genres occurred in the 1970s when some science-fiction writers tried to find ways to imagine alternatives to their society. But if the utopia presents an alternative to the present, science fiction is a neutral form, able to express positions in opposition to or in defence of the status quo; and with its widespread success the imagined futures of contemporary science fiction rarely imply or assert a critique of the present.

There are moments, as I've mentioned, when literary utopias have prospered, abetted by the existence of fertile generic ground, as was the case with the imaginary voyage in the seventeenth and eighteenth centuries, or science fiction in the 1970s. But literary utopias have also flourished at other moments, without the encouragement of existing literary forms, at the beginning of the nineteenth century, for instance, in the writing of Fourier and Saint-Simon (or in Marx and Engels). We have also seen historical moments when there were fewer literary utopias, but when utopianism – the desire for change, the refusal of the status quo – breaks into the real. One might argue that events in the Global South over the past decade or so constitute such a utopian moment, but in the developed countries of the North today, however, neither form of utopianism is much in evidence.

NOTES

1 Glen Negley and J. Max Patrick (eds.), *The Quest for Utopia: An Anthology of Imaginary Societies* (New York: Henry Schuman, 1952), p. 588.

2 Raymond Williams, *Marxism and Literature* (New York: Oxford University Press, 1977), pp. 187–8.

3 I would like to thank Nicholas Serruys for his helpful comments.

4 Lyman Tower Sargent, 'Three Faces of Utopianism Revisited', *Utopian Studies* 5:1 (1994), 9.

5 Like Sargent, 'Three Faces', p. 9, I think that it is important to distinguish the *utopia* (a term which I use to mean the eutopia or positive utopia) from the *dystopia* which follows the model of 'if this goes on': a future in which some aspect of the present had continued and worsened. This last term should be distinguished from the *anti-utopia* which is an equally dismal future, but one which is intended as a criticism of utopianism or of some particular eutopia.

6 Darko Suvin, *Metamorphoses of Science Fiction: On the Poetics and History of a Literary Genre* (New Haven: Yale University Press, 1979), p. 49; my italics.

7 John Clute and Peter Nicholls, *The Encyclopedia of Science Fiction* (London: Orbit Books, 1993), p. 314.

8 Suvin, *Metamorphoses*, pp. 6–7; italics in text. In the 'History of SF' entry in Clute and Nicholls, *The Encyclopedia of Science Fiction*, Peter Nicholls calls science fiction an 'impure genre ... which did not finally take shape until the late 19th century, although its separate elements existed earlier', p. 567.

9 'Strictly and precisely speaking, utopia is not a genre but the *sociopolitical sub-genre of science fiction*. Paradoxically, it can be seen as such only now that SF has expanded into its modern phase, "looking backward" from its englobing of utopia' (Suvin, *Metamorphoses*, p. 61).

10 B. F. Skinner, *Walden Two* (1948) (London: Macmillan, 1962).

11 Lyman Tower Sargent, *British and American Utopian Literature, 1516–1975* (New York: Garland, 1988).

12 In 1911, the magazine *Modern Electrics* began the publication of a serialized story by Gernsback that later became the novel *Ralph 124C 41+* (1925).

13 Jacques Sadoul in *Histoire de la science fiction moderne* (Paris: Albin Michel, 1973), writes that in its first three years of publication, the magazine included thirty stories by Wells, nine novels of Jules Verne and seven stories by Poe (pp. 61–2).

14 There is a long tradition of combinations of the two media, from *The Thing* and *The Invasion of The Body Snatchers* in the 1950s to the Alien films or the 2008 *Cloverfield* – another sign of science fiction's heterogeneous status.

15 Louis-Sébastien Mercier, *L'An 2440: Un rêve s'il en fut jamais* (translated into English as *Memoirs of the Year Two Thousand Five Hundred*, 1772) (1771).

16 Edward Bellamy, *Looking Backward 2000–1887* (1888), ed. Robert C. Elliott (Boston: Houghton Mifflin, 1966).

17 H. G. Wells, *The Time Machine* (1895) (London: Heinemann, 1937).

18 Mark Hillegas, *The Future as Nightmare: H. G. Wells and the Anti-Utopians* (New York: Oxford University Press, 1967), p. 5.

19 Aldous Huxley, *Brave New World* (1932) (Harmondsworth: Penguin, 1955).

20 H. Bruce Franklin, *Future Perfect: American Science Fiction of the Nineteenth Century: An Anthology* (New York: Oxford University Press, 1966), p. 391.

21 Chad Walsh, *From Utopia to Nightmare* (London: Geoffrey Bles, 1962).

22 Thomas Molnar, *Utopia: The Perennial Heresy* (New York: Sheed & Ward, 1967), p. 227.

23 John Wyndham, *The Chrysalids* (London: Michael Joseph, 1955); Theodore Sturgeon, *More than Human* (London: Victor Gollancz, 1954).
24 Frederik Pohl and C. M. Kornbluth, *The Space Merchants* (New York: Ballantine, 1953), pp. 155–6.
25 Samuel R. Delany, *The Einstein Intersection* (London: Victor Gollancz, 1967).
26 Ursula K. Le Guin, *The Dispossessed* (New York: Avon, 1974); Samuel Delany, *Triton* (London: Corgi, 1976); Joanna Russ, *The Female Man* (New York: Bantam Books, 1975); Suzy McKee Charnas, *Motherlines* (London: Gollancz, 1980).
27 Ursula K. Le Guin, *The Left Hand of Darkness* (New York: Ace, 1969).
28 Le Guin, *The Left Hand*, p. 93.
29 Marge Piercy, *Woman on the Edge of Time* (New York: Knopf, 1976).
30 Delany, *Triton*, ch. 10, p. 267.
31 Kim Stanley Robinson, *The Mars Trilogy* [*Red Mars* (1992), *Green Mars* (1993), *Blue Mars* (1996)] (New York: Bantam Spectra, 1992–6).
32 Tom Moylan, *Demand the Impossible: Science Fiction and the Utopian Imagination* (New York: Methuen, 1986), p. 10.
33 Ernest Callenbach, *Ecotopia* (London: Bantam Books, 1975).
34 Sally Miller Gearhart, *The Wanderground: Stories of the Hill Women* (Watertown, MA: Persephone Press, 1979).
35 Suvin, *Metamorphoses*, p. 49 (my italics).

BIBLIOGRAPHY

Bellamy, Edward, *Looking Backward 2000–1887* (1888), ed. Robert C. Elliott (Boston: Houghton Mifflin, 1966).
Callenbach, Ernest, *Ecotopia* (London: Bantam Books, 1975).
Charnas, Suzy McKee, *Motherlines* (London: Victor Gollancz, 1980).
Clute, John and Peter Nicholls, *The Encyclopedia of Science Fiction* (London: Orbit Books, 1993).
Delany, Samuel R., *The Einstein Intersection* (London: Victor Gollancz, 1967).
Triton (London: Corgi, 1976).
Franklin, H. Bruce, *Future Perfect: American Science Fiction of the Nineteenth Century: An Anthology* (New York: Oxford University Press, 1966).
Gearhart, Sally Miller, *The Wanderground: Stories of the Hill Women* (Watertown, MA: Persephone Press, 1979).
Hillegas, Mark, *The Future as Nightmare: H. G. Wells and the Anti-Utopians* (New York: Oxford University Press, 1967).
Huxley, Aldous, *Brave New World* (1932) (Harmondsworth: Penguin, 1955).
Le Guin, Ursula K., *The Left Hand of Darkness* (New York: Ace, 1969).
The Dispossessed (New York: Avon, 1974).
Mercier, Louis-Sébastien, *L'An 2440: Un rêve s'il en fut jamais* (translated into English as *Memoirs of the Year Two Thousand Five Hundred*, 1772) (1771).
Molnar, Thomas, *Utopia: The Perennial Heresy* (New York: Sheed & Ward, 1967).
Moylan, Tom, *Demand the Impossible: Science Fiction and the Utopian Imagination* (New York: Methuen, 1986).
Negley, Glen and J. Max Patrick (eds.), *The Quest for Utopia: An Anthology of Imaginary Societies* (New York: Henry Schuman, 1952).
Piercy, Marge, *Woman on the Edge of Time* (New York: Knopf, 1976).

Pohl, Frederik and C. M. Kornbluth, *The Space Merchants* (New York: Ballantine, 1953).

Robinson, Kim Stanley, *The Mars Trilogy* [*Red Mars* (1992), *Green Mars* (1993), *Blue Mars* (1996)] (New York: Bantam Spectra, 1992–6).

Russ, Joanna, *The Female Man* (New York: Bantam Books, 1975).

Sadoul, Jacques, *Histoire de la science fiction moderne* (Paris: Albin Michel, 1973).

Sargent, Lyman Tower, *British and American Utopian Literature, 1516–1975* (New York: Garland, 1988).

'Three Faces of Utopianism Revisited', *Utopian Studies* 5:1 (1994), 1–37.

Skinner, B. F., *Walden Two* (1948) (London: Macmillan, 1962).

Sturgeon, Theodore, *More than Human* (London: Victor Gollancz, 1954).

Suvin, Darko, *Metamorphoses of Science Fiction: On the Poetics and History of a Literary Genre* (New Haven: Yale University Press, 1979).

Walsh, Chad, *From Utopia to Nightmare* (London: Geoffrey Bles, 1962).

Wells, H. G., *The Time Machine* (1895) (London: Heinemann, 1937).

Williams, Raymond, *Marxism and Literature* (New York: Oxford University Press, 1977).

Wyndham, John, *The Chrysalids* (London: Michael Joseph, 1955).

7

PATRICK PARRINDER

Utopia and romance

> Romance is a figure with outstretched hands, yearning for the unattainable.
> E. M. Forster, *The Longest Journey*[1]

Utopia, the good place which is no place, is also the place at the end of the traditional fairy tale, where 'They all lived happily ever after.' If romance, as Forster says, is an expression of the yearning for the unattainable, then utopia is that which cannot be attained – the happy-ever-after which always eludes us no matter how near we draw to it. In utopian narratives, the blissful state fleetingly evoked in the fairy tale's final sentence is extended to a whole society, and fully and often pedantically spelt out. The fundamental purpose of both romances and utopias is to 'remake the world in the image of desire', but the image of desire in each case is very different.[2] The heart of romance are the physical and emotional torments suffered by its heroes and heroines and their determination in the face of adversity; utopia, by contrast, portrays a collective, not individual, reward for suffering humanity as a whole. If romance is Cinderella, then utopia is a fairy godmother not just to the heroine but to the whole world.

Romance and utopia have something in common but are in many ways opposites. It is with this in mind that we should approach the genre of the *utopian romance*, which came into its own with the spread of modern popular fiction on utopian and dystopian themes. At its high point in the late nineteenth century the utopian romance was an increasingly self-conscious genre, a narrative of love and adventure combined with the didactic or satirical portrayal of a supposedly utopian society. In utopian (as opposed to dystopian) romances, the excitements of love and adventure are normally experienced by a visitor to utopia, not by the utopians themselves, and for good reasons.

Love in the broad sense of sexuality and sexual relationships is a standard topic – though not always a very important one – throughout the utopian tradition, and most utopias belong somewhere on a continuum between the highly regulated and repressive at one extreme, and the promiscuous and libertine at the other. What are invariably absent from the classical utopia, however, are passion and its concomitants such as adventure and danger (although the more militaristic utopias may admit danger in conflicts with other states). Passion or romantic love is notoriously antisocial and, therefore, destabilizing, and it generally takes a visitor – whose very presence has a destabilizing influence – to introduce a 'love interest' into utopian narratives. All too often the result is a merely conventional or sentimental addition to the story, and the aesthetically satisfying utopian romance is a distinct rarity, as we shall see.

Utopian narrative is defined as the detailed and systematic description of a society better than, and in opposition to, the writer's own.[3] It is both a deliberate thought-experiment – hence an instrument of rational enquiry – and a fictional construction characterized by a greater or lesser degree of improbability. While the improbability of utopian narratives aligns them with the traditional literary romance, the requirement for detailed and systematic description is shared with the realistic novel, with which romance has long been sharply contrasted. One of the earliest writers to distinguish between romance and novel was the dramatist William Congreve, whose preface to *Incognita* (1692) describes the subject-matter of romance as the 'constant loves and invincible courage of heroes, heroines, kings and queens, mortals of the first rank, and so forth'. Romances are full of 'lofty language, miraculous contingencies, and impossible performances', while novels are 'of a more familiar nature'.[4] More than a century later Walter Scott, the founding father of historical romance, contrasted its reliance on 'marvellous and uncommon incidents' with the novel's representation of 'the ordinary train of human events, and the modern state of society'.[5] As will be seen from these definitions, literary romance is generally a backward-looking form, based on the myth of a past heroic age and equating mundaneness with modernity. Romance is nostalgic by definition, while utopia is – in intention, at least – forward-looking.

Nevertheless, the distinction between romance and novel, however long-established, tends to disappear on close analysis. Every novel contains romance elements, and nearly all fictional plotting relies on coincidences and repetitions which are, statistically speaking, improbable. In utopian texts, it is true, 'plot' in the sense of decisive narrative events or incidents is generally reduced to a minimum, its place being taken by description, explanation and justification of an unfamiliar state of society. Even utopias, however, allow some scope for 'marvellous and uncommon' events. The classical form of utopian narrative shows the visitor-protagonist arriving in a strange place, meeting the inhabitants, taking a guided tour, and settling down for some time before eventually sailing away. The story of the voyage, if not the period of utopian residence, can easily be furnished with shipwrecks and other adventure-story motifs, though the genre's inventor, Thomas More, was careful to avoid these.

The narrator of *Utopia*, Raphael Hythloday, refuses to give any account of the sea-monsters he and his companions may or may not have encountered:

> But as for monsters, because they be no newes, of them we were nothing inquisitive. For nothing is more easye to bee founde, then bee barkynge Scyllaes, ravening Celenes, and Lestrigones devourers of people, and suche lyke great, and incredible monsters. But to fynde Citizens ruled by good and holsome laws, that is an exceeding rare, and harde thyng.[6]

Like any serious reporter, Hythloday prefers to expound the 'good and holsome laws' of Utopia and their effects, leaving more sensational news to the romances which were the sixteenth-century ancestors of tabloid journalism. This self-denying ordinance was frequently ignored by More's successors, but it is in dystopian and anti-utopian fiction, where plotting is usually far more intensive, that romance elements come into their own. The typical dystopian narrative dramatizes the difficulties and dangers faced by an individual who is either a visitor or a dissident citizen. It is the foregrounding of difficulty and danger that accounts for the popular appeal of successful dystopian novels, so that works such as *Brave New World*, *Nineteen Eighty-Four* and *The Handmaid's Tale* enjoy a best-selling status that the classic utopian authors can only envy. Dystopias foreground the individuality, the self-absorption, and the capacity for emotion that novel-readers crave but the architects of utopian societies look down upon.

Since its beginnings in Plato's *Republic*, utopian thought has been characterized by moral condemnation of the craving for passion and longing for incident, and of the romance-writers who pander to it. Plato excludes the poets from his Republic because poetry has a habit of dwelling on the less savoury aspects of human behaviour. In English literature the two poets who most conspicuously sprang to the defence of their art against Plato's onslaught were Sir Philip Sidney and Percy Shelley; both, paradoxically, have a strongly utopian streak. Sidney's *Apology for Poetry* (1595) argues that the poet imagines a more perfect world than the world of nature: 'Her world is brazen, the poets only deliver a golden'; and Sidney has no hesitation in naming More's *Utopia* as an example of poetic creation.[7] His authority stands behind such extravagantly utopian texts as Margaret Cavendish's *The Blazing World* (1666), described by its author as a mixture of the 'romancical', the 'philosophical' and the 'fantastical'.[8] Sidney's own famous prose work *The Arcadia* (1580) pioneered the modern romance as a melodramatic saga of love and war, set in a distant, mythical past and written for a leisured and specifically female readership.[9] By a neat coincidence, his *Apology* was published posthumously in the same year that another great Elizabethan courtier, Sir Walter Raleigh, set out for Guyana in search of the goldmines of Eldorado. The ambiguity of the concept of a 'golden world' – past golden age or future Eldorado? – could not be more clearly illustrated than in the contrast between Sidney and Raleigh.

In Voltaire's *Candide* (1759) the hero briefly visits the utopian state of Eldorado, but cannot find happiness there.[10] Not only is he separated from his beloved Cunégonde, but he wants to show off the riches of Eldorado to the poor people of Europe he has left behind. Gold is so commonplace in Eldorado that it can be picked up on the streets, while in More's *Utopia* it is used for chamberpots. Once gold has lost its monetary value, its associations with beauty, mystery, glamour and lovers' promises all disappear. A 'golden world' is an image of romance, but nothing is more unromantic for its inhabitants than a utopia in which everything is made of gold. The utopians will take pride in their world – at least for the benefit of awestruck visitors – but they will no longer be excited by it. The heightened emotions necessary for romance are all on the side of the visitor. He (for it is always a he) embodies the motif of adventure thanks to his unexpected arrival in utopia and his surprising and disturbing discoveries there. He feels a growing horror at the contrast between this more perfect world and the world from which he has come, and as often as not he transfers his loyalties to the new society even as his return home (if not his physical expulsion from utopia) becomes inevitable. Frequently he falls in love not only with, but in utopia. The utopia which is also a love story became a commonplace from the eighteenth-century 'Age of Sensibility' onwards. James Henry Lawrence's *The Empire of the Nairs* (1811), possibly the first work to be explicitly described as a 'utopian romance' on its title page, follows its hero's search for complete sexual freedom in a series of worlds.[11] By the time that we reach William Morris's *News from Nowhere* (1890), subtitled *Or, an Epoch of Rest; Being Some Chapters of a Utopian Romance*, the visitor's arousal by and growing intimacy with a utopian female had become a more or less obligatory source of narrative momentum.[12]

The utopian romance is thus both a generic hybrid – a narrative combining melodramatic and improbable elements of love, mystery and adventure with a didactic utopian content – and something of a philosophical scandal. A visitor from our own (by definition, backward if not barbarous) world may very well become besotted with the charms of the utopians, but how is it possible that these feelings should be returned? And, if they are returned, how can the utopian society fail to condemn the resulting liaison? The utopians are superior to us not only culturally but biologically and genetically, since virtually every utopia impresses the visitor not only with its social arrangements but with the health, strength and beauty of its ordinary citizens. The utopians are more imposing and fairer to look upon than we are. Having achieved this eugenic advantage over all previous human societies, they must wish to protect and extend it. Sexual connection with a weaker and more backward specimen of humanity, such as the visitor from our own world, is necessarily dysgenic, and the utopian female who finds herself attracted to a male visitor must be somewhat maladjusted, if not a potential outlaw. Eugenic logic suggests that like should be paired off with like, and many utopias introduce a specifically eugenic element into the rituals of courtship: couples in More's Utopia, for example, must see one another naked (to expose any hidden physical defects) before consenting to a marriage contract. Romance, by contrast, rejects the arranged marriage and thrives on unforeseen passion and the attraction of opposites. Logic and passionate intensity are necessarily at odds. But even if the 'love interest' of romance is better suited to dystopian fiction, the triumph of libido over species improvement has proved an irresistible theme for some utopian writers as well.

It was not until the late nineteenth century that the novel, previously a poor relation of poetry and poetic drama, reached the height of its prestige among literary forms. Soon the literary world was divided between the champions of realism, taken to extremes in the naturalism of Emile Zola with its supposed affiliation to scientific method, and the advocates of a revival of fictional romance. Adventure-story writers such as Robert Louis Stevenson and Henry Rider Haggard specialized in heroic action in exotic locations far removed from the realists' concentration on the sordid banalities of modern urban life. In 1890 the popular novelist Hall Caine proclaimed 'The New Watchwords of Fiction' as (among others) Justice, Faith, Imagination, Beauty and Passion.[13] The romantic revival was strengthened by changes in the book market, including the break-up of the all-encompassing three-volume novel and the rapid growth of specialized genres of short fiction such as the detective story, the ghost story, science fiction (then known as 'scientific romance'), the children's novel and the Gothic thriller. Within a few years there appeared such popular classics as Stevenson's *Treasure Island* (1883) and *Dr Jekyll and Mr Hyde* (1886), Mark Twain's *The Adventures of Huckleberry Finn* (1885), Jerome K. Jerome's *Three Men in a Boat* (1889), the Sherlock Holmes stories, H. G. Wells's *The Time Machine* (1895) and *The War of the Worlds* (1898) and Bram Stoker's *Dracula* (1897). The utopian romances of Samuel Butler, W. H. Hudson, Edward Bellamy, William Morris and others constitute another of these specialized genres.

To some extent, the revival of romance was founded on the continuing popularity of earlier authors such as Walter Scott and the American novelist Nathaniel Hawthorne (1806–64).[14] Hawthorne is notable both for his critical advocacy of romance and for *The Blithedale Romance* (1852), a work that is not, strictly speaking, a utopian romance but a romance with a quasi-utopian setting.[15] The genre of romance, as he wrote in his preface to *The House of the Seven Gables* (1851), gives the writer 'a certain latitude' in contrast to the 'very minute fidelity, not merely to the possible, but to the probable and ordinary course of man's experience' expected of realistic fiction. Authors of romance set out to display human nature in a different context from that of mundane realism. Hawthorne nevertheless insisted that the fantastic element in modern romance should be kept to a minimum, the aim being to 'mingle the Marvelous rather as a slight, delicate, and evanescent flavour than as any portion of the actual substance of the dish offered to the public'.[16]

The Blithedale Romance, accordingly, portrays not an ideal state but a contemporary utopian community manifestly based on Hawthorne's own brief residence at Brook Farm, near Boston, ten years earlier. The romance elements in the story include the 'Veiled Lady', apparently a hypnotic subject who poses as a prophetess, and a plot based on hidden identity in which two rivals in love are finally discovered to be half-sisters. 'Blithedale' literally means 'Happy Valley', a traditional synonym for utopia, and Hawthorne's anti-utopian critique is manifest in the observations of his sceptical narrator Miles Coverdale. Not only is Coverdale quickly disillusioned by the conformist and anti-intellectual ethos of the community he has joined, but he finds himself the appalled witness of a love-tragedy culminating in a suicide. However committed they are, or were, to the aims of Blithedale, the protagonists in this tragedy have wider interests and uncontrollable desires which, in the end, must tear the community apart. Hawthorne's conservatism on this score was already implicit in his earlier critical preface, where he had stated that the romance 'sins unpardonably so far as it may swerve aside from the truth of the human heart'.[17] The truth of the heart, he implies, is unquestionable and unchanging, while the slightest deviation from it, however experimental or speculative in intent, must be condemned. Insofar as utopia relies on an improvement in human nature or a 'change of heart', the romance in Hawthorne's definition is necessarily anti-utopian.

A similar conclusion might be drawn from two extraordinary satirical works of the early 1870s which mark the inception of the modern utopian romance, Edward Bulwer-Lytton's *The Coming Race* (1871) and Samuel

Butler's *Erewhon* (1872).[18] Bulwer-Lytton had been a popular novelist for four decades before publishing *The Coming Race*, a formal utopia with long essay-like disquisitions on the language, customs, history and biological evolution of the Vril-ya, an underground super-civilization discovered by chance by an American mining engineer. The romance elements in the story consist of the narrator's adventures as he embarks on the potholing expedition that leads to the world underground, his moment of first meeting with the Vril-ya, and his eventual escape contrived by his host's daughter. The underground world is so spacious that the Vril-ya have developed wings and can fly; moreover, they possess a miraculous energy source, vril (apparently a form of nuclear energy), which poses an evident threat to terrestrial humanity. Although the romance elements in *The Coming Race* are somewhat marginal, they involve two highly influential modifications of the conventional structure of utopian narrative. The first is the presentation of the protagonist's arrival as a brief but sensational adventure story involving a specific set of what anthropologists call liminal experiences, while the second is the final hair's-breadth departure assisted by one or more utopian females.

To move from one world to another is to pass through a frontier zone or no man's land with several typical features. These include separation and isolation, the crossing of a forbidden boundary, entry into a timeless condition, the appearance of monstrous and marvellous forms, and an experience of death leading to rebirth.[19] All these liminal features distinguished by anthropologists in initiation ceremonies and other tribal rituals are also characteristic motifs of heroic adventure fiction and, therefore, of late nineteenth-century romances. In *The Coming Race*, accordingly, the two men who descend into the mineshaft feel separated from one another from the start. Not only does an underground descent suggest entry into the land of the dead, but the narrator's companion is almost too terrified to make the journey. Very soon there is a rock-fall which knocks the narrator unconscious and kills or stuns his companion. When a giant carnivorous reptile comes on the scene, the narrator abandons his friend and makes a hasty exit. No sooner has he fully entered the underground world than he meets his first Vril-ya and, quaking with fear, falls to his knees. Revived by the magical touch of a vril staff, he undergoes a symbolic rebirth but soon lapses into unconsciousness once again. Finally he makes a full recovery after being nursed by the Vril-ya for a period of days or weeks during which he loses all sense of time.

The description of the moment of first contact is notable for its effect of romantic sublimity:

> And now there came out of this building a form – human; was it human?
> ... It came within a few yards of me, and at the sight and presence of it an

indescribable awe and tremor seized me, rooting my feet to the ground. It reminded me of symbolical images of Genius or Demon that are seen on Etruscan vases or limned on the walls of Eastern sepulchres – images that borrow the outlines of men, and are yet of another race. It was tall, not gigantic, but tall as the tallest men below the height of giants … It wore on its head a kind of tiara that shone with jewels, and carried in its right hand a slender staff of bright metal like polished steel. But the face! it was that which inspired my awe and my terror. It was the face of man, but yet of a type of man distinct from our known extant races. The nearest approach to it in outline and expression is the face of the sculptured sphinx – so regular in its calm, intellectual, mysterious beauty.[20]

The society of the Vril-ya may be utopian – certainly it is well ordered, highly civilized and apparently peaceful – but they themselves are only ambiguously human. Described as both godlike and sphinx-like, their exoticism is conveyed through classical and Oriental imagery while the narrator uses the neutral term 'it' in the very moment of affirming their humanity. The sphinx, associated with the riddle of the future and the mystery of ageing, is at once animal, human and semi-divine. The narrator's instinctive terror at this first encounter is not misplaced, since, although they infuse him with vril (which clearly has medicinal properties), the Vril-ya eventually decide that he must be killed. As had earlier happened to Gulliver in Houyhnhnmland in book four of Swift's *Gulliver's Travels,* no sooner has the visitor to utopia conceived an intense desire to remain there than the utopians decide to get rid of him at all costs.

Gulliver received some kindness from his Houyhnhnm master and from another horse, the sorrel nag. Bulwer-Lytton's narrator is finally saved by his devoted protector and nurse, his host's daughter Zee. The Vril-ya operate a strict policy of racial exclusion and eugenics, so that the narrator could not possibly have been allowed to interbreed with one of them. Zee is no young innocent but an expert biologist and member of the College of Sages, besides being awesomely muscular and strong. Nevertheless, she falls for the terrestrial visitor and nobly contrives his escape just before the moment of judicial execution. Not only does this heroic action override the intellectual logic of her society, but – as often in the utopian romance – the narrator's symbolic rebirth has led to the imminent prospect of a second death. That he is able to return to the surface and warn his compatriots of the threat from below is entirely due to Zee's assistance. The theme of erotic romance belatedly introduced in the novel's final chapters is necessary to round off the story.

Although these episodes of arrival and departure identify *The Coming Race* as a utopian romance, they are largely conventional and can have placed few demands on an accomplished popular novelist such as Bulwer-Lytton. The core of his text lies in its extensive social descriptions laced with philosophical satire on contemporary targets, including American democracy and popular-scientific themes such as the Darwinian evolutionary theory. Apart from the 'first contact' moment quoted above, the emotional elements are distinctly muted and the protagonist's growing fear and frustration are barely felt. All this would change in later utopian romances, notably those by W. H. Hudson and William Morris.

Erewhon and its sequel *Erewhon Revisited* (1901) were the only works of fiction published during his lifetime by the essayist and controversialist Samuel Butler, who achieved posthumous fame as a novelist with his outspokenly anti-Victorian polemic *The Way of All Flesh* (1903). Little noticed when it first appeared, *Erewhon* became a popular classic in the early twentieth century thanks to its powerful though idiosyncratic satires on religion (the Musical Banks) and industrial civilization (the Book of the Machines). The romance elements in the story, which draw on Butler's youthful experiences as a sheep-farmer in New Zealand, are pleasing if somewhat inconsequential, and the same may be said of the author's back-to-front coinages, such as the narrator's utopian guide Mr Nosnibor and the name Erewhon itself. Where *The Coming Race* may have been rescued from obscurity by the recent growth of utopian studies, Butler's work has suffered from scholarly disparagement of its apparent inconsistencies and non sequiturs. That it does possess an underlying consistency, deriving from its satire on eugenic ideas, is a case I have argued elsewhere.[21] For example, the Erewhonians' medicalization of crime and criminalization of ugliness and disease make sense as a radical eugenic policy. Once again, the romance elements are somewhat intermittent, and few readers may take much notice of the forbidden love-affair with his host's younger daughter Arowhena which precedes the narrator's hasty departure. Threatened with imprisonment for his supposed attempt to reintroduce machinery into Erewhon – and secretly aided by no less a personage than the Queen of the country – he and Arowhena elope by balloon.

The first five chapters of *Erewhon*, describing a hazardous journey across an unexplored mountain range, introduce the liminal motifs of separation (the narrator parts company with his native guide Chowbok), transgression (he enters a forbidden valley), timelessness (he has a temporary fainting-fit, and later the Erewhonians confiscate his watch), monstrosity (he passes through a ring of hideous prehistoric statues) and death and rebirth (he is almost drowned while crossing a river in flood). Of these various ordeals, it is the passing of the ring of giant statues that most taxes the narrator's courage. The wind howls through the hollowed-out, 'superhumanly malevolent' figures with a sinister melody that he has earlier heard performed with frightful grimaces by Chowbok.[22] He falls down in a dead faint and then, as he proceeds downhill to the beautiful and fertile land he has glimpsed from afar, he foresees a second death much more horrible than the drowning he has just escaped. Above all, he fears being offered up as a human sacrifice in front of the giant statues. We are told that in the past the fair-haired, white-skinned Erewhonians did indeed make forays to capture Chowbok's dark-skinned ancestors and sacrifice them to the 'hideous guardians of the pass', in order to 'avert ugliness and disease from the Erewhonians them-selves'.[23] Some of their own uglier or more diseased citizens were once butchered at the same spot, but the average level of health, strength and beauty has improved so enormously that this is no longer necessary. The statues represent the origins of Erewhonian eugenics.

Since readers and critics of *Erewhon* have for the most part missed the point of the statues, it may be that Butler should be blamed for not mak-ing his intentions more explicit. Nevertheless, when *Erewhon* is read as a satire on eugenics it becomes clear that the adventure story at the begin-ning is much more than a preliminary to be got through as soon as pos-sible; the passing of the ring of statues offers the key to the full ghastliness of Butler's supposed utopia. The later episodes of the Musical Banks and the Colleges of Unreason are comparatively playful, distracting most of his readers from the novel's central message. Romance and utopia are closely bound up together in *Erewhon* even if it lacks the artistic unity of at least two of its successors, W. H. Hudson's *A Crystal Age* (1887) and William Morris's *News from Nowhere*.

William Henry Hudson, best known as a field naturalist and prolific nature essayist, wrote three full-length romances, two of which – *The Purple Land* (1885) and *Green Mansions* (1904) – are tales of adventure set in his native South America. *A Crystal Age*, published two years after *The Purple Land*, is his only utopian work.[24] In a digression towards the end of the earlier text, Hudson's narrator had attacked the idea of a utopian state: 'I hate all dreams of perpetual peace, all wonderful cities of the sun, where people consume their joyless monotonous years in mystic contemplations, or find their delight like Buddhist monks in gazing on the ashes of dead generations.'[25] Smith, the narrator of *A Crystal Age*, soon becomes frustrated and depressed in the arcadian society of the far future in which, after falling asleep in our own time, he inexplicably finds himself. He finds something sinister in the uneventful company of the Crystallites, who live together in large self-supporting households presided over by an ageing Father and Mother. At the beginning, as he wakes up in the far future, Smith undergoes the liminal ordeals of separation, transgression, timelessness, monstrosity (though here it is Smith who, caked with mud and earth from his centuries of premature burial, appears monstrous to himself) and symbolic death and rebirth. He falls asleep in a kind of open grave and, rising from the dead thousands of years later, he comes across a second open grave with a funeral procession coming towards it. The Crystallites are burying a young man whose death is never explained, but whose vacant place in their community Smith perhaps fills. The story ends with Smith's own apparent death in the new world; just how his narrative could have been transmitted back to our own time remains mysterious.

The Crystallites are descended from the last survivors of our industrial civilization, which destroyed itself in what for them is the dawn of history. They are strong, healthy, beautiful and long-lived thanks to their natural, vegetarian existence and their freedom from spiritual unrest and emotional conflict. Smith falls in love with Yoletta, the daughter of the house, but can detect no flicker of sexual interest in her friendliness towards him. There are no children in the household, and the men apart from the Father are all beardless. It is only when he meets the ailing Mother, whose existence has been concealed from him, that he finds someone who can understand his state of emotional unrest. Finally he discovers the sacred book of the household, *The Renewal of the Family*, which explains the mysteries of procreation into which he, as the chosen stranger, and Yoletta would presumably have been initiated. But it is too late: Smith has drunk a forbidden medicine which turns out to be a vial of poison. We can only guess that the same fate engulfed the dead young man who was his predecessor and, perhaps, his double.

The Crystallites have been delivered from what they see as the curse of unlimited fertility by a change in human biology, leading to a social structure resembling a beehive more than a human family. The price of utopian stability and happiness is castration, or at least the virtual elimination of male sexuality and female sexual response. Smith's intense suffering in the face of these mysteries reflects his isolation and bafflement in a future world he finds superficially appealing but, in the end, deeply alien. A happy ever-after has been attained (as, later, in the very different society of Huxley's *Brave New World*) by suppressing if not entirely eliminating what we regard as elemental human feelings. There is no longer any feeling of sexual romance, so we may assume that Yoletta would have married Smith without (in his eyes) ever returning his love; but the shadow of the old world remains potent in the aura of tragic suffering and unexplained loss surrounding the Mother.

What is entirely lacking from *A Crystal Age* is the satirical edge of most portrayals of anti-utopia; instead, Hudson's portrayal of an unromantic future is itself deeply romantic. The use of a far-future setting is integral to

this, since – in contrast to the ominous exaggerations and savage disillusionment of near-future visions – the far future, like the distant past, has dream-
like and nostalgic overtones. We respond to its unattainable beauty and are
not too much troubled if it is also, in some respects, deeply undesirable.
Faced with the spirituality and refinement of the Crystallites, the reader cannot entirely sympathize with Smith's hasty, impatient protests on behalf of
what are for him – and for us as his contemporaries – normal human feelings. The result is one of the most poignant works in the utopian tradition,
a fiction that is both other-worldly and intensely moving. In *A Crystal Age*
utopia and romance are at once philosophically incompatible and, at the
narrative level, inseparable. The context remains anti-utopian, so that the
challenge for writers after Hudson was to deploy the narrative structures of
romance within a positive future based on the nineteenth century's principal
utopian ideology, that of revolutionary socialism.

Before moving to the utopias of Bellamy and Morris, however, it should
be said that the lineal successor of the utopian romances considered so far
is not *Looking Backward* or *News from Nowhere* but H. G. Wells's anti-
utopian vision of the far future in *The Time Machine* (1895).[26] While direct
influence cannot be proved, the Eloi of *The Time Machine* live in a degenerate pastoral state rather like the Crystallites, while the Morlocks are a
sinister underground race like the Vril-ya. The first object that Wells's Time
Traveller encounters in the year 802,701 is the decaying statue of a White
Sphinx, offering another possible link to the sphinx-like Vril-ya as well as to
the ring of statues in *Erewhon*. The name of Butler's heroine, Arowhena, is
echoed in the Time Traveller's Eloi companion, the unfortunate Weena. The
Time Traveller's journey to the future incorporates the liminal ordeals that
we have found in the earlier texts (and that are absent from Bellamy's and
Morris's utopias). His hair's-breadth escape from the Morlocks on his time
machine is also in the familiar romance pattern. Most tellingly, he lacks a
utopian guide to the new world and has to puzzle out the future course of
evolution for himself, a feature that distinguishes *The Time Machine* from
The Coming Race and *Erewhon* but links it to *A Crystal Age*. The main
difference between the two protagonists is, perhaps, that Smith is an amateur botanist while the Time Traveller is a scientist and inventor of genius
who is seeking not the emotional truth but the logical explanation of the
post-human society he encounters. His highly superficial first impression –
that the pastoral Eloi are enjoying the fruits of a communist utopia – is
rapidly discredited. Instead, in the world of the Eloi and Morlocks the class
divisions of our own society have evolved into a bifurcation of the human
species, leading through separate evolutionary paths to a situation in which
one set of our remote post-human descendants preys on the other.

In *The Time Machine*, too, Wells's invention of a mechanical means of travelling through time has been recognized as marking a decisive turning point in the development from earlier romance forms such as the adventure story to modern science fiction.[27] The result is in sharp contrast to the utopias of Bellamy and Morris, where the adventure-story element is reduced to a bare minimum. Wells did the same when he came to write *A Modern Utopia* (1905), which was marketed as a work of speculative non-fiction employing a synthesis of philosophical discussion and imaginative narrative.[28] In neither *Looking Backward*, *News from Nowhere* nor *A Modern Utopia* does the visitor to utopia pass through a liminal experience. Bellamy's and Morris's protagonists fall asleep when somewhat beset by the day-to-day troubles of their own time and wake up in a better, happier and more just near future. Naturally, they fall in love in the new world. Can they remain in the society which each of them feels is his spiritual home, or must they return to our own time to spread the socialist message?

Bellamy's hero in *Looking Backward* (1888) is a contemporary Bostonian undergoing treatment for insomnia. A quack doctor puts Julian West to sleep rather too soundly, so that he wakes up more than a century later in the year 2000. In twenty-first-century Boston he is taken under the wing of an expert physician, Dr Leete, and becomes involved with Leete's daughter Edith, who (needless to say) enjoys the 'magnificent health' and 'physical superiority' exhibited by most of her fellow-citizens. As her father explains, the human race has undergone an enlightened process of eugenic purification and species improvement.[29] There is still room for further development, since blindness, deafness and other forms of disability still persist. At the same time, crime is regarded as a medical problem and criminals are sent for hospital treatment, just as they were in *Erewhon*. When Julian tells Dr Leete of his love for Edith we might expect the doctor to recoil in horror, since marriage to a man carrying the defective inheritance of pre-socialist society is hardly what a conscientious twenty-first-century eugenicist would desire for his daughter. But Julian is welcomed into the family of the future with open arms. There is a disturbing moment at the end of the novel when, in the middle of the night, he thinks he is back in dirty, poverty-stricken nineteenth-century Boston, but he wakes up in the Leetes' spacious house to discover it was only a nightmare. *Looking Backward* was an immensely influential novel in its time, probably the most significant vision of socialism ever produced in the United States, but as a utopian romance with a love-story at its centre it is largely inept.

News from Nowhere, originally serialized in Morris's socialist journal *The Commonweal*, was written to counter the political impact of *Looking Backward*. To Morris, Bellamy's prophecy of state socialism relying on a heavily industrial economy powered by conscripted labour was simply abhorrent; to many later readers, it must be said, *Looking Backward* offers an all too recognizable anticipation of modern advanced societies whether capitalist or socialist. Morris believed that every utopia is a personal projection, a reflection of its author's temperament, and one of his reasons for labelling *News from Nowhere* a 'utopian romance' was doubtless to give himself more leeway for self-expression than would normally be expected in a work of socialist propaganda. While it fulfils all the formal requirements of utopian description – the conducted tour, the account of utopian history and government, the answers to frequently voiced objections to the vision of society the author is putting forward – *News from Nowhere* also has a much more whimsical aspect, parading a series of Morrisian idiosyncrasies in front of the reader. His protagonist, William Guest, wakes up in the twenty-first century having gone to bed in Morris's own house in Hammersmith. Later he journeys upriver to the author's country retreat at Kelmscott Manor. On the way he meets a number of Morrisian avatars: antiquarians, craftworkers, bibliophiles and the like. If Guest can hardly believe his luck and wonders several times if his presence in utopia is no more than a dream, the reason is that this pastoral future England seems so exactly tailored to his own predilections. Responses to *News from Nowhere* often differ sharply, depending on the reader's level of tolerance (or the reverse) for such genial but sentimental self-indulgence.

William Morris, who wrote *News from Nowhere* in his mid-fifties, was a poet, a leading political radical, an original and successful interior designer and the author of verse romances including his collection of mythical tales, *The Earthly Paradise* (1868–70). *News from Nowhere* coincided with his turn to heroic prose romances set not in the future but in medieval or earlier times: *A Dream of John Ball* (1888), *The House of the Wolfings* (1889), *The Roots of the Mountains* (1890), *The Story of the Glittering Plain* (1890) and others. His sheer facility as a romance writer is astonishing, and would still be so if he had not combined it with editing *The Commonweal*, running his handicrafts firm and experimenting with book design and production at the Kelmscott Press. *News from Nowhere* is a highly accomplished blend of romance narrative and utopian construction, but it is more than that, since Morris handles the romance plot with a subtlety and delicacy at least rivalling *A Crystal Age*.

There is, to begin with, no suggestion of romance about Morris's twenty-first-century England, since Guest's arrival there is as sudden and prosaic as possible:

> Well, I awoke, and found that I had kicked my bedclothes off; and no wonder, for it was hot and the sun shining brightly. I jumped up and washed and hurried on my clothes, but in a hazy and half-awake condition, as if I had slept

for a long, long while, and could not shake off the weight of slumber. In fact, I rather took it for granted that I was at home in my own room than saw that it was so.[30]

Guest's brisk awakening conveys not only his obliviousness to his surroundings, but the fact that, apart from the unfamiliar heat (he had gone to bed on a cold winter's night), he is capable of feeling perfectly at home in the new world: 'there was still the Thames, sparkling under the sun, and near high water, as last night I had seen it gleaming under the moon'.[31] Although something like a century and a half has passed since 'last night', the Thames continues to flow throughout the story, offering a link to the old world but also a symbol of constant change since a stable riverside utopia is something of a contradiction in terms. The river's transience, however, will not become apparent until much later, when the romance mode has taken over from this apparently mundane opening. Effectively this happens during the narrative of the upriver journey (chapters 21–32), after the formal guided tour and description of utopia are virtually complete. During the journey Guest, who has already responded warmly to the beauty and kindness of the female utopians, meets Ellen, a young woman who seems to reciprocate his interest. She is something of an athlete, enabling Morris to fill his story with the technicalities of rowing upstream which have evidently not changed since the nineteenth century.[32]

Not only are Guest and Ellen soon sharing a boat, but she offers the nineteenth-century visitor a potential future together. Guest, who is in every sense much older than his companion, is not triumphant like Julian West but fearful and apprehensive. He seems to realize that the love of a girl of the future can be no more than an erotic fantasy, though Ellen herself does not know this. Arriving at Kelmscott on the upper Thames where they have supposedly gone to take part in the haymaking, Ellen draws him apart and into the old manor house, offering, as it were, a guided tour of the old world rather than the twenty-first-century England we have seen up to now. It is when they are alone together in an upstairs room that Guest sinks into a dream of the past, as if unconscious of Ellen's presence. Very soon after this the illusion of the future begins to dissolve, until Guest finds himself back in the nineteenth century and the story is recast as a dream narrative (although this will not explain the fact that he leaves our world in London and returns to it in Oxfordshire). It is, Morris finally suggests, a romance that conveys responsibility and political obligation, feeding back into the socialist cause and the attempt to realize utopia: in the novel's last words, a 'vision' rather than a mere 'dream'.[33]

Although *News from Nowhere* had a number of successors, none can match its artistic quality. Charlotte Perkins Gilman's *Herland* (1915) is remarkable in that, though it is a feminist portrayal of a female separatist utopia, once again there is a romance plot turning on a utopian's love affair with a male visitor.[34] H. G. Wells begins *A Modern Utopia* by rejecting *News from Nowhere* as unrealistic; instead he offers a second-order utopia, based on a synthesis of previous utopian constructions adjusted to what he sees as the demands of contemporary, and necessarily imperfect, human society. Romance is confined to the aspirations of the narrator's companion, the Botanist, a reluctant visitor to utopia whose main function in the text is to provide a little comic relief. Wells, however, is the author not only of an anti-utopian romance (*The Time Machine*) and an anti-romantic utopia, but of texts such as *In the Days of the Comet* (1906) and *Men Like Gods* (1923) which may be classed as utopian romance. Remarkably enough, Wells can also claim to have originated the typical narrative form of the modern dystopian novel, a story whose protagonist is a citizen of the future society from which he comes to feel increasingly excluded. The plot of the dystopian novel hinges on alienation, rebellion, victimization and (in most cases) final suppression. In two turn-of-the-century texts, *When the Sleeper Wakes* (1899; subsequently revised as *The Sleeper Awakes*, 1910) and 'A Story of the Days to Come' (1899), Wells describes a claustrophobic future city with all the features later associated with Zamyatin, Huxley, Orwell and others: the totalitarian state dominating an architecturally overwhelming, closed environment, the regimented and enslaved population and the intense pressure on individuals to conform or be liquidated. Although *The Sleeper*, as its title indicates, uses the familiar nineteenth-century device to transport its hero into the future, Wells's protagonist Graham is unlike, say, Julian West in becoming a significant political figure in the strife-torn new world. 'A Story of the Days to Come' portrays a very similar world to *The Sleeper*, except that the protagonist is neither a survivor from the twentieth century nor a charismatic leader but an ordinary, alienated future citizen, the precursor of Zamyatin's D-503, Huxley's Bernard Marx and Orwell's Winston Smith.[35]

The abandonment of the 'travelogue' structure in modern dystopian fiction reflects the normal location of dystopias in the near future of our advanced industrial societies rather than in some remote and unexplored region of earth. Not only had the 'sleeper' device to get the protagonist into the future become increasingly hackneyed, but the totalitarian dystopia is essentially a closed society offering neither exit nor entry. If a visitor were allowed to roam around freely it would not be truly dystopian. This means that the romantic motifs of danger, passion and suffering must all arise within the society, most often – as in *We* and *Nineteen Eighty-Four* – emerging as the consequence of an illicit love-affair. The novels of both Zamyatin and Orwell employ a somewhat weak protagon-ist seduced by a fascinating female who may or may not be an *agent pro-vocateur*. D-503 is initially a model citizen, but his lover 1-330 perceives his potential usefulness to the coming rebellion against the One State. Julia in *Nineteen Eighty-Four* is ostensibly a rebel from the waist down only, but the background to the novel's dramatic action remains slightly mys-terious and readers may wonder if possibly she is acting under orders. Nevertheless, Orwell's denouement hinges not only on Winston's arrest, interrogation and torture but upon the romantic anticlimax of his and Julia's mutual betrayal.

Within the closed world of the modern dystopia there remains, as often as not, a kind of secondary travelogue element, since the protagonist must be granted a varied social experience in order for the society to be described fully. There is a clear example of this in *Brave New World*, which begins with a group of new students on a conducted tour of the London Hatcheries and Conditioning Centre.[36] The students have under-gone the very processes of cloning and conditioning that are being dem-onstrated to them, but we must assume that their memories have been wiped in the interim. Now they are shown round on a strictly limited, 'need to know' basis. Later in the novel Bernard and Lenina visit the Savage Reservation which is a preserved fragment of the old world, and then the tourist motif is reversed as they bring John the Savage back to London. John, however – given the identity of his father and mother – is strictly a product of the New World, from which he finds that there is no escape except suicide.

In *Brave New World*, unlike *We* and *Nineteen Eighty-Four*, the romantic plot elements (such as the return of the Director's long-lost son and the Savage's love for Lenina) are distanced and reduced to farce by Huxley's pervasive stance of satirical detachment. The cynical World Controller Mustapha Mond, a scholarly hermit without any personal life, is in many ways the most admirable character. Huxley, in other words, portrays dis-sidence and disaffection within his dystopia while deliberately crushing any expectation of heroism. Neither John the Savage nor Bernard Marx can be taken seriously. The situation is very different in *We*, *Nineteen Eighty-Four* and the majority of modern dystopian novels, where the standard romance conventions of commercial fiction play a much greater part, however suc-cessful the novelist may be in creating a fiction that is both artistically sat-isfying and intellectually and politically challenging. Even if the heyday of the utopian romance is now long past, it seems safe to predict that new combinations of utopia and romance will continue to enthrall and, in most cases, to alarm the reading public.

NOTES

1   E. M. Forster, *The Longest Journey* (Oxford University Press, 1960), p. 248.
2   Cf. Gillian Beer, *The Romance* (London: Methuen, 1970), p. 79.
3   Cf. Vita Fortunati,'Utopia as a Literary Genre', in Vita Fortunati and Raymond Trousson (eds.), *Dictionary of Literary Utopias* (Paris: Honoré Champion, 2000), pp. 634–43, 637.
4   William Congreve, *Incognita*, in Paul Salzman (ed.), *An Anthology of Seventeenth-Century Fiction* (Oxford University Press, 1991), p. 474.
5   Walter Scott, 'Essay on Romance' (1822), quoted in Alexander Welsh, *The Hero of the Waverley Novels* (New Haven: Yale University Press, 1963), p. 13.
6   Sir Thomas More, *Utopia*, trans. Raphe Robynson (1551), in *Utopia with the 'Dialogue of Comfort'* (London and Toronto: Dent, and New York: Dutton, 1910), p. 17.
7   Sir Philip Sidney, 'An Apology for Poetry', in Walter Jackson Bate (ed.), *Criticism: The Major Texts*, 2nd edn (New York: Harcourt Brace Jovanovich, 1970), p. 85.
8   Margaret Cavendish (Duchess of Newcastle), *The Blazing World* (1666), in Salzman (ed.), *An Anthology*, p. 252.
9   Sir Philip Sidney, *The Countess of Pembroke's Arcadia* (1580) (Harmondsworth: Penguin, 1987).
10 Voltaire, *Candide, ou l'Optimisme* (London, 1759).
11 James Henry Lawrence, *The Empire of the Nairs*, 2nd edn (4 vols., London: T. Hookham, 1811).
12 William Morris, *News from Nowhere, Or, an Epoch of Rest* (1890), ed. James Redmond (London: Routledge, 1970).
13 See Kenneth Graham, *English Criticism of the Novel 1865–1900* (Oxford University Press, 1965), pp. 61–76, esp. p. 68.
14 *Ibid.*, p. 63.
15 Nathaniel Hawthorne, *The Blithedale Romance* (1852), ed. Seymour Gross and Rosalie Murphy (New York: Norton Critical Edition, 1978).
16 Nathaniel Hawthorne, *The House of the Seven Gables* (1851), ed. Robert S. Levine (New York: Norton Critical Edition, 2005), p. vii.
17 *Ibid.*
18 Sir Edward Bulwer-Lytton, *The Coming Race* (1871) (Peterborough, ON: Broadview, 2002); Samuel Butler, *Erewhon* (1872), ed. Peter Mudford (Harmondsworth: Penguin, 1985).
19 See Victor Turner, *Dramas, Fields, and Metaphors: Symbolic Action in Human Society* (Ithaca: Cornell University Press, 1974), esp. p. 273.
20 Bulwer-Lytton, *The Coming Race*, pp. 24–5.
21 Patrick Parrinder, 'Entering Dystopia, Entering *Erewhon*', *Critical Survey* 17:1 (2005), 6–21.
22 Butler, *Erewhon*, p. 66.
23 *Ibid.*, pp. 70, 96.
24 W. H. Hudson, *A Crystal Age* (London: T. Fisher Unwin, 1887).
25 W. H. Hudson, *The Purple Land: Being the Narrative of one Richard Lamb's Adventures in the Banda Oriental, in South America, as told by Himself*, 2nd edn (London: Duckworth, 1904), p. 338.

26 H. G. Wells, *The Time Machine* (London: William Heinemann, 1895).
27 See Darko Suvin, 'Wells as the Turning Point of the SF Tradition', in Suvin, *Metamorphoses of Science Fiction: On the Poetics and History of a Literary Genre* (New Haven: Yale University Press, 1979), pp. 208–21.
28 'I am aiming throughout at a sort of shot-silk texture between philosophical discussion on the one hand and imaginative narrative on the other.' H. G. Wells, 1925 'Preface' to *A Modern Utopia*, ed. Gregory Claeys and Patrick Parrinder (Harmondsworth: Penguin, 2005), p. 6.
29 Edward Bellamy, *Looking Backward 2000–1887*, ed. Robert C. Elliott (Boston: Houghton Mifflin, 1966), pp. 136, 161.
30 Morris, *News from Nowhere*, p. 3.
31 *Ibid.*
32 As it happens, *News from Nowhere* appeared less than a year after Jerome K. Jerome's comic saga of Thames rowing, *Three Men in a Boat*.
33 Morris, *News from Nowhere*, p. 182.
34 Charlotte Perkins Gilman, *Herland* (1915) (New York: Panther, 1979).
35 H. G. Wells, *When the Sleeper Wakes* (London: Harper, 1899); subsequently revised as *The Sleeper Awakes* (1910) (London: Penguin, 2005); 'A Story of the Days to Come' (1899), in Everett F. Bleiler (ed.), *Three Prophetic Science Fiction Novels of H. G. Wells* (New York: Dover, 1960).
36 Aldous Huxley, *Brave New World* (London: Chatto & Windus, 1932).

BIBLIOGRAPHY

Beer, Gillian, *The Romance* (London: Methuen, 1970).
Bellamy, Edward, *Looking Backward 2000–1887*, ed. Robert C. Elliott (Boston: Houghton Mifflin, 1966).
Bulwer-Lytton, Sir Edward, *The Coming Race* (1871) (Peterborough, ON: Broadview, 2002).
Butler, Samuel, *Erewhon*, ed. Peter Mudford (Harmondsworth: Penguin, 1985).
Cavendish, Margaret (Duchess of Newcastle), *The Blazing World* (1666), in Paul Salzman (ed.), *An Anthology of Seventeenth-Century Fiction* (Oxford University Press, 1991).
Congreve, William *Incognita*, in Paul Salzman (ed.), *An Anthology of Seventeenth-Century Fiction* (Oxford University Press, 1991).
Forster, E. M., *The Longest Journey* (Oxford University Press, 1960).
Fortunati, Vita, 'Utopia as a Literary Genre', in Vita Fortunati and Raymond Trousson (eds.), *Dictionary of Literary Utopias* (Paris: Honoré Champion, 2000), pp. 634–43.
Gilman, Charlotte Perkins, *Herland* (1915) (New York: Panther, 1979).
Graham, Kenneth, *English Criticism of the Novel 1865–1900* (Oxford University Press, 1965).
Hawthorne, Nathaniel, *The Blithedale Romance* (1852), ed. Seymour Gross and Rosalie Murphy (New York: Norton Critical Edition, 1978).
  The House of the Seven Gables (1851), ed. Robert S. Levine (New York: Norton Critical Edition, 2005).
Hudson, W. H., *A Crystal Age* (London: T. Fisher Unwin, 1887).

The Purple Land: Being the Narrative of one Richard Lamb's Adventures in the Banda Oriental, in South America, as told by Himself, 2nd edn (London: Duckworth, 1904).

Huxley, Aldous, *Brave New World* (London: Chatto & Windus, 1932).

Lawrence, James Henry, *The Empire of the Nairs*, 2nd edn (4 vols., London: T. Hookham, 1811).

More, Sir Thomas, *Utopia*, trans. Raphe Robynson [1551], in *Utopia with the 'Dialogue of Comfort'* (London: Dent, and New York: Dutton, 1910).

Morris, William, *News from Nowhere, Or, an Epoch of Rest*, ed. James Redmond (London: Routledge, 1970).

Orwell, George, *Nineteen Eighty-Four* (London: Secker & Warburg, 1949).

Parrinder, Patrick, 'Entering Dystopia, Entering Erewhon', *Critical Survey* 17:1 (2005), 6–21.

Salzman, Paul (ed.), *An Anthology of Seventeenth-Century Fiction* (Oxford University Press, 1991).

Scott, Walter, 'Essay on Romance' (1822), quoted in Alexander Welsh, *The Hero of the Waverley Novels* (New Haven: Yale University Press, 1963).

Sidney, Sir Philip, 'An Apology for Poetry', in Walter Jackson Bate (ed.), *Criticism: The Major Texts*, 2nd edn (New York: Harcourt Brace Jovanovich, 1970).

The Countess of Pembroke's Arcadia (1580) (Harmondsworth: Penguin, 1987).

Suvin, Darko, 'Wells as the Turning Point of the SF Tradition', in Suvin, *Metamorphoses of Science Fiction: On the Poetics and History of a Literary Genre* (New Haven: Yale University Press, 1979), pp. 208–21.

Turner, Victor, *Dramas, Fields, and Metaphors: Symbolic Action in Human Society* (Ithaca: Cornell University Press, 1974).

Voltaire, *Candide, ou l'Optimisme* (London, 1759).

Wells, H. G., *A Modern Utopia*, ed. Gregory Claeys and Patrick Parrinder (Harmondsworth: Penguin, 2005).

'A Story of the Days to Come' (1899), in Everett F. Bleiler (ed.), *Three Prophetic Science Fiction Novels of H. G. Wells* (New York: Dover, 1960).

The Sleeper Awakes, ed. Patrick Parrinder (London: Penguin, 2005).

The Time Machine (London: William Heinemann, 1895).

When the Sleeper Wakes (London: Harper, 1899).

8

ALESSA JOHNS

Feminism and utopianism

Feminists have joined in celebrating and critiquing utopianism. On the one hand they have profited from the socio-political changes that visions of better societies have impelled; on the other, they have called into question utopias that depict static perfection – societies so ideal that they have nowhere to go, rely on rigid hierarchies and use coercion to maintain their perfect order. Thomas More's *Utopia* (1516) epitomizes the traditional version: it is fully mapped, boasting uniform towns that are geometrically organized with a centrally located seat of power from which the sovereign can conduct surveillance. Infrastructure supports the discipline of inhabitants; architecture and institutions encourage certain behaviours and discourage others. Ancient books, repeated rituals, pervasive symbols and signs ground authority in the traditional utopia. Clothing is issued and regulated. Dissenters are expelled or incarcerated. Such traditional utopias have also been called 'classical', 'blueprint', or 'end-state' utopias, and many critics have concurred that, even though inhabitants are provided for, such visions are distasteful. Despite readers' admiration for the wit and inventiveness of More's *Utopia*, few would want to live there. Women in particular have fared poorly in traditional blueprint utopias, where they have been forced to labour endlessly and bow to humourless patriarchs.

Consequently feminist utopian authors and critics have generally side-stepped the blueprint form to privilege instead a 'process' or 'reproductive' or 'critical' model.[1] What is surprising, and what will be explored here, is that this form of process-oriented feminist utopianism is not new. I will argue that it is not merely the product of what is called the first-, second- and third-wave feminism of the nineteenth, twentieth and twenty-first centuries. Instead, process-oriented utopianism characterizes a large part of feminist utopian writing beginning in the late middle ages and continuing to today – from Christine de Pizan to Sarah Scott to Ursula K. Le Guin – and it appears emphatically in Enlightenment Britain: that is, *before* what is considered the modern women's movement. Such trans-historical persistence does not imply any essential female psychology; instead, it suggests continuity in many feminists' reactions to socio-cultural arrangements in the Anglo-American world (and arguably in the West in general) that have remained deeply patriarchal despite significant political and economic changes over time.

Before I address the tenacity and salient characteristics of process-oriented feminist utopianism, it will be well to consider more generally why the utopian imagination has been crucial for feminists even though classic works in the genre have treated women so poorly. Three reasons stand out. First, gender equality has never fully existed, so it must be imagined if it is to become a subject of conscious thought and discussion. According to Anne Mellor, 'Those seeking a viable model of a non-sexist society must ... look to the future; their model must be constructed first as a utopia.'[2] Second, given the limited political, economic and social clout of feminists, they have sought out cultural modes, especially artistic and literary representations, as the most eligible means of making a different future comprehensible to the largest possible audience. The utopian literary mode, so open to imaginative construction and unhindered theorizing, has therefore always appeared useful to feminist authors. However, the fully mapped, blueprint variety has never been obligatory even if it has been the most prominent, and part of what is prized even in the traditional utopia is the flair with which an author conceives of unexpected cultural practices. Utopia as thought-experiment has consistently offered ways of altering people's perceptions, of making the familiar seem strange. Consequently, third, veering from the traditional utopia has given feminists a socially viable course of discursive and ideological deviance. As Darby Lewes has written of the late nineteenth century, 'the dialectical and ambiguous genre of lost outsiders in disorienting worlds mirrored women's own situation' in a society where on the one hand they were told they were central to human existence and morally accountable yet, on the other hand, lived lives in which they were legally without status, politically voiceless and domestically subordinated.[3]

Therefore utopia has long been a fitting and crucial vehicle for women's critique. One of the few modes available for feminist theorizing and the articulation of alternatives, it became particularly helpful when increasing literacy, wealth and access to books opened the literary marketplace to European women in the eighteenth century. It is consequently no surprise that, after a lull in the production of utopian literature in the early nineteenth century, modern feminists returned to utopian visions to express their desires for a more just and equitable society in the late nineteenth and early twentieth centuries, and that the liberation movements of the 1970s gave rise to another flowering of feminist utopianism.

Still, some feminist theorists today wonder whether the idea of utopia retains resonance. Sally Kitch has recently proposed 'post-utopian approaches to feminist thought' that favour what she calls realism over imagined improvements. 'Without utopianism feminism can more readily recognize contingent truths, inevitable conflicts, and complex motivations and loyalties, as it addresses the problems it can name. Realistic feminist thought can embrace the serendipity and vagaries of human life, identity, relationships, and institutions.'[4] Others suggest that the pressures of our plural world and of socio-cultural emphases on differences in nationality, race, ethnicity, class, sexuality, ability and religion as well as gender all underscore the complexities of our transnational world and raise the question whether feminism itself, with its origins in well-to-do, white, western culture, remains a feasible political force. Given the enormous concerns of today, old forms of feminist agitation appear to some to make little sense, and the depiction of alternative worlds through interventions in utopian writing appears to them wholly ineffectual. However, countering such pessimism are others who suggest that feminists today need utopian ideas more than ever. Strategies for empowering women and subaltern groups, they argue, are constantly thwarted by reactionary political and social forces, and feminists, men as well as women, need to 'take time out to dream'; they insist that utopian literature facilitates the imaginative speculation necessary for generating new liberating strategies in a globalized world.

Anglo-American feminism is therefore at a crossroads in the early twenty-first century. I will side with the hopeful to suggest that a look at the utopian visions of feminist authors through the centuries shows not only how the idea of utopia can and should remain useful, but also how early authors actually address some of the very reservations raised by current critics. Feminist writers of the past reacted creatively and imaginatively to substantial pressures under complicated circumstances of their own, and the surprising historical continuities at the heart of their concerns led to representations, intelligent and sensitive, from which we can glean courage and learn.

Utopia resists classification because the very idea is so vast, spanning not only literary works but also experimental communities, political programmes and psychological proclivities. However, creating categories helps to counter hasty dismissals of the literature – sometimes denigrated as subliterary precisely because of its perceived amorphousness – by offering conceptual frameworks that allow us profitably to analyse and evaluate it. In considering the categories below we need to keep in mind that distinctions in feminist utopias sometimes constitute shifts away from the traditional model rather than stark oppositions, that not all feminist utopias necessarily reveal all characteristics and that some traditional utopias display 'process' characteristics too. It is useful to avoid thinking in terms of opposed sets of texts and to envisage instead continua created by a series of points on a graph. The horizontal axis would chart generic *form*, moving from the static, blueprint variety on the left to the process-oriented form on the right; the vertical axis would consider *content* and chart its way from patriarchal or sexist representations at the bottom to feminist ones at the top. On such a graph the texts I discuss below would be the plotted points clustered with significant density at the top right area. There would of course be a few outlying texts that, though containing feminist traits, landed short of the top right corner by virtue of following a static model, as some critics have suggested concerning Margaret Cavendish's *Blazing World*, Mary Bradley Lane's *Mizora* or Sheri Tepper's *Gate to Women's Country*. And there would likely be some that, though containing process traits, would not be plotted as feminist, for instance William Morris's *News from Nowhere*. Such a graph would also reveal some process-oriented feminist utopias to be male-authored (for example Samuel Delany's *Triton* or Kim Stanley Robinson's *Pacific Edge*). Envisioning such a diagram helps us to fathom the complexity and variety of this vast literature while highlighting meaningful trends.

To attempt to do justice to the variety of texts, I offer numerous examples from different historical periods; at the same time I hope to explain how works respond to specific historical contexts even as they demonstrate trans-historical continuities. I focus necessarily on a few prominent texts and consider the four main periods of greatest feminist utopian output: first, the late middle ages and beginning of the early modern period, when the *querelle des femmes*, the debate over women, encouraged Christine de Pizan to compose *The Book of the City of Ladies* (1404–5) and its sequel, *The Book of the Three Virtues* (1405); second, the 'long eighteenth century', when increasing wealth due to colonialism and trade spurred debates about luxury and the meaning of the good life, as in Mary Astell's *Serious Proposal* (1694) and Sarah Scott's *Millenium Hall* (1762); third, the late nineteenth and early twentieth century, when socialist ideas and the end of the Civil War in the United States brought about vast political shifts and women, along with freed slaves, sought suffrage and greater sway, lending impetus to Frances Harper's *Iola Leroy* (1892) and Charlotte Perkins Gilman's *Herland* (1915); and fourth, the 1970s, when feminists wished to give shape to their needs and desires after the New Left failed adequately to press for women's rights, traceable in works such as Ursula K. Le Guin's *The Dispossessed* (1974) and Marge Piercy's *Woman on the Edge of Time* (1976).[5]

The most prominent distinction characterizing feminists' utopian expression, as I have suggested, is that it has generally favoured process-oriented utopianism instead of adhering to the better-known 'classic', 'blueprint', 'end-state' model.[6] But why have so many feminists preferred this mode, and in what does such utopianism consist? Five features seem most salient in lending to feminist utopias their process-oriented character: (1) Feminist utopias see education and intellectual development as central to the individual and to women's empowerment; (2) they embrace a view of human nature as malleable and social rather than determined, fallen and individualist; (3) they favour a gradualist approach to change, a cumulative approach to history and a shared approach to power; (4) they view the non-human natural world as dynamic rather than as an inert receiver of human impulses; and (5) they are usually pragmatic. These features, I suggest, follow from an author's viewing issues from the perspective of female subjection and from a knowledge that change cannot be undertaken alone; what allows for transhistorical continuity in spite of historical and other significant differences between writers is the feminists' shared commitment to exposing and undoing injustices experienced by women and subalterns in patriarchy.

1. Centrality of education

The most common thread in feminist utopian writing is the emphasis on education. Though this theme appears also in traditional utopias, education tends there to remain tangential, whereas it becomes the fulcrum in feminists' works all the way into the twentieth century. Through most of western history, women have had far less access to education than men, and they have seen this lack as key to their subordinate status. Viewing female history and the accomplishments of celebrated women, feminists often ask: since it is clear women are educable and their minds are as keen as their brothers', why are they denied access to the means of developing their intellects? Feminist utopias therefore pay enormous attention to education of all types.

Some feminist utopian authors approach education through *institutions*, which are often described in great detail, including buildings, subjects of instruction and timetables. Mary Astell's *Serious Proposal to the Ladies* calls for the establishment of a female monastery where women attend to the cultivation of their souls as they study theology and philosophy and develop significant friendships. In Sarah Scott's *Sir George Ellison* (1766) the Millenium Hall women generously set up a school system for girls of all classes, though they less liberally ensure that the girls remain planted in those classes: 'third-rank' women who are to become servants or 'wives to men in small trades' learn writing and accounts, washing, baking, brewing and milking; 'second-rank' girls with 'no prospect of considerable fortunes' study economics, sewing, cooking and drawing; and 'first rank' girls follow an ambitious academic curriculum including music, arithmetic, science, history, geography, languages, religion, 'the less abstruse parts of astronomy, natural philosophy, ethics, and the rational parts of metaphysics'.[7] Unlike later utopias, early feminist visions often reinforce class hierarchies, even though they insist that *all* women are to gain substantial freedoms and that society as a whole is to profit: witness Clara Reeve's *Plans of Education* (1792), which suggests that institutions of learning, including girls' academies, will help Britain approach the ideal of 'Utopia ... where every order is kept in its proper state, and none is allowed to encroach upon, or oppress another'.[8] In the same year, however, *A Vindication of the Rights of Woman* appeared from the pen of the radical Mary Wollstonecraft; it is a text no less concerned than Reeve's to create a productive populace and it also takes the servant class for granted, but it critiques the aristocracy viciously, arguing that virtue is most likely to reside in the middle ranks. *A Vindication* calls for public co-education of girls and boys, suggesting that this would lead to rational relationships between the sexes, encourage early marriages, and make women more attentive mothers, better companions and more involved citizens.[9]

Wollstonecraft's ideas made their way to America. Frances Wright, influenced by Wollstonecraft as well as by Robert Owen, saw schools as a way to 'perfect the free institutions of America' in 1829: 'a nation to be strong, must be united; to be united, must be equal in condition; to be equal in condition, must be similar in habits and in feeling; to be similar in habits and in feeling, *must be raised in national institutions, as the children of a common family, and citizens of a common country*'.[10] In Mary Bradley Lane's *Mizora* (1880–1) the narrator sees the virtues of the Mizoran women's education and resolves that 'it is the duty of every government to make its schools and colleges, and everything appertaining to education – FREE'.[11] In the nineteenth century economic and political shifts spurred more far-reaching discussions not only of the interconnections among class, gender and nation but also race. African American author Frances Harper in *Iola Leroy* views education as the means for uplifting former slaves and thereby demonstrates its double efficacy in empowering not only the female sex ('every woman ought to know how to earn her own living') but also freed blacks. Her biracial protagonist Iola refuses to pass for white, and, finding family members and bringing them together into a utopian community after the Civil War, works to teach blacks self-reliance in the American south.[12]

In other feminist utopias education is portrayed through *reading*, either casual, formally interpreted in group settings, or prescribed in syllabi. Thus in the utopic girls' school of Sarah Fielding's *The Governess* (1749) education occurs through proctored discussions of didactic stories. Mary Hamilton offers reading lists in the *Duchess de Crui* (1777) and builds an octagonal library at the centre of her utopian *Munster Village* (1778). She addresses explicitly the issue of process or the reproductive power of education, which, she argues, 'is productive of infinite advantages, extending its influence to society, and may operate upon posterity to the end of the world'.[13] In Ursula Le Guin's *The Dispossessed* the protagonist Shevek, a physicist and inhabitant of the egalitarian, anarchistic moon Anarres, is handed a book by his mentor and directed to teach himself the Iotic language of the rival planet Urras through solitary study. He is also told to keep his knowledge a secret, which perplexes him since it is 'a situation so new to him and morally so confusing that he had not yet worked it out'.[14] Knowledge is to be shared; the idea of intellectual property appears oxymoronic. On Anarres females receive the same educational opportunities as men do, but on Urras, Shevek is startled to find, the huge University is 'exclusively male … and [is] not organized federatively but hierarchically, from the top down' (65).

Despite women's increasing access to education and libraries through the twentieth century, feminists have not left off insisting on the continued relevance of reading, though the ways the issue is framed have changed in a world shaped by new media. In a dystopian work such as Margaret Atwood's *The Handmaid's Tale* (1986) the dangers of digitization are depicted in the fundamentalist Republic of Gilead, where people's identities are stolen electronically and books outlawed and burned. The female narrator Offred, desperately greedy for the intellectual stimulation of words, devours even a shabby, antiquated issue of *Vogue* magazine illicitly acquired through her Commander. Together they play a furtive game of Scrabble.

Education in feminist utopias is also fostered through *conversation*, which can train girls in current affairs, language and critical thinking. In her *Essay in Defence of the Female Sex* (1696) Judith Drake suggests that girls were in fact more adept socially than boys because they participated in discussions of books rather than pursuing a classical education, which emphasized Latin and Greek.[15] The popularity of eighteenth-century salons and bluestocking gatherings underscored the profit of conversation, as Hannah More put it in her poem *The Bas-Bleu, or Conversation* (1787):

> Ah! wherefore wise, if none must hear?
> Our intellectual ore must shine,
> Not slumber idly in the mine.
> Let education's moral mint
> The noblest images imprint;
> Let taste her curious touchstone hold,
> To try if standard be the gold;

But 'tis thy commerce, Conversation,
Must give it use by circulation;
That noblest commerce of mankind,
Whose precious merchandize is MIND![16]

Britain's increasingly commercial and imperial economy offered a certain momentum for feminists, even as feminists themselves sometimes noted how their position paralleled that of ruthlessly colonized subalterns. Mary Wollstonecraft in *A Vindication* laments: 'Is sugar always to be produced by vital blood? Is one half of the human species, like the poor African slaves, to be subject to prejudices that brutalize them ...? Is not this indirectly to deny woman reason?'[17] Recognizing the costs of British prosperity, feminists nonetheless also saw that coffee houses, tea tables and salon gatherings could become utopian spaces in which women moved, conversed and increased their knowledge alongside men.

Even later, after national plans of schooling were drawn up in Britain and the United States, Charlotte Perkins Gilman's *Herland* stressed that in the utopia education is 'our highest art', the source of citizens' 'real growth'.[18] Herlanders attend lectures as a public benefit, in stark contrast to citizens of Thomas More's Utopia who, wishing to gain learning, attend talks in their 'spare time ... before daybreak' so as not to waste work hours, and they engage in conversations merely to 'amuse themselves' rather than to profit intellectually;[19] brain work is reserved for a hand-selected elite. Shevek's education in Le Guin's *The Dispossessed* occurs through animated conversations with friends as he is growing up and with mentors as he is developing his professional interests. He keeps his theories about time in his head, discussing them casually at gatherings, while Urrasti physicists assume that what is crucial must be written down and therefore clear his computer to get at his ideas. Looking to women's traditions, feminist authors have recognized the significant extent to which knowledge has been passed on orally; the dialogue that dominates utopian writing dovetails conveniently with feminists' hope that the power of spoken words will influence people, expand knowledge and increase women's freedoms.

Finally, education appears in feminist utopias occurring through *example*, allowing women to become empowered by following dynamic models. Pizan, in *The Book of the City of Ladies*, shapes her legendary into an allegorical utopian city filled with all of history's good women, thereby creating a place where a mother sets 'a good example of integrity and learnedness' for her daughter and all are encouraged 'to cultivate virtue, to flee vice, to increase and multiply our City, and to rejoice and act well'.[20] Participating in the *querelle des femmes*, Pizan sought to revise and thereby lend a feminist impulse to Boccaccio's *De mulieribus claris* (*On Famous Women*). The main theme of Mary Astell's *Serious Proposal* is also imitation, in particular the imitation of Christ. Astell wishes women of the female monastery to copy the pious, Christ-like behaviour of those around them, to improve their souls through a 'holy emulation which a continual view of the brightest and most exemplary Lives will excite in us'.[21] While it has been argued that Thomas More, also inspired by the monastic model, sought to curtail social emulation in Utopia as a way of combating the sin of pride, feminists have used the idea of imitation from an optimistic viewpoint: copying positive models will increase the amount and range of ethical behaviour and enhance women's lives and their chances for salvation. Harper contrasts the examples of Iola Leroy's employers Mr Cohen and Mr Cloten to show how a businessman should model the equitable treatment of his black employees in order to create fair working conditions,[22] while in *The Female Man* (1975) Joanna Russ uses as negative examples the despicable behaviour of men in the different worlds she describes – a New York party host and a Manlander boss who insult and make passes at women – in order to expose misogyny and justify the violent attacks they then suffer from Janet and Jael.[23]

From the middle ages to today feminists of various ideological bents have been aware of the benefits of education and sought to further knowledge on all levels. Learned ladies were in the past often socially derided – as Rectitude puts it in Pizan's *Book of the City of Ladies*, 'many foolish men have claimed [that it is bad for women to be educated] because it displeased them that women knew more than they did'[24] – but feminists have not allowed this prejudice to impede study in their utopian visions, where they imagine access to knowledge that happens openly, avidly and regularly, and is seen to encompass all aspects of life. Feminists repeatedly argue that women will become better mothers and friends, more productive citizens and more devout believers if they are given access to books and training. Often women are depicted as instructors, and the implication is that their teaching will replicate itself as students, male as well as female, become tutors themselves, furthering virtue and happiness. The perpetuation and extension of knowledge is a crucial part of the reproductive utopian process.

2. Human nature adaptable and social

In keeping with the belief that people can be educated, most feminist utopian authors suggest that human psychology can be amended. Where Thomas More saw human nature as fallen, as likely to give way to sin unless checked by institutions and surveillance, feminists have generally viewed human beings as at least partially alterable from within. Thus feminist utopias reveal a faith in behaviour modification, looking to stories, conversation, education and play to teach new habits, goals and values. One could argue that this tendency emerges from a model of childrearing, and it certainly may be influenced by women's longstanding roles as mothers and nurturers; yet, in feminist utopias this process happens socially, in communities and tribes, rather than strictly within nuclear families. Feminists emphasize that inhabitants, instead of simply learning traditional family functions, absorb the aims of the society as a whole and muster the motivation to act morally.

Even before Locke's *Essay Concerning Human Understanding* (1690) feminists furthered the idea that individuals' experience shaped their development ('nurture versus nature'). Pizan's *Book of the City of Ladies*, where models of virtue persuade readers to become models of virtue themselves, implies a view of human beings not only motivated by vanity and self-interest (they wish to stand out), but also capable of altering their actions. Astell in the seventeenth century similarly counts on such vanity as she wishes to 'decoy' women who lack sufficient 'Piety to read a Book for its Usefulness' into seeking the gratification of reading a book by a woman and unexpectedly being edified by it.[25] Sarah Scott in the eighteenth century builds games into her stories so that vain people will evolve into utopian subjects. Thus a coquettish wife is told to accompany her husband into the country and to read romances. These will stimulate desires she will then redirect towards her husband, making him her hero and curtailing her egotistic wishes to be desired by other men. After romances, 'more rational Studies were to succeed; that after being taught how to love, she might learn what was lovely, the better to place her Affections, and to deserve those of others'.[26] Even the marital relationship is to open out into social affinity. In Marge Piercy's utopian Mattapoisett, inhabitants seek to 'educate the senses, the imagination, the social being, the muscles, the nervous system, the intuition, the sense of beauty – as well as memory and intellect' to prevent individual isolation and to create instead 'a net of connecting'.[27] An important exception would appear to be the separatist communities from which men have been banished – as Scott's Millenium Hall, Gilman's Herland, or Gearhart's Wanderground (1979) – suggesting that men are irremediably power-hungry or violent and will insist on the reinstatement of patriarchal forms of dominance if allowed admittance. Yet, with a notable exception like Russ's *Female Man*, even in these works trustworthy men appear, for example D'Avora and the narrator in *Millenium Hall*, Jeff and Van in *Herland*, or the 'gentles' in *Wanderground*; these characters offer alternative versions of masculinity and sexuality and imply the possibility of new, egalitarian forms of interaction between the sexes.

Feminist utopian authors have drawn on their understanding of how women and underlings in general have persuaded people subtly when they have had little power to command. In her *Book of the Three Virtues*, also called *The Treasure of the City of Ladies* (1405), Pizan acknowledges that a woman's power derives not from herself but from her rank; if she wishes to achieve her ends she needs to be an effective psychologist and able manager of those around her. The whole book offers advice to women of different ranks about how this can be accomplished. Pizan draws a remarkable conclusion that anticipates social contract theory; most people, even princes, are in fact in the same dependent situation and would do well to act accordingly: 'Although the prince may be lord and master of his subjects, the subjects nevertheless make the lord and not the lord the subjects ... he must necessarily keep their affections, not by harshness but in such a way that from this love comes fear, or otherwise his authority is in peril.'[28] This astute analysis of the derivation of power underscores how deeply even an early feminist assessed the subaltern's position of dependence and how central a topic to feminists has been the tiptoeing through different types of subjection. Sarah Fielding describes the pain of what was called the dependent 'toadeater', which is 'a Metaphor taken from a Mountebank's Boy's eating Toads, in order to shew his Master's Skill in expelling Poison ... And the Metaphor may be carried on yet farther, for most People have so much the Art of tormenting, that every time they have made the poor Creatures they have in their power *swallow a Toad*, they have given them something to expel it again, that they may be ready to swallow the next thing.'[29] To survive, the dependant must become a careful reader of personalities, knowing when and how to avoid manipulation but being able to exploit opportunities for improving a pitiful situation by appealing to the conscience or self-interest of superiors. Feminist utopian authors, conceiving their narratives by looking from the position of the underling, have no illusions about people's capacities for oppression, and yet they hold out a hope in the canny and persuasive strengths of the powerless: sometimes even those wielding authority will be educated to mercy or even taught the advantages of fully accepting utopian values.

Central to such utopian values, whether traditional or feminist, is the importance of the community. In traditional works the group does not attain the same level of intensity as it does in feminist ones, where not only comradeship but love, intimacy and spiritual connection characterize the ties between members. In Astell's *Serious Proposal* the women's community will offer the chance for sacred friendship:

> We shall have opportunity of contracting the purest and noblest Friendship; a Blessing, the purchase of which were richly worth all the World besides! For she who possesses a worthy Person, has certainly obtain'd the richest Treasure. A Blessing that Monarchs may envy, and she who enjoys is happier than she

who fills a Throne! A Blessing, which next to the love of GOD, is the choicest Jewel in our Caelestial Diadem … [I]f we cannot spare a hearty Good-will to one or two choice Persons, how can it ever be thought, that we shou'd well acquit our selves of that Charity which is due to all Mankind? For Friendship is nothing else but Charity contracted; it is … a kind of revenging ourselves on the narrowness of our Faculties, by exemplifying that extraordinary Charity on one or two, which we are willing, but not able to exercise towards all.[30]

Astell uses the attractive metaphors of jewels and crowns, speaking of purchase and possession, to persuade both her wealthy, worldly readers and the Princess to whom she dedicated this work that communal feeling, distilled into friendship, must be dearer than power and material acquisition. Sarah Fielding's *David Simple* (1744) is, in the words of the subtitle, about the protagonist's 'Search of a Real Friend'. After many trials he succeeds, and the novel ends with two weddings which form a community where all 'contribute to the Happiness of the others'.[31] Fielding repeatedly depicts communities of shared property, work and emotion in order to counter the pervasive acquisitiveness of the early capitalism of her time. The narrator concludes: 'It is impossible for the most lively Imagination to form an Idea more pleasing than what this little Society enjoyed, in the true Proofs of each other's Love: And, as strong a Picture as this is of real Happiness, it is in the power of every Community to attain it.'[32] The early twentieth-century American male visitor to Gilman's Herland likewise describes how the inhabitants 'thought in terms of the community';[33] 'all the surrendering devotion our [American] women have put into their private families, these women put into their country and race. All the loyalty and service men expect of wives, they gave, not singly to men, but collectively to one another.'[34] In Gearhart's *Wanderground* the hill women live pastorally without the trappings of industrialized society, and emotion moves as freely as wealth between the female members. In Russ's *Female Man*, Le Guin's *Dispossessed*, and Piercy's Mattapoisett, the inhabitants are sexually free from puberty onward, even if monogamy is sometimes chosen.

Feminist utopias offer varied approaches to sexuality and motherhood and parenting – in some, reproduction occurs through parthenogenesis, in some through heterosexual intercourse; in some, children are part of families, in others they become offspring of the entire community, and in others there is a combination of both approaches – and earlier visions are more likely than later nineteenth or twentieth-century ones to depict hierarchical social arrangements. Nonetheless, there is a strong overall tendency to revise the 'family' into an egalitarian unit, not based on sex or blood ties alone, in which love – more than mere allegiance or family identification – inspires people and binds the community. Gender roles are more visible in earlier texts, but work is equally distributed and, crucially, feeling circulates in even exchange so that emotional needs and desires are satisfied.

3. Gradualist change, cumulative history, shared power

The dependant's perspective also dominates feminist utopian approaches to history, to change through time. Traditional utopias tend to rely on revolutionary substitution, abrupt regime change, for the origin of the society and then on a subsequent perpetuation of dictated social forms and rituals. The reader of More's *Utopia* finds out in a few sentences how 'Utopus ... conquered the country and gave it his name', overpowered the natives, quickly made the peninsula into an island, and subdued the 'neighboring peoples, who ... were struck with wonder and terror at his success'.[35] Power there is manifestly patriarchal: 'The oldest of every household ... is the ruler. Wives are subject to their husbands, children to their parents, and generally the younger to their elders.'[36] Rituals sustain the distribution of power by reinforcing social roles and hierarchies. Absolutist political power is the model for the early traditional utopia, where a divine-right sovereign demands blind obedience and has the authority to command by fiat.

By contrast, feminist utopias across the centuries tend to depict shared power and promote gradual reform and ongoing change. They avoid revolutionary shifts, build their societies piecemeal and adjust them little by little. Pizan's Reason tells the narrator of the *Book of the City of Ladies*: 'you will set the foundations deep to last all the longer, and then you will raise the walls so high that they will not fear anyone'; and after this Rectitude decides 'that our construction is quite well advanced, for the houses of the City of Ladies stand completed all along the wide streets ... It is therefore right that we start to people this noble City now.'[37] In *Millenium Hall* Scott shows how inhabitants appear there one by one, gradually forming the society which gains in residents until more houses need to be purchased: accommodation to circumstances expresses their attitude towards time and change. Hamilton's Munster Village is slowly created and inhabited. Harper's Iola Leroy first needs to find her family and then seeks to expand outward to create and educate a community. Gilman explains the evolving history of the Herlanders: 'their time-sense was not limited to the hopes and ambitions of an individual life'.[38] The mindset is long-term and geared to social adjustments. In Le Guin's *The Dispossessed* couples on Anarres wanting to live in partnership simply build a room onto an existing structure, 'and long, low, straggling buildings might thus be created room by room, called "partners' truck trains"'.[39] As a need arises, the inhabitants of utopia respond.

Adaptation to circumstances literally shapes the societies: form follows function. Instead of building identical cities simultaneously, feminist utopians fill one house or community and then settle another. No master plan governs; instead, one improvement leads to another and one event to the next. A recognition of contingency therefore characterizes much feminist utopian thought, and to respond effectively a decentralized, quasi-anarchistic form of government often emerges. Non-hierarchical decision-making characterizes the small communities that dominate feminist utopian writing. According to Joanna Russ, the general classlessness in 1970s feminist utopias fosters a dispersion of power and therefore the capacity for directing change through time. This classlessness is so 'pervasive … e.g., the informality of tone, the shifting of jobs from person to person, the free choice of jobs whenever possible – that the authors' not discussing their worlds' forms of government seems neither ignorance nor sloppiness'.[40] In *The Female Man* Russ, in the voice of Joanna, suggests that men have always been the history makers – 'Men succeed. Women get married. Men fail. Women get married … Men start wars. Women get married. Men stop them. Women get married. Dull, dull' – so a woman must become a man if she is to achieve agency and self-determination, or, alternatively, she can remove herself, work towards and inhabit a lesbian separatist society like Janet's Whileaway.[41] Le Guin depicts Anarres as an anarchistic society, as does Piercy Mattapoisett. But even Scott's eighteenth-century Millenium Hall, dominated by an oligarchy of high-ranking women, makes a point of emphasizing women's self-determination: inhabitants should be free to decide how they spend their time; they should be at liberty to leave or withdraw when they wish. Women's freedom begins with the right to come and go, to participate or not.

And the vision is so attractive it proliferates. Feminists imagine one utopia which then often spills over into another, so that utopia expands by replication. Pizan's *Book of the City of Ladies* spills over into its sequel, the *Treasure*; Mary Astell's *Serious Proposal* moves from Part I to Part II; Sarah Scott's *Millenium Hall* begets *Sir George Ellison*. Readers want to know what happens to the society next, but whereas traditional utopias have reached their perfection, feminist utopias create a reproductive inner energy that leads naturally to multiplication. Their inner logic about how utopia is achieved piecemeal and then expanded through the cascading efforts of dependants concludes in an ongoing reproduction of ideal societies and literary sequels. In later texts new worlds expand into the future, with movement back and forth between the societies: Russ shuttles between the 1969 world and the future Whileaway; Le Guin moves between Anarres and Urras; Piercy shifts from modern-day New York to Mattapoisett and back again. Characters move beyond their world, often through time-travel, in order to effect present and future change. Thus the message spreads through space and time, and the literary utopias operate on the level of form as well as content, opening out beyond their bounds rather than reinforcing a limited, traditional insularity.

Indeed the notion of proliferation, coming from the dependant's view of power and politics, shapes the feminist utopian view of history: it is not the traditional fantasy of suddenly summoning Eden. Instead it is a theory of history as accumulation, the combined power of many small, discrete events issuing in large impacts. According to Sarah Scott, 'Upon these common, and frequent acts, depends in great measure the happiness of those connected with us. Great injuries or great benefits are seldom in our power; the opportunities for either are few.'[42] In Piercy's *Woman on the Edge of Time* utopian Mattapoisett is only one of several futures that are possible, and even that future society turns out to be engaged in struggle against reactionary forces. Connie, the twentieth-century protagonist, is contacted to become involved in the future war. With courage gained through communication with Mattapoisett, she musters the resolve to rebel against the oppressive forces in the present, thereby weakening the reactionary powers of the cyborgs and tyrants against whom the Mattapoisettians of the future are fighting. Piercy thus emphasizes the importance of each individual's resolve in countering socio-political oppression. American works of the 1970s such as Rita Mae Brown's *Rubyfruit Jungle*, Russ's *The Female Man* and Piercy's *Woman on the Edge of Time* all 'favor … a movement *toward* utopia in a journey of many small steps … Change, they maintain, is … the sum total of changes we ourselves create day by day in the process of living', in the words of Angelika Bammer.[43]

Scott in the eighteenth century expressed this rationale to address the question of historiography on a national level. In her view,

> what is looked upon by the public eye as the effects of national resentment for national injuries, and spreads the most extensive destruction, sometimes originally arises from the private views of the lowest officer in the monarch's service, as the greatest river has its source under ground; in its first appearance little more than a bubbling rivulet, scarcely perceptible, till uniting with every stream it meets in its progress, it swells gradually into a river, whose torrent at length destroys every thing that opposes its course.[44]

Scott responded as a feminist utopian writer to new theories of philosophical history in her time, which argued that great movements, leaders and nations are what make history and that this is therefore what written histories should include. She countered that it is smaller forces, the collective acts of individuals that cause the wheels to turn; grand events are only the most visible manifestations of less conspicuous catalysts. She argued with Samuel Johnson for the importance of *biographical* history: the virtuous example of an individual could have a social efficacy surpassing the story of two nations at odds; effective struggle against negative social forces depended on people's united ethical actions. Pizan anticipated Scott. Her medieval *Book of the City of Ladies* is populated with women from the ancient world, from legend, from the Bible and from the recent past in order to revise history so that women attain their deserved place. Modern feminists echo these views. In Gearhart's *Wanderground* Remember Rooms exist for the hill women to weave their various individual stories together into a grand narrative: 'from countless seemingly disconnected episodes the women had pieced together a larger picture' in order that the full story of women's experience can be witnessed.[45] In Le Guin's *Dispossessed*, Shevek proffers two images for the inscription of time, images which posit both the forward-moving actions of individuals and the meaning-conferring, enclosing shape of grand narrative: 'there is the arrow, the running river, without which there is no change, no progress, or direction or creation. And there is the circle or the cycle, without which there is chaos, meaningless succession of instants, a world without clocks or seasons or promises.'[46] The first is sequence, the second simultaneity, which Shevek struggles to reconcile in his General Theory of Time.

Feminists have suggested that this dual perspective is critical. Change must happen gradually through time, a 'succession of instants', but a clear picture of events, discernible at a glance, must direct the forward movement. To formulate a reasonable plan for the future a distinct understanding of history is necessary, but individual women's stories must be gathered together in order for the full scope of women's long oppression to be understood. Grand narratives depend on the individual stories of which they are composed, just as powerful princes depend on their various underlings, just as events are influenced by hidden causes: the two forms of understanding history, like the distribution of power between the sovereign and the subject, exist in dialectical relationship. To achieve a freer future, then, not only must images of the past motivate critical discernment in the present, but images of possible alternatives must also guide the steps to be taken.

4. Dynamic view of the environment

The work of modern feminists has often coincided with the values of environmentalism, and yet it is not only the modern feminist movement that has recognized how capitalism has affected the Earth's 'others'. Earlier utopian feminists shared this tendency; familiarity with the position of the dependant and the exploited sensitized authors to the plight of abused nature, and the language used was often overtly political. In Scott's *Millenium Hall* the ladies create a landscape corresponding to eighteenth-century ideas about the English garden, with picturesque vistas, a grotto and a temple of solitude, but at the same time they seek to foster indigenous flora and fauna even when British colonizers eagerly displayed exotic species in their personal zoos and cabinets of curiosities. On the Millenium Hall estate 'the wood is well peopled with pheasants, wild turkies, squirrels and hares, who live so unmolested, that they seem to have forgot all fear, and rather to welcome than fly those who come amongst them. Man never appears there as a merciless destroyer; but the preserver, instead of the tyrant of the inferior part of the creation.'[47] In the early nineteenth century Mary Shelley probed the possibilities of man as 'merciless destroyer' in her dystopian science fictions *Frankenstein* (1818) and *The Last Man* (1826), which warn of the consequences of human culture failing adequately to accommodate non-human nature.

By the twentieth century technology appeared to offer not only dangers but also some irresistible advantages. The visitors to Herland admire the women's ingenious inventions; at the same time these women plant a variety of trees with 'due regard ... paid to seasonable crops' and follow a careful programme of composting wherein 'everything which came from the earth went back to it. The practical result was ... an increasingly valuable soil ... instead of the progressive impoverishment so often seen in the rest of the world.'[48] Mary Bradley Lane's *Mizora*, as an exception, sees technological development as benign; when the narrator observes that science allows the Mizorans 'to supercede Nature', her guide responds: 'By no means. It has only taught us how to make her obey us.'[49] This overriding optimism is uncommon in feminist works; the view is generally tempered by caveats. For example, in Piercy's *Woman on the Edge of Time* the future society of Mattapoisett has developed a sophisticated means of reproducing human life in the laboratory and concomitantly become a rural village with meandering goats and chickens; Luciente explains that 'We of Mattapoisett are famous for our turtles and our geese. But our major proteins are plant proteins. Every region tries to be ownfed ... Self-sufficient as possible in proteins.'[50] By contrast Luciente time-travels to twentieth-century New York and is interested to see how a toilet works, fascinated to learn about garbage collection and shocked to find that the rumours about 'the Age of Greed and Waste' are true: 'to burn your compost! To pour your shit into the waters others downstream must drink! That fish must live in! Into rivers whose estuaries and marshes are links in the whole offshore food chain!'[51] Technological innovation is matched by environmental awareness.

Late twentieth-century feminist utopian writers sometimes suggest a special connection of women to nature. According to Joanna Russ some authors 'go beyond the problems of living in the world without disturbing its ecological balance into presenting their characters as feeling a strong emotional connection to the natural world'.[52] In Gearhart's *Wanderground* the hill women live in 'a green world'[53] without modern conveniences, surviving in a nature which speaks to them, where they themselves converse with trees and ride winds and life is based on natural rhythms. In Le Guin's *Dispossessed*, Takver's 'concern with landscapes and living creatures was passionate … It was strange to see Takver take a leaf into her hand, or even a rock. She became an extension of it, it of her.'[54] Shevek himself looks over a Urras valley of green fields and hedgerows and trees bordered by hills, 'blue fold behind blue fold, soft and dark under the even, pale grey of the sky' and concludes that 'this is what a world is supposed to look like' (52–3). Ambassador Keng later points to the paradisal qualities of Urras in order to expose how her land, Terra, is 'a ruin. A planet spoiled by the human species … We controlled neither appetite nor violence; we did not adapt' (279). By contrasting dusty Anarres and ruined Terra with Urras's beautiful land but flawed society, Le Guin warns of environmental exploitation and pollution, emphasizes the need for careful stewarding of the natural world, and points to the unlikelihood of any culture's achieving full perfection; hence the book's subtitle of 'ambiguous utopia' and the importance of Anarres's 'ongoing revolution'. With her treatment of the environment and the socio-political effects on it, Le Guin, following the lead of feminist utopian authors before her, indicates the need for adaptability, for constant change, for self-control and never-ending evaluation: she sees this as a crucial part of the process towards utopia.

The process-oriented character of feminist environmentalism folds into its other concerns. Feminist utopian authors have from the beginning sought to 'speak for the trees', to use the phrase of Dr Seuss's Lorax, since the trees cannot speak for themselves. Though authors view the specifics of nature and its cultivation variously, the plant and animal world is generally represented not as a passive recipient of human endeavour, but as a powerful, dynamic, potentially dying or potentially deadly force that must be respected and that affects human actions even as human actions have an impact on it.

5. Pragmatism

Feminist utopians are 'nothing if not practical', as Gilman writes of the Herlanders.[55] In Russ's Whileaway, the girls learn things that are 'heavily practical: how to run machines, how to get along without machines, law, transportation, physical theory, and so on. They learn gymnastics and mechanics. They learn practical medicine. They learn how to swim and shoot.'[56] While authors embrace the freedom to theorize offered by the utopian genre, they emphasize the material over the transcendent, the physical over the metaphysical, the action over the idea. Achieving utopia will, in their view, require industriousness and involvement, an energetic engagement with people, environment and things. Shevek confesses in Le Guin's *The Dispossessed* that there is in Anarres actually no alternative: 'Our society is practical. Maybe too practical, too much concerned with survival only. What is idealistic about social cooperation, mutual aid, when it is the only means of staying alive?'[57] Feminists therefore come upon their pragmatism in a straightforward way, since only a collective effort can generate the socio-political changes necessary to improve women's lives.

Erin McKenna has in fact argued that the most useful feminist utopias dovetail with philosophical pragmatism to offer the most compelling method today of moving towards a freer global future, thereby attaining broader feminist ends. 'Intricately linked through business relations, environmental concerns, advances in technology, vulnerability to disease (such as AIDS), and fear of nuclear devastation, we need visions that take this connectedness into account and prepare people to cope with the multiplicity and complexity of possibilities the future may hold.'[58] In particular John Dewey's notion of the 'end-in-view', McKenna argues, will allow for difference and accommodate the need for experimentation and change: the 'end-in-view' is a provisional goal that derives from a critical understanding of the present – including 'an awareness of the relational nature of ourselves and our environment' – and from the development of expectations and desires for the future. 'We are finite developmental creatures who must grow and adapt to both our changing physical and changing social environments in order to survive. This means there can be no set goals, no predetermined unchanging goods or ends. Instead, there is a continuous chain of ends-in-view becoming means for new ends-in-view which become means for new ends-in-view' (85). McKenna suggests that process-oriented feminist utopias provide the critical foresight necessary for good ends-in-view to be discerned; the utopias are visions that help to organize and structure present experience and dissatisfaction towards a desirable, workable purpose in the future.

Other feminists agree. Drucilla Cornell suggests that freedom can only be attained through a universal access to 'the imaginary domain', of which utopia is a part. 'Utopianism has always been tied to the imagination, to visions of what is truly new. A world in which we could all share in life's glories would be one radically different from our own society. Yet what is possible always changes as we change with the transformations we try to realize.'[59] Angelika

Bammer argues that recent shifts of feminist utopian attention to questions of race and class reveal an 'anticipatory pragmatism ... able to accommodate the vagaries of change because it thinks of change in concrete and practical terms'; it is 'the concrete-utopia-in-process'.[60]

This conception coincides with the view of utopia's most prominent theorist, Ernst Bloch. Bloch was a 'warm' Marxist who disagreed with Karl Marx and Friedrich Engels's disparagement of utopias as escapist and ineffectual. His idea of the 'not-yet' lines up significantly with Dewey's notion of the 'end-in-view' and with feminists' characterization of that goal as furthered by utopian writing. It is part of 'anticipatory consciousness', an awareness of possibilities that have not yet taken shape but that could one day be effected. Bloch focuses on the daydream, the way the individual's desires come to consciousness as visions, allowing people to organize their discontent with the present. He shows how art and culture capture the daydream and thereby serve the function of catalyzing hope and sketching a roadmap for achieving a better future. McKenna may discuss more specifically how process-model utopian writing in particular allows people to perceive the desirable 'end-in-view', but the notion is the same as Bloch's: of an ongoing mental process aided by art to understand and functionalize the otherwise inchoate quality of hopes and desires for a different and better future.[61]

The broad tendencies I have outlined from feminist utopian writing since the middle ages distinguish a process-oriented feminist utopian impulse different from the mainstream tradition. By looking at education, human psychology, epistemology, nature and method from the perspective of women's subordination, feminist utopian authors have conceived different worlds that seek to alter patriarchy and improve the lives of society's powerless. There has been both repetition and change. While I have pointed to recurring themes, it is also clear that in different historical periods adjustments have occurred. And given the positive changes in western women's lives over the past centuries it would be hard to deny that feminists have helped to transform those lives, not to mention lent strength to other movements of liberation for people of different races, ethnicities, sexualities and abilities. Pressure for public education, calls for women's independence and suffrage, demands for a women's history, movements to save the environment: all these endeavours have been furthered by and to that extent are indebted to images conceived in feminist utopian writing.

Critics rightly decry the many injustices and problems our societies face, from poverty to prejudice to war to global warming. The endless list of threats and dangers has spawned an increasing number of dystopian writings. A hopeless outlook is for many all too real today, in 2008, when the administration in Washington has instigated war, recklessly handled the economy, squandered resources, reversed policies that existed to protect the environment, exacerbated social divisions and alienated allies. Because of these developments, commentators such as Seyla Benhabib, Jürgen Habermas, David Harvey, Fredric Jameson and Russell Jacoby have repeatedly called for a return to utopian imagining. Richard Rorty has asserted that utopian social hope remains 'the noblest imaginative creation of which we have record'.[62] And recent scholarship suggests that this hope has been no less prevalent in non-western societies than in western ones. Centuries of utopian writing demonstrate how feminists time and again have relied on utopia in order to posit a viable as opposed to an unattainable future. Their repeated contributions suggest that utopia will recur as a force for transforming discontent into critique and desire into practical political action.

NOTES

I would like to thank Sean Burgess, Colin Milburn, Nicole Pohl and Christopher Reynolds for invaluable suggestions on a draft of this essay.

1 Angelika Bammer emphasizes process in her study of 1970s utopianism, *Partial Visions: Feminism and Utopianism in the 1970s* (London: Routledge, 1991); Erin McKenna suggests the term 'process model' in *The Task of Utopia: Politics and Culture in an Age of Apathy* (New York: Basic Books, 2001); Alessa Johns discusses the 'reproductive utopian model' in *Women's Utopias of the Eighteenth Century* (Urbana: University of Illinois Press, 2003); Tom Moylan speaks of 'critical utopia' in *Demand the Impossible: Science Fiction and the Utopian Imagination* (New York: Methuen, 1986); and Peter Fitting employs the phrase 'critical and utopian' in 'The Modern Anglo-American SF Novel: Utopian Longing and Capitalist Cooptation', *Science-Fiction Studies* 6:1 (1979), 59–76. These scholars are not examining identical sets of utopian texts, so they are not covering exactly the same ground; however, all suggest that feminist interventions have precipitated such new terms and formulations. Nicole Pohl sees the seeds of the critical utopia in a sceptical tradition of Enlightenment thinking in '"The Emperess of the World": Gender and the Voyage Utopia', in Nicole Pohl and Brenda Tooley (eds.), *Gender and Utopia in the Eighteenth Century* (London: Ashgate, 2007), pp. 121–132. For expanded discussion of twentieth-century 'critical' utopias see Jennifer Burwell, *Notes on Nowhere: Feminism, Utopian Logic, and Social Transformation* (Minneapolis: University of Minnesota Press, 1997); Ruth Levitas, *The Concept of Utopia* (Syracuse University Press, 1996); Lucy Sargisson, *Contemporary Feminist Utopianism* (London: Routledge, 1996); and Frances Bartkowski, *Feminist Utopias* (Lincoln: University of Nebraska Press, 1989).
2 Anne Mellor, 'On Feminist Utopias', *Women's Studies* 9 (1982), 241–62, 243.
3 Darby Lewes, *Dream Revisionaries: Gender and Genre in Women's Utopian Fiction 1870–1920* (Tuscaloosa: University of Alabama Press, 1995), p. 13.
4 Sally Kitch, *Higher Ground: From Utopianism to Realism in American Feminist Thought and Theory* (University of Chicago Press, 2000), p. 12.

5 Christine de Pizan, *The Book of the City of Ladies* (1404–5), trans. Earl Jeffrey Richards (New York: Persea, 1982) and *The Treasure of the City of Ladies, or The Book of the Three Virtues* (1405), trans. Sarah Lawson (Harmondsworth: Penguin, 1985); Mary Astell, *A Serious Proposal to the Ladies* (1694), ed. Patricia Springborg (Peterborough, ON: Broadview, 2002); Sarah Scott, *A Description of Millenium Hall* (1762), ed. Gary Kelly (Peterborough, ON: Broadview, 1995); Frances E. W. Harper, *Iola Leroy; or, Shadows Uplifted* (1892) (Boston: Beacon Press, 1987); Charlotte Perkins Gilman, *Herland* (1915), ed. Denise D. Knight (Harmondsworth: Penguin, 1999); Ursula K. Le Guin, *The Dispossessed* (New York: Avon Books, 1974); Marge Piercy, *Woman on the Edge of Time* (New York: Knopf, 1976).

6 More's *Utopia* will be the principal example of that model, since it is the foundational and best-known text, but there are others that could serve as well, e.g., Bacon's *New Atlantis*, Berington's *Sig. Gaudentio*, Paltock's *Peter Wilkins*, Griggs's *Imperium in Imperio*, Bellamy's *Looking Backward* and Wells's *A Modern Utopia*.

7 Sarah Scott, *History of Sir George Ellison* (1766), ed. Betty Rizzo (Lexington: KY: University Press of Kentucky, 1996), pp. 95–7.

8 Clara Reeve, *Plans of Education* (London: T. Hockham & J. Carpenter, 1792), p. 71.

9 Mary Wollstonecraft, *A Vindication of the Rights of Woman* (1792), ed. Carol H. Poston, 2nd edn (New York: Norton, 1988).

10 Frances Wright, 'Of Existing Evils, and Their Remedy', in Susan S. Adams (ed.), *Reason, Religion, and Morals* (New York: Humanity Books, 2004), pp. 219, 209. Wright founded the biracial utopian community of Nashoba, Tennessee in 1825.

11 Mary E. Bradley Lane, *Mizora: A Prophecy* (1880–1) (Boston: Gregg Press, 1975), p. 32.

12 Frances E. W. Harper, *Iola Leroy; or, Shadows Uplifted* (1892) (Boston: Beacon Press, 1987), pp. 205, 210. For a discussion of this novel within a context of African American utopian writing, see M. Giulia Fabi, *Passing and the Rise of the African American Novel* (Urbana: University of Illinois Press, 2001), pp. 44–71.

13 Mary Hamilton, *Letters from the Duchess de Crui* (London: 1777), vol. 1, p. 42.

14 Ursula K. Le Guin, *The Dispossessed* (New York: Avon Books, 1974), pp. 85, 89.

15 Judith Drake, *Essay in Defence of the Female Sex* (London: S. Butler, 1696).

16 Hannah More, *The Bas-Bleu, or Conversation* (1787), in *Selected Writings of Hannah More*, ed. Robert Hole (London: Pickering & Chatto, 1995).

17 Mary Wollstonecraft, *A Vindication of the Rights of Woman* (1792), ed. Carol H. Poston, 2nd edn (New York: Norton, 1988), pp. 144–5.

18 Charlotte Perkins Gilman, *Herland* (1915), ed. Denise D. Knight (Harmondsworth: Penguin, 1999), pp. 83, 61.

19 Thomas More, *Utopia* (1516) trans. and ed. Robert M. Adams, 2nd edn (New York: Norton, 1992), pp. 37, 38.

20 Pizan, *The Book of the City of Ladies*, pp. 111, 257. Pizan's text, though written in French, first appeared in print in England and was translated into English by Bryan Ansley in 1521.

21 Mary Astell, *A Serious Proposal to the Ladies* (1694), ed. Patricia Springborg (Peterborough, ON: Broadview Press, 2002), p. 35.

22 Harper, *Iola Leroy*, pp. 210–12.

23 Joanna Russ, *The Female Man* (Boston: Beacon, 1975).

24 Pizan, *The Book of the City of Ladies*, p. 154.

25 Mary Astell and John Norris, *Letters Concerning the Love of God*, ed. E. Derek Taylor and Melvyn New (Aldershot: Ashgate, 2005), p. 66.

26 Sarah Scott, *Journey Through Every Stage of Life* (London: n.p., 1754), vol. 5, p. 67.

27 Marge Piercy, *Woman on the Edge of Time* (New York: Knopf, 1976), p. 132.

28 Christine de Pizan, *The Treasure of the City of Ladies, or The Book of the Three Virtues* (1405), trans. Sarah Lawson (Harmondsworth: Penguin, 1985), p. 49.

29 Sarah Fielding, *The Adventures of David Simple* (1744), ed. Malcolm Kelsall (Oxford: Oxford University Press, 1994), p. 113.

30 Astell, *A Serious Proposal*, pp. 35–6.

31 Fielding, *Adventures of David Simple*, p. 304.

32 *Ibid.*, pp. 304–5.

33 Gilman, *Herland*, p. 80.

34 *Ibid.*, pp. 95–6.

35 More, *Utopia*, pp. 31–2.

36 *Ibid.*, p. 41.

37 Pizan, *The Book of the City of Ladies*, pp. 12, 116.

38 Gilman, *Herland*, p. 80.

39 Le Guin, *The Dispossessed*, p. 89.

40 Joanna Russ, 'Recent Feminist Utopias', in *To Write Like a Woman: Essays in Feminism and Science Fiction* (Bloomington: Indiana University Press, 1995), p. 137.

41 Russ, *The Female Man*, pp. 126, 203–4.

42 Sarah Scott, *History of Sir George Ellison* (1766), ed. Betty Rizzo (Lexington, KY: University Press of Kentucky, 1996), p. 91.

43 Bammer, *Partial Visions*, p. 104.

44 Sarah Scott, *History of Gustavus Ericson* (London: A. Millar, 1761), pp. v–vi.

45 Sally Miller Gearhart, *The Wanderground: Stories of the Hill Women* (Boston: Alyson, 1979), p. 23.

46 Le Guin, *The Dispossessed*, p. 180.

47 Scott, *Millenium Hall*, p. 69.

48 Gilman, *Herland*, pp. 80–1.

49 Mary Bradley Lane, *Mizora: A Prophecy* (1880–1) (Boston: Gregg Press, 1975), p. 104.

50 Piercy, *Woman*, p. 62.

51 *Ibid.*, p. 47.

52 Russ, 'Recent Feminist Utopias', p. 137.

53 Gearhart, *Wanderground*, p. 125.

54 Le Guin, *The Dispossessed*, p. 150.

55 Gilman, *Herland*, p. 114.

56 Russ, *The Female Man*, p. 50.

57 Le Guin, *The Dispossessed*, p. 109.

58 McKenna, *The Task of Utopia*, p. 161.

59 Drucilla Cornell, *At the Heart of Freedom: Feminism, Sex, and Equality* (Princeton University Press, 1998), pp. 8, 186.
60 Bammer, *Partial Visions*, pp. 161–2.
61 Ernst Bloch, *The Principle of Hope* (1959), trans. Neville Plaice, Stephen Plaice and Paul Knight (3 vols., Cambridge, MA: MIT Press, 1995), vol. 1.
62 Seyla Benhabib, *Situating the Self: Gender, Community, and Postmodernism in Contemporary Ethics* (London: Routledge, 1992) and 'Sexual Difference and Collective Identities: The New Global Constellation', *Signs* 24:2 (1999), 335–61; Jürgen Habermas, *The Structural Transformation of the Public Sphere* (1962) (Cambridge, MA: MIT Press, 1991) and *The Philosophical Discourse of Modernity* (Cambridge, MA: MIT Press, 1987); David Harvey, *Spaces of Hope* (Berkeley: University of California Press, 2000); Russell Jacoby, *The End of Utopia: Politics and Culture in an Age of Apathy* (New York: Basic Books, 1999) and *Picture Imperfect: Utopian Thought for an Anti-Utopian Age* (New York: Columbia University Press, 2005); Fredric Jameson, *Archaeologies of the Future: The Desire Called Utopia and Other Science Fictions* (London: Verso, 2007); Richard Rorty, *Philosophy and Social Hope* (Harmondsworth: Penguin, 1999), p. 277.

BIBLIOGRAPHY

Astell, Mary, *A Serious Proposal to the Ladies* (1694), ed. Patricia Springborg (Peterborough, ON: Broadview, 2002).
Astell, Mary and John Norris, *Letters Concerning the Love of God*, ed. E. Derek Taylor and Melvyn New (Aldershot: Ashgate, 2005).
Atwood, Margaret, *The Handmaid's Tale* (Toronto: McClelland & Stewart, 1985).
Bammer, Angelika, *Partial Visions: Feminism and Utopianism in the 1970s* (London: Routledge, 1991).
Bartkowski, Frances, *Feminist Utopias* (Lincoln: University of Nebraska Press, 1989).
Benhabib, Seyla, *Situating the Self: Gender, Community, and Postmodernism in Contemporary Ethics* (London: Routledge, 1992).
  'Sexual Difference and Collective Identities: The New Global Constellation', *Signs* 24:2 (1999), 335–61.
Bloch, Ernst, *The Principle of Hope* (1959), trans. Neville Plaice, Stephen Plaice and Paul Knight (3 vols., Cambridge, MA: MIT Press, 1995).
Burwell, Jennifer, *Notes on Nowhere: Feminism, Utopian Logic, and Social Transformation* (Minneapolis: University of Minnesota Press, 1997).
Cornell, Drucilla, *At the Heart of Freedom: Feminism, Sex, and Equality* (Princeton University Press, 1998).
Drake, Judith, *Essay in Defence of the Female Sex* (London: S. Butler, 1696).
Fabi, M. Giulia, *Passing and the Rise of the African American Novel* (Urbana: University of Illinois Press, 2001).
Fielding, Sarah, *The Adventures of David Simple* (1744), ed. *Malcolm Kelsall* (Oxford University Press, 1994).
Fitting, Peter, 'The Modern Anglo-American SF Novel: Utopian Longing and Capitalist Cooptation', *Science-Fiction Studies* 6:1 (1979), 59–76.

Gearhart, Sally Miller, *The Wanderground: Stories of the Hill Women* (Boston: Alyson, 1979).

Gilman, Charlotte Perkins, *Herland* (1915), ed. Denise D. Knight (Harmondsworth: Penguin, 1999).

Habermas, Jürgen, *The Structural Transformation of the Public Sphere* (1962) (Cambridge, MA: MIT Press, 1991).

The Philosophical Discourse of Modernity (Cambridge, MA: MIT Press, 1987).

Hamilton, Mary, *Letters from the Duchess de Crui* (London, 1777).

Memoirs of the Marchioness de Louvoi (London, 1777).

Munster Village (London, 1778).

Harper, Frances E. W., *Iola Leroy; or, Shadows Uplifted* (1892) (Gloucester: Dodo Press, 2007).

Harvey, David, *Spaces of Hope* (Berkeley: University of California Press, 2000).

Jacoby, Russell, *The End of Utopia: Politics and Culture in an Age of Apathy* (New York: Basic Books, 1999).

Picture Imperfect: Utopian Thought for an Anti-Utopian Age (New York: Columbia University Press, 2005).

Jameson, Fredric, *Archaeologies of the Future: The Desire Called Utopia and Other Science Fictions* (London: Verso, 2007).

Johns, Alessa, 'Thinking Globally, Acting Locally: Enlightenment Utopianism for 21st-Century Feminists?', in Nicole Pohl and Brenda Tooley (eds.), *Gender and Utopia in the Eighteenth Century* (London: Ashgate, 2007), pp. 163–78.

Women's Utopias of the Eighteenth Century (Urbana: University of Illinois Press, 2003).

Kitch, Sally, *Higher Ground: From Utopianism to Realism in American Feminist Thought and Theory* (University of Chicago Press, 2000).

Lane, Mary E. Bradley, *Mizora: A Prophecy* (1880–1) (Boston: Gregg Press, 1975).

Le Guin, Ursula K., *The Dispossessed* (New York: Avon Books, 1974).

Levitas, Ruth, *The Concept of Utopia* (Syracuse, NY: Syracuse University Press, 1996).

Lewes, Darby, *Dream Revisionaries: Gender and Genre in Women's Utopian Fiction 1870–1920* (Tuscaloosa: University of Alabama Press: 1995).

McKenna, Erin, *The Task of Utopia: A Pragmatist and Feminist Perspective* (Lanham: Rowman & Littlefield, 2001).

Mellor, Anne, 'On Feminist Utopias', *Women's Studies* 9 (1982), 241–62.

More, Hannah, *The Bas-Bleu, or Conversation* (1787), in *Selected Writings of Hannah More*, ed. Robert Hole (London: Pickering & Chatto, 1995).

More, Thomas, *Utopia* (1516), trans. and ed. Robert M. Adams, 2nd edn (New York: Norton, 1992).

Morris, William, *News from Nowhere* (1890), ed. Clive Wilmer (Harmondsworth: Penguin, 1993).

Moylan, Tom, *Demand the Impossible: Science Fiction and the Utopian Imagination* (New York: Methuen, 1986).

Scraps of the Untainted Sky: Science Fiction, Utopia, Dystopia (Boulder, CO: Westview Press, 2000).

Piercy, Marge, *Woman on the Edge of Time* (New York: Fawcett, 1976).

Pizan, Christine de, *The Book of the City of Ladies* (1404–5), trans. Earl Jeffrey Richards (New York: Persea, 1982).

The Treasure of the City of Ladies, or The Book of the Three Virtues (1405), trans. Sarah Lawson (Harmondsworth: Penguin, 1985).

Pohl, Nicole, '"The Emperess of the World": Gender and the Voyage Utopia', in Nicole Pohl and Brenda Tooley (eds.), *Gender and Utopia in the Eighteenth Century* (London: Ashgate, 2007), 121–32.

Reeve, Clara, *Plans of Education* (London: T. Hockham & J. Carpenter, 1792).

Rorty, Richard, *Philosophy and Social Hope* (Harmondsworth: Penguin, 1999).

Russ, Joanna, *The Female Man* (Boston: Beacon, 1975).

To Write Like a Woman: Essays in Feminism and Science Fiction (Bloomington: Indiana University Press, 1995).

Sargisson, Lucy, *Contemporary Feminist Utopianism* (London: Routledge, 1996).

Scott, Sarah, *A Description of Millenium Hall* (1762), ed. Gary Kelly (Peterborough, ON: Broadview, 1995).

History of Gustavus Ericson (London: A. Millar, 1761).

History of Sir George Ellison (1766), ed. Betty Rizzo (Lexington, KY: University Press of Kentucky, 1996).

Journey Through Every Stage of Life (London: n.p., 1754).

Shelley, Mary, *Frankenstein; or, The Modern Prometheus* (London, 1818).

The Last Man (London: Henry Colburn, 1826).

Tepper, Sheri S., *The Gate to Women's Country* (New York: Doubleday, 1988).

Wollstonecraft, Mary, *A Vindication of the Rights of Woman* (1792), ed. Carol H. Poston, 2nd edn (New York: Norton, 1988).

Wright, Frances, *Reason, Religion, and Morals*, ed. Susan S. Adams (New York: Humanity Books, 2004).

9

LYMAN TOWER SARGENT

Colonial and postcolonial utopias[1]

Introduction: The nature of colonization

Europeans established two types of colonies. One was designed primarily to exploit the labour of the inhabitants and the natural resources of the country, with the Congo and India prime examples. The second, while still exploiting the natural resources of the country and sometimes the labour of the inhabitants, was primarily for settlement; most of the North and South American colonies, New Zealand and South Africa are examples. A variant of the second that became indistinguishable from it occurred in some of the Australian colonies, in which one of the purposes of the colonial power was to get rid of undesirables of various sorts. The settler colonies produced a rich harvest of utopias; the colonies designed to exploit generally did not.

The settlement colonies served the purposes of the settlers as well as those of the home country. Most settlers wanted to improve their own lives and some had a specific utopian vision in mind. Those who voluntarily travelled significant distances in often horrible conditions hoped either to practise a way of life they were unable to practise in the home country or to improve their lives materially or both. Probably the overwhelming majority of voluntary colonists were what are now disparagingly called economic immigrants. They travelled because they believed that the new place was sufficiently different that they would be able to move up the economic and social ladders, and, in particular, they often aspired to own their own property. Many failed, many returned home and many, particularly among the Irish who, due to the famine, could not return home, moved from colony to colony until they put down roots somewhere or died.

For settlers one of the motivations was that most basic utopia of all – a full stomach, decent shelter and clothing and a better future for themselves and their children. This most fundamental utopia has always inspired most immigration, and it was basic to settler colonization. Other colonists were driven by the desire to practise their religion freely or to organize their lives differently economically, politically and socially. As such they were more explicitly utopian in that they wanted to be able to live a specific vision of the good life. The best known of these colonial visions are religious, such as the Puritans settling Massachusetts Bay Colony in what became the United States, but most were smaller and followers of a charismatic leader such as those who followed the Reverend Norman MacLeod from Scotland to Nova Scotia and then to Australia before finally settling in Waipu, New Zealand, where their descendants still live.

Much of the utopianism of colonization was like a sales pitch, plausible but really too good to be true. But the immigrants wanted to be sold something too good to be true and actively participated in being conned. The Irish song 'The Glorious and Free United States of America' encourages immigration by saying, 'If you labour in America, In riches you will roll.'[2] What many of them found is suggested in song titles like 'Many a Fool Sailed Across the Sea'[3] and 'The Irish Emigrant's Lament'.[4] But most stayed in the colonies and imposed a European culture on the earlier inhabitants or got rid of the earlier culture by killing the inhabitants. That process was never entirely successful, and in the current era of postcolonialism modified forms of indigenous cultures are developing or there is a growing admixture of earlier forms with European ones.

Neither the colonial nor the postcolonial should be oversimplified. The colonies differed radically. They were settled at different times between the early seventeenth and the mid-nineteenth centuries. They varied significantly in climate, geography and natural resources, and the indigenous peoples they confronted differed greatly. Also, there were both very wealthy and extremely poor colonists and some colonists did not move up the economic ladder as they hoped; some even fell down it.[5] There were also female and male colonists, and their experiences could be very different. And the colonists also brought with them different religions and ethnicities. We generally hear about the successful male colonists, although the specific experiences of the women and the different religious and ethnic groups have begun to be documented in some countries.

There were also variations in perceptions of the colonized and in the policies towards them as well as important differences among the colonized, which the colonizer often did not recognize. There were differences of gender, wealth, status, power and tribe, all of which meant that the responses of the colonized varied, and these differences continued into the postcolonial period.

The relationships between colonization and utopianism

Wherever the basic bibliographical work has been done, it is clear that settler colonies have produced a rich harvest of utopian literature and projects.
The British colonies in North America and the South Pacific, the Spanish
colonies in the Americas and the Portuguese colony of Brazil have been
particularly prolific. And the reasons are not hard to find. In all of these colonies people chose to give up the familiar for the unknown or little known
hoping to find or build a better life. And new or revised social and political
institutions and economic patterns had to be created. As a result, the whole
process of colonial settlement can be seen as a type of utopianism.

The traditional way of thinking about immigration is to argue that people
were pushed from their country of origin by the dystopian conditions there
and pulled to the new country by the utopian vision of a better life. As with
many simple explanations of complex phenomena, this one does not fit all
settler colonies at all times.[6] But it still fits much of the history of immigration and colonization. The songs sung by immigrants and the letters they
sent home are instructive. There are two sets of voyage songs, one in port
before leaving and one about the sea voyage, and these divide into troubled
and untroubled. There are rapacious immigration agents and kindly helpers
and terrible voyages versus easy voyages. The same duality continues on
landing, with songs saying that people were helped or ripped off, with relatively easy settlement and integration into the new country versus horrendous problems with settlement and integration. Of course, there is another
group of songs that reflect those immigrants who die, utterly fail and drop
below the worst of the old country, or, for a lucky few in this group, quickly
return home.

Another group of songs about the experiences in the new country follow
a similar pattern, with the utopia found through hard work or alternatively
the new world no better or even worse than the dystopian old world. And
even for those who find their dream to some extent, there is homesickness
and nostalgia and desire for the old land, with Irish songs in particular tending to utopianize particular places in Ireland.

Either homesickness or failure led many to return home; in some places
and some periods this was as high as 50 per cent. In New Zealand there is a
famous book, 'Taken In'; Being, A Sketch of New Zealand Life (1887) published under the pseudonym 'Hopeful', by an immigrant who turned around
and went home, and there are songs about the simple joys of reintegrating
into the area and community that had been abandoned.[7] The Irish, who
could not return, produced a real Diaspora, and they might more accurately
be thought of as refugees. While a few people returned to Ireland over the

years, the first major return was in the recent past in response to the Celtic
Tiger economy, and this return has offset a significant drop in the birth rate
in Ireland.

The letters home follow a similar pattern except that they tend to be more
utopian than the songs.[8] Food is a major concern; in the letters from New
Zealand there are constant references to being able to eat meat, and letters
from the United States Midwest generally stress the abundance available,
although sometimes at high prices. A Swedish song, 'The America Song'
reflects the myth of incredible abundance:

> Chickens and other fowl rain down,
> Cooked well-done, and what is more
> Fly in on the table
> With knife and fork in their thigh.[9]

Such myths, called Cockaigne, can be found throughout the history of utopianism, and generally stress food.

However often the images of streets paved with gold or the superabun-
dance of food may have been repeated, the overwhelming majority of immigrants expected hard work on arrival, and certainly the letters they wrote
back emphasize that, albeit often with the added message that you get more
for your hard work in the new country than the old. It isn't easy; some of
the natives and even some of your fellow immigrants will exploit or even
rob you if given a chance.

The greater equality in the new country is another recurring theme; you
are treated as an equal. Letters from New Zealand, for example, regularly
refer to workers eating at the same table as the farm owner and being served
the same food. And they stress that what counts is what an individual does,
not what their ancestors had done.

Access to land is another positive feature of the new country. Even though
you will have to work hard, you will be able to own enough land to make a
decent living for yourself and your family. The letters do not generally represent the new country as an earthly paradise. The message is generally that
if you come and work hard you can live much better than in the old country,
and you will be able to achieve this within a few years of landing.

Most of the immigration literature centres on men. The songs regularly
refer to either pining for the woman left behind who will join the immigrant
when he can afford it or to the heartless woman left behind who found a
new man as soon as the immigrant left. There are letters on the good prospects for marriage for the single women who immigrate. But there are also
some letters from women commenting on the log cabin with a dirt floor or
other conditions that make their life worse than in the old country, even

if it is better for men. A New Zealand pamphlet called *A Few Words to Emigrants' Wives* (*c.* 1870) makes the point particularly well:

> The house itself, it must be understood in the first instance, will be both smaller and ruder than the residence that would be occupied by persons of the same [artisan] class in England. It will, most likely, have mud floors under foot, and no ceiling at all over head. It will be destitute of closets and cupboards, and the chances are be without even a pantry. The sacred kitchen will be the most wretched-looking and repulsive apartment in the tenement – small, without a single shelf, board, or fitting of any kind; and with a huge cavernous space, raised some yard or so from the ground, to do duty as a fire-place. Here, without range, stove, or oven, and over a wood fire kindled on the bare hearth, all the roasting, boiling, and baking, and all the general business of the culinary department have to be performed. The utmost that must be looked for in the way of convenience, is, the fixing of a couple of iron bars, for the saucepan and kettle to stand upon, above the embers.[10]

But, there are many letters from women, both married and single, who find the new country all they hoped for, a real utopia in comparison to the old country.

Thomas More's *Utopia*, in which the word 'utopia' was coined, is also the first utopia to raise the issue of colonies, and it does so in a way that demonstrates that colonies are intended to support the home country, not primarily to fill the needs of the colonists. Utopia's colonies were generally achieved through conquest, and they were mostly used to offload surplus population. But in the case of Utopia, if the population of the home country dropped, the people who had been sent to the colonies were brought back. It could hardly be made clearer that the colonies were to serve the interests of the home country. The colonies also provided cheap labour, with some of the original inhabitants choosing to improve their lives by becoming slaves in Utopia.

The spaces chosen for settlement were not empty but inhabited, and the settler utopia was always accompanied by dystopias for the indigenous inhabitants. And until the late twentieth century, utopian literature was written almost exclusively by the colonizers. The current inhabitants of settler colonies would not be allowed to stand in the way of the desire or need to relocate.

More's Utopians simply did not consider the inhabitants of the area to be colonized to be important, and this attitude is frequently repeated in utopian literature set in colonies. Although in most cases the indigenous dystopia was a side effect of settlement, there were even a number of utopias written, like Theodor Hertzka's *Freiland: Ein sociales Zukunftsbild* (1890), that envisioned the displacement of the indigenous population to create the utopia. *Freiland* became an actual project but was unsuccessful. And James Burgh's 1764 *An Account of the First Settlement, Laws, Form of Government, and Police, of the Cessares* concerns the established of a Protestant colony in an 'uninhabited' area of South America. Also, Robert Pemberton's 1854 *The Happy Colony* specifies the creation of a community in an area of New Zealand that was heavily populated by Maori as if there was no one there at all. And in his *In Darkest England and The Way Out* of 1890 General William Booth, founder of the Salvation Army, intends to send the people he has rescued from the streets of English cities first to communities in the countryside where they will become sober and trained and then to communities in the colonies, where, he says, there are millions of acres of 'useful land' that can be purchased 'almost for the asking' in South Africa, Canada and Western Australia. None of these works considered the people living on the land or their displacement as relevant.[11]

One common theme in both British utopian literature and the utopias produced in the colonies is the collapse of Britain and the shift of power, culture and learning to the former colonies, now either independent or the dominant members of the British Empire. The most famous expression of this is 'Macaulay's New Zealander', where Thomas Babington Macaulay refers to a future in which 'some traveller from New Zealand shall, in the midst of a vast solitude, take his stand on a broken arch of London Bridge to sketch the ruins of St. Paul's'.[12] The earliest depictions of the transfer to the colonies are both from 1769 and the centres of both power and culture are now in North America.[13] And titles like *The New-Zealander on London Bridge; or, Moral Ruins of the Modern Babylon* (1878) and *History of the Decline and Fall of the British Empire* (1884 and 1890) were common. In addition, writers such as Edward Gibbon, Horace Walpole, Percy Bysshe Shelley and Anna Barbauld say similar things.[14]

Utopianism in the colonies

All settler colonies produced works that depicted the future of the colony in utopian terms, and descriptions of the United States and New Zealand in particular described the landscape in terms reminiscent of traditional utopian genres like the earthly paradise and arcadia. And in these new places questions that appeared to have been settled had to be asked anew. Who should rule? How should property be held? With no aristocracy, should one be created and, if not, why should some people have more power and property than others? Should women be subservient to men? With women clearly working alongside men, why can't they own property in their own right or vote? Who should be educated and what should they learn? Can children be educated so that they will be useful in the new circumstances? The classic authors of Greece and Rome were the basis of education in Britain, and many in the colonies thought such an education irrelevant to the colonies' needs, so should tradition or need dominate? If need dominated, what, with colonists regularly being called uncultured, did this say about culture? Should the mother country dominate her successful children? All these questions, and many more, are explored in colonial utopias, because they were the issues people were discussing.

Many, mostly those with power and property, wanted to continue with the institutions brought from the mother country. Others, and they were the majority, wanted change. And utopian literature, movements and communities responded with a wide range of proposals.

The creation of new institutions is seen most obviously in the United States, where the original thirteen colonies were founded by different groups for different purposes, with the Puritans in New England and the Society of Friends (Quakers) in Pennsylvania being the most clearly utopian.

John Winthrop (1588–1649), the first governor of Massachusetts Bay Colony, is famously quoted as saying that the Puritans came to the new world to build a 'citty upon a hill'. This has generally been interpreted as a utopian statement, and the Puritans did settle in America with the utopian intent of building a society in which they could put their beliefs fully into practice. And as early as 1641 John Cotton published *Abstract of Lawes of New England, As they are now established*, describing laws taken from Scripture that he argued should be adopted to help create that better place. Since Cotton moved to America in 1633, this can be considered the earliest utopia written by a colonist.[15]

Winthrop's famous statement is followed by the warning that 'the eyes of all people are upon us' so that if they fail to create their better world they will be a laughing stock,[16] and this combination of warning and vision was typical of the Puritan outlook. The Puritans thought they knew what was right, but as frail human beings there was a good chance they would fail. The belief that people may be incapable of creating a world that fits their dreams feeds a strong current of anti-utopianism in the United States.

Pennsylvania is often seen as the most utopian of the colonies, but its founder William Penn was pulled between the dream of an egalitarian society and the need to create a successful and prosperous colony, and the former usually gave way to the latter. At the same time, Pennsylvania was significantly better than any of the other colonies in its treatment of the American Indians who lived there.[17]

The Puritans and the Quakers and the Roman Catholics in Maryland came to America to be able to practise their religion freely, but the idea of freedom of religious practice was still a utopian ideal. The first intentional or utopian community, which existed briefly in Delaware in 1659, was founded by the Dutchman Pieter Plockhoy on the basis of freedom of belief; Roger Williams famously established freedom of religion in Rhode Island after being expelled from Massachusetts; Thomas Jefferson thought that his most important acts were the authorship of the 'Declaration of Independence' and the 'Act for Establishing Religious Freedom' adopted by Virginia in 1779; and the United States Bill of Rights added freedom of religion to the Constitution. Most of the early intentional communities in the United States were religious and established by Dutch, English or German immigrants who came to North America specifically to realize their dream of being able to live fully in accordance with their religious beliefs.

The creation of new institutions like freedom of worship and the forms of government established first in the constitutions of each of the colonies as they became states, then in the Articles of Confederation and finally in the Constitution and the Bill of Rights, are the most utopian aspects of the experience of the United States as thirteen colonies came together to form the first 'new nation'. Most other colonies did not establish as radically new institutions as in the United States but modified institutions modelled on European or, later, United States precedent, with varying degrees of adaptation to local conditions.

The first utopian literature actually published in a colony (British North America) was the 1753 'A General Idea of the College of Mirania' by William Smith.[18] And throughout the period of the American Revolution and the creation of the new institutions, many utopias, both original and reprinted from English sources, were published, primarily in newspapers, the main means of communication at the time. And utopian literature and utopian communities continued to be published and established in the United States from that time to the present.

In Canada in 1888 William Douw Lighthall published *The Young Seigneur; or, Nation-Making* under the pseudonym Wilfrid Châteauclair.[19] *The Young Seigneur* focuses on what is a central concern of much Canadian thought and literature, French–English relations. The pseudonym, half English and half French, is indicative of the desire expressed to create a nation out of the bifurcated (not yet recognized to be at least trifurcated in that the indigenous inhabitants did not count) elements of what was becoming Canada. The explicit eutopia contained within the book argues that a nation must have a clear ideal, and that when it develops one, Canada will become 'The Perfect Nation'. To accomplish this Canadians will need to work together as one nation, which they were far from being in 1888, and which still bedevils them. From Lighthall in 1888 to the most recent Canadian works, the single issue that has most agitated Canadian writers of utopias is national unity, most often focusing on Québec, but sometimes concerned with either the West or Atlantic Canada. In some utopias the disintegration of Canada has been presented not simply as a question of Québec but as a situation in which there is simply nothing that holds Canada together. For example, in *Canada Cancelled Because of Lack of Interest* (1977) by Eric Nicol and Peter Whalley, Canada has disintegrated into a number of colonies or protectorates of other countries.[20]

In English writing regarding Québec the issue of separation has usually been treated satirically, with the future Québec either poor or authoritarian. Needless to say, French writing on the subject is different. From the earliest text of 1839, 'Mon voyage à la Lune' by Aimé-Nicolas Aubin, Québécois utopianism focuses on independence from English Canada.[21]

Well before Australia was discovered by Europeans, it had been the setting for numerous utopias, mostly in French.[22] But the reality of settlement was almost equally divided between the utopian and the dystopian in that while some of the early settlements were established with the same set of utopian expectations as in other settlement colonies, others were established as places to send convicts from Britain and were in essence prisons. In addition, the treatment of the indigenous inhabitants was among the worst of all the settlement colonies, and it remains one of the worst situations for native peoples anywhere in the world. There is a strong racist streak in Australian utopianism, with a particular emphasis on Asians, and Asians faced severe restrictions in Australia until the middle of the twentieth century.

Australia was a difficult place to settle. It has a thin band of fertile land that runs from the middle north around the east coast to the middle south and another in the southwest. In the middle of the country is a huge desert, the 'empty middle'. And the entire country is prone to extreme drought with periodic torrential rains and regular huge wildfires. Thus, those who settled in the Australian colonies found themselves in a frequently recalcitrant and dystopian environment, and there is a strong tradition of Australian writers presenting Australia in dystopian terms.

Still, there has been a powerful utopian stream that argued that even in this difficult setting, a new beginning and a better life were possible. In 1852 John Dunmore Lang published a very early plea for Australian independence, entitled *Freedom and Independence for the Golden Lands of Australia*. In it and in a number of later editions Lang presented a future united Australia, including New Zealand, in which the poor of Britain can become self-sufficient, and he contends that this vision will only be possible with independence.[23]

But the most significant aspect of Australian utopianism has been in practical attempts to put utopia in place. While historically the number of Australian intentional communities was not great, from the 1970s on Australia has produced more such communities per capita than any country other than Israel.[24] And the Garden City Movement, which started in Britain with Ebenezer Howard's 1898 *To-Morrow: A Peaceful Path to Real Reform* (better known under the title of the 1902 second edition *Garden Cities of To-Morrow*), has had a greater impact in Australia than in any other country.[25]

South Africa has a deeply divided utopian tradition in that most utopian literature well into the twentieth century depicted the system of racial division or apartheid in positive terms, and after that the same system was depicted almost universally in dystopian terms.[26] A subset of the first category is literature depicting the ending of apartheid and the establishment of black rule in dystopian terms. The shift between the two categories appears to have taken place between the early sixties and the late seventies, with, for example Garry Allighan's 1961 *Verwoerd – A Look-back from the Future* picturing the eutopia of apartheid, and almost all works published after the late seventies, like Christopher Hope's 1984 *Kruger's Alp*, taking the opposite position.[27]

The settler colony with the strongest utopian tradition, with the possible exception of the United States, is New Zealand. The origins of colonization were explicitly utopian in that Canterbury was designed to reproduce the social hierarchy of Britain without the aristocracy or the truly poor, Otago was to become the homeland for Scottish Presbyterians, and the literature throughout the country designed to attract immigrants likened it to paradise and gave the country names like Britain of the South and Better Britain. And the early intention was to create better relations with the indigenous inhabitants than had been achieved in other settler colonies.[28]

New Zealanders came to believe that it was possible to create a utopia in New Zealand. At times many believed that such a utopia had been created, and a popular name for the country is godzone, from the poem 'God's Own Country' by Tom Bracken. As a result, until the depression of the 1930s New Zealand utopias tended to be practical proposals meant to be implemented rather than depictions of complete societal transformation, although they often suggested that such transformation would be the ultimate result of their proposed reforms.

New Zealand is best known as the country that in 1893 was the first to give women the right to vote, but the most important reform movements from the colonial perspective were various proposals to change the pattern of land ownership. In many colonies earlier settlers were able to get large tracts of the best land, often by deception, theft or murder. Later settlers who wanted to have their own farm were unable to do so and had to work for the earlier settlers or could only get poor land. And in many colonies, the early settlers got the land, hired others to work it, and returned to the home country to live well off the profits. This pattern was much resented by the later settlers and led to various proposals to take the land back and redistribute it. The most utopian of such proposals were land nationalization and the single tax on land, but the idea of nationalizing land was never very popular because settlers wanted to own their land.

The single tax on land, an idea developed by the American author Henry George in his *Progress and Poverty* (1879), was based on the idea that everyone had an equal, God-given right to land.[29] George proposed abolishing all taxes except one on land. This would, he argued, force landowners to use the land productively or sell, thus making more land available to the landless. George also argued that the value of any land was created by the community, through its location and the demand for its products. Thus, a tax on land was simply returning to the community the value that the community had produced. The single tax was extremely popular in Australia, where it is still used, Ireland and New Zealand, areas in which huge estates, often owned by absentee owners, kept new land unavailable. In New Zealand, while the single tax was never implemented for long, it was part of the agitation that led to the breakup of many of the largest estates, making land available to later immigrants.

The countries of Latin and South America repeat all the themes of the other colonies with, over time, the added dimension of relations with the United States, which was seen as both a utopian goal for immigration and a dystopian country dominating weaker countries. In the late twentieth century this becomes a common theme in utopian literature. Conflicts between rich and poor have been particularly strong in Latin and South America, and one of the reasons for the dystopian image of the United States was the perception, often accurate, that it supported the rich against the poor. The Mexican revolution in particular had strong utopian elements, and there was an attempt to redistribute land collectively with the formation of communities called *ejidos* or cooperative farms.

Colonies in space

While many utopias have been located on the moon, as utopian literature became a common part of science fiction, colonization imagery was shifted to space, with colonies established on the planets, moons or asteroids of the solar system, artificial satellites within the solar system, or planets anywhere in the galaxy. In most cases these colonies repeat the pattern of colonies on Earth both with regard to their relations with the home planet and with the indigenous inhabitants where they exist.

One thread of this shift to space, one intended quite seriously by some enthusiasts, is the establishment of colonies in habitats orbiting Earth, much bigger versions of the space station currently being built. These habitats are generally placed at the Lagrange point, the place between the Earth and the Moon where a satellite will stay in orbit indefinitely without being pulled out of orbit by either body. Since these colonies are close to Earth but still separate, just as the earlier colonies were close but not too close to the home country, they play out almost all the issues that actually occurred in those colonies but without the issues raised by indigenous inhabitants. Habitats at this point became a standard trope in science fiction, with the United States author Mack Reynolds publishing five novels set there between 1979 and 1985, the Australian author George Turner depicting a conflict between the colony in space and Earth in his *Yesterday's Men* (1983), and other writers depicting the struggle of the colony for independence from Earth.[30]

Such colonies are generally designed to do two things Earth needs done, the two things that earlier colonies were also designed to do, absorb excess population and feed the home economy. One of the reasons for building the space station is that it is believed that certain manufacturing processes will be possible outside Earth's gravity that are not possible on Earth, and a number of the experiments carried out during the trips of the United States space shuttle were designed to test this. The result envisioned by science-fiction writers is similar to that of the colonies founded earlier on Earth, a slowly growing dissatisfaction with being seen as an appendage designed solely to support Earth, followed by an independence movement, conflict sometimes leading to war, and, in some cases, independence.

The planet-based colonies are also designed to offload population, but as often they are primarily intended to provide Earth with raw materials that either have been depleted on Earth or do not exist on Earth at all or to provide luxury goods that do not exist on Earth. Often the sole reason for the colony is to exploit a planet's resources. But a few had different aims, just as the purposes of Earth-based colonies reflected different objectives. In many cases, planets are chosen so that a religious group can practise its beliefs without outside interference and entire planets used solely as prisons are quite common in the literature. For example, in his 1961 *Planetary Agent X*, Mack Reynolds depicts a future in which both religious and political groups colonize planets so as to be able to exclude non-believers, and Quaker colonies have been depicted in Joan Slonczewski's 1980 *Still Forms on Foxfield* and Judith Moffett's 1987 *Pennterra*, while in her 2003 *Snare*

Katharine Kerr depicts as dystopia a planet colonized by Islamic fundamentalists.[31] Examples of planets used as prisons include Piers Anthony's 1967 *Chthon* and William C. Dietz's 1989 *Prison Planet*.[32]

But often there are indigenous inhabitants that pose problems, whether the colony is for exploitation or settlement or both. The most common scenario suggests that humanity has learned nothing from its experiences on Earth, an example being Ursula K. Le Guin's 1972 'The Word for World is Forest'.[33] An alternative version that is quite common is one in which Earth itself has been colonized by aliens. Brian W. Aldiss's 1960 'X for Exploitation' (also known as *Bow Down to Nul* and *The Interpreter*) depicts such a situation, and an author's note says it was written to show the dystopian nature of imperialism.[34]

Indigenous utopianism and the emergence of postcolonial utopianism

The original inhabitants' idea of the good life inconveniently did not include having their land stolen, being enslaved, and being slaughtered. Because native cultures were so thoroughly destroyed, we know very little with certainty about the nature of indigenous utopianism in settler colonies or in most of the exploitative colonies. Most of the indigenous cultures were transmitted orally, and the deliberate destruction of indigenous religions resulted in the loss of some of the myths that almost certainly included utopian elements. We have a text, 'The Great Law of Peace', from the tribes of eastern forests of North America which describes an ideal political system, but this is an isolated text with uncertain status, and there were many different cultures among the indigenous peoples of North America.[35] The great exceptions are India and Ireland, where we have literatures from the pre-colonial period. And the early Buddhist texts from Southeast Asia have strong utopian elements. We also have written records from the great civilizations of Latin and South America, but these have not been looked at from the point of view of utopianism.

Many changes have come about in the postcolonial period either because, as in Africa, the colonized came to power, or, as in Canada and New Zealand, to improve the situation of the colonized. And the European utopian ideas of freedom and equality, taught to the colonized, demonstrated the disjunction between belief and practice, and provided independence movements with the intellectual tools needed to confront their masters. Ideas that had once been explicitly utopian in Europe and put into practice to at least some extent became again utopian for those seeking independence.

The recreated sense of the traditional cultures are presented by the contemporary cultures as the reality of the past, but these recreations are purified, made more utopian, than what we know of the actual pasts. The interesting point about these recreated pasts is that there are similarities across widely diverse cultures from different parts of the globe. Thus, today there is a commonality about indigenous representations of their ideal pasts, which stresses closeness to nature, including flora, fauna and physical features like mountains and rivers.

One of the ways that the colonized tried to counteract the dystopia brought to them by the colonizer was to adopt aspects of the colonizers' religion. One of the most common results was the growth of millennial movements among the colonized. In North America, the Ghost Dance religion of the Plains Indians, which ultimately led to the massacre of the Indians at Wounded Knee, has been studied as utopian.[36] Millennial movements among the Maori in New Zealand produced both major armed opposition to the colonizers and an important peaceful non-resistance movement. They were also defeated, but in New Zealand some of them did not disappear but remain as both religious and political movements among the Maori, who are now courted by pakeha (non-Maori) politicians.

There have also been a few works by descendants of the colonizers depicting the indigenous culture defeating the colonists and establishing a better society. Examples include Martin Cruz Smith's 1970 *The Indians Won*, Ernest Callenbach's 1994 'Chocco' and Pamela Sargent's 1999 *Climb the Wind: A Novel of Another America*.[37]

At the same time, many indigenous peoples are using the perceived utopia of their pasts to attempt to depict a better life today for their peoples. For example, in his 1973 *Two Thousand Seasons*, the Kenyan writer Ayi Kwei Armah describes a re-envisioned African past as an egalitarian utopia.[38] Utopia is still a powerful and effective dream for the dispossessed.

The countries of Latin and South America again follow the same pattern of generally very poor treatment of and relations with their indigenous peoples, and the utopias written by the colonizer either ignore the original inhabitants altogether or justify their extinction. And again in a few cases, the descendants of the original inhabitants have provided an alternative utopia. Currently this is most notable in the Zapatista movement in Mexico, which has both fought the Mexican government sufficiently successfully to control some territory itself and has provided a utopian justification for doing so. This image has proven to be quite attractive outside Mexico and that attraction has contributed to the success of the movement.

Although postcolonialism is a very complex subject, postcolonial utopianism is initially the re-presentation of both the past and the future as seen by others besides the settlers and the exploiters. This means that utopias written from the point of view of the indigenous are frequently dystopian projections of what the settlers and exploiters had presented positively.[39] Two Australian examples were written by men who adopted Aboriginal identities. Both *Doctor Wooreddy's Prescription for Enduring the End of the World* (1983) by Colin Johnson/Mudrooroo and *Walg* (1983) by B. Wongar (born Sreten Bozic but adopted into his wife's tribe) describe the vicious dystopia of white Australian treatment of Aborigines.[40] The American Indian writer Sherman Alexie in 'The Farm' (1996) describes the Indian reservation as dystopian, and in *Gardens in the Dunes* (1999) Leslie Marmon Silko, another American Indian writer, describes the white treatment of Indians as a dystopia.[41] The Ghanaian writer Kodwo Abaidoo in his 1995 *Black Fury* and the Nigerian writer Buchi Emechta in her 1983 *The Rape of Shavi* describe similar experiences in their countries.[42]

Leslie Marmon Silko's 'One World, Many Tribes' (1991) describes the gathering of the tribes to reclaim the land with brief notes on how the world will be healed in the future.[43] 'Ngati Kangaru' by Patricia Grace describes a Maori eutopia in which the Maori take back Aotearoa/New Zealand using the same techniques, but only the peaceful ones, that were used in the pakeha (European) settlement to take the land from the Maori.[44] And on Australia Day 1988 the Aboriginal activist Burnum Burnum declared Aboriginal possession of England, raising the Aboriginal flag on the English coast at Dover.[45] None of these works by contemporary indigenous authors is seriously hopeful, and Silko's *Ceremony* (1977), which discusses what might constitute appropriate ceremonies for Dine (Navajo) in the twentieth century, illustrates why hope is hard to come by. In Australia there is a poem, 'The Aboriginal Charter of Rights' by Oodgeroo Noonuccal, that is a strong statement of the Aboriginal position, but despite the title it still is asking for equality, not yet demanding it.[46]

A second postcolonial move is found in the influence of indigenous belief systems on utopias written by the descendants of both the colonized and the colonizers. The most profound impact appears to be in New Zealand, where most literary utopianism from the late twentieth century on incorporates Maori beliefs and practices. Examples include Lora Mountjoy's 1984 *Deep Breathing* and Chris Baker's 2000 *Kokopu Dreams* and 2006 *Shadow Waters*.[47]

A third postcolonial move can be seen in a novel like *Black Rainbow* (1992) by Albert Wendt, a Samoan/New Zealand writer, who presents a number of different perspectives on the same dystopian future, which, as in George Orwell's *Nineteen Eighty-Four* (1949), is systematically erasing the history of the country.[48] Such erasure has been the actual but not necessarily deliberate practice in many colonies where the treatment of the indigenous population is conveniently forgotten. Only in 2008, after a change of government, did the Australian government apologize to its Aboriginal citizens for the way they had been treated throughout most of Australian history, and the issue is still hotly debated by Australian historians. A similar process has been and is still taking place in many ex-colonies and has not yet started in others.

The multiple perspectives of Wendt's novel are typical of postcolonial literature, but they are used somewhat less often in the utopias because they are designed to make a political point and the authors want to ensure that the point gets across to the reader. Still, there are extremely complex postcolonial utopias like New Zealander Ian Wedde's *Symme's Hole* (1986) and Australian Terry Dowling's Rynosseros series that make their points in their multi-dimensional novels.[49]

Conclusion

As has been shown, utopianism was an important part of the process of colonization, and in all the settler colonies it has continued from the time of settlement to the present. In some of these countries there is both a utopianism of the colonizer and a different utopianism of the colonized, and in a few cases, most notably in New Zealand, the two have partially blended, with the utopianism of the descendants of the colonizers integrating themes from the utopianism of the colonized.

There were some indigenous utopian traditions in the colonies that emerged from colonies primarily designed for exploitation rather than settlement, but the greatest growth of utopianism in these countries came with postcolonialism and images of independence and a better life free from colonial domination. And it has continued with images of a better life free from the corrupt system that too often replaced the corrupt colonial regime.

Thus, it can be argued that utopianism has been most important in countries that were once colonies. This utopianism was initially based on themes drawn from the colonial power, but over time it became different as it was adapted to the conditions in the new country.

NOTES

1 The word colony derives from Greek and Latin and was first used in English as early as the sixteenth century in its modern meaning, which refers to a settlement in a new country with ties back to the parent country. There are some problems as to what countries can be considered to have been colonies. For example, Ireland is now generally treated as having been or, given Northern Ireland, still being a colony, but it was not so treated until sometime in the twentieth century.

2 Robert L. Wright (ed.), *Irish Emigrant Ballads and Songs* (Bowling Green University Popular Press, 1975), p. 491.

3 Theodore C. Blegan and Martin B. Rudd (eds. and trans.), songs harmonized by Gunnar J. Malmin, *Norwegian Emigrant Songs and Ballads* (Oxford University Press, 1936), p. 93.

4 Wright (ed.), *Irish Emigrant Ballads and Song*, p. 505.

5 For an example of someone who went down the social scale after immigrating, see Miles Fairburn, *Nearly Out of Heart and Hope: The Puzzle of a Colonial Labourer's Diary* (Auckland University Press, 1995).

6 For a consideration of the push-pull interpretation, see James Belich, 'Settler Utopianism? English Ideologies of Emigration, 1815–1880', in John Morrow and Jonathan Scott (eds.), *Liberty, Authority, Formality: Political Ideas and Culture, 1600–1900: Essays in Honour of Colin Davis* (Exeter: Imprint Academic, 2008), pp. 213–34.

7 'Hopeful' [pseud.], *Taken In; Being, A Sketch of New Zealand Life* (London: W. H. Allen & Co., 1887).

8 In one sense this is surprising in that the letters reflect experience in the new land, but there are fewer letters from the disillusioned; the failures are less likely to write home (who wants to report failure?), and those who die or return are also unlikely to write home.

9 Robert L. Wright, *Swedish Emigrant Ballads* (Lincoln: University of Nebraska Press, 1965), p. 39.

10 *A Few Words to Emigrants' Wives* (London: Jarrold and Sons, [*c.* 1870]), unpaginated.

11 Theodor Hertzka, *Freiland: Ein sociales Zukunftsbild* (Leipzig: Verlag von Duncker & Humblot, 1890); James Burgh, *An Account of the First Settlement, Laws, Form of Government, and Police, of the Cessares* (London: Ptd for J. Payne, 1764), reprinted in Gregory Claeys (ed.), *Utopias of the British Enlightenment* (Cambridge University Press, 1994), pp. 71–136; Robert Pemberton, *The Happy Colony* (London: Saunders & Otley, 1854); General William Booth, *In Darkest England and The Way Out* (London: Salvation Army, 1890).

12 [Thomas Babington Macaulay, 1st Baron Macaulay (1800–59)], review of *The Ecclesiastical and Political History of the Popes of Rome, during the Sixteenth and Seventeenth Centuries* by Leopold Ranke, *Edinburgh Review or Critical Journal* 72:145 (October 1840), 228.

13 *Private Letters from an American in England to his Friends in America* (London: Ptd. for J. Almon, 1769), also entitled *Anticipation, or The Voyage of an American to England in the Year 1899, in a series of letters, humourously describing the supposed situation of this Kingdom at that Period* (London: Ptd. for W. Lane, 1781), reprinted in Gregory Claeys (ed.), *Modern British Utopias 1700–1850* (8 vols., London: Pickering & Chatto, 1997), vol. 3, pp. 341–412; and Rationales [pseud.], 'Remarks which are supposed will be made in this Kingdom, by two North American travellers in the year one thousand nine hundred and forty-four', *The Literary Register or Weekly Miscellany* (Newcastle upon Tyne, England), 1 (1769), 98–9.

14 On this literature, see David Skilton, 'Contemplating the Ruins of London: Macaulay's New Zealander and Others', *Literary London: Interdisciplinary Studies in the Representation of London* (March 2004), http://homepages.

gold.ac.uk/london-journal/march2004/skilton.html. Accessed 11 September 2008.

15 John Cotton, *Abstract of Lawes of New England* (London: F. Coules & W. Ley, 1641).

16 John Winthrop, *Life and Letters of John Winthrop* (2 vols., Boston, MA: Ticknor & Fields, 1864–7), vol. 2, p. 19.

17 For a sustained argument that Pennsylvania was founded to be a utopia, see Isaac Sharpless, *A Quaker Experiment in Government* (Philadelphia, PA: A. J. Ferris, 1898).

18 William Smith, 'A General Idea of the College of Mirania' (New York: J. Parker & W. Weyman, 1753).

19 Wilfrid Châteauclair [pseud.] [William Douw Lighthall], *The Young Seigneur; or, Nation-Making* (Montreal: W. Drysdale & Co., 1888).

20 Eric Nicol and Peter Whalley, *Canada Cancelled Because of Lack of Interest* (Edmonton: Hurtig, 1977).

21 Napoléon Aubin [pseud.], 'Mon voyage à la Lune', *Le Fantasque* (Québec City, QC: 1839), reprinted in *Napoléon Aubin*, ed. Jean-Paul Tremblay (Montréal, QC: Editions Fides, 1972), pp. 31–40.

22 On this literature, see John Dunmore, *Utopias and Imaginary Voyages to Australia: A lecture delivered at the National Library of Australia, 2 September 1987*, Occasional Lecture Series, No. 2 (Canberra: National Library of Australia, 1988); William [Lawrence] Eisler, *The Furthest Shore: Images of Terra Australis from the Middle Ages to Captain Cook* (Cambridge University Press, 1995); David Fausett, *Writing the New World: Imaginary Voyages and Utopias of the Great Southern Land* (Syracuse University Press, 1993); and Bernard Smith, *European Vision and the South Pacific*, 2nd edn (Sydney, NSW: Harper & Row, (1984).

23 John Dunmore Lang, *Freedom and Independence for the Golden Lands of Australia* (London: Longman & Co., 1852).

24 See Bill Metcalf (ed.), *From Utopian Dreaming to Communal Reality: Cooperative Lifestyles in Australia* (Sydney, NSW: UNSW Press, 1995).

25 See Robert Freestone, *Model Communities: The Garden City Movement in Australia* (Melbourne: Thomas Nelson Australia, 1989).

26 Any generalization about South African utopian literature is based primarily on the literature published in English because there has been almost no study of the literature published in Afrikaans and little has been translated. On South African utopianism, see N. J. C. van den Bergh, *The National States in South Africa and Utopian Thought* (KwaDlangezwa, South Africa: University of Zululand, 1982); Michael Green, 'Future Histories', in his *Novel Histories: Past, Present, and Future in South African Fiction* (Johannesburg: Witwatersrand University Press, 1997), pp. 233–87; and Ralph Pordzik, 'Nationalism, Cross-Culturalism, and Utopian Vision in South African Utopian and Dystopian Writing 1972–92', *Research in African Literatures* 32:3 (Fall 2001), 177–97.

27 Garry Allighan, *Verwoerd – A Look-back from the Future* (London: Boardman, 1961); Christopher Hope, *Kruger's Alp* (London: Heinemann, 1984).

28 See Dominic Alessio, 'Promoting Paradise: Utopianism and National Identity in New Zealand, 1870–1930', *New Zealand Journal of History* 42:1 (April 2008), 22–41.

29 Henry George, *Progress and Poverty* (New York: D. Appleton & Co., 1880).

30 George Turner, *Yesterday's Men* (London: Faber & Faber, 1983).

31 Mack Reynolds [Dallas McCord], *Planetary Agent X* (New York: Ace, 1961); Joan Slonczewski, *Still Forms on Foxfield* (New York: Ballantine, 1980); Judith Moffett, *Isaac Asimov Presents Pennterra* (New York: Congdon & Weed, 1987); Katharine Kerr, *Snare* (London: Harper Collins, 2003).

32 Piers Anthony, *Chthon* (New York: Ballantine Books, 1967), William C. Dietz, *Prison Planet* (New York: Ace, 1989).

33 Ursula K. Le Guin, 'The Word for World is Forest', in Harlan J. Ellison (ed.), *Again, Dangerous Visions* (Garden City, NY: Doubleday, 1972), pp. 32–117.

34 Brian W. Aldiss, 'X For Exploitation', *New Worlds Science Fiction* 31:92–32:94 (March–May 1960), 4–42, 78–110, 112–14, 78–123. Republished as *Bow Down to Nul* (New York: Ace, 1960).

35 A version, under the title, 'The Constitution of the Iroquois Nations', is available at www.indigenouspeople.net.iroqon.htm. Accessed 11 September 2008.

36 See, for example, B. C. Mohrbacher, 'The Whole World is Coming: The 1890 Ghost Dance Movement as Utopia', *Utopian Studies* 7:1 (1996), 75–85.

37 Martin Cruz Smith, *The Indians Won* (New York: Belmont, 1970); Ernest Callenbach, 'Chocco', in Kim Stanley Robinson (ed.), *Future Primitive: The New Ecotopias* (New York: Tor, 1994), pp. 189–213; Pamela Sargent, *Climb the Wind: A Novel of Another America* (New York: HarperPrism, 1999).

38 Ayi Kwei Armah, *Two Thousand Seasons* (Nairobi: East African Publishing House, 1973).

39 While some texts from indigenous communities have been translated, many have not, so although there have been suggestions that utopias exist in African and Indian languages, it has so far been impossible to confirm this.

40 Colin Johnson/Mudrooroo, *Doctor Wooreddy's Prescription for Enduring the End of the World* (Melbourne: Hyland House, 1983); B. Wongar, *Walg* (New York: Dodd, Mead, 1983).

41 Sherman Alexie, 'The Farm', *The Raven Chronicles* (Fall 1996), 51–6. Reprinted in Kateri Akiwenzie-Damm and Josie Doublas (eds.), *Skins: Contemporary Indigenous Writing* (Alice Springs, NT: Jukurrpa Books, 2000), pp. 42–56; Leslie Marmon Silko, *Gardens in the Dunes* (New York: Simon & Schuster, 1999).

42 Kodwo Abaidoo, *Black Fury* (Accra, Ghana: Woeli Publishing Services, 1995); Buchi Emechta, *The Rape of Shavi* (London: Ogwugwu Afor Co./Ibuza, Nigeria: Umuezeokolo, 1983).

43 Leslie Marmon Silko, 'One World, Many Tribes', in Silko, *Almanac of the Dead* (New York: Simon & Schuster, 1991), pp. 707–63.

44 Patricia Grace, 'Ngati Kangaru', in *The Sky People and Other Stories* (Auckland: Penguin, 1994), pp. 25–43.

45 See 'The Burnum Burnum Declaration' in Anita Heiss and Peter Minter (eds.), *The Macquarie PEN Anthology of Aboriginal Literature* (Crows Nest, NSW: Allen & Unwin, 2008), pp. 124–5. Burnum Burnum was known as Henry Penrith before taking back his Aboriginal name.

46 Oodgeroo Noonuccal, 'The Aboriginal Charter of Rights', in Heiss and Minter (eds.), *The Macquarie PEN Anthology*, pp. 445–6. Originally published as by Kath Walker, *The Dawn is at Hand: Selected Poems* (London: Marion Boyars,

1992), pp. 60–1. Oodgeroo Noonuccal was known as Kath Walker before taking back her Aboriginal name. She was the author of the first book by an Aboriginal woman and the first book of poetry by an Aboriginal. The poem was first read at the 5th Annual Meeting of the Federal Council for the Advancement of Aborigines and Torres Strait Islanders in 1962.

47 Lora Mountjoy, *Deep Breathing* (Auckland: New Women's Press, 1984); Chris Baker, *Kokopu Dreams* (Wellington: Huia Publishers, 2000) and *Shadow Waters* (Wellington: Huia Publishers, 2006).

48 Albert Wendt, *Black Rainbow* (Harmondsworth: Penguin, 1992); George Orwell, *Nineteen Eighty-Four* (London: Secker & Warburg, 1949).

49 Ian Wedde, *Symme's Hole* (Auckland: Penguin, 1986).

BIBLIOGRAPHY

A Few Words to Emigrants' Wives (London: Jarrold and Sons, [c. 1870]).

Abaidoo, Kodwo, *Black Fury* (Accra, Ghana: Woeli Publishing Services, 1995).

Aldiss, Brian W., 'X For Exploitation', *New Worlds Science Fiction* 31:92–32:94 (March–May 1960), 4–42, 78–110, 112–14, 78–123. Reprinted as *Bow Down to Nul* (New York: Ace, 1960).

Alessio, Dominic, 'Promoting Paradise: Utopianism and National Identity in New Zealand, 1870–1930', *New Zealand Journal of History* 42:1 (April 2008), 22–41.

Alexie, Sherman, 'The Farm', *The Raven Chronicles* (Fall 1996), 51–6. Reprinted in Kateri Akiwenzie-Damm and Josie Doublas (eds.), *Skins: Contemporary Indigenous Writing* (Alice Springs, NT: Jukurrpa Books, 2000), pp. 42–56.

Allighan, Garry, *Verwoerd – A Look-back from the Future* (London: Boardman, 1961).

Anthony, Piers, *Chthon* (New York: Ballantine Books, 1967).

Armah, Ayi Kwei, *Two Thousand Seasons* (Nairobi: East African Publishing House, 1973).

Aubin, Napoléon [pseud.], 'Mon voyage à la Lune', *Le Fantasque* (Québec City, QC: 1839), reprinted in *Napoléon Aubin*, ed. Jean-Paul Tremblay (Montréal, QC: Editions Fides, 1972), pp. 31–40.

Baker, Chris, *Kokopu Dreams* (Wellington: Huia Publishers, 2000).
  Shadow Waters (Wellington: Huia Publishers, 2006).

Belich, James, 'Settler Utopianism? English Ideologies of Emigration, 1815–1880', in John Morrow and Jonathan Scott (eds.), *Liberty, Authority, Formality: Political Ideas and Culture, 1600–1900: Essays in Honour of Colin Davis* (Exeter: Imprint Academic, 2008), pp. 213–34.

Blegan, Theodore C. and Martin B. Rudd (eds. and trans.), songs harmonized by Gunnar J. Malmin, *Norwegian Emigrant Songs and Ballads* (London: Oxford University Press, 1936).

Booth, General William, *In Darkest England and The Way Out* (London: Salvation Army, 1890).

Burgh, James, *An Account of the First Settlement, Laws, Form of Government, and Police, of the Cessares* (London: Ptd for J. Payne, 1764), reprinted in Gregory

Claeys (ed.), *Utopias of the British Enlightenment* (Cambridge University Press, 1994), pp. 71–136.

Callenbach, Ernest, 'Chocco', in Kim Stanley Robinson (ed.), *Future Primitive: The New Ecotopias* (New York: Tor, 1994), pp. 189–213.

Châteauclair, Wilfrid [pseudo. for William Douw Lighthall], *The Young Seigneur; or, Nation-Making* (Montreal; W. Drysdale & Co., 1888).

Claeys, Gregory (ed.), *Utopias of the British Enlightenment* (Cambridge University Press, 1994).

Cotton, John, *Abstract of Lawes of New England* (London: F. Coules & W. Ley, 1641).

Dietz, William C., *Prison Planet* (New York: Ace, 1989).

Dunmore, John, *Utopias and Imaginary Voyages to Australia: A lecture delivered at the National Library of Australia, 2 September 1987*, Occasional Lecture Series, No. 2 (Canberra: National Library of Australia, 1988).

Eisler, William [Lawrence], *The Furthest Shore: Images of Terra Australis from the Middle Ages to Captain Cook* (Cambridge University Press, 1995).

Emechta, Buchi, *The Rape of Shavi* (London: Ogwugwu Afor Co./Ibuza, Nigeria: Umuezeokolo, 1983).

Fairburn, Miles, *Nearly Out of Heart and Hope: The Puzzle of a Colonial Labourer's Diary* (Auckland University Press, 1995).

Fausett, David, *Writing the New World: Imaginary Voyages and Utopias of the Great Southern Land* (Syracuse University Press, 1993).

Freestone, Robert, *Model Communities: The Garden City Movement in Australia* (Melbourne: Thomas Nelson Australia, 1989).

George, Henry, *Progress and Poverty* (New York: D. Appleton & Co., 1880).

Grace, Patricia, 'Ngati Kangaru', in *The Sky People and Other Stories* (Auckland: Penguin, 1994), pp. 25–43.

Green, Michael, 'Future Histories', in *Novel Histories: Past, Present, and Future in South African Fiction* (Johannesburg: Witwatersrand University Press, 1997), pp. 233–87.

Heiss, Anita and Peter Minter (eds.), *The Macquarie PEN Anthology of Aboriginal Literature* (Crows Nest, NSW: Allen & Unwin, 2008).

Hertzka, Theodor, *Freiland: Ein Sociales Zukunftsbild* (Leipzig: Verlag von Duncker & Humblot, 1890).

Hope, Christopher, *Kruger's Alp* (London: Heinemann, 1984).

'Hopeful' [pseud.], *Taken In; Being, A Sketch of New Zealand Life* (London: W. H. Allen & Co., 1887).

Johnson, Colin/Mudrooroo, *Doctor Wooreddy's Prescription for Enduring the End of the World* (Melbourne: Hyland House, 1983).

Kerr, Katharine, *Snare* (London: Harper Collins, 2003).

Lang, John Dunmore, Freedom and Independence for the Golden Lands of Australia (London: Longman & Co., 1852).

Le Guin, Ursula K., 'The Word for World is Forest', in Harlan J. Ellison (ed.), *Again, Dangerous Visions* (Garden City, NY: Doubleday, 1972), pp. 32–117.

[Macaulay, Thomas Babington, 1st Baron Macaulay (1800–59)], review of *The Ecclesiastical and Political History of the Popes of Rome, during the Sixteenth and Seventeenth Centuries*, by Leopold Ranke, *Edinburgh Review or Critical Journal* 72:145 (October 1840).

Metcalf, Bill (ed.), *From Utopian Dreaming to Communal Reality: Cooperative* [*Co-operative* on cover] *Lifestyles in Australia* (Sydney, NSW: UNSW Press, 1995).

Moffett, Judith, *Isaac Asimov Presents Pennterra* (New York: Congdon & Weed, 1987).

Mohrbacher, B. C., 'The Whole World is Coming: The 1890 Ghost Dance Movement as Utopia', *Utopian Studies* 7:1 (1996), 75–85.

Mountjoy, Lora, *Deep Breathing* (Auckland: New Women's Press, 1984).

Nicol, Eric and Peter Whalley, *Canada Cancelled Because of Lack of Interest* (Edmonton: Hurtig, 1977).

Orwell, George, *Nineteen Eighty-Four* (London: Secker & Warburg, 1949).

Pemberton, Robert, *The Happy Colony* (London: Saunders & Otley, 1854).

Pordzik, Ralph, 'Nationalism, Cross-Culturalism, and Utopian Vision in South African Utopian and Dystopian Writing 1972–92', *Research in African Literatures* 32:3 (Fall 2001), 177–97.

Private Letters from an American in England to his Friends in America (London: Ptd. for J. Almon, 1769), also entitled *Anticipation, or The Voyage of an American to England in the Year 1899, in a series of letters, humourously describing the supposed situation of this Kingdom at that Period* (London: Ptd for W. Lane, 1781), reprinted in Gregory Claeys (ed.), *Modern British Utopias 1700–1850* (8 vols., London: Pickering & Chatto, 1997), vol. 3, pp. 341–412.

Rationales [pseud.], 'Remarks which are supposed will be made in this Kingdom, by two North American travellers in the year one thousand nine hundred and forty-four', *The Literary Register or Weekly Miscellany* (Newcastle upon Tyne, England), 1 (1769), 98–9.

Reynolds, Mack [Dallas McCord], *Planetary Agent X* (New York: Ace, 1961).

Sargent, Pamela, *Climb the Wind: A Novel of Another America* (New York: HarperPrism, 1999).

Sharpless, Isaac, *A Quaker Experiment in Government* (Philadelphia, PA: A. J. Ferris, 1898).

Silko, Leslie Marmon, *Gardens in the Dunes* (New York: Simon & Schuster, 1999).
'One World, Many Tribes', in *Almanac of the Dead* (New York: Simon & Schuster, 1991), pp. 707–63.

Skilton, David, 'Contemplating the Ruins of London: Macaulay's New Zealander and Others', *Literary London: Interdisciplinary Studies in the Representation of London* (March 2004).

Slonczewski, Joan, *Still Forms on Foxfield* (New York: Ballantine, 1980).

Smith, Bernard, *European Vision and the South Pacific*, 2nd edn (Sydney, NSW: Harper & Row, [1984]).

Smith, Martin Cruz, *The Indians Won* (New York: Belmont, 1970).

Smith, William, 'A General Idea of the College of Mirania' (New York: J. Parker & W. Weyman, 1753).

Turner, George, *Yesterday's Men* (London: Faber & Faber, 1983).

van den Bergh, N. J. C., *The National States in South Africa and Utopian Thought* (KwaDlangezwa, South Africa: University of Zululand, 1982).

Wedde, Ian, *Symme's Hole* (Auckland: Penguin, 1986).

Wendt, Albert, *Black Rainbow* (Harmondsworth: Penguin, 1992).

Winthrop, John, *Life and Letters of John Winthrop* (2 vols., Boston, MA: Ticknor & Fields, 1864–7).

Wongar, B., *Walg* (New York: Dodd, Mead, 1983).

Wright, Robert L. (ed.), *Irish Emigrant Ballads and Songs* (Bowling Green University Popular Press, 1975).

10

JACQUELINE DUTTON

'Non-western' utopian traditions

> In the red (dead) heart of Australia
> Utopia is a place.
> Though it bears a Western name
> It is not a Western space.
> But a sign that social dreaming
> Can have a different face.

Utopia and utopianism are often perceived to be primarily western constructs – western dreams of a better world, an ideal existence or a fantastic future. This is undoubtedly due to the fact that the definition, design and development of utopian literatures and theories have emerged from western examples of the genre and practice. Whether we consider the dawn of utopia as the moment when Thomas More created the neologism *utopia* in 1516, or seek its roots further back in Plato's *Republic* or St Augustine's *City of God*, the overwhelming majority of references to the (pre-)history of utopia point to western traditions and worldviews as its foundations. If the West is deemed to be the source of utopia, it is hardly surprising that the proliferation of definitions and theories that have contributed to critical studies of the genre are also mainly produced by and adhere to western academic models. But as western scholarship has evolved, so too have the rules determining the shape of utopia. From a literary genre, it has become a paradigm that can be applied to a wide variety of disciplines and endeavours, including architecture, music, visual arts, politics, philosophy, sociology and even psychology. The parameters of the theory have changed accordingly, to encompass a broader range of utopian expressions – the spirit of utopia (Ernst Bloch), the desire for utopia (Ruth Levitas), critical utopias and critical dystopias (Tom Moylan) and utopianism (Krishan Kumar). Relaxing many of the generic and theoretical constraints of the traditional literary genre allows Lyman Tower Sargent's inclusive reading of utopianism as 'social dreaming'. This new broader definition prompts us to consider whether interpretations of utopia and utopianism might have been in existence all

223

around the world, throughout history, without necessarily being recognized by the West. Questioning the epistemological foundations of utopia as a western way of imagining the ideal society is therefore at the core of this study of 'non-western' utopian traditions.

Through acknowledging the diversity in representations of utopia in the West, researchers in the field have opened up understanding of multiple western traditions of utopianism. The same comprehensive approach should now be applied to all cultures to ascertain where, when, how and why 'non-western' utopian traditions appear and whether they manifest particular forms of intercultural imaginaries of the ideal. To focus momentarily on the dilemma of designation, it must be noted that the binary oppositions of 'western' and 'non-western' as categories of utopian representations are utterly inadequate. While these terms are often used by critics seeking to deconstruct Orientalist and hierarchical systems of interpretation – from Edward Saïd to Gayatri Spivak and Homi Bhabha – they perpetuate an un-desirable insistence on defining the 'rest' of the world in relation to the West. Instead of portraying the plurality of independent cultural traditions, this dichotomy cements an interdependency that is detrimental on both sides of the somewhat arbitrary East–West divide. It is clear that western uto-pias take on such radically different forms as Gabriel de Foigny's paradise for hermaphrodites in Australia, described in *The Southern Land Known* (1676), juxtaposed against the constitution of an Israeli *kibbutz* or a Soviet manifesto, or Marge Piercy's surrealist novel *Woman on the Edge of Time* (1976).[1] It is equally evident that 'non-western' utopias draw on so many different traditions and worldviews that such a reductive classification becomes useless. Rather than using the negative term of 'non-western' to refer to utopian visions that arise in cultures beyond the previously demar-cated limits of the western genre, this study seeks to explore new ways of expressing the range of utopian possibilities that are becoming apparent in different cultures. With its historically West-centred description of theory and practice, the concept of utopia may no longer be broad enough to en-compass the full scope of social dreamings. 'Intercultural imaginaries of the ideal' may be a more appropriate and neutral term for this study of several different traditions of speculative and idealistic thought grounded in the projection of a better society.

What makes us think that, after centuries of concentrating on the western traditions of utopia and utopianism, there may be a whole range of other traditions that express similar frameworks in which to imagine ways of im-proving our existence? The answer to this question requires reconsideration of the origins of utopia in the West, and a systematic search for comparable representations of an ideal time, place or way of being in other cultures. It is widely recognized that four major mythical models of felicity contribute to the genesis of the utopian genre: the Golden Age, the Land of Cockaigne, the Millennium and the Ideal City.[2] As the earliest representation of an ideal place and time, the Golden Age can be seen as the most pivotal source of social dreaming in the West. Most utopian scholars agree that even if we do not consider the descriptions of the Golden Age in Hesiod's *Works and Days*, Ovid's *Metamorphoses* and Virgil's *Eclogues* as utopias in the strict sense of the term, they nevertheless constitute the foundations of the genre. These texts, and many others that pre-date the Renaissance creation of Thomas More, are included in *The Utopia Reader*[3] and feature in most anthologies and studies as part of the pre-history of utopia. If the Golden Age is a vision of a time of harmony and happiness that influences the development of utopia in the West, and this mythical model has widespread significance in almost every culture in the world, it may therefore provide the key to understanding the development of intercultural imaginaries of the ideal in other contexts.

This chapter seeks to provide an overview of comparative utopian studies, tracing the argument for and against the development of this field of scholarship, as well as offering some examples that indicate the presence of imagined ideal societies in a range of cultures that are not considered part of the western utopian tradition. Beginning with the case against the existence of utopia outside the western canon, this study will examine the reasons for excluding 'non-western' models from the rich and diverse research on utopia as both a literary genre and a social experiment. It will then track the growing critical support for comparative utopian studies as a means for considering intercultural imaginaries of the ideal society or desires for an alternative order in 'non-western' cultures. Following this exposition of the ideological debate surrounding comparative utopian studies, this chapter will present various schema that outline the possible pathways by which utopianism may have developed in cultures outside the West. It will identify alternative approaches to imagining the ideal in culturally specific foundational stories to ascertain the existence of diversity in pre-More utopian traditions. It will also determine which particular tendencies persist in post-More projections of a better place to be, in order to demonstrate how the influence of local cultures is maintained concurrently even as the western utopian model is introduced and extended. In this way, this study will attempt to advance understanding of how 'non-western' utopian traditions may have been established and elaborated according to fundamentally different cultural paradigms to those that define the western utopian tradition.

Until recently, the debate around the existence of 'non-western' utopian traditions has not attracted serious attention from many critics, who have been otherwise engaged in defining, delimiting and often defending the nebulous concept of utopia, not to mention its ever-evolving avatars of dystopia, anti-utopia and their critical counterparts. Most of the scholarship on the subject has therefore privileged the western model of utopia, and it has been proposed that the only country outside the West to produce a real and ongoing utopian tradition is China. However, there is substantial evidence to suggest that most cultures generate – if not utopias corresponding to the western design – then at least some representations of an imaginary ideal place or time that do reflect similar preoccupations to those observed in western utopian writings and practices.

In exploring utopian traditions outside the western canon, the main obstacle to be overcome is resistance from certain scholars who, in contributing to the process of defining utopia, have opposed comparative utopian studies, and indeed dismissed the notion that 'non-western' utopias might exist. Despite the 1970s awakening to postcolonial and postmodern perspectives, Frank and Fritzie Manuel maintained that although earthly paradises and blessed isles of felicity exist in most world cultures, there is no real evidence of utopian fiction or practice beyond the borders of the West:

> There are treatises on ideal states and stories about imaginary havens of delight among the Chinese, the Japanese, the Hindus and the Arabs, but the profusion of Western utopias has not been equaled in any other culture. Perhaps the Chinese have been too worldly and practical, the Hindus too transcendental to recognize a tension between the Two Kingdoms and to resolve it in the myth of a heaven on earth which lies at the heart of utopian fantasy.[4]

Those scholars who have considered the question whether 'non-western' utopias do actually exist have more often than not answered in the negative, and a particularly strong stance by Krishan Kumar might seem difficult to refute: 'Utopia is *not* universal. It appears only in societies with the classical and Christian heritage, that is, only in the West.'[5] He concedes that China may have demonstrated some indications of utopian tendencies, but then rejects those representations immediately:

> The claim has been made that China has an authentic utopian tradition. Particular emphasis is put on the Confucian concept of *ta-t'ung*, a Golden Age of 'Great Unity' or 'Great Togetherness'; the Taoist concept of *t'ai-p'ing*, the 'Great Harmony' ... the important thing, surely, is that none of these 'utopian' elements cohered into a true utopia as they did in the West.[6]

The study of Chinese utopias was certainly the most fertile area of scholarship on utopia in 'non-western' cultures during the twentieth century, producing over thirty articles, books and theses in English. These works are divided between those providing a utopian reading of Chinese communist ideology,[7] those that consider only the representations of utopia that correspond to the western definition following the influence of Thomas More's *Utopia*,[8] and those that draw on Confucian and neo-Confucian expressions of an ideal society as evidence of an independent tradition of utopianism in China.[9] The preponderance of research into ancient and pre-modern Chinese imaginaries of the ideal attests to a shared conviction amongst these international scholars that a Chinese utopian tradition does exist.

There has also been interest in the development of utopian practices in Japanese culture, especially since the publication in 1971 of Seiji Nuita's article 'Traditional Utopias in Japan and the West: A Study in Contrast',[10] which opened up English-language research in the area. His list of utopias from Tokugawa and Meiji Japan serves to demonstrate the inspiration of the western utopian model during the 1880s, with the publication of twenty utopias during this period of intense modernization in Japan. Nuita argues that the Japanese 'energy of consciousness' is not sufficiently dissociated from nature to encourage the Japanese to give birth to utopian visions, and therefore Japanese utopias are necessarily derived from western standards. However, the following essay in this volume does suggest the presence of a Japanese utopian tradition prior to the Meiji period, influenced by Neo-Confucianism and adapted by Japanese intellectuals of the Tokugawa period.[11] Other important work in Japanese[12] recognizes the relevance of utopian thought in Japanese culture. However, until recently, much of the research in Japan has focused on particular western utopian thinkers and writers, especially Thomas More,[13] Robert Owen,[14] William Morris[15] and H. G. Wells.[16] Coming through English Literature and Comparative Literature disciplines now are studies in English that are invaluable contributions to East–West comparative utopian studies accessible to an English readership.[17]

In addition to this work on Chinese and Japanese utopian traditions, research on African, Indian, Islamic, Australian, New Zealand and indigenous utopias has been growing in the past decades, taking up a comparative perspective. There remains in these studies a tendency to seek out applications of the western model of utopia in these 'non-western' representations of the desire for an alternative society or order, which does not challenge the epistemological foundations of utopia as a western way of imagining the ideal society. This may be the fundamental flaw in previous approaches to understanding utopias outside the West. Adam B. Seligman's edited volume *Order and Transcendence: The Role of Utopias and the Dynamics of Civilizations* (1989) questions the hegemonic role of the utopian paradigm as a product of western civilization, in the most convincing attempt at providing a comprehensive exploration of comparative utopias to date.[18] But the recurring feature of this and the other comparative utopian studies mentioned is a reliance on the western definition and terminology of utopia that may not be an appropriate method for examining imaginaries of the ideal space, place, order or time in an intercultural context.

In spite of these sporadic forays into comparative utopian studies, assertions regarding the exclusively western heritage of utopia have continued to dominate research in the area, largely uncontested, right up to the turn of the millennium. During the lead-up to the year 2000, when all manner of predictions were appearing – from the Millennium Bug to the end of the world – there was a substantial surge in creative and critical work on utopia, including the highly successful and popular international exhibitions on utopia at the Bibliothèque Nationale de France and at the New York Public Library entitled: 'Utopie: la quête de la société idéale en Occident / Utopia: The Search for the Ideal Society in the Western World'. The very title of the exhibition equates 'utopia' with the 'West', a view upheld in Roland Schaer's contribution to the accompanying publications, in which he adopts a very narrow approach to defining the term: 'In the strictest sense of the word, utopia came into being at the beginning of the sixteenth century [...] the history of utopia necessarily begins with Thomas More.'[19] The following essay by Lyman Tower Sargent demonstrates a much more inclusive perspective: 'Not every culture appears to have utopias brought about through human effort that pre-date knowledge of Thomas More's *Utopia*, but such utopias do exist in China, India, and various Buddhist and Islamic cultures.'[20] The clear divide between these two standpoints offers evidence that the comparative debate in the field of utopian studies must now be taken more seriously. Although the western focus of the exhibitions and publications accounts for and may justify the explicit rejection of Islamic and Chinese utopian traditions, for example, it seems to have launched a concerted counter-movement to expose the under-represented sources of 'non-western' utopian traditions, the intercultural imaginaries of the ideal society.

The innovative study by Ralph Pordzik of the utopian novel in New English Literatures, *The Quest for Postcolonial Utopia*,[21] begins the wave of publications that challenge the western utopian model as the starting point for discussion. Pordzik draws our attention to the 'particular genre that has been neglected in the course of the revision process initiated in literary criticism: the utopian novel and its related literary forms' (1) and attempts to remedy this oversight by analysing a corpus of 'utopian fiction written in English-speaking countries all over the world' (1). Through examples as diverse as Tung Lee's *The Wind Obeys Lama Toru* (1976) from India and Alasdair Gray's *Lanark* (1987) from Scotland, he contends that postcolonial utopias defy generic and cultural boundaries in ways that break with western utopian traditions to promote 'epistemological otherness' (130). The resulting texts resemble globalized heterotopias, transcending national and western models in their fictions of the future. In its emphasis on the 'post-western' utopia – going beyond the western traditions – Pordzik's study suggests new ways of reading the contemporized and hybridized postcolonial utopia at the endpoint of the evolutionary process away from the West.

More focused on excavating the foundations of alternative utopian traditions, which is also the aim of the present study, are the contributions of Zhang Longxi to the current debate.[22] Zhang has added vital and convincing elements to the argument that a Chinese utopian tradition has both roots and branches, continuing to grow in different directions from its western counterparts. His work was also included in the 2005 volume of essays entitled *Thinking Utopia: Steps into Other Worlds*,[23] based on lectures and talks given at an interdisciplinary conference on the subject at Hagen in 2001. This volume includes several indications that the debate on comparative utopias is gaining momentum: Lyman Tower Sargent builds on his brief declaration in the 2000 exhibition publication: 'The single most important fact is that each country, and within the United Kingdom each constituent nation, has its own utopian tradition that differs from the others.'[24] He indicates that what is now being written in both fictional and critical modes makes it difficult to ignore the contemporary presence of 'non-western' utopias and therefore less reasonable to contest their historical development alongside western examples of the genre.

Kumar's contribution to *Thinking Utopia: Steps into Other Worlds* shows that his views have not changed substantially since his earlier denial of 'non-western' utopian traditions. He does, however, question his own competence in making such pronouncements, mitigating his previous statements with a tentative discussion of how various Chinese utopias were infused with western utopian thought and practice or Christian millenarianism.[25] Kumar defers to the other specialists in the Chinese utopian tradition, including Zhang Longxi and Dorothy Ko. The latter author's chapter focuses on the body, revealing that the corporal trope appears to have a completely different significance in western and Chinese utopian traditions.[26]

In addition to these contributions to the field, three comparative utopias workshops have been organized in Australia, at the University of Melbourne (2005) and at Monash University (2007 and 2010).

By way of an introduction to the ideological debate surrounding comparative utopian studies, this overview of progress in the field serves to position the following attempt to question the epistemological foundations of utopia as a western way of imagining the ideal society. Returning to the foundations of the western utopian traditions, it will reconsider the defining influence of its mythical and religious origins in the Golden Age and the Garden of Eden. It will then present a series of schema outlining comparable representations of an ideal time or place in 'non-western' cultures in order to trace the possible pathways from these founding myths, religions and worldviews through to interpretations of imaginary ideal societies. In this way, this study will endeavour to avoid the hegemonic tendencies of inflicting a western mode of thinking onto 'non-western' cultural traditions. It is not seeking to identify an established western paradigm by applying a utopian overlay to intercultural imaginaries of the ideal. Rather, it is proposing a forensic examination of the evidence that most cultures generate stories as a means of imagining a better way of being in the world, in order to track the different influences at work in 'non-western' utopian thought.

To reconsider the notion of the Golden Age as the epistemological foundation of utopia in the western world, it is clear that myth has an important role in the development of utopia in the West. Myths such as the Golden Age and its avatars of Eldorado, the Garden of Eden, Atlantis and Arcadia, the Platonic Ideal City, the Augustinian Theodicy, the Land of Cockaigne and the Millennium all provide the foundational material from which utopia has been elaborated. Indeed, it is this western mythological basis for utopia that has been cited as one of the principal reasons for utopia being the sole possession of the West – the Manuels and Kumar argue that cultures not grounded in these founding myths cannot therefore produce utopias. So the significance of mythology in the western utopian tradition is twofold – it is both a defining feature and a prerequisite condition.

Extrapolating from this, we can posit that projections of alternative societies may well arise from founding myths in 'non-western' cultures, tracing a similar pathway from the collective unconscious to individual conceptions of the desire for a different social order. But of course, an intervening influence in the western trajectory to utopia is religion, which may therefore have an effect on 'non-western' examples as well. The impact of religion on the shape of utopia is in fact the core subject of Adam B. Seligman's introductory essay 'The Comparative Study of Utopias' in the volume *Order and Transcendence*.[27] He focuses on the relation of utopian drives to the salvational doctrines of the great world-historical religions and analyses their place not only within theodicies, but as alternatives to established models of salvation. Inspired by Norman Cohn's insight that the challenge to traditional values that engendered millennial movements was in essence 'the supposed defection of the authority traditionally responsible for regulating relations between society and the powers governing the cosmos',[28] Seligman proposes to analyse the nature of relations between society and the cosmos. But he limits the scope of possible cultures for analysis to those where Axial religions have emerged to produce a fundamental restructuring of the terms of relations between mundane and transcendent orders. That is, according to Karl Jaspers and S. N. Eisenstadt's studies, the cultures of ancient Israel, Christianity, ancient Greece, China, Hinduism, Buddhism and Islam. While the potential of Seligman's approach is evident and well developed in the volume, it precludes consideration of all those cultures where the dominant worldview does not profess a marked separation between mundane and transcendent orders, such as many of the indigenous beliefs of Australia, New Zealand and the Pacific region, the animistic religions of the Americas and even Japanese Shinto.

As this study of comparative utopias aims to provide a methodology that is applicable to all cultural traditions, it would seem contradictory to follow the limiting parameters proposed by Seligman's approach, which effectively circumscribes the study of comparative utopias through reference to comparative religions. Although it is clear that religion must be taken into account in comparative utopian studies, it is equally clear that using comparative mythology as a starting point, rather than comparative religions, allows for inclusion of the greatest range of cultures within the scope of the study.

Seligman raises one other point that makes an important link between mythology and utopia – namely that existing research trends on cosmic meaning in millennial and utopian movements have concentrated on the structural conditions giving rise to images of a Golden Age, rather than analysing the cultural assumptions underlying the very idea of a Golden Age.[29] He advocates instead an inquiry into the symbolic factors accounting for the existence of a critical stance towards a particular social order, paying closer attention to the core symbols of a culture and to their relation to a broader transcendent system of meaning. The papers in his edited volume strive to achieve this aim, focusing on the so-called world-historical religions already mentioned. In contrast, the strategy that this study is proposing, using comparative mythology in conjunction with comparative religions, seeks to fulfil similar goals, but reaches beyond those religious limits to encompass any given culture. In this way, it may be possible to discover more culturally specific terms and methods for identifying and analysing 'non-western' conceptions of an alternative social dreaming.

Almost all cultures have foundation stories or myths expressing an avatar of the ancient Hellenistic Golden Age, including Zoroastrian views of Dilmun, the Ramarajya – reign of the Rama in Hindu history, the Garden of Eden in Judeo-Christian beliefs, *datong* (Great Unity) in Confucianism, *taiping* (Great Equality) in Taoism, the 'Dreaming' in the indigenous Australian worldview, the first Caliphate or Medinan regime in Islamic thought, and

Nirvana, the Pure Land of Eternal Happiness in ancient Indian Buddhism. These collective representations of a better way of being are indisputably sources for imagining an ideal society. However, whether or not there is concurrent or subsequent development of utopian writings and practices in these cultures can only be determined via a systematic study of the individual projections of ideal societies that are elaborated from the foundation stories and myths of the culture in question.

Let us start with the traditions of utopianism that are the closest and most intertwined with the western model, and the ones that have indeed been almost fully integrated into mainstream scholarship on utopia – the Jewish utopian traditions. While Christianity and Judaism share the same founding story of perfect happiness in the Garden of Eden, expressed in the Jewish Bible or Old Testament, the Christian vision of the ideal society on Earth is mediated by the salvational and unifying orders of the Eucharist. Inspiring utopian movements as diverse as the Anabaptists at Münster and the Mormons in Utah, Christian utopian thought differs from Jewish utopian traditions, principally in its interventional stance through activities and rituals within the institution of the Church to prepare for individual salvation, rather than relying solely on millennial predictions for access to an ideal Christian community.[30] The Christian focus on the individual is perhaps responsible for the first examples of the utopian literary genre during the Renaissance, and the continuing tradition of Christian literary projections representing individualized visions of an alternative existence. In contrast, Jewish traditions have produced many more social movements and community projects with millennial underpinnings than individually authored literary projections of the ideal place.

Jewish utopian traditions provide a revealing example of how a form of utopianism that is closely related to the western utopia diverges from the dominant model. Although Judaism shares with Christianity the Golden Age origins in the Genesis stories of the Garden of Eden, it also privileges the beginnings of institutionalized Jewish faith and culture, centred firstly around the Tabernacle of Moses, and then the First Temple built by King Solomon on the Temple Mount in Jerusalem in the tenth century BCE. The destruction of the First Temple by the Babylonians during the sixth century BCE was followed by a period of Jewish exile in Babylon and the beginnings of the Jewish Diaspora. However, under the reign of the more tolerant Persian King Koresh, the 'children of exile' started to return to Jerusalem around 540 BCE and began the construction of the Second Temple, completed in 515 BCE, which heralded a flourishing new era for Jerusalem and Judaism. When the Second Temple was destroyed by the Romans around 70 CE, the systematic persecution and enslavement of the Jews marked the end of what may be considered the Golden Age of Jewish practice and cultural development in Jerusalem, and provoked eschatological visions of a Third Temple, coinciding with the coming of the Messiah. The messianic predictions of the reconstruction of the centre of Judaism in Jerusalem are therefore closely related to the particular historical traditions of an ideal existence in Jewish thought.

A subsequent period of religious tolerance under Muslim rule in Spain from the eighth to the eleventh centuries is often referred to as the 'Golden Age' of Jewish culture in Spain. It was shortly after this time of relative harmony that Judah HaLevi, having experienced the first Crusade, composed the famous philosophical novel *The Kuzari* (c. 1140), also known as the *Book of Argument and Proof in Defense of the Despised Faith*. This novel, written in the form of a dialogue between the King of the Khazars and representatives of various belief systems – Christian, Muslim and Jewish – is based on the real conversion of the Khazars to Judaism at the end of the eighth century. However, HaLevi reinterprets the events through the prism of idealism, presenting a utopian vision of the Kingdom of Khazaria, located between the Black Sea and the Caspian Sea and ruled by an enlightened leader. This work also served as an inspirational force for Zionism and Jewish nationalism, as well as exercising an influence on subsequent theological and Kabbalistic writings of the Middle Ages.

Zionism represents a multi-faceted utopian variation on the messianic predictions of the Third Temple and the potential for creating an ideal kingdom for the Jewish people on Earth. Zionism reinforces the links between the Jewish people and Jerusalem that have existed since the founding of the First Temple, but negates the necessity for divine intervention, thus creating a more political programme for action born of human agency. While some rabbinical forms of Zionism emerged early in the nineteenth century, it was towards the end of the century that Austro-Hungarian journalist Theodor Herzl founded the political Zionist movement, outlining his programme in *The Jewish State* (1896) and writing a utopian novel *Altneuland* (1902) describing the Zionist utopia that he dreamed of creating in Eretz Israel (Palestine).[31] It is a multicultural vision of socio-religious tolerance, set in a modern, industrialised land of future abundance and harmony. From the First Zionist Congress in Basel (1897) to the British Mandate (1922), various strands of Zionism identified themselves – from political to cultural, practical to religious – each promoting a different cause for the Zionist State. From practical Zionism came the first *kibbutz*, Kibbutz Degania in 1909 at Sejera, launching a movement in collective farming that reflected the socialist ideals of the early settlers in Palestine. By the time the Jewish state of Israel was established on 15 May 1948, it was clear that the Zionist dream of a pluralistic, multicultural utopia that Herzl had projected was far from the reality of Jewish–Arab relations and the tensions and violence in the region may make us wonder whether utopianism is a justifiable practice. Works like Michael Higger's *The Jewish Utopia* (1932), which states that 'A Jewish utopia begins where Wells leaves off',[32] only serve to fuel the controversy surrounding Zionism in its more extreme forms, whereas the collective farming movement of the *kibbutz* has inspired socialist utopian movements all over the world, with surprisingly successful effects in Japan.

As Jewish utopian traditions have suffered much due to radical Zionism, and the ongoing disputes and violence that continue to shatter any hopes for peace in the Gaza Strip, Islamic utopianism has been denigrated and indeed reviled through association with the rise of political Islam and radical fundamentalism. The cultural and ideological relationship that can be tracked from the founding utopian Jewish ideals of redemption to the development of later utopian movements may also be identified in the original Islamic visions of the ideal existence to demonstrate the influence of these underlying cultural premises on contemporary issues in Muslim projections of utopia.

In his introduction to *The Pursuit of the Millennium*, Norman Cohn emphasizes the pervasive influence of messianic and millennial beliefs throughout the Middle Ages. Although his references are almost exclusively based in Christian theology and practices, it is clear that Islam, having originated and spread during this period, bears the distinctive traces of millennial thought, which impacts in turn on the Islamic utopian vision. According to Muslim historians the birth of Islam dates from the Prophet Muhammad's first revelation in the year 610 to the collection of all subsequent revelations in a single written text of the Qur'an by the first Caliph in 632–4.[33] The period that is considered to be the Golden Age of Islam in most Muslim traditions begins with the first gathering of the Prophet and his followers in Mecca to flee persecution and establish the first Caliphate in Medina. This pilgrimage or *hijra* in 633 marks the beginning of the Muslim calendar, according to which Islamic events are observed. The Golden Age or Medinan regime that followed is remembered as the period of 'pure Islam', when Muslims were blessed with military, economic and cultural dominance due to their faithful observance of the Qur'an and the community or *ummah* of believers.[34] As the coherence and influence of the Muslim community was progressively eroded, the Medinan regime became more intimately associated with the ideal of return to a primordial state of harmony and grace through conservative religious practice of the Qur'an.

The millennial vision is not explicit in the Qur'an, but constant references to the afterlife and resurrection to paradise attest to the importance of belief in a final end, giving sense and purpose to the links between the earthly existence and the next life in heaven. The 'return to God', involving both the process of return in the physical world and the destination in itself – the life to come – is also present in the Qur'an (7:29). This concept gives rise to two principal pathways in the physical world that define the purpose of life – the return to God through obedience to the revealed Law, leading to divine transcendence, and the return to God through realization of the divine element immanent in all creation, indicating a more active participation in the eschatological project.[35] While the Apocalyptic message and descriptions of a garden Paradise (9:72) also feature in the Qur'an, this text contains no truly millennial descriptions or exhortations.[36] These millennial tendencies and the messianic figure of the Mahdi appear only in the hadith, which contains 'the attested reports of the sayings, actions, and tacit approvals and accounts of the Prophet Muhammad',[37] collated early in the eighth century. The Mahdi concept has differing influence according to the Muslim tradition. Sunni Muslims have not particularly embraced the millenarian or messianic movements, but there have been some examples of millenarianism in Mahdist movements, Sufi-influenced, or more politically charged movements in times of crisis, from the early Abbasid revolution in the eighth century, and Ibn Tumart of the Berber Almohads, whose strict doctrine dominated Muslim Spain during the twelfth century, to the Sudanese Mahdist movement of Muhammad Ahmad ibn 'Abd Allah in the late eighteenth century.[38] In Shi'ism, however, the messianic doctrine is much stronger and serves as a focus for devotional longing for the Twelfth Imam, the spiritual and political successor to the Prophet, whose presence legitimizes a political order.[39] Both Sunni and Shi'ite readings of the hadith have also produced visions of a utopian period in which the world will return to an ideal state of justice, harmony and truth, when the Mahdi ruler defeats the Dajjal, representative of the forces of evil. Essentially, two nascent utopian tendencies come through the founding texts of Islam: the more individualistic desire for transcendence through religious observation, and the more communal millennial projection of an ideal state ruled by a charismatic figure. Neither of these tendencies gives much importance to free will, social organization or democracy as part of the utopian project.

Such visions are evidence of the culturally specific conceptions in Islamic utopian traditions that emerge through the religious texts. In contrast, Islamic philosophical thought offers a series of utopian possibilities that are grounded in western philosophical models, adhering to the conventions established by Plato and Aristotle. The celebrated treatises of Abu Nasr al-Farabi (c. 870–950), also known as 'the Second Teacher', the 'First' being Aristotle, include two major contributions to the utopian corpus: *Ara Ahl al-Madina al-Fadila* (The Virtuous City) and *Kitab tashil as-Saadah* (The Attainment of Happiness), which constitutes the first part of *The Philosophy of Plato and Aristotle*.[40] The first Islamic philosopher to separate philosophy and theology, al-Farabi proposes that reason should take precedence over religion and revelation, not only because philosophy predates religion, but also due to its association with intellectual perception rather than imagination. His design for the virtuous city is therefore aligned with the premises of Plato's *Republic*, recommending the enlightened philosopher as the ideal 'king' or leader. While drawing on the western philosophical model, al-Farabi nevertheless integrates religious preoccupations as his ideal Muslim State provides opportunity for improved physical and political conditions as well as salvation through religious observation. His doctrine of happiness and its role in the ideal city is still anchored in Islamic beliefs, which are complemented by the study of philosophy, sciences and religion. Although his Neoplatonism potentially contradicts the utopian visions arising from transcendental and millennial tendencies in Islamic religious texts, al-Farabi's philosophical utopias represent important examples of the genre that attest to its capacity for cultural hybridity.

Several literary representations of utopia also appeared during the Middle Ages, depicting the desire for a better way of being, built on the Islamic foundations of the ideal of paradise attainable through the realization of God's immanence in all creation. One of these is the *Rubaiyat* of Omar Khayyam, a Persian astronomer and mathematician, who wrote this collection of around 1,000 poems in the early twelfth century. The first Arabic philosophical novel, *The History of Hayy Ibn Yaqzan (Philosophus Autodidactus)* by Arab philosopher Abu Bakr Ibn Tufail, came from twelfth-century Islamic Spain. This novel inspired a critical response from the Syrian polymath, Ibn al-Nafis, in *The Treatise of Kamil on the Prophet's Biography (Theologus Autodidactus)* in the thirteenth century, which evolved into the first example of a science-fiction novel.[41] All of these texts had a significant impact in both the Islamic world and in the West, but the most ambiguous and widely cited and translated is the *Rubaiyat*. The mystical vision of Omar Khayyam has led to associations with Sufism, but it is clear that the various translations have transmogrified the meaning of the original composition by privileging certain poems, orders and language. Quoting from Edward Fitzgerald's fifth edition of 1889, which are the best-known if not the most faithful translations, some verses seem to profess the realization of the ideal in the present:

> XII
> A Book of Verses underneath the Bough,
> A Jug of Wine, a Loaf of Bread – and Thou

Beside me singing in the Wilderness –
Oh, Wilderness were Paradise enow!
XIII
Some for the Glories of This World; and some
Sigh for the Prophet's Paradise to come;
Ah, take the Cash, and let the Credit go,
Nor heed the rumble of a distant Drum!

Others indicate a utopian vision of a better future, shaped by human agency:

XCIX
Ah, Love, could you and I with Him conspire
To grasp this sorry Scheme of Things entire,
Would we not shatter it to bits – and then
Remould it nearer to the Heart's Desire!

The *Rubaiyat* does not present a description of the physical incarnation of the ideal place, but it does explore the relationship between the cultural aspects of social dreaming and nature, as well as the role of human agency, or free will, in the conception of the utopian vision. These are important philosophical contributions to the Islamic utopian tradition that were later taken up more by western utopian traditions than in Islamic ones.

The History of Hayy Ibn Yaqzan was written during the fairly repressive and intolerant society of twelfth-century Islamic Spain. The influence of the messianic figure, Berber Mahdi Ibn Tumart, founder of the Almohads, was widespread, and his doctrine had particular importance in determining the strict doctrine of belief and conduct that made persecuted heretics of those who did not embrace its puritan principles. However, even under this fundamentalist regime, the Caliphs and rulers allowed certain privileged philosophers to question the sacred texts in private, creating a divide between private philosophical speculation and public practical politics. Ibn Tufail was one of the chosen ones, and his text draws on philosophical reasoning and mystical Sufi traditions to demonstrate the virtues of divesting oneself of material possessions and needs, in order to achieve enlightenment. It is the story of a child reared by a gazelle in isolation on a deserted island, prefiguring Daniel Defoe's *Robinson Crusoe* (1719), and pursuing the ideal of scientific discovery, self-education and the contemplative life of philosopher as a kind of utopian vision of an autarchic society. Ibn Tufail's text represents an implicit criticism of the contemporary regime demanding absolute obedience and being intolerant of individualistic pursuits such as philosophical or mystical interpretations of human or divine existence.

The utopian vision of Ibn al-Nafis discussed in *The Treatise of Kamil on the Prophet's Biography (Theologus Autodidactus)* (1268–77) proposes a more developed version of Ibn Tufail's text in that the child reared in seclusion is integrated into society when castaways shipwrecked on his island home take him to the 'civilized' world. Drawing on his expertise as a scientist – he is best known as the first physician to describe pulmonary circulation – and as a Sunni theologian – Ibn al-Nafis combined scientific reasoning and Islamic philosophy to provide a fictional portrait of the autodidact's revelatory experiences in contact with external influences and interactions. The narrative takes on a predictive tone towards the end, with reference to the end of the world, resurrection and the afterlife, which accounts for its identification with the science-fiction genre. In attributing value to the individual's interactions within a community, this text presents the search for reason and revelation as equally important components of the utopian future.

Despite their important contribution to Islamic philosophy and thought, these literary utopias of the Middle Ages have exercised less influence on contemporary representations of Islamic utopianism than the founding examples of the Medinan regime and Mahdism. The literary depictions of an ideal society lack the vital stimulus that is deemed necessary to constitute a programme of political and social action. Although the Medinan regime was also apolitical and accomplished, rather than planned and actively achieved in its historical incarnation, when its purity and integrality became the goal of fundamentalist movements, it took on utopian dimensions as a valorized model to be re-enacted through political engagement and social programmes. The Islamic radicalism that has emerged from this recent politicized incarnation of the Medinan regime relies on the specification of fundamentalism and the precise and imminent interpretation of the original pristine model.[42] And it is this political form of fundamentalist Islam that underpins Islamic utopian movements in the contemporary period, including the very different examples of the Islamic Republic of Iran and the Taliban.

While they cannot be readily aligned in terms of their motives, processes or outcomes, both of these entities have been described as Islamic utopias. The utopianism that inspired the Iranian Revolution of 1979 had its roots in Navvab Safavi's ideal Islamic social system detailed in his *Barnameh-ye Enqelabi-ye Fada'ian-Eslam* (1950). This 'eclectic combination of a simplistic notion of Islamic theology and ethics and a pedestrian vision of the existing society in the 1940s in Iran'[43] was the basis for the revival of religious fundamentalism in Iran. The vision of a theocracy ruled by the *velayat-e-faqih*, the guardianship of the clerical authority, propounded by the leader of the Revolution, Ayatollah Khomeini, together with the Marxist ideals of the ideological father of the Revolution, the 'Islamic Utopian' Ali-Shari'ati,[44] led to the creation of the Islamic Republic of Iran in 1979. The subsequent foundation of the first Islamist State demonstrates how the politicization of Islam in Iran could result in the reformist fundamentalism (or neo-fundamentalism) necessary to provoke active political and social programmes for change.

In contrast, the Taliban derives from the *salafi* strand of Islamic utopianism, promoting the exact reconstruction of a past historical moment – the Golden Age of Islam – in the present. This gesture is activated through reinstating the reign of unadulterated purity, characterized by military strength, cultural superiority and unity among the *ummah* of believers.[45] Temporality is not relevant and must be denied to allow the reversibility of time and the re-enactment of the ideal society.[46] Evidently, the politicization of Islam encouraged by the *salafi* utopian ideal is more radical and reactionary than political Islam in Iran. Contesting the forces of colonization and globalization, *salafi* thought engenders such radicalism as Wahhabite fundamentalism in Saudi Arabia and *jahilryya*, specifying that non-Islam is to be converted into Islamic order, as an actual presence.[47] Sayyid Qutb and the Muslim Brotherhood of Egypt also resorted to the safety of an imagined past in their *salafi* utopia of subjective unity. The influence of these *salafi* traditions on the Taliban is well documented, and the strict interpretation of Shari'a law in Afghanistan under Taliban rule from 1996 to 2001 attests to their desire to recreate the moment of past purity in the present through radical and violent action. The Taliban's sweeping reforms, driving out the Mujahideen warlords and bandits, and establishing a more stable though repressive regime, seemed to indicate initially a positive improvement for the Afghan population. However, the imposition of the Taliban's utopian vision for a return to the Golden Age of Islam, with its violent ambitions of *jihad*, holy war, as well as *al-Jannah*, the paradise of the after-life, proved too extreme.

As the historical and contemporary examples outlined demonstrate, Islamic utopias tend to manifest either a messianic tradition related to Mahdism, or a radicalism that attempts to re-enact the Medinan regime through specifying fundamentalist political and social action. The chiliastic and eschatological forces at play may resemble those observed in other religious traditions. However, Islamic utopianism remains inextricably linked to the cultural valorization of the unadulterated purity of the Golden Age of Islam, rather than embracing the possibility of reason and revelation through interaction, as expressed in some of the Islamic literary utopias of the Middle Ages. The inherently subjective nature of an ideal society based on the *uncodified* law of Shari'a leaves free will, social organization, democracy and political progress out of the social equation.

The representations of a Golden Age of Hinduism have been equally influential on Hindu utopian visions and literature. Known as the *Krita Yuga*, or *Krta Yuga*, and closely related to the *Satya Yuga*, the first era of purity and perfection lasts for 4,000 divine years or 1,728,000 human years, according to the *Mahabharata* and various other Hindu sacred texts. The subsequent degradation of humanity to its current state of disorder in the *Kali Yuga* can be compared to the eschatological cycles in other belief systems, promising a renewal of the Golden Age after a period of total destruction. In literary terms, the Golden Age was expressed in most detail in the *Ramayana*, the Sanskrit epic dating from around 400 BCE, and attributed to the Hindu sage, Valmiki. This text traces the life and deeds of Lord Rama, prince of the city of Ayodhya, capital of the Kosalas, which is described as a kind of Golden Age, with the qualities of an ideal realm of righteousness and equality. Throughout the trials and suffering that Rama must endure, he epitomizes the example of *dharma*, fulfilling his duties and retaining his piety and humanism to become the ideal, enlightened and just leader of the democratic kingdom of *Ramarajya*.

The *Ramayana* inspired many poetic visions of utopian harmony throughout history, ranging from the Tamil poet Kambar's *Kambaramayanam*, composed during the twelfth century, to the Hindi poet Tulsidas's sixteenth-century *Ramcharitmanas*, popular in northern India. The permanence of this ideal society in Indian cultural representations of utopian felicity can be seen through its continued presence in television serials, films and songs, and a futuristic version of the epic, *Ramayan 3392 A.D.* by Deepak Chopra and Shekhar Kapur, was published as a comic-book series beginning in 2006 and is currently being made into a film.

The most culturally specific aspects of this Hindu utopian vision are the underpinning characteristics of *dharma*, the virtue, righteousness and duty to oneself and society according to principles of the cosmic order, in combination with equal rights and socio-religious freedom in a true democracy. These were the qualities that Mohandas K. Gandhi (1869–1948) identified in the *Ramayana* as the sources for creating a better society in an independent India. Gandhi's utopian writings and actions were explicitly grounded in the same principles as those described in the kingdom of *Ramarajya*, as stated in his speech at a public meeting in Bhopal on 10 September 1929, published in *Young India*:

> By Ramarajya I do not mean Hindu Raj. I mean by Ramarajya Divine Raj, the Kingdom of God. For me Rama and Rahim are one and the same deity. I acknowledge no other God but the one God of truth and righteousness.
>
> Whether Rama of my imagination ever lived or not on this earth, the ancient ideal of Ramarajya is undoubtedly one of true democracy in which the meanest citizen could be sure of swift justice without an elaborate and costly procedure. Even the dog is described by the poet to have received justice under Ramarajya.[48]

He later described the ideal society of independent India in utopian terms that emphasize the interconnectedness of the individuals within the society, but the necessity for individual self-discipline and salvation as well as collective salvation:

> Independence must begin at the bottom. Thus, every village will be a republic or a panchayat having full powers. It follows, therefore, that every village has to be self-sustained and capable of managing its affairs, even to the extent of defending itself against the whole world. It will be trained and prepared to perish in the attempt to defend itself against any onslaught from without. Thus ultimately, it is the individual who is the unit. This does not exclude dependence on the willing help from neighbours or from the world. It will be a free and voluntary play of mutual forces. Such a society is necessarily highly cultured in which every man and every woman knows what he or she wants and, what is more, knows that no one should want anything that the others cannot have with equal labour.
>
> In this structure composed of innumerable villages, there will be ever widening, never ascending, circles. Life will not be a pyramid with the apex sustained by the bottom. But will be an oceanic circle whose centre will be the individual always ready to perish for the village, the latter ready to perish for the circle of villages, till at last the whole becomes one life composed of individuals, ever humble, sharing the majesty of the oceanic circle of which they are integral units.
>
> Therefore, the outermost circumference will not wield power to crush the inner circle, but will give strength to all within and will derive its own strength from it. I may be taunted with the retort that this is all Utopian and, therefore, not worth a single thought. If Euclid's point, though incapable of being drawn by any human agency, has an imperishable value, my picture has its own for mankind to live. Let India live for this true picture, though never realizable in its completeness. We must have a proper picture of what we want, before we can have something approaching it. If there ever is to be a republic of every village in India, then I claim verity for my picture in which the last is equal to the first, or, in other words, no one is to be the first and none the last.[49]

The complex interactions between individuals and cultural transformation in Gandhi's utopian vision have been studied in detail,[50] and represent another determining aspect of the Hindu utopia, distinguishable in certain previous utopian movements, such as the twelfth-century Kanphata Panth.[51]

In essence, the Golden Age described in the *Ramayana* is the culturally specific model for the Hindu utopia, the utopia that Gandhi hoped to see realized on earth in the present through the action of individuals towards Indian independence:

> Friends have repeatedly challenged me to define independence. At the risk of repetition, I must say that independence of my dream means Ramarajya i.e.,

the Kingdom of God on earth. I do not know what it will be like in Heaven. I have no desire to know the distant scene. If the present is attractive enough, the future cannot be very unlike.[52]

The Golden Age to which Chinese utopian thought often refers is based upon the concepts of *datong* in Confucianism and *taiping* in Taoism. As in various other cultural representations of happier past times, both of these philosophical traditions privilege the primordial existence of unity and equality. The Great Unity of *datong* suggests a social vision that promotes public good rather than individual interest, harmonious interpersonal relationships through mutual support, and competent, elected leaders.[53] The Great Equality of *taiping* emphasizes the natural equilibrium of heaven and earth, but maintains the hierarchical social structures in place provided that there is fair treatment of subjects by the rulers.[54]

While the ideas of *datong* and *taiping* constitute the basic foundations for Chinese utopian visions, Zhang Longxi's research points to the secular nature of Confucian thought as the integral impetus for elaborating the ideal of a better future. Rather than positing a religious ideal of an era of harmony between divine and mundane beings, the Confucian *Analects* express respect and nostalgic longing for the ancient dynasty of Zhou under the rule of King Wen, considered as 'the perfect model for moral conduct and kingly rule'.[55] It is this earthly incarnation of a better society that inspires hope for improvement in the future, to be achieved not through re-enacting the spiritual conditions of that earlier time nor depending on the presence of a messianic leader, but by individual efforts of self-discipline and following of the ancient rites.[56] The individual's action is therefore the determining factor that revives the social and ethical aspects of the previous model and thereby contributes to creating a better existence in the future. Building on the Confucian ideal of the perfectibility of human nature, Mencius extrapolated on its inherent goodness to propose the possibility of a 'humane government'.[57]

The philosophies of Confucius and Mencius open the way for a secular Chinese utopianism that is complemented by the concepts of *datong* and *taiping*, and that finds its earliest literary expression in the poem 'Big Rat' (*Shuo shu*). This folk song from the *Book of Poetry* refers to a 'land of happiness' in which the narrator longs to rest, which according to Zhang articulates the 'desire for a better way of being' that Ruth Levitas designates as the essential element of utopia.[58] The most famous Chinese literary utopia is Tao Yuanming's (365–427) *Peach Blossom Spring*, the story of a fisherman who discovers a hidden community of peace, harmony and equality through a cave under a mountain. Impossible to locate once he has left it, the utopian community's mysterious qualities add to its otherworldliness, yet its inhabitants and characteristics are described in very practical terms. It is their individual labour and cooperative organization that render their society a more desirable one than the oppressive feudal regimes with high taxes and tyrannical rulers that dominated in contemporary China.

Several later versions of this utopian tale transform its inhabitants into immortals living in a fairyland, which may have been the inspiration for more fanciful utopias, such as Wang Yucheng's (954–1001) letter written by a seafarer of a barbarian tribe,[59] and Li Ruzhen's *Romance of Flowers in the Mirror*, designated as China's equivalent of *Gulliver's Travels*. However, Tao Yuanming's original vision of a simple, agrarian society that draws on the description of *datong* is the most culturally specific tradition of Chinese utopian thought that can be traced through to contemporary times. Kang Youwei's late nineteenth-century interpretation of Confucian ideas of *datong* in his *Book of Great Unity* was influenced by western utopian thought and movements, including Charles Fourier, Edward Bellamy and Darwinian theories, but nevertheless drew on Chinese history and classical texts to describe a world of racial and sexual equality, with public management of all economic and social services.[60] Although Mao Zedong considered Kang Youwei a pioneer in his efforts to find the path to Great Unity, he was obviously critical of western influences that detracted from the ideal of the 'people's republic'. Mao maintained the Chinese utopian vision of Great Unity in his 'dictatorship of the people',[61] but brought socialist and communist ideologies to the fore to engender the inherent problems of translating utopia into reality.

The Confucian utopian vision has also produced a series of feminist utopias, from Luo Maodeng's sixteenth/seventeenth-century work *Sanbao's Expedition to the Western Ocean*, and the late eighteenth-century narratives by Chen Duansheng, *The Destiny of the Next Life* (*Zai shengyuan*), and Xia Jingqu, *Humble Words of an Old Rustic* (*Yesou Puyan*), to Bai Hua's recent novel of an idyllic matriarchal community in *The Remote Country of Women*.[62] Revealing an evolution in the role of women in Chinese utopian texts, these examples also present culturally specific visions of a better future for women with particular models that reference Chinese history and philosophy, including the movement from individual to collective female rule.

The influence of Chinese Confucianism in Japanese thought became clearly visible during the nationalistic regimes of the Tokugawa period, but had been a strong presence since the introduction of Neo-Confucianism to Japan during the twelfth century, having entered Japan via Korea during the third century and attracted interest from intellectuals when the Chinese writing system appeared around the beginning of the fifth century. However, there were also the competing belief systems and philosophies of

Buddhism and Taoism, as well as the indigenous Japanese belief system of Shinto.

Although deemed to be the foundational religion of Japan, the Shinto view of the cosmos is a complex worldview that contains influences from various parts of Asia and even Oceania. According to this belief system, the physical universe is divided into five parts, each governed by the appropriate *kami* or gods. First, there is the High Plain of Heaven (*Takamanohara*) where many of the most important *kami* reside. Earth is the second part, and beneath the Earth lies the kingdom of the dead and of evil spirits (*Yomi no Kuni*). The oceans make up the fourth part, called *Watatsûmi no Kuni*, the domain of all kinds of creatures, from ordinary fish to dragon kings. Somewhere across the sea lies the fifth part: *Tokoyo no Kuni*, which is 'a utopian land whose denizens neither age nor die'.[63]

The original reading of the mythical place of *Tokoyo no Kuni* resembles a Golden Age of coexistence and harmony, when the gods provided for the needs of humankind. As the home of the gods, a place of holy spirits and divine powers, *Tokoyo no Kuni* represented the dynamic of the life cycle, combining revival and eternity. However, the geographical location of *Tokoyo no Kuni* had not been suggested at this stage. It existed nowhere in real terms therefore it could exist anywhere in imaginary terms. In his analysis of *Tokoyo no Kuni* as a utopian construct, Yasunaga Toshinobu relies on this inherent mutability of *Tokoyo no Kuni* in order to explain the variations in its conceptual and formal expressions.

From its initial incarnation in the *Fudoki* as the elusive resting place of the gods, *Tokoyo no Kuni* gradually became more closely associated with the first Emperor of divine lineage, Iwarebiko, and as a resting place for immortal souls of the dead. In both the *Kojiki* and the *Nihon Shoki*, it is suggested that the Eternal Land of *Tokoyo no Kuni* is at Kumano, which was also the entrance to the underworld of *Yomi no Kuni*. This coincides with the original description of *Tokoyo no Kuni* as linked to the dynamic of the whole life cycle – from harvest, regeneration and renewal to death. However, when the closer relationship between the Emperor and *Tokoyo no Kuni* was established, the notion of death that was associated with *Yomi no Kuni* had to be separated from the living Emperor and *Tokoyo no Kuni*. Thus *Yomi no Kuni*, which was then identified as being in the west at Izumo, became the opposing pole that propelled *Tokoyo no Kuni* to the opposite site of Japan, to the east, to the so-called island of Ise.

Around the seventh or eighth century therefore, the concept of *Tokoyo no Kuni* changed dramatically. Whereas previously *Tokoyo no Kuni* existed only as an abstract and ideological figure that transcended the limits of human society, its association with the Emperor changed it into a tangible island,

Ise. The association with the real, living being of the Emperor imparted a more concrete, earthly form to the projection of *Tokoyo no Kuni*, thereby diminishing its mythical and abstract characteristics. In return, the Emperor became the personification of bliss, consistency and eternity that were previously represented by *Tokoyo no Kuni*, in a reciprocal interchange of qualities and characteristics. Although *Tokoyo no Kuni* remained a sacred place, it became more realistic and accessible – something to strive for in the present. At this point, it loses its original representation of the dynamic life cycle yet remains pertinent as the symbol of eternity. In poems from the *Kojiki* and *Manyoshu*, *Tokoyo no Kuni* is evoked merely as a figurative expression, having lost some of its dynamism as well as its role as the object of human desire and transcendence.

The particular feature of the Japanese utopian vision that emerges from Shinto beliefs is therefore its mutability and ambiguity. The representation of a blissful Golden Age can be either life or death, divine or human, geographically identifiable or personified by the Emperor. With the introduction of Buddhist and Confucian philosophies and beliefs, the Japanese conception of a better place was modified, and a messianic tradition evolved out of the society of discontent and inequality of the Middle Ages. The saviour was named *Miroku*, after the Maitreya bodhisattva, and it was said that the world of *Miroku* would be realized when all evils disappeared from the Earth. In other words, it was up to the people to bring about the descent of *Miroku* to Earth, by striving for equality, sharing the same ideals and abolishing hierarchies and social classes. Human effort in a communal society was the key to creating a better existence. However, this schema was further transformed by the notion that *Miroku* would descend whether or not the people were able to achieve harmony within their everyday lives. This more appealing vision of deliverance from the miserable earthly existence is described in the Heian period texts *The Tale of Genji (Genji Monogatari)* by Murasaki Shikibu and the anthology of folk tales *The Tales of Long Ago (Konjaku Monogatari)*, which depict the world of *Miroku* as the joyful place where the human emotions are liberated.

Various messianic uprisings and breakaway factions of unruly monks represent the most active participation in a utopian practice during the Middle Ages, until the oppressive reign of the Tokugawa period made such overt subversion impossible. Implicit rebellion through indulging in the delights of the floating world, *ukiyo*, became the most evident representation of the imaginary of the ideal in Edo Japan. The mutable and ambiguous nature of *Tokoyo no Kuni* is reinstated in the Japanese utopian vision of *ukiyo*, with its fleeting pleasures and ephemeral beauty to be enjoyed in the moment. *Ukiyo* began as a Buddhist term, used in classical poetry during the Heian period to translate the fundamental sadness associated with the vain, impure world of earthly suffering. The transitory, impermanent and worthless nature of human existence as a dream, a 'life as vain dust', remains relevant in the later mutations of the term, but it is the pursuit of happiness through earthly pleasures that is emphasized in the Tokugawa period, as demonstrated in the much-cited passage by Asai Ryoi from *Tales of the Floating World (Ukiyo Monogatari)* (1661):

> Living only for the moment, turning our full attention to the pleasures of the moon, the snow, the cherry blossoms and the maple leaves; singing songs and drinking wine, diverting ourselves in just floating, floating; caring not a whit for the pauperism staring us in the face, refusing to be disheartened, like a gourd floating along with the river current: this is what we call *ukiyo* – the floating world …[64]

Like *Tokoyo no Kuni*, *ukiyo* is both an elusive realm that exists nowhere in geographical terms, and yet is apparently identified within the walled areas filled with teahouses and geisha quarters of Tokyo's *Yoshiwara*, or red-light district. The ambiguities inherent in the Golden Age of Japanese utopian thought seem therefore to be a permanent feature of this utopian tradition, following through into *ukiyo* and pervading even contemporary utopian literature from Japan, such as Haruki Murakami's *Hard Boiled Wonderland and the End of the World* (1985). The cultural specificity of the Japanese utopian tradition appears to arise from the combination of Shinto and Buddhist belief systems and stories, rather than from the Confucian and Neo-Confucian organizational structures that were adopted by the Tokugawa regime in particular.

A final example of a utopian tradition that arises from a very different worldview is the indigenous Australian belief in the 'Dreaming'. As a representation of the kind of diversity in belief systems that exists in indigenous cultures all over the world, the oral tradition of the indigenous Australian utopian vision can be seen as one of the many 'non-western' utopian traditions that does not coincide with western models for creating a better society on Earth. Even the representation of the Golden Age in indigenous Australian cosmology does not correspond to the past or cyclical temporalities that the Golden Age tends to express in the other worldviews and traditions already outlined. In fact, the translation of indigenous Australian experience of creation stories as the 'Dreamtime' by early ethnographers Baldwin Spencer and F. J. Gillen has been corrected to eradicate the reference to time.[65] Their English translation of the Aranda term *altjiranga ngambakala* as 'Dreamtime' imposes a western creationism ideology with its linear version of time on the circular logic of indigenous Australian experiences of the Dreaming as past, present and future combined. Although it is not really an adequate rendering of this experience that has many different names in the various indigenous Australian languages, the 'Dreaming' has become a more or less accepted term of reference, signifying the eternal nature of all things, from dreams, to ceremony, to law and everyday living.

Despite the inherent atemporality of the 'Dreaming', there was, however, a period during which the ancestral beings rose up from the beneath the earth to give form to the world, creating the land and leaving tangible traces, such as rocks, rivers, islands and lakes, as well as founding intangible orally transmitted rituals, laws and customs. These features are recorded for eternity in a series of stories and songs that represent the indigenous Australian cosmology. Although these events occurred within a certain historical context, they are timeless and have been referred to as 'everywhen'.[66] And while the ancestors returned to the earth after finishing their work, they remain intrinsically linked to the land of their creation and are alive in the evidence of their passage. In order to maintain the living cosmos of the ancestors and continue the existence of its living inhabitants, the stories and songs must be regularly reproduced in balance and awareness of all the other parts of the system, according to what Deborah Bird Rose calls a 'reflexive moral relationship of care'.[67]

The constant reproduction of the experience of the Dreaming in order to maintain the living system of the cosmos may suggest that the harmony and abundance of the creative origins of country will also be repeated in the past, present and future. However, stories, songs and rituals indicate that there has been a diminishing in both the size of inhabitants and creatures in the indigenous Australian context, and their abundance, demonstrating a slow degradation of living conditions compared to the original abundance and bounty of the land. This may be related to a kind of Golden Age paradigm, but it in no way equates to the moral opposition between an idyllic past and an evil present that can be identified in many other cultural traditions. The notion of a more heroic era in the past is incompatible with the idea of continuity in indigenous Australian cosmology. The ancestors continue to live beyond all the conditions to which their descendants are subject, since such conditions are the result of the activities of the ancestral beings themselves.[68]

Given that the 'Dreaming' implies the uninterrupted flow of action by individuals in collaboration with communities across all eternity, it may be possible to interpret the indigenous Australian worldview as essentially utopian through its constant expression of social dreaming. Alternatively, it may seem that their entire existence is so tightly interconnected that it could not accommodate a different kind of social dreaming and therefore cannot incorporate any change in imagining a better way of being. The unfortunate response to this apparent dilemma is of course that the European invasion of Australia destabilized the harmonious system in place by introducing competing demands on indigenous peoples, places and politics, leading to a disruption of their system, whether or not it is defined as utopian. Although some indigenous Australian peoples have continued to reproduce the cultural practices necessary to maintain their traditional links to the land, others have been impeded from contributing to their heritage and some of the stories, songs and rituals have been lost, along with many indigenous lives, lands and rights.

According to the essential points of the system of the 'Dreaming' described by Deborah Bird Rose, 'the system has the potential to get out of balance and to be brought back into balance', but 'there is no hierarchy, no central agency' to act as the arbiter of the system.[69] The system is working at its best when homeostatic, when nothing happens to signify marked change. However, when significant new change has occurred, as evidenced by the arrival of Europeans and their detrimental impact on the system, it would seem that there must be new strategies to bring the system 'back into balance'. It may be in this realm that different utopian visions and actions can become part of indigenous Australian social dreaming.

Among these new utopian visions to redress the balance are indigenous Australian civil rights movements and land rights claims, artistic and musical expressions and, more recently, literary representations of social and political ideals. All of these incarnations of indigenous Australian utopian thought have been forced to confront contradiction and redefinition of experiences of the 'Dreaming' within the dominant worldview of western social norms. Land rights have for example been debated as inconsistent with an indigenous Australian worldview regarding ownership of the land, as notions of private property were not part of the original systems in place. However, the intervening western experience of dispossession of traditional country obliged such recourse through land claims to have access to sacred sites, such as Uluru (formerly Ayers Rock), which has been restored to the traditional owners of the area, the local Pitjantjatjara people.

Similar tensions between indigenous Australian worldviews and western terms of authenticity and originality have been raised in relation to indigenous art. 'Artistic' interpretations of the ahistorical otherness of the work seek to perpetuate its distance, rather than allowing the dynamic relationship between different ways of being that utopian interpretation provides.[70] A utopian reading of indigenous desert painting would focus less on the representational, 'artistic' elements as its principal desire is 'to return the art to the country from which it came'.[71]

Land rights, artistic expressions and several other issues come together in exemplary new strategies for bringing the 'Dreaming' back into balance through the model of the indigenous community of Utopia, in northern Australia. The community of Utopia, around 250 km north-east of Alice Springs, has attracted much attention as a positive model for indigenous societies. Named by the first white pastoralists in the area, possibly re-interpreting the local Alyawarr and Anmatyerr peoples' word for big sandy hill 'uturupa' as 'Utopia', it was one of the first successful indigenous land claims in 1976, with artists from the area playing an important part in establishing traditional ownership through cultural connections with the land. Emily Kame Kngwarreye, her adopted daughter Barbara Weir, Kathleen Petyarre, Gloria Petyarre, Ada Bird, Edie Holmes, Michelle Holmes, Gloria Ngal, Poly Ngal and Minnie Pwerle, are among the artists who have contributed to the celebrated status of Utopia as an artistic centre.

More recently, Utopia has become a positive model for indigenous health and well-being, as a ten-year study published in March 2008 has revealed lower than expected morbidity and mortality.[72] It is also a model for future social and environmental sustainability in the Northern Territory. With the decentralized organization of around 1,000 people in sixteen outstations, known as homelands, dispersed over about 10,000 km^2, Utopia does not correspond to western ideals of a cohesive community, but promotes indigenous ideals of connectedness to culture, family and land. It is a society whose economic success is based on artistic creation, undertaken mainly by women, offering opportunities for self-determination as well as cultural expression. The community is supported by western health and social services, which are adapted to the needs of its indigenous members. This example of bringing the 'Dreaming' back into balance through land rights claims, artistic development and reconnecting to traditional ways of being in the world demonstrates the successful co-existence of indigenous and western social ideals within an explicitly utopian vision for improving the life of indigenous peoples in Australia.

The practical and artistic expression of new strands of indigenous utopian thought that have arisen to counter the negative effects of western colonization on indigenous Australian utopian traditions retain their cultural specificity that links them to the stories, songs, laws and rituals of the 'Dreaming'. They have been complemented by recent literary expressions of utopian visions as diverse as Archie Weller's fantastic novel set in the future *Land of the Golden Clouds* (1998) and Alexis Wright's epic *Carpentaria* (2007).[73] Both novels encode messages of utopian hope through reproduction of traditional stories and wisdom: 'Anyone can find hope in the stories: the big stories and the little ones in between.'[74] Indigenous Australian utopian visions therefore continue to develop and thrive in various media and actions to present alternative models and better ways of being in the world.

This partial overview of some Jewish, Islamic, Hindu, Chinese, Japanese and indigenous Australian ideals of a better existence on Earth provides an indication of potential cultural differences in the ways that utopia might be perceived according to different worldviews and belief systems. However, there are of course a myriad of nuances within the traditions presented in this chapter and countless cultures that could not even be considered within the scope of this study. It is hoped that the variety of ways of imagining an improved society will be further explored in specialized studies of culturally specific utopian traditions as well as in comparative research.

In conclusion, it is clear that by reconsidering the origins of utopia in the West, it is possible to identify comparable representations of an ideal time, place or way of being in 'non-western' cultures. The key example of the Golden Age in western traditions has been used as the point of reference in this study, but there are certainly other criteria or tropes that could be employed with similar or equally revealing results, such as the other founding myths of western utopianism: the Land of Cockaigne, the Millennium and the Ideal City. In any event, this study has shown that intercultural imaginaries of the ideal exist both in texts that pre-date More's *Utopia*, as well as in those that are influenced by the western model, but retain qualities derived from the particular local traditions that underpin them. Whether or not we choose to refer to these culturally differentiated representations of social dreaming using the western term of 'utopia' may persist as a point of contention in contemporary studies of utopian thought. But based on the evidence available to us regarding the diverse belief systems and worldviews, cultural manifestations and socio-political movements that demonstrate fundamentally utopian visions, it seems that the desire for a better way of being in the world is indeed a universal concept.

NOTES

1 Gabriel de Foigny, *La Terre Australe connue* (*The Southern Land Known*) (1676), ed. Pierre Ronzeaud (Paris: Société des Textes Français Modernes, 1990); Marge Piercy, *Woman on the Edge of Time* (New York: Knopf, 1976).
2 See for example, J. C. Davis, *Utopia and the Ideal Society: A Study of English Utopian Writing, 1516–1700* (Cambridge University Press, 1981); Krishan Kumar, *Utopia and Anti-Utopia in Modern Times* (Oxford and New York: Blackwell, 1987); Roland Schaer, Gregory Claeys and Lyman Tower Sargent (eds.), *Utopia: The Search for the Ideal Society in the Western World* (New York: Oxford University Press, 2000).

3 Gregory Claeys and Lyman Tower Sargent (eds.), *The Utopia Reader* (New York University Press, 1999).

4 Frank E. Manuel and Fritzie P. Manuel, *Utopian Thought in the Western World* (Cambridge, MA: Belknap Press, 1979), p. 1.

5 Kumar, *Utopia and Anti-Utopia*, p. 19.

6 *Ibid.*, p. 428.

7 See Maurice Meisner, 'Utopian Goals and Ascetic Value in Chinese Communist Ideology', *Journal of Asian Studies* 28:1 (November 1968), 101–10; Stuart R. Schram, 'To Utopia and Back: A Cycle in the History of the Chinese Communist Party', *China Quarterly* 87 (September 1981), 407–39.

8 See Hsiao Kung-Chuan, *A Modern China and a New World: K'ang Yu-Wei, Reformer and Utopian, 1858–1927* (Seattle: University of Washington Press, 1975); Kang Youwei, 'In the Age of One World: A Chinese Utopia', *UNESCO Courier* 37 (November 1984), 31–4; Chang Hui-Chuan, 'Literary Utopia and Chinese Utopian Literature: A Generic Appraisal', dissertation, University of Massachusetts, 1986, AAI8612022; Qingyun Wu, *Female Rule in Chinese and English Literary Utopias* (Syracuse University Press, 1995).

9 See Wolfgang Bauer, *China and the Search for Happiness: Recurring Themes in Four Thousand Years of Chinese Cultural History*, trans. Michael Shaw (New York: Seabury Press, 1976); James Chester Cheng, *Chinese Sources for the Taiping Rebellion 1850–1864* (Hong Kong University Press, 1963); Scott Lowe, *Mo Tzu's Religious Blueprint for a Chinese Utopia: The Will and the Way* (Lewiston, ME: The Edwin Mellen Press, 1992); Frederic L. Bender, 'Sagely Wisdom and Social Harmony: The Utopian Dimension of the Tao Te Ching', *Utopian Studies* 1:2 (1990), 123–43; Julia Ching, 'Neo-Confucian Utopian Theories and Political Ethics', *Monumenta Serica* 30 (1972–3), 1–56; Sarit Helman, 'Turning Classic Models into Utopias: The Neo Confucianist Critique', in Adam Seligman (ed.), *Order and Transcendence: The Role of Utopias and the Dynamics of Civilizations* (Leiden: E. J. Brill, 1989), pp. 93–110; Forest Lin, 'Utopias East and West: On the Relationship Between Ancient and Modern Chinese Ideals', *Alternative Futures* 3:3 (Summer 1980), 15–31; Dudley Tyng, 'The Confucian Utopia', *Journal of the American Oriental Society* 54 (March 1934), 67–9; Wang Pi-Twan Huang, 'Utopian Imagination in Traditional Chinese Fiction', dissertation, University of Wisconsin-Madison, 1980, AAI8107053.

10 Seiji Nuita, 'Traditional Utopias in Japan and the West: A Study in Contrast', in David Plath (ed.), *Aware of Utopia* (Urbana: University of Illinois Press, 1971), pp. 12–32.

11 George B. Bikle, Jr, 'Utopianism and the Planning Element in Modern Japan', in Plath (ed.), *Aware of Utopia*, pp. 33–54.

12 See Yasunaga Toshinobu, *Nihon no yutopia shiso: komyun e no shiko* (Utopian Thought in Japan: The Communal Inclination), *Kyoyo sensho* 13 (Tokyo: Hosei Daigaku Shuppankyoku, 1971); Takayanagi Shun'ichi, *Yutopiagaku kotohajime* (An Introduction to the Study of Utopias) (Tokyo: Fukutake Shoten, 1983).

13 Akio Sawada, *Thomas More in Japan* (Tokyo: Sophia University, Renaissance Institute, 1978).

14 Atsushi Shirai, 'A Century of Owen Studies in Japan', in Chishichi Tsuzuki (ed.), *Robert Owen and the World of Co-operation* (Tokyo: Robert Owen Association

of Japan, 1992), pp. 195–209; Atsushi Shirai, 'The Impact of Owenism in Japan', *Communal Studies* 5 (1985), 59–64.

15 Kawabata Yasuo, 'Otsuki Kenji to Morris Kinen-sai' (Kenji Otsuki and the William Morris Centenary Exhibition in Tokyo), in Fujita Haruhiko (ed.), *The Arts and Crafts and Nippon (Japan)* (Kyoto: Shibun-kaku, 2003); Kawabata Yasuo, 'William Morris to Arts and Crafts Undo' (William Morris and the Arts and Crafts Movement), in A. Hisamori *et al.*, *Interia de Yomu Igirisu shosetu (Reading English Novels in Terms of 'Interior')* (Kyoto: Minerva Shobo, 2003).

16 Sakyo Komatsu, 'H. G. Wells and Japanese Science Fiction', trans. by the author with Judith Merril, Tesu Yano and Robert M. Philmus, in Darko Suvin and Robert M. Philmus (eds.), *H. G. Wells and Modern Science Fiction* (Lewisburg: Bucknell University Press, 1977), pp. 179–90.

17 Yoriko Moichi, 'Japanese Utopian Literature from the 1870s to the Present and the Influence of Western Utopianism', *Utopian Studies* 10:2 (1999), 89–97; Angela Yiu, 'Atarashikimura: The Intellectual and Literary Contexts of a Taisho Utopian Village', *Japan Review* 20 (2008), 203–30; Koon-Ki Tommy Ho, 'Why Utopias Fail: A Comparative Study of the Modern Anti-Utopian Traditions in Chinese, English and Japanese Literatures', dissertation, University of Illinois-Urbana, 1986, AAI8623320; William J. Burton, 'In a Perfect World: Utopias in Modern Japanese Literature', dissertation, University of Washington, 2002, UMI3062920.

18 Adam B. Seligman (ed.), *Order and Transcendence: The Role of Utopias and the Dynamics of Civilizations* (Leiden: E. J. Brill, 1989).

19 Roland Schaer, 'Utopia: Space, Time, History', in Roland Schaer, Gregory Claeys and Lyman Tower Sargent (eds.), *Utopia: The Search for the Ideal Society in the Western World* (New York: Oxford University Press, 2000), p. 3.

20 Lyman Tower Sargent, 'Utopian Traditions: Themes and Variations, in Schaer, Claeys and Sargent (eds.), *Utopia*, p. 8.

21 Ralph Pordzik, *The Quest for Postcolonial Utopia: A Comparative Introduction to the Utopian Novel in New English Literatures* (New York: Lang, 2001). See also Nicholas Brown, *Utopian Generations: The Political Horizon of Twentieth Century Literature* (Princeton University Press, 2005).

22 See for example Zhang Longxi, 'The Utopian Vision, East and West', *Utopian Studies* 13:1 (Winter 2002), 1–21; and Zhang Longxi, *Allegoresis: Reading Canonical Literature East and West* (Ithaca: Cornell University Press, 2005).

23 Jörn Rüsen, Michael Fehr and Thomas W. Rieger (eds.), *Thinking Utopia: Steps into Other Worlds* (Oxford: Berghahn Books, 2005).

24 Lyman Tower Sargent, 'The Necessity of Utopian Thinking: A Cross-national Perspective', in Rüsen, Fehr and Rieger (eds.), *Thinking Utopia*, pp. 1–16, 2.

25 Krishan Kumar, 'Aspects of the Western Utopian Tradition', in Rüsen, Fehr and Rieger (eds.), *Thinking Utopia*, pp. 17–31, 26.

26 Dorothy Ko, 'Bodies in Utopia and Utopian Bodies in Imperial China', in Rüsen, Fehr and Rieger (eds.), *Thinking Utopia*, pp. 89–103.

27 Adam B. Seligman, 'The Comparative Study of Utopias', in Seligman (ed.), *Order and Transcendence*.

28 Norman Cohn, *The Pursuit of the Millennium* (New York: Oxford University Press, 1972), p. 40.

29 Seligman, 'The Comparative Study of Utopias', p. 5.
30 *Ibid.*, p. 14.
31 Theodor Herzl, *Der Judenstaat (The Jewish State)* (Leipzig and Vienna: M. Breitenstein's Verlags-Buchhandlung, 1896); *Altneuland (The Old New Land)* (Leipzig: Hermann Seemann Nachfolger, 1902).
32 Michael Higger, *The Jewish Utopia* (Baltimore: The Lord Baltimore Press, 1932), p. 6.
33 M. A. S. Abdel Haleem, 'Qur'an and hadith', in Tim Winter (ed.), *The Cambridge Companion to Classical Islamic Theology* (Cambridge University Press, 2008), pp. 19–20.
34 Maryam El-Shall, 'Salafi Utopia: The Making of the Islamic State', http://clogic. eserver.org/2006/el-shall.html
35 Marcia Hermansen, 'Eschatology', in Winter (ed.), *The Cambridge Companion to Classical Islamic Theology*, pp. 308–24, 310–11.
36 *Ibid.*, p. 316.
37 Abdel Haleem, 'Qur'an and hadith', p. 22.
38 Hermansen, 'Eschatology', p. 315.
39 *Ibid.*, p. 315.
40 Abu Nasr al-Farabi, *Ara Ahl al-Madina al-Fadila* (The Virtuous City*) and Kitab tashil as-Saadah* (The Attainment of Happiness), in Charles E. Butterworth, *The Philosophy of Plato and Aristotle by Alfarabi*, trans. Muhsin Mahdi, foreword by Thomas L. Pangle (revised edn) (Ithaca: Cornell University Press, 2001).
41 Edward Fitzgerald, *Rubaiyat of Omar Khayyam*, 5th edn (1889); Abu Bakr Ibn Tufail, *The History of Hayy Ibn Yaqzan (Philosophus Autodidactus)*, trans. George N. Atiyeh, in R. Lerner and M. Mahdi (eds.), *Medieval Political Philosophy* (Ithaca: Cornell University Press, 1963), pp. 134–62; Ibn al-Nafis, *The Theologus Antodidactus of Ibn al-Nafis*, ed. with an introduction, translation and notes by Max Meyerhof and Joseph Schacht (Oxford: Clarendon Press, 1968).
42 Aziz Al-Azmeh, *Islam and Modernities* (London: Verso, 1993), p. 98.
43 Sohrab Behdad, 'Islamic Utopia in Pre-Revolutionary Iran: Navvab Safavi and the Fada'ian-e Eslam', *Middle Eastern Studies* 33:1 (January 1997), 53.
44 Ali Rahema, *An Islamic Utopian: A Political Biography of Ali Shari'ati* (London: I. B. Tauris, 1998). See also Arshin Adib-Moghaddam, *Iran in World Politics: The Question of the Islamic Republic* (London: Hurst & Co., 2007), pp. 31–82.
45 El-Shall, 'Salafi Utopia', http://clogic.eserver.org/2006/el-shall.html
46 Al-Azmeh, *Islam and Modernities*, pp. 96–7.
47 *Ibid.*, p. 99.
48 Mohandas K. Gandhi, *Young India* (19 September 1929), 305. See the *Collected Works of Mahatma Gandhi Online* available at www.gandhiserve.org/cwmg/ cwmg.html
49 Mohandas K. Gandhi, 'Independence', *Harijan* (28 July 1946). See *Collected Works of Mahatma Gandhi Online*.
50 Richard G. Fox, *Gandhian Utopia: Experiments With Culture* (Boston: Beacon Press: 1989).

51 Harriet Hartman, 'Can a Hindu Utopia be a Moslim Utopia? Examples from 12th Century India and Beyond', in Seligman (ed.), *Order and Transcendence*, pp. 111–25.
52 Mohandas K. Gandhi, 'Independence', *Harijan* (5 May 1946), 116. See *Collected Works of Mahatma Gandhi Online*.
53 Zhang, *Allegoresis*, p. 188.
54 *Ibid.*, p. 190.
55 *Ibid.*, p. 174.
56 *Ibid.*, pp. 174–5.
57 *Ibid.*, p. 177
58 *Ibid.*, p. 180.
59 *Ibid.*, pp. 192–3.
60 *Ibid.*, p. 199.
61 *Ibid.*, p. 203.
62 For more details on these utopias, please see Qian Ma, *Feminist Utopian Discourse in Eighteenth-Century Chinese and English Fiction: A Cross-Cultural Comparison* (Aldershot: Ashgate, 2004) and Qingyun Wu, *Female Rule*.
63 John W. Hall *et al.* (eds.), *The Cambridge History of Japan*, vol. 1 (Cambridge University Press, 1988–99), p. 329.
64 See Howard Hibbett, *The Floating World in Japanese Fiction* (New York: Oxford University Press, 1959).
65 Baldwin Spencer and F. J. Gillen, *The Arunta* (Oosterhout, Netherlands: Anthropological Publications, 1996), p. 306.
66 W. E. H. Stanner, *White Man Got No Dreaming: Essays 1938–1973* (Canberra: Australian National University Press, 1979), p. 24.
67 Cited in Lynne Hume, 'Accessing the Eternal: Dreaming "the Dreaming" and Ceremonial Performance', *Zygon* 39:1 (March 2004), 239.
68 Eleazar M. Meletinsky, Guy Lanoue and Alexandre Sadetsky, *The Poetics of Myth* (London: Routledge, 2000), p. 201.
69 Deborah Bird Rose, 'Life and Land in Aboriginal Australia', in Maxwell John Charlesworth, Françoise Dussart and Howard Morphy (eds.), *Aboriginal Religions in Australia: An Anthology of Recent Writings* (Aldershot: Ashgate Publishing, 2005), p. 207.
70 Darren Jorgensen, 'Martian Utopias, Land Rights and Indigenous Desert Painting', *Australian Cultural History* 23 (2004), 107.
71 *Ibid.*, p. 116.
72 K. G. Rowley *et al.*, 'Lower than Expected Morbidity and Mortality for an Australian Aboriginal Population: 10-year follow-up in a decentralised community', *Medical Journal of Australia* 188 (2008), 283–7.
73 Archie Weller, *Land of the Golden Clouds* (St Leonard's, NSW: Allen & Unwin, 1998), Alexis Wright, *Carpentaria* (Artarmon, NSW: Giramondo, 2007).
74 Wright, *Carpentaria*, p. 12.

BIBLIOGRAPHY

Abdel Haleem, M. A. S., 'Qur'an and hadith', in Tim Winter (ed.), *The Cambridge Companion to Classical Islamic Theology* (Cambridge University Press, 2008).

Adib-Moghaddam, Arshin, *Iran in World Politics: The Question of the Islamic Republic* (London: Hurst & Company, 2007), pp. 31–82.

Al-Azmeh, Aziz, *Islam and Modernities* (London: Verso, 1993).

Al-Farabi, Abu Nasr, *Ara Ahl al-Madina al-Fadila* (The Virtuous City) *and Kitab tashil as-Saadah* (The Attainment of Happiness), in Charles E. Butterworth, *The Philosophy of Plato and Aristotle by Alfarabi*, trans. Muhsin Mahdi, foreword by Thomas L. Pangle (revised edn) (Ithaca: Cornell University Press, 2001).

Al-Nafis, Ibn, *The Theologus Autodidactus of Ibn al-Nafis*, ed. with an introduction, translation and notes by Max Meyerhof and Joseph Schacht (Oxford: Clarendon Press, 1968).

Bauer, Wolfgang, *China and the Search for Happiness: Recurring Themes in Four Thousand Years of Chinese Cultural History*, trans. Michael Shaw (New York: Seabury Press, 1976).

Behdad, Sohrab, 'Islamic Utopia in Pre-Revolutionary Iran: Navvab Safavi and the Fada'ian-e Eslam', *Middle Eastern Studies* 33:1 (January 1997).

Bender, Frederic L., 'Sagely Wisdom and Social Harmony: The Utopian Dimension of the Tao Te Ching', *Utopian Studies* 1:2 (1990), 123–43.

Bikle, George B., Jr, 'Utopianism and the Planning Element in Modern Japan', in David Plath (ed.), *Aware of Utopia* (Urbana: University of Illinois Press, 1971), pp. 33–54.

Brown, Nicholas, *Utopian Generations: The Political Horizon of Twentieth Century Literature* (Princeton University Press, 2005).

Burton, William J., 'In a Perfect World: Utopias in Modern Japanese Literature', dissertation, University of Washington, 2002, UMI3062920.

Chang, Hui-Chuan, 'Literary Utopia and Chinese Utopian Literature: A Generic Appraisal', dissertation, University of Massachusetts, 1986, AAI8612022.

Cheng, James Chester, *Chinese Sources for the Taiping Rebellion 1850–1864* (Hong Kong University Press, 1963).

Ching, Julia, 'Neo-Confucian Utopian Theories and Political Ethics', *Monumenta Serica* 30 (1972–3), 1–56.

Claeys, Gregory and Lyman Tower Sargent (eds.), *The Utopia Reader* (New York University Press, 1999).

Cohn, Norman, *The Pursuit of the Millennium* (New York: Oxford University Press, 1972).

Davis, J. C., *Utopia and the Ideal Society: A Study of English Utopian Writing, 1516–1700* (Cambridge University Press, 1981).

El-Shall, Maryam, 'Salafi Utopia: The Making of the Islamic State', http://clogic. eserver.org/2006/el-shall.html

Fitzgerald, Edward, *Rubaiyat of Omar Khayyam*, 5th edn (1889).

Foigny, Gabriel de, *La Terre Australe connue* (The Southern Land Known) (1676), ed. Pierre Ronzeaud (Paris: Société des Textes Français Modernes, 1990);.

Fox, Richard G., *Gandhian Utopia: Experiments With Culture* (Boston: Beacon Press: 1989).

Gandhi, Mohandas K., *Collected Works*, available at www.gandhiserve.org/cwmg/cwmg.html <https://owa.ghul.zc.uk/exchwe/bin/redir.asp?URL=http://www.gandhiserve.org/cwmg/cwmg.html>

Hall, John W. *et al.* (eds.), *The Cambridge History of Japan*, vol. 1 (Cambridge University Press, 1988–99).

Hartman, Harriet, 'Can a Hindu Utopia be a Moslim Utopia? Examples from 12th Century India and Beyond', in Adam Seligman (ed.), *Order and Transcendence: The Role of Utopias and the Dynamics of Civilizations* (Leiden: E. J. Brill, 1989), pp. 111–25.

Helman, Sarit, 'Turning Classic Models into Utopias: The Neo Confucianist Critique', in Adam Seligman (ed.), *Order and Transcendence: The Role of Utopias and the Dynamics of Civilizations* (Leiden: E. J. Brill, 1989), pp. 93–110.

Hermansen, Marcia, 'Eschatology', in Tim Winter (ed.), *The Cambridge Companion to Classical Islamic Theology* (Cambridge University Press, 2008), pp. 308–24.

Herzl, Theodor, *Altneuland (The Old New Land)* (Leipzig, Hermann Seemann Nachfolger, 1902).

Der Judenstaat (The Jewish State) (Leipzig: M. Breitenstein's Verlags-Buchhandlung, 1896).

Hibbett, Howard, *The Floating World in Japanese Fiction* (New York: Oxford University Press, 1959).

Higger, Michael, *The Jewish Utopia* (Baltimore: The Lord Baltimore Press, 1932).

Ho, Koon-Ki Tommy, 'Why Utopias Fail: A Comparative Study of the Modern Anti-Utopian Traditions in Chinese, English and Japanese Literatures', dissertation, University of Illinois-Urbana, 1986, AAI8623320.

Hsiao Kung-Chuan, *A Modern China and a New World: K'ang Yu-Wei, Reformer and Utopian, 1858–1927* (Seattle: University of Washington Press, 1975).

Hume, Lynne, 'Accessing the Eternal: Dreaming "the Dreaming" and Ceremonial Performance', *Zygon* 39:1 (March 2004).

Ibn Tufail, Abu Bakr, 'The History of Hayy Ibn Yaqzan (Philosophus Autodidactus)', trans. George N. Atiyeh, in R. Lerner and M. Mahdi (eds.), *Medieval Political Philosophy* (Ithaca: Cornell University Press, 1963), pp. 134–62.

Jorgensen, Darren, 'Martian Utopias, Land Rights and Indigenous Desert Painting', *Australian Cultural History* 23 (2004), 107.

Kawabata Yasuo, 'Otsuki Kenji to Morris Kinen-sai' (Kenji Otsuki and the William Morris Centenary Exhibition in Tokyo), in Fujita Haruhiko (ed.), *The Arts and Crafts and Nippon (Japan)* (Kyoto: Shibun-kaku, 2003).

'William Morris to Arts and Crafts Undo' (William Morris and the Arts and Crafts Movement), in A. Hisamori *et al.*, *Interia de Yomu Igirisu shosetu (Reading English Novels in Terms of 'Interior')* (Kyoto: Minerva Shobo, 2003).

Kang Youwei, 'In the Age of One World: A Chinese Utopia', *UNESCO Courier* 37 (November 1984), 31–4.

Ko, Dorothy, 'Bodies in Utopia and Utopian Bodies in Imperial China', in Jörn Rüsen, Michael Fehr and Thomas W. Rieger (eds.), *Thinking Utopia: Steps into Other Worlds* (New York: Berghahn Books, 2005), pp. 89–103.

Komatsu Sakyo, 'H. G. Wells and Japanese Science Fiction', trans. by the author with Judith Merril, Tesu Yano and Robert M. Philmus, in Darko Suvin and Robert M. Philmus (eds.), *H. G. Wells and Modern Science Fiction* (Lewisburg: Bucknell University Press, 1977), pp. 179–90.

Kumar, Krishan, 'Aspects of the Western Utopian Tradition', in Jörn Rüsen, Michael Fehr and Thomas W. Rieger (eds.), *Thinking Utopia: Steps into Other Worlds* (New York: Berghahn Books, 2005), pp. 17–31.

Utopia and Anti-Utopia in Modern Times (New York: Blackwell, 1987).

Lin, Forest, 'Utopias East and West: On the Relationship Between Ancient and Modern Chinese Ideals', *Alternative Futures* 3:3 (Summer 1980), 15–31.

Lowe, Scott, *Mo Tzu's Religious Blueprint for a Chinese Utopia: The Will and the Way* (Lewiston, ME: The Edwin Mellen Press, 1992).

Manuel, Frank E. and Fritzie P. Manuel, *Utopian Thought in the Western World* (Cambridge, MA: Belknap Press, 1979).

Meisner, Maurice, 'Utopian Goals and Ascetic Value in Chinese Communist Ideology', *Journal of Asian Studies* 28:1 (November 1968), 101–10.

Meletinsky, Eleazar M., Guy Lanoue and Alexandre Sadetsky, *The Poetics of Myth* (London: Routledge, 2000).

Moichi Yoriko, 'Japanese Utopian Literature from the 1870s to the Present and the Influence of Western Utopianism', *Utopian Studies* 10:2 (1999), 89–97.

Nuita Seiji, 'Traditional Utopias in Japan and the West: A Study in Contrast', in David Plath (ed.), *Aware of Utopia* (Urbana: University of Illinois Press, 1971), pp. 12–32.

Piercy, Marge, *Woman on the Edge of Time* (New York: Knopf, 1976).

Plath, David (ed.), *Aware of Utopia* (Urbana: University of Illinois Press, 1971).

Pordzik, Ralph, *The Quest for Postcolonial Utopia: A Comparative Introduction to the Utopian Novel in New English Literatures* (New York: Lang, 2001).

Qian Ma, *Feminist Utopian Discourse in Eighteenth-Century Chinese and English Fiction: A Cross-Cultural Comparison* (Aldershot: Ashgate, 2004).

Qingyun Wu, *Female Rule in Chinese and English Literary Utopias* (Syracuse University Press, 1995).

Rahema, Ali, *An Islamic Utopian: A Political Biography of Ali Shari'ati* (London and New York: I. B. Tauris, 1998).

Rose, Deborah Bird, 'Life and Land in Aboriginal Australia', in Maxwell John Charlesworth, Françoise Dussart and Howard Morphy (eds.), *Aboriginal Religions in Australia: An Anthology of Recent Writings* (Aldershot: Ashgate Publishing, 2005).

Rowley, K. G. *et al.*, 'Lower than Expected Morbidity and Mortality for an Australian Aboriginal Population: 10-year follow-up in a decentralised community', *Medical Journal of Australia* 188 (2008), 283–7.

Rüsen, Jörn, Michael Fehr and Thomas W. Rieger (eds.), *Thinking Utopia: Steps into Other Worlds* (New York: Berghahn Books, 2005).

Sargent, Lyman Tower, 'The Necessity of Utopian Thinking: A Cross-national Perspective', in Jörn Rüsen, Michael Fehr and Thomas W. Rieger (eds.), *Thinking Utopia: Steps into Other Worlds* (New York: Berghahn Books, 2005), pp. 1–16.

'Utopian Traditions: Themes and Variations', in Roland Schaer, Gregory Claeys and Lyman Tower Sargent (eds.), *Utopia: The Search for the Ideal Society in the Western World* (New York: Oxford University Press, 2000).

Sawada, Akio, *Thomas More in Japan* (Tokyo: Sophia University, The Renaissance Institute, 1978).

Schaer, Roland, 'Utopia: Space, Time, History', in Roland Schaer, Gregory Claeys and Lyman Tower Sargent (eds.), *Utopia: The Search for the Ideal Society in the Western World* (New York: Oxford University Press, 2000).

Schaer, Roland, Gregory Claeys and Lyman Tower Sargent (eds.), *Utopia: The Search for the Ideal Society in the Western World* (New York: Oxford University Press, 2000).

Schram, Stuart R., 'To Utopia and Back: A Cycle in the History of the Chinese Communist Party', *The China Quarterly* 87 (September 1981), 407–39.

Seligman, Adam B., 'The Comparative Study of Utopias', in Seligman (ed.), *Order and Transcendence*.

Seligman, Adam (ed.), *Order and Transcendence: The Role of Utopias and the Dynamics of Civilizations* (Leiden: E. J. Brill, 1989).

Shirai, Atsushi, 'A Century of Owen Studies in Japan', in Chishichi Tsuzuki (ed.), *Robert Owen and the World of Co-operation* (Tokyo: Robert Owen Association of Japan, 1992), pp. 195–209.

'The Impact of Owenism in Japan', *Communal Studies* 5 (1985), 59–64.

Spencer, Baldwin and F. J. Gillen, *The Arunta* (Oosterhout, Netherlands: Anthropological Publications, 1996).

Stanner, W. E. H., *White Man Got No Dreaming: Essays 1938–1973* (Canberra: Australian National University Press, 1979).

Takayanagi Shun'ichi, *Yutopiagaku kotohajime* (An Introduction to the Study of Utopias) (Tokyo: Fukutake Shoten, 1983).

Tyng, Dudley, 'The Confucian Utopia', *Journal of the American Oriental Society* 54 (March 1934), 67–9.

Wang Pi-Twan Huang, 'Utopian Imagination in Traditional Chinese Fiction', dissertation, University of Wisconsin-Madison, 1980, AAI8107053.

Weller, Archie, *Land of the Golden Clouds* (St Leonard's, NSW: Allen & Unwin, 1998),

Wright, Alexis, *Carpentaria* (Artarmon, NSW: Giramondo, 2007).

Yasunaga Toshinobu, *Nihon no yutopia shiso: komyun e no shiko* (Utopian Thought in Japan: The Communal Inclination), *Kyoyo sensho* 13 (Tokyo: Hosei Daigaku Shuppankyoku, 1971).

Yiu, Angela, 'Atarashikimura: The Intellectual and Literary Contexts of a Taisho Utopian Village', *Japan Review* 20 (2008), 203–30.

Zhang Longxi, *Allegoresis: Reading Canonical Literature East and West* (Ithaca: Cornell University Press, 2005).

'The Utopian Vision, East and West', *Utopian Studies* 13:1 (Winter 2002), 1–21.

II

BRIAN STABLEFORD

Ecology and dystopia

Introduction

The terms 'ecology' and 'dystopia' were first improvised from their Greek roots in the mid-nineteenth century. The former was used by Henry David Thoreau in 1858 before being formally defined as a branch of biology seven years later by Ernst Haeckel, while the latter was by employed by John Stuart Mill in 1868.

A basic awareness of ecological relationships had been a necessary concomitant of agricultural endeavour since the first crops were sown and the first animals domesticated; farming is, in essence, a matter of creating, sustaining and improving artificial ecosystems. The application of the scientific method to agricultural practice had made considerable impacts long before Haeckel identified a science of ecology, but Thoreau's usage was more closely connected to an increasing sensitivity to the complexity of natural processes, which changed the significance of the word 'nature' in philosophical discourse and popular parlance, where it was often rendered, with a degree of personification impregnated with mystical homage, as 'Nature'. Thoreau was continuing a tradition summarized in Ralph Waldo Emerson's *Nature* (1836), which owed a good deal to the Romantic movements of Europe; Romantic poets often elaborated their responses to Nature and celebrated supposed communions therewith.

In addition to its scientific definition, the term 'ecology' retained these mystical connections throughout the twentieth century. It was the mystical rather than the scientific aspects of ecology which forged a crucial bond with the history of utopian thought, helping to redefine notions of eutopia (and hence of dystopia) and eventually necessitating the coinage of the term 'ecotopia'; the notion of 'Nature' was central to that bonding process.

The personification of Nature was begun by the exponents of 'natural theology', who attempted to employ the study of Creation as a means of cultivating a better understanding of the mind of God. As doubts about

God's existence spread in the nineteenth century and theories of evolution provided an alternative to Creation as an explanation of the ecosphere's richness and complexity, it became possible – and, indeed, increasingly popular – to see Nature not as a means of reading the divine mind, but as a sort of divine mind in its own right. This was not welcome news to everyone, as exemplified by Alfred Lord Tennyson's reference in *In Memoriam* (1850) to 'Nature red in tooth and claw', but the idea of an implicitly cruel Nature was always in competition with the notion of an essentially benign Mother Nature – who was proverbially supposed to know best, however mysterious her ways of movement might be. The notion that Nature was blessed with an inherent 'balance' or 'harmony' became commonplace, and ecological representations of the complex relationships identifiable within ecosystems were routinely invoked as alleged proof of that contention.

The mystical aspect of ecology retained the concept of sin, tacitly if not explicitly, although its adherents were forced to reconceive sin as a trangression of 'laws of Nature' rather than Mosaic commandments. Whereas Genesis had explicitly established the natural world as something specifically made for human exploitation, and thus subject to human dominion, mystical ecology reversed that priority, making human beings part of Nature and subject to its imperatives. This inversion was bound to have an effect on utopian speculation, particularly in terms of the ways in which eutopian ambitions might run into trouble.

The alteration of perspective was dramatically illustrated by the arguments employed in Thomas Robert Malthus's *Essay on the Principle of Population as it Affects the Future Improvement of Society* (1798), which suggested that debates regarding the precise political shape of a future utopian state were pointless, because *all* futuristic dreams of universal peace and plenty were impossible of achievement, on ecological grounds. Malthus argued that food supply can only increase arithmetically, while population tends to increase exponentially. The logical result of this imbalance, he contended, is that human societies always require numerical restriction by war, famine and disease, formerly notorious as Horsemen of the Apocalypse but scientifically re-labelled as 'Malthusian checks'.

Malthus provided a stern challenge to the philosophy of progress developed in pre-revolutionary France by Anne-Robert Turgot and the Marquis de Condorcet, whose fundamental thesis was that technological advancement and social advancement went hand-in-hand: that increasing scientific knowledge and technological sophistication favoured and facilitated the growth of liberty, equality and fraternity. The specific formulation of the thesis inevitably generated a shadowy antithesis in the form of fears that at least some advances in technology might actually be detrimental to the ends of social justice, inhibiting rather than furthering the ideals in question; although a superficial inspection of the broad sweep of history seemed to favour the thesis, Malthus lent imaginative fuel to the antithesis.

Malthus was forced to modify his argument in subsequent editions of the *Essay* to take aboard criticisms made by William Godwin and other English philosophers of progress. He accepted that voluntary restriction of population might be possible by the exercise of 'moral restraint' – but he clearly had no faith in the likelihood that future generations might exercise such moral restraint. He was not alone in this suspicion – and it was in order to assist consideration of the darker aspects of future possibility, including Malthusian anxieties, that the word 'dystopia' was eventually coined.

In Malthus's time, the most apparent cutting edge of progress in 'applied ecology' was the calculated transplantion of crops in the development of colonies. Joseph Banks, as president of the Royal Society, played a leading role in defining the scientific missions of British naval expeditions; it was he who commissioned William Bligh to transplant breadfruit from Tahiti to the Caribbean colonies, and made sure that the *Providence* completed the mission in 1793 after the *Bounty*'s crew mutinied in 1791. Banks's immediate motive for augmenting the collection of plants held at the Royal Botanic Gardens at Kew, for which he assumed responsibility in 1798, was to discover and develop resources for the use of the colonists of Australia. In the wake of the American War of Independence, Thomas Jefferson, George Washington and John Quincy Adams similarly recognized the naturalization and cultivation of useful plants as a vital economic necessity for the success of the new nation.

The establishment of 'plantations' of every kind was the heart of colonial endeavour, and it is hardly surprising that a keen appreciation of the problems involved in their maintenance developed in the nineteenth century. The branches of biology that grew rapidly in that period tended to be guided by those imperatives, as evidenced by such works as Thaddeus William Harris's pioneering entomological study *Treatise on Some of the Insects of New England Which are Injurious to Vegetation* (1842). The primary function of the US Entomological Commission, established in 1877 under the directorship of Charles V. Riley, was to coordinate endeavours in pest control. The first textbooks of ecology were produced in this context, and were thus of considerable interest to utopian experimenters, whose endeavours were very often formulated as colonial settlements.

Colonial adventurism was routinely justified, in moral terms, by the notion that the native societies of colonizable lands were intrinsically bad because they were 'savage' – innately inclined to brutal violence of every sort, including human sacrifice and cannibalism – and thus direly in need of progress towards civilization. Eighteenth- and nineteenth-century fiction lent robust ideological support to this notion, especially in the adventure stories featured in British 'boys' books' and the fledgling American genre of the Western. As civilized society came under attack by such eighteenth-century philosophers as Jean-Jacques Rousseau, however, a contrarian anthropological myth was born which conceived of unspoiled tribal societies as innocent, peaceful, happy and paradisal – a model to which some French commentators attempted to accommodate the actual islands of the remote Pacific Ocean, especially Tahiti. This idea, too, became a staple of nineteenth-century romance, albeit a far less obvious one; it eventually spawned an entire sub-genre of quasi-nostalgic 'lost race stories', because it had to be admitted that very few actual tribal societies provided convincing candidates of paradisal innocence, peacefulness and happiness.

The Rousseauesque notion of technological development as a process of intrinsic spoliation of primal innocence was further augmented by nostalgic contrasts between rural life and life in the new industrial towns that were springing up all over Europe. Although such towns were sometimes allowed, like the curate's egg, to be 'good in parts', the idea took deep root that they had archetypally bad places within them. The coal mines where the fuel to drive steam engines was produced became, in the eyes of some commentators, the core of a modern Dantean Hell, whose outer circles were formed by the 'slums' that grew up in the vicinity of factories where steam engines were used in the production of goods. Some commentators refused to be selective; the English reformer William Cobbett wrote off the whole of London as 'the Great Wen', neatly encapsulating the horror that early nineteenth-century sceptics felt as they observed the unfolding of the industrial revolution. William Blake may not have meant his reference in 'Jerusalem' (1804) to 'dark Satanic Mills' to be taken literally, but it was frequently read that way.

Cities had always had a dystopian aspect of this sort; the first laws to abate smoke production and restrict garbage disposal in London had been enacted by the English Parliament in 1273 and 1388. The dramatic growth of cities in the nineteenth century amplified the problem alarmingly, however; the modernization of London's sewer system was inspired by the 'Great Stink' of the 1850s, which made the citybound banks of the river Thames – including the stretch on which the Houses of Parliament stood – quite unendurable. Futuristic images of eutopian cities, from Louis-Sébastien Mercier's pioneering account of Paris in *L'An deux mille quatre cent quarante* (1771; tr. as *Memoirs of the Year Two Thousand Five Hundred*) onwards, were often optimistic that technological progress would enable cities to become much cleaner, but it is hardly surprising that the Great Stink generated a certain scepticism in that regard.

The original meaning of the word 'pollution' had a moral and spiritual context, referring to defilement or desecration rather than common-or-garden uncleanliness, and the increasing use of the term 'environmental pollution' with reference to problems of industrial waste disposal retained a plangent echo of that implication. In effect, pollution became the first and foremost of the deadly ecological sins. The idea of dystopia was infected with this consciousness at birth, and the history of the idea has, inevitably, seen a gradual and inexorable increase in its elaboration within the context of ecological mysticism and science. The idea of ecology was similarly infected; the historical development of the science has been haunted by the imagery of disaster and the festering anxieties that lie at the core of dystopian romance and satire.

Immiseration, pollution and alienation in early speculative fiction

The narrative of the first significant dystopian satire, Émile Souvestre's *Le monde tel qu'il sera* (1846; tr. as *The World As It Shall Be*), makes only passing reference to the extent of industrial spoliation, but the illustrations accompanying the text – which are reproduced in the English translation of 2004 – were more explicit, the cityscapes being notable for their murky atmospheres. The same is true of the illustrations of the city of Stahlstadt in the first edition of Jules Verne's *Les cinq cents millions de la bégum* (1879; developed from a first draft by Paschal Grousset; tr. as *The Begum's Fortune*), which is similarly reproduced in early translations issued by Sampson Low *et al*. Verne's textual description of life in the 'City of Steel' – hypothetically located in Oregon – depicts the extreme regulation of time and effort within the vast factory complex and its associated mine in a much more earnest fashion than Souvestre, and its awareness of the effects of environmental pollution is correspondingly grim.

Even in Verne's Stahlstadt, however, let alone its eutopian counterpart Frankville, technology enables pollution to be held at bay where required; the centre of Stahlstadt is a privileged enclave centred on a beautiful tropical park, populated with plants and animals transplanted from distant parts of the globe. The most obvious impact of nineteenth-century reality on literary imagery of this sort was the lesson of social division: the notion that bad places were for the abandonment of the poor, while the rich and privileged could and would build exclusive eutopian microcosms. In naturalistic and speculative fiction alike, eutopia and dystopia often sat side by side, as two sides of the same coin, the eutopia of the few being built at the expense of the dystopia of the many.

Striking instances of this pattern of thought can be found in many alarmist futuristic fantasies. In the first significant American dystopian romance, Ignatius Donnelly's *Caesar's Column* (1890, initially bylined Edmund Boisgilbert), the dystopia of the masses proves to be a fertile breeding ground for an unprecedentedly vengeful revolution; the titular column is erected from the skulls of its victims. In H. G. Wells's *The Time Machine* (1895) the imagery of social division attained a new extreme in the contrast between the effetely eutopian society of the Eloi and the nightmarish dystopian underworld of the Morlocks.

The immiseration that takes place in such conventional dystopian locations as Stahlstadt is, to a large extent, a straightforward representation of the actuality of nineteenth-century slum life; it is a matter of living in squalid conditions in a spoiled environment with barely enough to eat. There is, however, another significant element to which Verne and Grousset pay particular attention: the fact that the lives of the factory workers are excessively regulated by the nature of their labour and their shift-patterns, to the point where they become mechanized themselves. This was a well-established nineteenth-century anxiety, dating back to the Romantic movements. When Thomas Carlyle suggested in 'Signs of the Times' (1829) that the modern era ought to be characterized as an 'Age of Machinery', he complained bitterly that 'mechanical genius' had not restricted itself to the management of physical and external factors but had invaded the internal and spiritual aspects of human life.

Carlyle's essay elevates Mechanism to the status of a satanic counterpart to Nature, similarly personalized as an elementary force of malevolence – and this was the status it assumed in much dystopian fiction. The most obvious corollary of this opposition, in the context of literary didacticism, is the mechanization of time. One of the principal defining features of Nature is its relationship with the temporal cycles of the day and the year, while one of the key features of technological society is its domination by clocks.

The oppressive regulation of time is responsible for much of the distress of the downtrodden citizens of Verne's Stahlstadt, and was increasingly seen as a fundamental defining feature of dystopian existence. It was given striking visual representation in Fritz Lang's film *Metropolis* (1926) after extensive literary development in such novels as H. C. Marriott-Watson's *Erchomenon; or, The Republic of Materialism* (1879), Owen Gregory's *Meccania* (1918) and Yevgeny Zamyatin's *We* (1921; tr. 1924). In *Les condamnés à mort* (1920; tr. as *Useless Hands*) by 'Claude Farrère' (Charles Bargone) the misery of mechanized labour reaches breaking-point when the process of automation achieves its logical end-point, but the enclosed eutopia of the elite is well defended by heavy artillery. In Karel Čapek's

R.U.R. (1920) the artificial 'robot' labourers which support a similar euto-pian elite find a means of overcoming their own enforced automatism once the oppressive elite has been exterminated, but that merely takes the whole historical process back to square one.

The notion that the division between the major classes of society would inevitably become wider, the condition of the rich tending towards eutopia and freedom while that of the poor tended towards dystopia and mech-anization, had been widely popularized by Karl Marx. The first volume of *Das Kapital* (1867; tr. as *Capital*) had made free use of ecological analogies in representing the essential relationship between the classes in terms of parasitism, predation and vampirism, as well as giving a new meaning to the term 'alienation' in speaking of the relationship between workers and their produce. The latter term was, however, already confused by another new meaning which gave that term a quasi-ecological context, in speaking of human alienation from Nature by virtue of the Carlylean mechanization of every aspect of day-to-day life.

Marxism offered a potential solution to the immiseration of the pro-letariat in terms of revolution, while other socialists – including H. G. Wells – preferred to pin their hopes on evolutionary reform, but the record of literary commentary gives little evidence of widespread faith in either solution. Literary accounts of hypothetical societies did, however, become increasingly suspicious of the eutopian qualifications of the idle existence that social elites already led, which were often presumed to be in the process of a gradual exaggeration towards absurdity. Enclaves of the sort found in the heart of Stahlstadt and taken to their extreme in the lifestyle of the Eloi were routinely judged by literary commentators to be false eutopias, symp-tomatic of morbid social stagnation. That notion could easily be detached from the imagery of social division; Walter Besant's *The Inner House* (1888), which extrapolates the consequences of a technology of longevity, imagi-nes an entire society that has fallen victim to spiritual stagnation, while James Elroy Flecker's *The Last Generation* (1908) looks forward satirically to a near future in which the human race, having become too keenly aware of the ineradicable dystopian aspects of its existence, refuses to perpetuate itself any longer.

Early speculative fictions based in a conscious ecological awareness some-times went to extremes in rejecting the notion that an ideal society could ever be founded on the artifices of civilized luxury. A graphic extrapola-tion of Cobbett's notion of London as a Great Wen is in Richard Jefferies's *After London; or, Wild England* (1885), in which the capital has been reduced to a bleak scar of ineradicable pollution and the quality of English life has been restored by a technological retreat. W. H. Hudson's

A Crystal Age (1887) is an extreme extrapolation of the principles of eco-logical mysticism, in which harmonious ecological relationships become a frankly supernatural means to the establishment of a peculiar matriarchal eutopia. Hudson's best-selling exotic romance *Green Mansions* (1902) is just as wholehearted in its assertions, maintaining that all extant human societies, from the most savage to the most civilized, are equally alienated from ecological harmony and uniformly dystopian in consequence.

Early fantasies of runaway future pollution usually took the form of moralistic disaster stories rather than dystopian romances; W. D. Hay's *The Doom of the Great City* (1880) and Robert Barr's 'The Doom of London' (1892) – both of which feature catastrophic smogs – are ringing accounts of richly deserved punishment. On the other hand, the traditional link between cleanliness and godliness came to seem rather dubious if God were replaced by Nature, because – however well-balanced its harmony might be – Nature did seem to have a sort of essential dirtiness. The early development of dys-topian romance and satire showed as much evidence of fear of excessive cleanliness as fear of spreading pollution. Excessive cleanliness was fre-quently seen as a manifestation of the excessive orderliness of Mechanism, construed in opposition to the beautiful untidiness of Nature.

Writers involved in the Decadent movements of the *fin-de-siècle* defiantly celebrated artificiality in all its aspects but they were working in conscious opposition to a perceived majority whose members considered technological artificiality to be somehow intrinsically awful, even while they drew extrava-gantly and enthusiastically on the particular opportunities it presented. *Fin-de-siècle* Romantic literature made much of the symbolism of Pan, the Graeco-Roman god of Arcadia, who was widely employed as a figurehead of Nature, and Romantic utopianism routinely favoured the nostalgic imagery of Arcadian pastoral existence over that of eutopian city-states.

In consequence of these lines of thought, most futuristic fantasies of the late nineteenth and early twentieth centuries, irrespective of whether they featured exaggerated social division or wholesale social reform, accepted the notion that the most fundamental social evil – the essential seed of dys-topia – was the abstraction of human beings from a supposedly harmonious relationship with the natural environment and its inherent rhythms: a per-nicious form of alienation that was equally corrupting in its effects on the rich and the poor.

Enemies of the rational state

The argument that the severance of human beings from Nature is a kind of ultimate folly is strikingly exemplified by the futuristic horror stories collected in S. Fowler Wright's *The New Gods Lead* (1932), which offer a scathing indictment of the values of technocracy and the perversity of the worship of the 'new gods', here named as Comfort and Cowardice. Fowler Wright's argument is that eutopians who see the good life in terms of a leisurely existence supported by all the luxuries of modern technology are woefully mistaken, and that the quality of human life depends on their engagement in a healthy struggle for existence against the vicissitudes of Nature – a Nature whose redness in tooth and claw is an essential component of its harmony, to be celebrated rather than regretted. He went on to recapitulate James Elroy Flecker's image of a future society that becomes literally suicidal by virtue of its own existential sickness in *The Adventure of Wyndham Smith* (1938).

The novel that now has the reputation of being the first great dystopian satire of the twentieth century, Aldous Huxley's *Brave New World* (1932), is fully conscious of the incipient hypocrisy of this kind of nostalgic Romanticism, and was enabled by that acute consciousness to set a new standard in black comedy. Huxley had sketched out an earlier ambiguous utopia in the unashamedly nostalgic *Crome Yellow* (1920), whose later chapters feature an enthusiastically ominous description of a coming 'Rational State'. In *Brave New World* that model is greatly elaborated, and considerably enriched by input from an alternative prospectus for the future offered by J. B. S. Haldane in *Daedalus; or, Science and the Future* (1923).

Haldane's essay looks forward optimistically to a day when biotechnology has secured the food supplies of an expanding population and 'ectogenetic' children born from artificial wombs can be biologically modified at will; in *Brave New World* Huxley combined the latter notion with technologies of social conditioning to form a system ensuring that all the citizens of his rigidly stratified future society are content with their various stations and capabilities. This was to become a central motif of much late twentieth-century dystopian fiction: the notion that future inhabitants of a bad society might be conditioned gladly to celebrate their own alienation added a vital element of insult to injury.

Haldane was careful to preface the image of the future contained in *Daedalus* with a cautionary observation that there is always extreme initial resistance against 'biological inventions', because they are invariably perceived, at first, as blasphemous perversions. He was certainly right about that, as the literary response to his essay clearly demonstrated. Huxley's was not the first, and was certainly not the last dystopian satire based on its anticipations; Julian Huxley – a fellow biologist and close friend – got in ahead of his younger brother with 'The Tissue-Culture King' (1926), which describes the nightmarish use made of Haldanian biotechnologies by a taboo-laden African tribal society. As if the scepticism of his friend were not hard enough to bear, Haldane's sister, Naomi Mitchison, produced grim futuristic fantasies based on the essay's key motifs in *Solution Three* (1975) and *Not by Bread Alone* (1983), although she diplomatically waited until he was dead before publishing them. Muriel Jaeger's *Retreat from Armageddon* (1936) offered a more even-handed response, although the optimistic side of the case is somewhat undermined by the fact that the dialogue takes place between intellectuals hiding in a bunker from the threat of a potentially apocalyptic world war.

Brave New World is a more ambiguous text than many of its modern commentators assume; final judgment in the debate between Mustapha Mond and John Savage regarding the merits and limitations of the future it depicts is delivered by the latter's suicide, when he realizes that he cannot resist the seductions that the world of artifice has to offer. A similar ambiguity is reflected in E. M. Forster's criticism of technological eutopianism, 'The Machine Stops' (1909), which concentrates its criticism on the essential precariousness of an overprotective technological environment.

Huxley's suggestion that the inhabitants of a future dystopia might be conditioned to like it was an extrapolation of an anxiety common among the literate middle class that the fondest ambitions of society's ill-educated 'masses' were inherently dystopian, judged by the tastes and preferences of literate and literary people. John Stuart Mill's father, James Mill, had been a Utilitarian eutopian who believed that the universalization of literacy would drive bad fiction to extinction, but the first prophet of dystopia had observed the falsity of that prediction; by the time Huxley wrote *Brave New World* its absurd naivety was painfully manifest. By that time, the appeal of 'pulp fiction' was incontestable.

Although the American genre of pulp 'science fiction' was established by its founder, Hugo Gernsback, as a propagandistic medium for the calculated celebration of the advancement of technology, it was rapidly infected by anxieties regarding the ultimate results of the worship of Fowler Wright's 'new gods'. Laurence Manning and Fletcher Pratt produced a striking account of 'The City of the Living Dead' (1930), in which civilized humankind gladly retreats into synthetic experience, preferring life in what would nowadays be called 'virtual reality' to the vicissitudes of natural existence.

The demands of popular melodrama ensured that pulp science-fiction writers would be more interested in representations of rebellion against evil futures than peaceful accommodation to pleasant ones, but that imperative cannot entirely account for the anxieties manifest in the SF genre from its inception regarding the 'decadence' that might overtake human societies addicted to the comforts of technology. The fear of creeping decadence is, however, intrinsically muted, and has an obvious solution. John Savage could not, in the end, escape the seductiveness of Mustapha Mond's corrupt world, but when E. M. Forster's Machine stopped, its minions had no alternative but to return to the challenging wilderness, and Fowler Wright's Wyndham Smith was eager to do the same, in the hope that his descendants might learn to belong there again. Such dystopian societies are not manifestly or actively evil; their worst feature is, in fact, the hollowness of their eutopian pretence. Wholehearted dystopian imagery, in the first half of the twentieth century, required the kind of active vindictiveness in the deployment of technology and authority that was only displayed in political fantasies that set out to stigmatize some particular party as an incarnation of evil.

There was no shortage of such political fantasies in the first half of the century, their production being greatly encouraged by such actual instances of outrageous tyranny as Josef Stalin's regime in Russia and Adolf Hitler's in Germany. The tradition eventually culminated in George Orwell's *Nineteen Eighty-Four* (1949), whose careful excesses only served to emphasize the assumption that technological development unaided by tyrannical brutality could not plausibly be seen as an intrinsic road to hell. In spite of its tight focus on the politics of tyranny, however, *Nineteen Eighty-Four* retains an element of nostalgic Nature-worship in its depiction of Winston Smith's brief escape to an enclave of rural harmony.

Orwell's classic borrowed much of its narrative energy from anxieties left over from the Second World War, and the decade following the end of the war produced other memorable dystopias provoked by the same anxieties. Those with an ecological component to their anxieties included several accounts of extreme pollution in the wake of atomic warfare; Aldous Huxley's *Ape and Essence* (1948) is, in this respect, a much more contemptuous comedy than *Brave New World*. The most successful Orwellian fantasy, save for the original, was Ray Bradbury's *Fahrenheit 451* (1953), which brought the literary man's fear of the illiterate masses into uniquely sharp focus in its portrayal of future 'firemen' whose job is to burn books and thus prevent the spread of the kinds of grief which, according to Ecclesiastes, inevitably stem from wisdom and the kinds of sorrow produced by the increase of knowledge. Here, too, a nostalgic regard for Nature is carefully conserved, and it is the wilderness that ultimately provides a refuge for the last custodians of literary value.

Orwellian political dystopias continued to appear for some thirty years, but they gradually faded from view. Ecological concerns were never irrelevant to these works, which routinely employed notions of alienation and pollution as well as conserving a certain Romantic nostalgia, but ecological issues rudely barged their way into the foreground of futuristic fiction in the 1950s and 1960s, with the result that the political issues central to Orwellian novels were gradually forced out to the margins. The disenchantment with political systems fostered by Orwellian dystopias helped to feed the conviction that the essential problem afflicting eutopian ambitions lay outside the arena of party politics, arising from such ecological problems as population expansion and environmental pollution, whose potential ill-effects put those of tyranny somewhat in the shade. The perception gradually grew that politicians of every stripe, however well-intentioned they might be, were all hirelings of the Rational State, unwitting slaves of Mechanism and hapless instruments of dystopia, impotent even to perceive, let alone to contend with the impending ecological crisis.

The resurgence of Malthusian anxieties in speculative fiction

Anxiety regarding the possibility of ecological disaster was sharpened in the United States between the two World Wars by the emergence of the Midwestern 'Dust Bowl', which received considerable literary attention in contemporary novels. These anxieties were extrapolated in the SF magazines by such alarmist fantasies as Nathan Schachner's 'Sterile Planet' (1937) and Willard E. Hawkins's 'The Dwindling Sphere' (1940), while more respectable novels foregrounding the potential problems of soil exhaustion included A. G. Street's *Already Walks Tomorrow* (1938) and Edward Hyams's *The Astrologer* (1950). In spite of such hiccups, though, the expansion of food supply had kept pace with the actual expansion of global population throughout the nineteenth and early twentieth centuries, soothing the anxiety that Malthus had tried to spread. Food-producers were still showing considerable enterprise in mid-century, participating in a 'green revolution' based on the selective breeding of crop-plants which increased their yields markedly.

In parallel with the success of food production technologies, on the other hand, dramatic improvements in hygiene and the treatment of bacterial infections had lessened the impact of the most powerful of the Malthusian checks, facilitating an increase in global population that was increasingly likened in popular parlance to an 'explosion'. In the spring of 1955 a number of interested parties formed the Population Council, whose eleven-strong committee became a significant disseminator of propaganda regarding the dangerous rapidity of world population growth. The March 1956 issue of *Scientific American* carried an alarmist article on 'World Population' by Julian Huxley, which assisted the Council's efforts.

The successes of modern technology in augmenting food production and reducing mortality rates seemed, in this context, merely to be postponing an inevitable disaster, which would be all the more catastrophic for its postponement. In the meantime, it seemed, society's attempts to sustain a vast population, or interrupt its expansion by draconian means, might be forced to become desperately ingenious. Anxiety was further heightened in the following decade, widely popularized by a best-selling account of *The Population Bomb* (1968) by Paul Ehrlich. Ehrlich dramatized his warnings in a fictionalized futuristic vision of 'Ecocatastrophe' (1969), and similar images of future social collapse became commonplace. Literary accounts of desperate holding actions multiplied with equal rapidity, producing a rich spectrum of dystopian satires and futurological horror stories.

Literary accounts of 'the population problem' had begun to appear in some profusion in the SF magazines before the Population Council was formed. Stories addressing the idea as a problem requiring ingenious solution were already commonplace in 1954. In that year Isaac Asimov's *The Caves of Steel* offered a conscientiously even-handed analysis of the kinds of living conditions that a huge population would have to adopt and learn to love, while Damon Knight's gentle satire 'Natural State' (revised for book publication as *Masters of Evolution*) provided a modest account of the biotechnological improvisations that might be necessary to sustain an overcrowded world, and Kurt Vonnegut Jr's brutal black comedy 'The Big Trip Up Yonder' re-emphasized the hopelessness of the expectation that any such situation could long endure. The Council's propagandizing familiarized the idea, assisting earnest projections to push further and further ahead in dramatizing the search for imaginative solutions and satirical projections to become increasingly bitter.

The dystopias produced in this context were not all despairing. Robert Silverberg's *Master of Life and Death* (1957) maintains a certain pragmatic optimism in its depiction of a day in the hectic life of the bureaucrat responsible for the difficult organization of Malthusian moral restraint. Lester del Rey's *The Eleventh Commandment* (1962) tries to find some compensation for the continued harassments of the Malthusian checks in terms of the logic of natural selection. James Blish and Norman L. Knight's *A Torrent of Faces* (1967) bravely attempts to identify the advantages of the explicitly Fascist organization that a vast population might require. John Brunner's *Stand on Zanzibar* (1968) conscientiously dissects its overpopulated global society to expose its hopeful and heart-warming elements as well as nasty and frustrating aspects in multitudinous vignettes of everyday existence.

On the other hand, blackly comic projections published in the same period became increasingly sharp. The bureaucrats in Frederik Pohl's 'The Census Takers' (1956) are more coldly methodical in meeting their targets than Silverberg's. In C. M. Kornbluth's 'Reap the Dark Tide' (1958;

reprinted as 'Shark Ship') members of tribal societies exiled to the oceans by virtue of population pressure on land return to shore to discover the relics of the inevitable ecocatastrophe. The effects of inevitability in the vignette of everyday existence featured in J. G. Ballard's 'Billenium' (1961) are all the more telling for their careful understatement. Harry Harrison's *Make Room! Make Room!* (1966) adapts Jonathan Swift's 'modest solution' to the alleged problem of overpopulation in eighteenth-century Ireland to a twentieth-century near future. Robert Sheckley's 'The People Trap' (1968) adapts the American improvisation of the Land Race to the acquisition of scarce property in the smogbound Jungle City of future New York.

As Malthusian anxieties began to play a leading role in popular debate, a US pressure group calling for Zero Population Growth attempted to make strategic use of dystopian fiction by promoting a science-fiction anthology, *Voyages: Scenarios for a Ship Called Earth* (1971) edited by Rob Sauer and a movie named for its own acronym, *Z.P.G.* (1971; novelized as *The Edict* by screenwriter Max Ehrlich). The year 1971 was a particularly fruitful one for overpopulation dystopias; it also saw the production of Robert Silverberg's *The World Inside*, in which huge Urban Monads accommodate the population of an entire city on every floor while the surrounding fields are subjected to ever more intense agricultural exploitation; T. J. Bass's *Half Past Human*, in which decadent Nebishes have had to adopt a troglodytic existence while the world surface is entirely devoted to agricultural production and Gordon R. Dickson's *Sleepwalker's World*, in which the broadcast energy that keeps food factories running at full capacity also maintains the vast population in a state of quiescent hibernation. The issue was, however, rarely isolated thereafter, save for carefully focused low key satires like John Hersey's *My Petition for More Space* (1974). The notion that an increase in environmental pollution was an inevitable concomitant of increasing population was the first significant complication to be introduced into the pattern of expectation, but others followed swiftly in its train, including the possible exhaustion of fossil fuels and – eventually – global warming due to industrial carbon dioxide emissions.

Anxieties regarding the effects of environmental pollution were dramatically reinforced by Rachel Carson's best-selling *Silent Spring* (1962), whose influence reinforced Malthusian anxieties and encouraged their elaboration. The boom year of 1971 was followed by another in 1972, which saw the publication of a large number of compound ecological dystopias and disaster stories. In John Brunner's *The Sheep Look Up* and Philip Wylie's *The End of the Dream* pollution becomes a crucial Malthusian check, as civilization drowns ignominiously in its own wastes. In Gordon R. Dickson's *The Pritcher Mass* and William Jon Watkins and Gene Snyder's *Ecodeath* mutations caused by pollution produce new parasitic organisms, whose spread forces survivors into sealed environments – which, like the similar retreats featured in Andrew J. Offutt's *The Castle Keeps*, soon become unendurable as well as indefensible.

Throughout the 1970s and the subsequent decades of the twentieth century, ecological anxieties played a central role in futuristic fiction, both within and without the generic ghetto of labelled science fiction. The notion that the twenty-first century would be an era of unprecedented ecological crisis, highly likely to lead to a temporary or permanent collapse of civilization, became so firmly entrenched in speculative fiction as virtually to be taken for granted.

Environmentalism and posthumanism

The anxieties fostered in the aftermath of *Silent Spring*'s publication lent considerable impetus to a burgeoning environmental protection movement, whose advocates relegated overpopulation to the status of a single aspect of a broader problem. The ideology of the movement was summarized in *The Environmental Handbook* (1970), edited by Garrett de Bell, and propagandized by such works as Richard Lillard's *Eden in Jeopardy: Man's Prodigal Meddling with His Environment* (1966), J. Clarence Davis's *The Politics of Pollution* (1970) and James Ridgeway's *The Politics of Ecology* (1971). Green Parties were founded in several European countries, and such pressure groups as Friends of the Earth (founded in 1969) and Greenpeace (launched in 1971) became significant as lobbyists. Greenpeace also sponsored direct action for publicity purposes, often undertaken by its first naval vessel, *Rainbow Warrior*.

Garrett Hardin, the editor of *Population, Evolution, and Birth Control: A Collage of Controversial Ideas* (1964) went on to sketch out a new discipline of 'ecological economics' in a classic essay published in *Science*, 'The Tragedy of the Commons' (1968). 'Classical' economists had always regarded population growth as a good thing, because it encouraged economic growth, and had also argued that the collective effect of the individual pursuit of personal advantage was an increase in the wealth of the whole society, but Hardin turned those arguments on their head. Wherever people were granted free access to a natural resource, he argued – as in the 'commons' where all and sundry had once been entitled to graze their herds – the pursuit of individual advantage would inevitably lead to the overexploitation, spoliation and eventual annihilation of the resource.

The more obvious corollaries of Hardin's argument included the propositions that because the oceans are treated as a commons by fishermen, and the atmosphere is treated as a commons by producers of carbon dioxide, then the oceans are doomed to be denuded of fish and the atmosphere will be subject to catastrophic warming. From this perspective, the whole earth is bound to become dystopian as it lurches towards terminal disaster. As Hardin's essay was widely reprinted and its ideas circulated, the notion that a world ruled by the principles of classical economics was doomed to spoliation, and ultimately to self-destruction, became increasingly common in futuristic fiction, even though the dominant political culture of the United States came increasingly under the influence of 'economic fundamentalists' zealously devoted to the free-market principles of classical economics.

Hardin's hard-headed alarmism was complemented by a dramatic resurgence of ecological mysticism. The notion that the entire ecosphere could be regarded as a single entity possessed of homeostatic systems akin to those regulating conditions within an individual body, first broached by Vladimir Vernadsky in *The Biosphere* (1926; tr. 1986), was popularized in spectacular fashion by James Lovelock's 'Gaia hypothesis,' elaborated in *Gaia: A New Look at Life on Earth* (1973). Although not mystical in itself, the language in which the Gaia hypothesis was couched lent tremendous encouragement to those who desired to construe it as if it were; Gaia displaced Pan as the most popular repersonification of Nature, although the *frisson* of panic remained.

The case for an actual technological retreat as the only viable means of averting a dystopian Tragedy of the Commons was forcefully made in Ernest Callenbach's millenarian tract *Ecotopia: A Novel about Ecology, People and Politics in 1999* (1978). Its future history describes the secession from the USA of the western seaboard states, whose new masters establish a new low-tech society based on the principle of ecological sustainability. The unofficial religion of the new state is a species of Gaian mysticism – whose rituals helped to license the popular description of environmentalists as 'tree-huggers' – and its folkways gladly embrace the principles of 'alternative technology' laid out in such texts as Ernst Schumacher's *Small is Beautiful* (1973).

Callenbach's new term caught on more widely, to the extent that Kim Stanley Robinson eventually produced a showcase SF anthology entitled *Future Primitive: The New Ecotopias* (1994), which collected works operating on the assumption that contemporary 'megacities' cannot serve as models for future development but are, instead, 'demonstrations of a dysfunctional social order' – a prospectus that condemns all images of future urban life to the status of dystopias. This supposition is dramatically illustrated by the imagery of the most flamboyant sub-genre of late twentieth-century SF, 'cyberpunk' fiction, in which megacities like the Sprawl featured in William

Gibson's *Neuromancer* (1984) and its sequels become the ultimate urban jungles, relative to which the wide-open virtual plains of cyberspace become a kind of Heavenly frontier, complete with a nascent God as well as exotic gunslingers.

Although such Gaia-conscious dystopian novels as David Brin's *Earth* (1990) tried hard to maintain a note of optimism in depicting global attempts to cope with ongoing problems of pollution and induced climate change, there was a near-universal consensus among literary commentators that any envisaged 'solutions' to Hardin's cold equations – including heroic escapes into virtual reality – could only be local and temporary. *Neuromancer*'s alternative term for cyberspace was adopted as the title of a trilogy of films begun with *The Matrix* (1999) in which a manufactured virtual reality maintains a semblance of contemporary life in a future whose 'actual' landscapes attempted a visual summation of dystopian nightmares – imagery replicated to a lesser degree in numerous other movies produced in the wake of Ridley Scott's highly influential *Bladerunner* (1982).

By the time that cyberpunk fiction made its debut, the myth of the Space Age – the notion that the future of humankind would consist of a gradual but illimitable colonization of the universe – had foundered on the realization that the 1969 moon landing really was just one small step, impotent in the short term to facilitate a second. It was obvious by that time that the construction and maintenance of mini-ecospheres required for any expansion into orbital space would be far more problematic than earlier images of spaceships, space stations and space colonies had imagined.

The cyberpunk writers who paid more attention than William Gibson to the possible terms of a human expansion into actual space, most notably Bruce Sterling – in the Shaper/Mechanist series launched in 1982, which culminated in *Schismatrix* (1985) – presumed that such colonization would be as rich in eutopian experimentation as the colonization of the Americas, but with no better result. Indeed, the didactic conclusion of the Shaper/Mechanist series is that effective space colonization is an inherently post-human project – a conclusion so compelling in its logic that it formed the fundamental assumption of the next sub-generic boom within SF: a 'new space opera' whose spacefaring characters are, by necessity, subjected to genetic engineering and/or cyborgization, except for those whose intelligence is purely artificial.

Although most posthumanist fiction is resolutely, flamboyantly and disingenuously upbeat, the fact that J. B. S. Haldane's observation about the initial imaginative impact of 'biological inventions' still holds true ensures that the entire spectrum of such fiction retains a curious 'dystopian glamour', in which the vicissitudes of ultra-mechanized urban life tend to be transformed into healthy challenges akin to those provided by Nature to S. Fowler Wright's exiles from the sterile eutopia of comforts. Genetic engineering and cyborgization may be regarded as processes of ecological adaptation or ecological defiance, according to one's point of view – taken, in either case, towards a new logical extreme – but in either case, their invocation in futuristic fiction changes the rules of the utopian game.

Although early commentators on the possibility of a posthuman future felt free to be straightforwardly horror-stricken by such imagery, after the fashion of David Bunch's depiction of a cyborg dystopia in *Moderan* (1971), the majority of post-cyberpunk commentators adopted a calculatedly ironic ambiguity, as they had to do. Science-fictional attempts to describe mature posthuman societies, such as those contained in Damien Broderick's *The White Abacus* (1997), Karl Schroeder's *Permanence* (2002), Robert Reed's *Sister Alice* (2003) and Justine Robson's *Natural History* (2003) defy classification as eutopias or dystopias precisely because the societies they describe *are* posthuman, and therefore exceed the capacity of terms designed to reflect the extremes of human ambition and anxiety. Where posthuman possibilities are extravagantly displayed – the most extravagant example to date is the story-sequence collected in Charles Stross's *Accelerando* (2005) – nineteenth-century anxieties about the creeping 'mechanization' of human life and the 'alienation' of human existence from Nature are inevitably overturned, lost in a fetishistic celebration of mechanization and alienation, which regard the merely human with casual contempt.

Dystopia now

As the twentieth century drew to a close, anxieties about environmental pollution – which had broadened out by degrees from vulgar smoke and slag to embrace heavy metals, radioactive wastes, non-biodegradable organic compounds preserved and concentrated within the food chain and aerosol propellants depleting the ozone layer – became increasingly focused again on a single problem: the threat of global warming caused by emissions of carbon dioxide.

Although many politicians maintained a state of denial for some time after the issue was first raised, a 1992 Earth Summit issued a resolution calling for world carbon dioxide levels to be stabilized at 1990 levels by the year 2000. The Berlin Mandate of 1995, renewed by the Kyoto Protocol of 1997, adopted a higher target and a longer deadline, but was still reduced to futility by the refusal of the United States to ratify the agreement and the non-involvement of China, whose ultra-rapid programme of industrialization had already become a major source of accelerating carbon dioxide emissions. While these developments were under way, however, reportage of the problem changed its tone markedly, as a tendency developed for every item of inclement weather to be interpreted as a sign that global warming was already under way, and that its momentum was gathering pace.

As with other ecological problems, global warming was something for which every human individual was to some degree responsible, although some individuals and organizations were obviously guiltier than others. This unequal sharing of guilt was dramatized in the notion of a 'carbon footprint': the dark dystopian stain left on the earth's surface by the passage through life of every human being and industrial endeavour. Although endeavours of all kinds contributed to an individual's carbon footprint, censure became concentrated on those seen to be the most sinful, in particular the habit of driving 'gas-guzzling' cars and the custom of using cheap air travel to take foreign holidays: present indulgences assisting in the precipitation of a present crisis.

The carbon footprint was not the only stigma of ecological sin widely attributed to human individuals in the early twenty-first century, nor was it the one that generated the most anxiety and shame; that dubious honour was given to the phenomenon of obesity, which was subject to a similar quasi-scientific formulation in the 'body mass index'. While a carbon footprint was only something figuratively left behind, body fat was something people carried around inside them. It thus became the most visible manifestation of the hedonistic over-indulgence – further exemplified by the cheap foreign holidays that were popularly considered to be a key contributor to carbon footprints – that seemed both to constitute and to be hastening the dystopian degradation and ecocatastrophic destruction of the world.

Hedonism always had a bad press in dystopian fiction, since Odysseus first encountered the listless Lotus Eaters; its seductive but destructive appeal underlies the essential irony of 'The City of the Living Dead', *Brave New World* and many other twentieth-century accounts of the siren song of technology. The argument obtained a particularly explicit summary in James E. Gunn's *The Joy Makers* (1961), whose first part describes the acquisition of political power by Hedonics, Inc – a corporation whose slogan is 'Your Happiness is Our Business', which persuades individuals to sign over all their wealth in return for a guarantee of permanent happiness. In the novel's second part, a Hedonic Council that has inherited absolute political power plans to sweep away all humankind's natural dissatisfactions by means of drugs and psychosurgery – with the result that the third part finds the entire race cocooned in the foetal bliss of artificial wombs, attended by a dutiful Mechanism that is in no danger of stopping, but is instead ambitious to export this paradigm of paradise throughout the universe. Arguments of this sort, which became increasingly common as the century progressed, not only endorsed and re-emphasized Malthus's suspicion that human beings would never be willing to pay the cost of achieving eutopia in the currency of moral restraint, but suggested strongly that the battle was already lost, and that dystopia had come to stay.

Although dystopian dramas of environmental spoliation by overpopulation and pollution had not been reluctant to point out that the enemy was not so much an implacable external force as our own lack of moral restraint, the addition of perceptible global warming to the list of the world's political problems and the drastic exaggeration of individual anxieties about obesity played a major role in switching the emphasis of popular rhetoric to the magnification of individual responsibility and the careful cultivation of an individual sense of ecological sin. When the drafters of the American constitution had added the pursuit of happiness to life and liberty as an inalienable human right they had assumed that the pursuit of happiness was, on the whole, a good thing, and an essential component of the eutopian quest. As the twentieth century drew towards its close, however, hedonism had been redefined as a road to dystopia and obesity, the latter being construed not as a sign of wealth and jollity but as the epitome of morbid dysfuctionality.

Literary attempts to anticipate the adaptations that global civilization might yet have to make in order to cope with the 'greenhouse effect' induced by carbon dioxide emissions began to appear in some profusion as the twentieth century ended and the twenty-first century began. Notable examples tending towards political fantasy rather than straightforward disaster stories include Bruce Sterling's *Distraction* (1998), Norman Spinrad's *Greenhouse Summer* (1999), William Sanders's 'When this World is All on Fire' (2001) and Kim Stanley Robinson's *Forty Signs of Rain* (2004). What is primarily notable about all these works, as well as the temper of almost all reportage of the unfolding ecocatastrophe, is the absence of the slightest vestige of trust in the possibility that the exercise of moral restraint might slow the catastrophe down, let alone prevent it proceeding to its climax.

The placement of dreams of future eutopia with an ecological perspective has wrought a gradual but inexorable transformation in the significance of dystopian imagery. Such dystopian imagists as Ray Bradbury and John Brunner were fond of arguing that they were not trying to predict the future but to prevent it, updating images of Stahlstadt in the hope of evoking a reaction that would favour the development of Frankville. By the end of the twentieth century, however, such arguments had lost their force, because the recognition that the unfolding ecocatastrophe could not be halted, or even slowed down, put Frankville out of reach, at least until the catastrophe had run its course. Dystopian images of the near future can no longer avoid the burden of their own inevitability; Orwellian fears of future tyranny can no longer make more than a marginal difference to the tenor of contemporary pessimism.

Insofar as twenty-first-century futuristic fiction set on Earth retains a eutopian component, its eutopias are necessarily postponed until the aftermath of an environmental collapse. The near universal assumption of such fiction is that dystopia has already arrived, in embryo, and that its progress to maturity is unavoidable. Having calculated the amount of landbound ice that might eventually be melted into the oceans, we know that the impending Deluge will not be as all-consuming as its mythical prototype, but that will not make it very much easier to endure. Nor does the knowledge that we have brought dystopia upon ourselves by our pursuit of material comforts provide much imaginative solace, even to the kind of people who relish opportunities to say 'I told you so.'

BIBLIOGRAPHY

Asimov, Isaac, *The Caves of Steel* (Garden City, NY: Doubleday, 1954).
Ballard, J. G., 'Billenium', *New Worlds*, November 1961.
Barr, Robert, 'The Doom of London', *The Idler*, November 1892.
Bass, T. J., *Half Past Human* (New York: Ballantine, 1971).
Besant, Walter, *The Inner House* (Bristol: Arrowsmith, 1888).
Blish, James and Norman L. Knight, *A Torrent of Faces* (Garden City, NY: Doubleday, 1967).
Bradbury, Ray, *Fahrenheit 451* (New York: Ballantine, 1953).
Broderick, Damien, *The White Abacus* (New York: Avon Eos, 1997).
Brunner, John, *The Sheep Look Up* (New York: Harper, 1972).
    Stand on Zanzibar (Garden City, NY: Doubleday, 1968).
Bunch, David, *Moderan* (New York: Avon, 1971).
Callenbach, Ernest, *Ecotopia: A Novel about Ecology, People and Politics in 1999* (Berkeley, CA: Banyan Tree, 1978).
Čapek, Karel, *R.U.R.: A Fantastic Melodrama* (Garden City, NY: Doubleday Page, 1923).
Carlyle, Thomas, 'Signs of the Times', *Edinburgh Review*, June 1829.
Carson, Ruth, *Silent Spring* (Boston: Houghton Mifflin, 1962).
Davis, J. Clarence, *The Politics of Pollution* (New York: Pegasus, 1970).
De Bell, Garrett (ed.), *The Environmental Handbook* (New York: Ballantine, 1970).
Del Rey, Lester, *The Eleventh Commandment* (Evanston, IL: Regency, 1962).
Dickson, Gordon R., *The Pritcher Mass* (Garden City, NY: Doubleday, 1972).
    Sleepwalker's World (Philadelphia: Lippincott, 1971).
Donnelly, Ignatius [as Edmund Boisgilbert, M.D.], *Caesar's Column: A Story of the Twentieth Century* (Chicago: F. J. Schulte, 1890).
Ehrlich, Paul R., 'Ecocatastrophe', *Ramparts* 8 (1969), 24–28.
    The Population Bomb (New York: Ballantine Books, 1968).
Farrère, Claude [Charles Bargone], *Les Condamnés à Mort* (Paris: Édouard Joseph, 1920).

Flecker, James Elroy, *The Last Generation: A Story of the Future* (London: New Age, 1908).

Forster, E. M., 'The Machine Stops', *Oxford and Cambridge Review* (Michaelmas Term, 1909).

Gibson, William, *Neuromancer* (New York: Ace, 1984).

Gunn, James E., *The Joy Makers* (New York: Bantam, 1961).

Haldane, J. B. S., *Daedalus; or, Science and the Future* (London: Kegan Paul, Trench & Trubner, 1923).

Hardin, Garrett, 'The Tragedy of the Commons', *Science* 162 (1968), 1243–8.

Harrison, Harry, *Make Room! Make Room!* (Garden City, NY: Doubleday, 1966).

Hawkins, Willard E., 'The Dwindling Sphere', *Astounding Stories*, March 1940.

Hay, W. D., *The Doom of the Great City* (London: Newman, 1880).

Hersey, John, *My Petition for More Space* (New York: Knopf, 1974).

Hudson, W. H., *A Crystal Age* (London: T. Fisher Unwin, 1887).
  Green Mansions (London: Duckworth & Co., 1904).

Huxley, Aldous, *Ape and Essence* (New York: Harper, 1948).
  Brave New World (London: Chatto & Windus, 1932).
  Crome Yellow (London: Chatto & Windus, 1921).

Huxley, Julian, 'The Tissue-Culture King', *Amazing Stories*, October 1927).
  'World Population', *Scientific American, March* 1956.

Hyams, Edward, *The Astrologer* (London: Longmans Green, 1950).

Jaeger, Muriel, *Retreat from Armageddon* (London: Duckworth, 1936).

Jefferies, Richard, *After London; or, Wild England* (London: Cassell & Co., 1885).

Knight, Damon, 'Natural State', *Galaxy*, January 1954; reprinted as *Masters of Evolution* (New York: Ace, 1959).

Kornbluth, C. M., 'Reap the Dark Tide', *Vanguard*, June 1958; reprinted as 'Shark Ship'.

Lillard, Richard, *Eden in Jeopardy: Man's Prodigal Meddling with His Environment* (New York: Knopf, 1966).

Lovelock, James, *Gaia: A New Look at Life on Earth* (Oxford University Press, 1973).

Malthus, T. R., *An Essay on the Principle of Population; or, a View of its Past and Present Effects on Human Happiness; with an Inquiry into our Prospects Respecting the Future Removal or Mitigation of the Effects which it Occasions. A New Edition, very much Enlarged* (London: Printed for J. Johnson by T. Bensley, 1803 [First edition 1798]).

Manning, Laurence and Fletcher Pratt, 'The City of the Living Dead', *Science Wonder Stories*, May 1930.

Mitchison, Naomi, *Solution Three* (London: Dennis Dobson, 1975).
  Not by Bread Alone (London: Marion Boyars, 1983).

Offutt, Andrew J., *The Castle Keeps* (New York: Berkley, 1972).

Orwell, George, *Nineteen Eighty-Four* (London: Secker & Warburg, 1949).

Pohl, Frederik, 'The Census Takers', *The Magazine of Fantasy & Science Fiction*, February 1956.

Reed, Robert, *Sister Alice* (New York: Tor, 2003).

Ridgeway, James, *The Politics of Ecology* (London: Dutton, 1971).

Robinson, Kim Stanley, *Forty Signs of Rain* (New York: Bantam Spectra, 2004).

Robinson, Kim Stanley (ed.), *Future Primitive: The New Ecotopias* (New York: Tor, 1994).

Robson, Justine, *Natural History* (London: Macmillan, 2003).

Sanders, William, 'When this World is All on Fire', *Asimov's Science Fiction Magazine*, October 2001.

Sauer, Rob (ed.), *Voyages: Scenarios for a Ship Called Earth* (New York: Ballantine, 1971).

Schachner, Nathan, 'Sterile Planet', *Astounding Stories*, July 1937.

Schroeder, Karl, *Permanence* (New York: Tor, 2002).

Schumacher, Ernst, *Small is Beautiful: A Study of Economics as if People Mattered* (London: Bond & Briggs, 1973).

Sheckley, Robert, 'The People Trap', *The Magazine of Fantasy & Science Fiction*, June 1968.

Silverberg, Robert, *Master of Life and Death* (New York: Ace, 1957).

 The World Inside (Garden City, NY: Doubleday, 1971).

Souvestre, Émile, *Le Monde tel qu'il sera* (Paris: W. Coquevert, 1846).

Spinrad, Norman, *Greenhouse Summer* (New York: Tor, 1999).

Sterling, Bruce, *Distraction* (New York: Bantam, 1998).

 Schismatrix (New York: Arbor House, 1985).

Street, A. G., *Already Walks Tomorrow* (London: Faber & Faber, 1938).

Stross, Charles, *Accelerando* (New York: Tor, 2005).

Verne, Jules [with Paschal Grousset], *Les cinq cents millions de la bégum* (Paris: Hetzel, 1879; tr. as *The Begum's Fortune*, London: Sampson Low, Marston, Searle and Rivington, 1880).

Vonnegut, Kurt, Jr, 'The Big Trip Up Yonder', *Galaxy*, January 1954.

Watkins, William Jon and Gene Snyder, *Ecodeath* (Garden City, NY: Doubleday, 1972).

Wells, H. G., *The Time Machine* (London: Heinemann, 1895).

Wright, Sydney Fowler, *The Adventure of Wyndham Smith* (London: Jenkins, 1938).

 The New Gods Lead (London: Jarrolds, 1932).

Wylie, Philip, *The End of the Dream* (Garden City, NY: Doubleday, 1972).

Yanarella, Ernest J., *The Cross, the Plow and the Skyline: Contemporary Science Fiction and the Ecological Imagination* (Parkland, FL: Brown Walker, 2001).

FURTHER READING

Albinski, Nan Bowman, *Women's Utopias in British and American Fiction* (London: Routledge, 1988).

Alexander, Peter and Roger Gill (eds.), *Utopias* (London: Duckworth, 1984).

Alkon, Paul E., *The Origins of Futuristic Fiction* (London: University of Georgia Press, 1987).

Armytage, W. H. G., *Heavens Below: Utopian Experiments in England, 1560–1960* (London: Routledge & Kegan Paul, 1960).

  Yesterday's Tomorrows: A Historical Survey of Future Societies (London: Routledge & Kegan Paul, 1968).

Atkinson, Geoffrey, *The Extraordinary Voyage in French Literature before 1700* (New York: Columbia University Press, 1920).

Baczko, Bronislaw, *Utopian Lights: The Evolution of the Idea of Progress* (London: Paragon Press, 1989).

Bailey, J. O., *Pilgrims Through Space and Time: Trends and Patterns in Scientific and Utopian Fiction* (London: Argus, 1947).

Bartkowski, Frances, *Feminist Utopias* (Lincoln: University of Nebraska Press, 1989).

Beaumont, Matthew, *Utopia Ltd.: Ideologies of Social Dreaming in England 1870–1900* (Leiden: Brill, 2005).

Berneri, Marie, *Journey Through Utopia* (London: Routledge & Kegan Paul, 1950).

Bloch, Ernst, *The Principle of Hope* (3 vols., Oxford: Basil Blackwell, 1986).

Booker, M. Keith, *The Dystopian Impulse in Modern Literature* (Westport, CT: Greenwood Press, 1994).

Braunthal, Alfred, *Salvation and the Perfect Society* (Amherst: University of Massachusetts Press, 1979).

Claeys, Gregory (ed.), *Late Victorian Utopias* (6 vols., London: Pickering and Chatto, 2008).

  (ed.), *Modern British Utopias, 1700–1850* (8 vols., London: Pickering and Chatto, 1997).

  (ed.), *Restoration and Augustan British Utopias* (Syracuse, NY: Syracuse University Press, 2000).

  (ed.), *Utopias of the British Enlightenment* (Cambridge University Press, 1994).

Claeys, Gregory and Lyman Tower Sargent (eds.), *The Utopia Reader* (New York University Press, 1999).

Clarke, I. F., *The Pattern of Expectation 1644–2001* (London: Jonathan Cape, 1979).

Cohn, Norman, *The Pursuit of the Millennium* (London: Secker & Warburg, 1947).

Davis, J. C., *Utopia and the Ideal Society: A Study of English Utopian Writing 1516–1700* (Cambridge University Press, 1981).

Eaton, Ruth, *Ideal Cities: Utopianism and the (Un)Built Environment* (London: Thames and Hudson, 2002).

Eliav-Feldon, Miriam, *Realistic Utopias: The Imaginary Societies of the Renaissance 1516–1630* (Oxford: Clarendon Press, 1982).

Elliott, Robert, *The Shape of Utopia: Studies in a Literary Genre* (University of Chicago Press, 1970).

Erasmus, Charles, *In Search of the Common Good: Utopian Experiments Past and Future* (Glencoe: The Free Press, 1977).

Eurich, Nell, *Science in Utopia* (Cambridge, MA: Harvard University Press, 1967).

Fausett, David, *Writing the New World: Imaginary Voyages and Utopias of the Great Southern Land* (Syracuse, NY: Syracuse University Press, 1993).

Ferguson, John, *Utopias of the Classical World* (London: Thames & Hudson, 1975).

Firchow, Peter Edgerly, *Modern Utopian Fictions from H. G. Wells to Iris Murdoch* (Washington, DC: The Catholic University Press of America, 2007).

Fogarty, Robert S., *American Utopianism* (Itasca, IL: F. E. Peacock, 1972).
   Dictionary of American Communal and Utopian History (Westport, CT: Greenwood Press, 1980)

Fortunati, Vita and Raymond Trousson, *Dictionary of Literary Utopias* (Paris: Honoré Champion, 2000).

Friesen, John W. and Virginia Lyons Friesen, *The Palgrave Companion to North American Utopias* (London: Palgrave-Macmillan, 2004).

Goodwin, Barbara, *Social Science and Utopia: Nineteenth Century Models of Social Harmony* (Hassocks: Harvester Press, 1978).

Goodwin, Barbara and Keith Taylor, *The Politics of Utopia* (New York: St Martin's Press, 1983).

Gove, Philip Babcock, *The Imaginary Voyage in Prose Fiction* (New York: Columbia University Press, 1941).

Hansot, Elizabeth, *Perfection and Progress: Two Modes of Utopian Thought* (Cambridge, MA: MIT Press, 1974).

Hertzler, Joyce, *The History of Utopian Thought* (London: Macmillan, 1923).

Hillegas, Mark R., *The Future as Nightmare: H. G. Wells and the Anti-Utopians* (Carbondale: Southern Illinois University Press, 1967).

Holstun, James, *A Rational Millennium: Puritan Utopias of Seventeenth-Century England and America* (Oxford University Press, 1987).

Jameson, Fredric, *Archaeologies of the Future: The Desire Called Utopia and Other Science Fictions* (London: Verso, 2005).

Johns, Alessa, *Women's Utopias of the Eighteenth Century* (Urbana: University of Illinois Press, 2003).

Kamenka, Eugene (ed.), *Utopias* (Oxford University Press, 1987).

Kateb, George, *Utopia and its Enemies* (Glencoe: The Free Press, 1963).

Kenyon, Timothy, *Utopian Communism and Political Thought in Early Modern England* (London: Pinter Publishers, 1989).

Kumar, Krishan, *Utopia and Anti-Utopia in Modern Times* (Oxford: Basil Blackwell, 1987).

Utopianism (Buckingham: Open University Press, 1991).

Kumar, Krishan and Stephen Bann (eds.), *Utopias and the Millennium* (London: Reaktion Books, 1993).

Lasky, Melvin, *Utopia and Revolution* (University of Chicago Press, 1976).

Leslie, Marina, *Renaissance Utopias and the Problem of History* (London: Cornell University Press, 1998).

Levitas, Ruth, *The Concept of Utopia* (Syracuse, NY: Syracuse University Press, 1990).

Mannheim, Karl, *Ideology and Utopia: An Introduction to the Sociology of Knowledge* (New York: Harcourt, Brace & Co., 1936).

Manuel, Frank, *The Prophets of Paris* (New York: Harper & Row, 1965).

(ed.), *Utopias and Utopian Thought* (Boston: Beacon Press, 1965).

Manuel, Frank and Fritzie P. Manuel, *Utopian Thought in the Western World* (Cambridge, MA: The Belknap Press of Harvard University Press, 1979).

(eds.), *French Utopias: An Anthology of Ideal Societies* (New York: Schocken Books, 1971).

Margolis, Jonathan, *A Brief History of Tomorrow* (London: Bloomsbury, 2000).

Marin, Louis, *Utopics: The Semiological Play of Textual Spaces* (Atlantic Highlands: Humanities Press, 1984).

McCord, William, *Voyages to Utopia* (New York: W. W. Norton, 1989).

Morton, A. L., *The English Utopia* (London: Lawrence & Wishart, 1952).

Moylan, Tom, *Demand the Impossible: Science Fiction and the Utopian Imagination* (London: Methuen, 1986).

Scraps of the Untainted Sky: Science Fiction, Utopia, Dystopia (Boulder, CO: Westview Press, 2000).

Mumford, Lewis, *The Story of Utopias* (New York: Viking Press, 1950).

Nicolson, Marjorie, *Voyages to the Moon* (London: Macmillan, 1948).

Parrinder, Patrick, *Shadows of the Future: H. G. Wells, Science Fiction and Prophecy* (Syracuse, NY: Syracuse University Press, 1995).

Pfaelzer, Jean, *The Utopian Novel in America 1886–1896: The Politics of Form* (University of Pittsburgh Press, 1984).

Pohl, Nicole and Brenda Tooley (eds.), *Gender and Utopia in the Eighteenth Century* (London: Ashgate, 2007).

Polak, Fred, *The Image of the Future* (2 vols., New York: Oceana, 1961).

Pordzik, Ralph, *The Quest for Postcolonial Utopia: A Comparative Introduction to the Utopian Novel in the New English Literatures* (Oxford: Peter Lang, 2001).

Rees, Christine, *Utopian Imagination and Eighteenth Century Fiction* (London: Longman, 1996).

Sargent, Lyman Tower, *British and American Utopian Literature, 1516–1975* (New York: Garland, 1988).

Schaer, Roland, Gregory Claeys and Lyman Tower Sargent (eds.), *Utopia: The Search for the Ideal Society in the West* (New York: Oxford University Press, 2000).

Seligman, Adam B. (ed.), *Order and Transcendence: The Role of Utopias and the Dynamic of Civilizations* (Leiden: E. J. Brill, 1989).

Shklar, Judith, *After Utopia: The Decline of Political Faith* (Princeton University Press, 1957).

Sutton, Robert P., *Communal Utopias and the American Experience: Secular Communities, 1824–2000* (Westport, CT: Praeger, 2004).

Taylor, Keith, *The Political Ideas of the Utopian Socialists* (London: Frank Cass, 1982).

Trahair, Richard C. S., *Utopias and Utopians: An Historical Dictionary* (London: Fitzroy Dearborn, 1999).

Tuveson, Ernest, *Millennium and Utopia: A Study in the Background of the Idea of Progress* (Berkeley: University of California Press, 1949).

Venturi, Franco, *Utopia and Reform in the Enlightenment* (Cambridge University Press, 1971).

Wagar, W. Warren, *Terminal Visions: The Literature of Last Things* (Bloomington: Indiana University Press, 1982).

Walsh, Chad, *From Utopia to Nightmare* (London: Geoffrey Bles, 1962).

Wegner, Phillip E., *Imaginary Communities: Utopia, the Nation, and the Spatial Histories of Modernity* (Berkeley: University of California Press, 2002).

INDEX

Cambridge Companions to ...

AUTHORS

David Mamet edited by Christopher Bigsby

Thomas Mann edited by Ritchie Robertson

Christopher Marlowe edited by
Patrick Cheney

Herman Melville edited by Robert S. Levine

Arthur Miller edited by Christopher Bigsby
(second edition)

Milton edited by Dennis Danielson
(second edition)

Molière edited by David Bradby and
Andrew Calder

Toni Morrison edited by Justine Tally

Nabokov edited by Julian W. Connolly

Eugene O'Neill edited by Michael Manheim

George Orwell edited by John Rodden

Ovid edited by Philip Hardie

Harold Pinter edited by Peter Raby
(second edition)

Sylvia Plath edited by Jo Gill

Edgar Allan Poe edited by Kevin J. Hayes

Alexander Pope edited by Pat Rogers

Ezra Pound edited by Ira B. Nadel

Proust edited by Richard Bales

Pushkin edited by Andrew Kahn

Rabelais edited by John O'Brien

Rilke edited by Karen Leeder and
Robert Vilain

Philip Roth edited by Timothy Parrish

Salman Rushdie edited by
Abdulrazak Gurnah

Shakespeare edited by Margareta de Grazia
and Stanley Wells (second edition)

Shakespearean Comedy edited by
Alexander Leggatt

Shakespeare on Film edited by
Russell Jackson (second edition)

Shakespeare's History Plays edited by
Michael Hattaway

Shakespeare's Last Plays edited by
Catherine M. S. Alexander

Shakespeare's Poetry edited by
Patrick Cheney

Shakespeare and Popular Culture edited by
Robert Shaughnessy

Shakespeare on Stage edited by Stanley Wells
and Sarah Stanton

Shakespearean Tragedy edited by
Claire McEachern

George Bernard Shaw edited by
Christopher Innes

Mary Shelley edited by Esther Schor

Shelley edited by Timothy Morton

Sam Shepard edited by Matthew C. Roudané

Spenser edited by Andrew Hadfield

Laurence Sterne edited by Thomas Keymer

Wallace Stevens edited by John N. Serio

Tom Stoppard edited by Katherine E. Kelly

Harriet Beecher Stowe edited by
Cindy Weinstein

August Strindberg edited by
Michael Robinson

Jonathan Swift edited by Christopher Fox

J. M. Synge edited by P. J. Mathews

Tacitus edited by A. J. Woodman

Henry David Thoreau edited by
Joel Myerson

Tolstoy edited by Donna Tussing Orwin

Mark Twain edited by Forrest G. Robinson

Virgil edited by Charles Martindale

Voltaire edited by Nicholas Cronk

Edith Wharton edited by Millicent Bell

Walt Whitman edited by Ezra Greenspan

Oscar Wilde edited by Peter Raby

Tennessee Williams edited by
Matthew C. Roudané

August Wilson edited by Christopher Bigsby

Mary Wollstonecraft edited by
Claudia L. Johnson

Virginia Woolf edited by Susan Sellers
(second edition)

Wordsworth edited by Stephen Gill

W. B. Yeats edited by Marjorie Howes and
John Kelly

Zola edited by Brian Nelson

TOPICS

The Actress edited by Maggie B. Gale and
John Stokes

The African American Novel edited by
Maryemma Graham